NATION OF GRAFFITI ARTISTS

Est. 1974 ▶ NYC

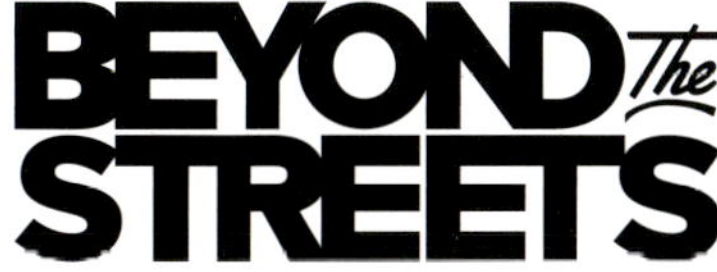

GINGKO PRESS

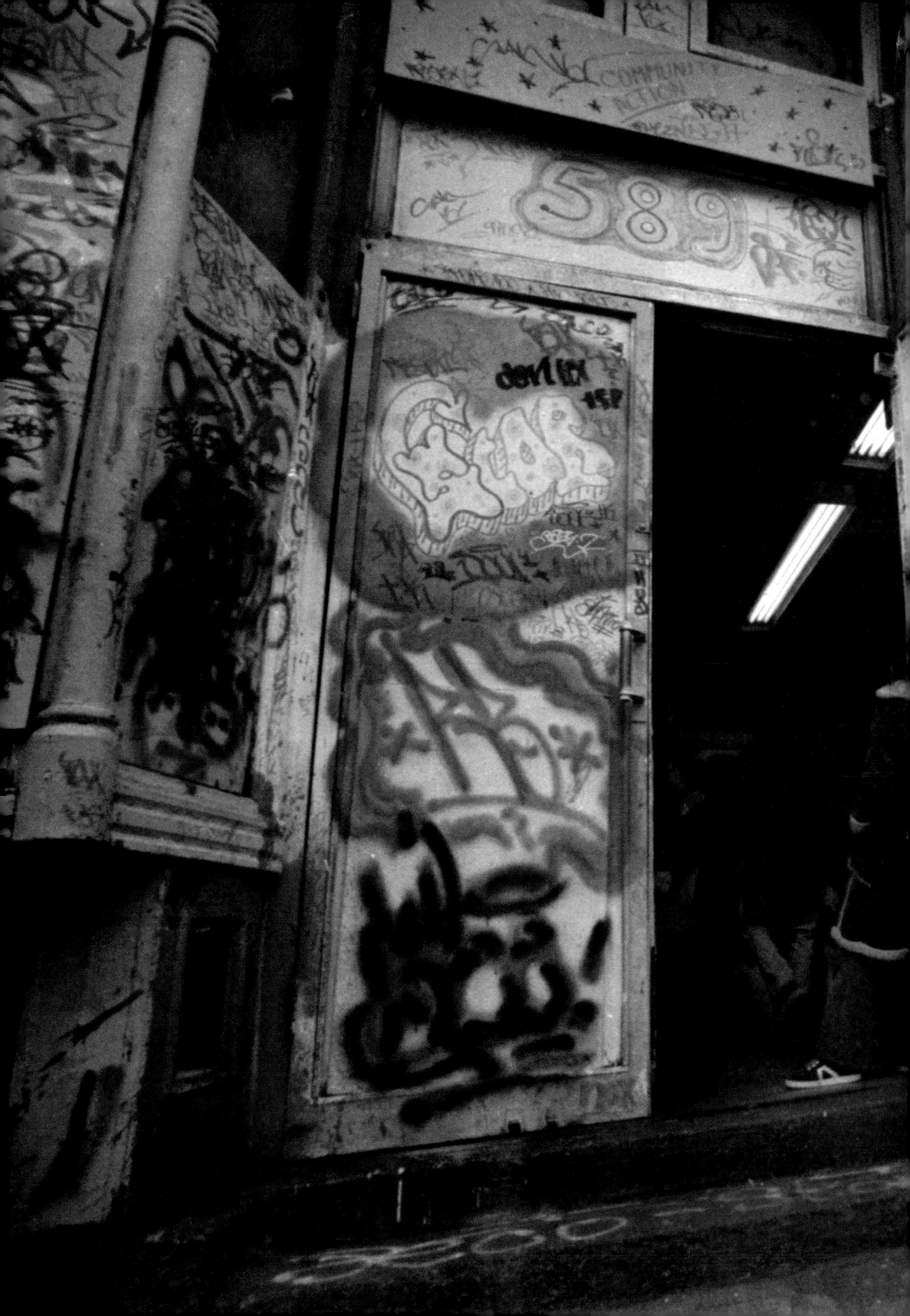

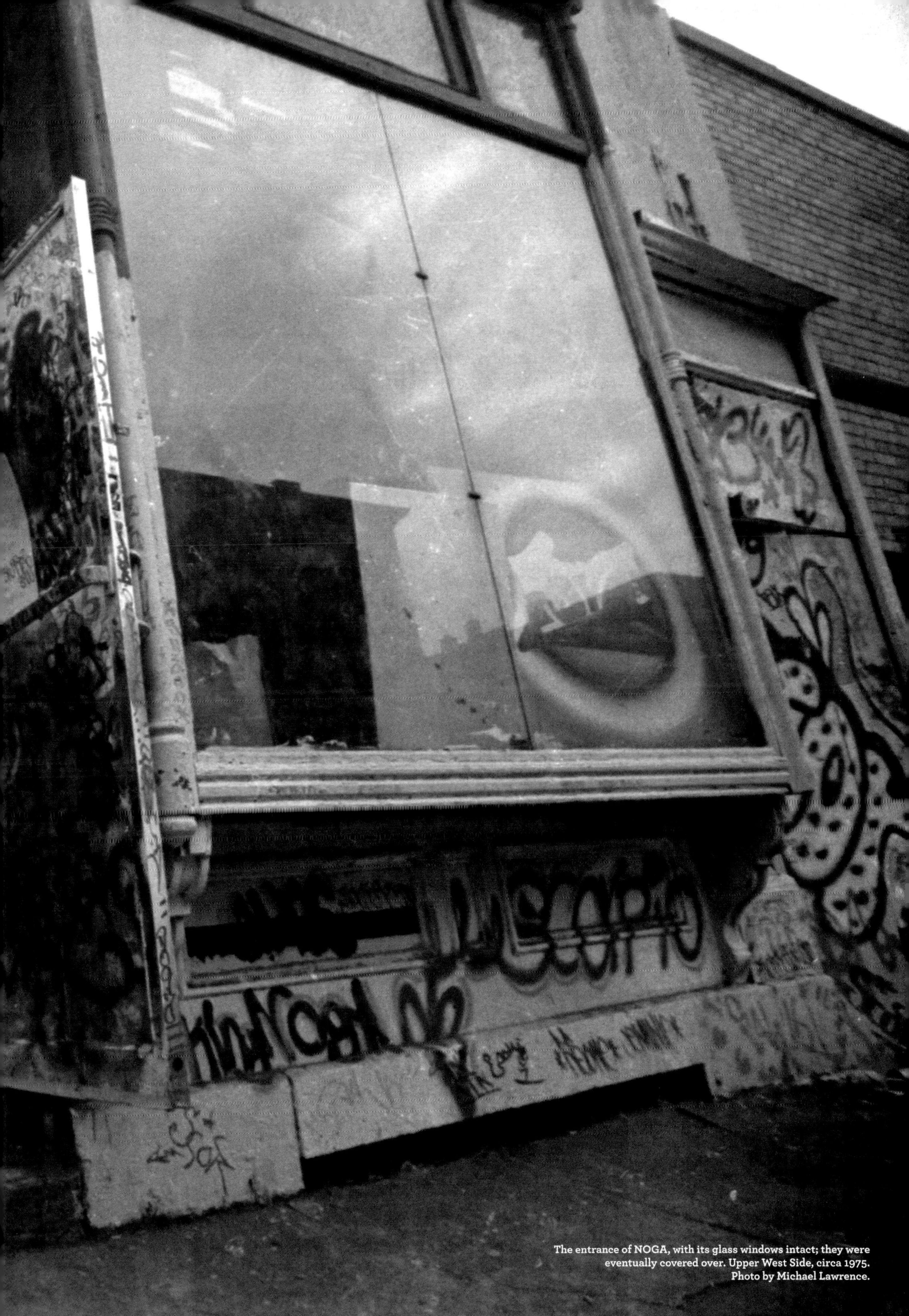

The entrance of NOGA, with its glass windows intact; they were eventually covered over. Upper West Side, circa 1975. Photo by Michael Lawrence.

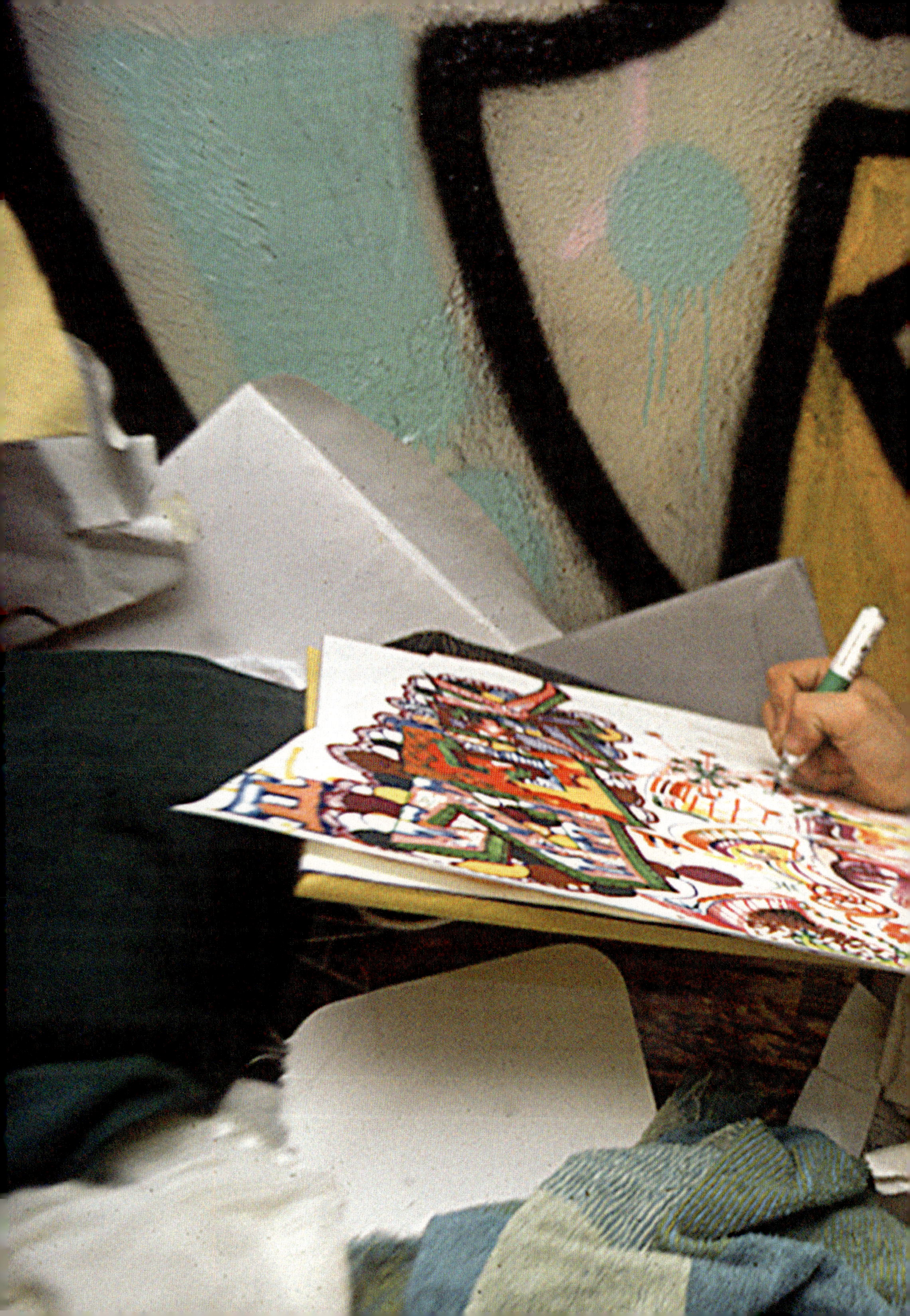

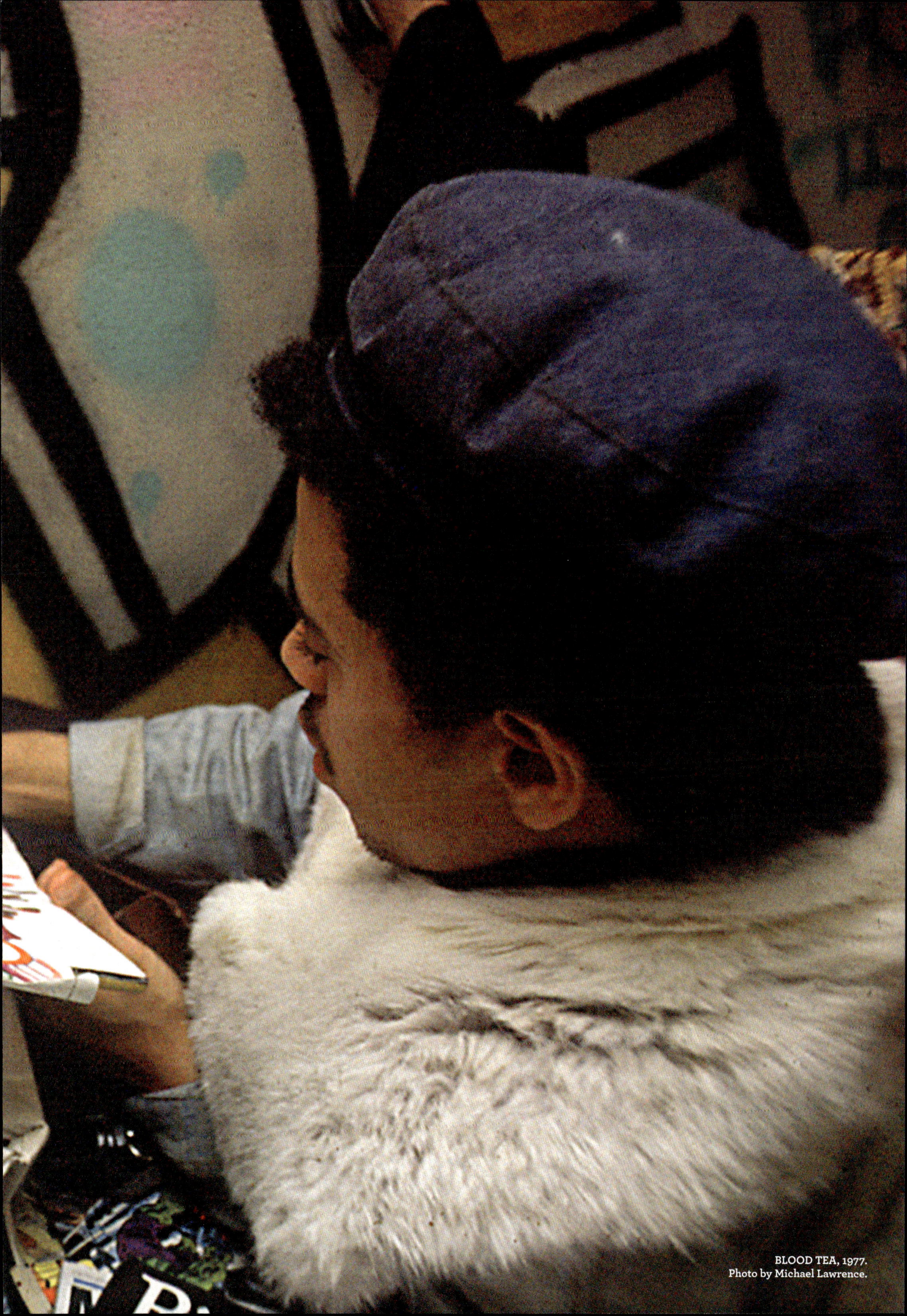

BLOOD TEA, 1977.
Photo by Michael Lawrence.

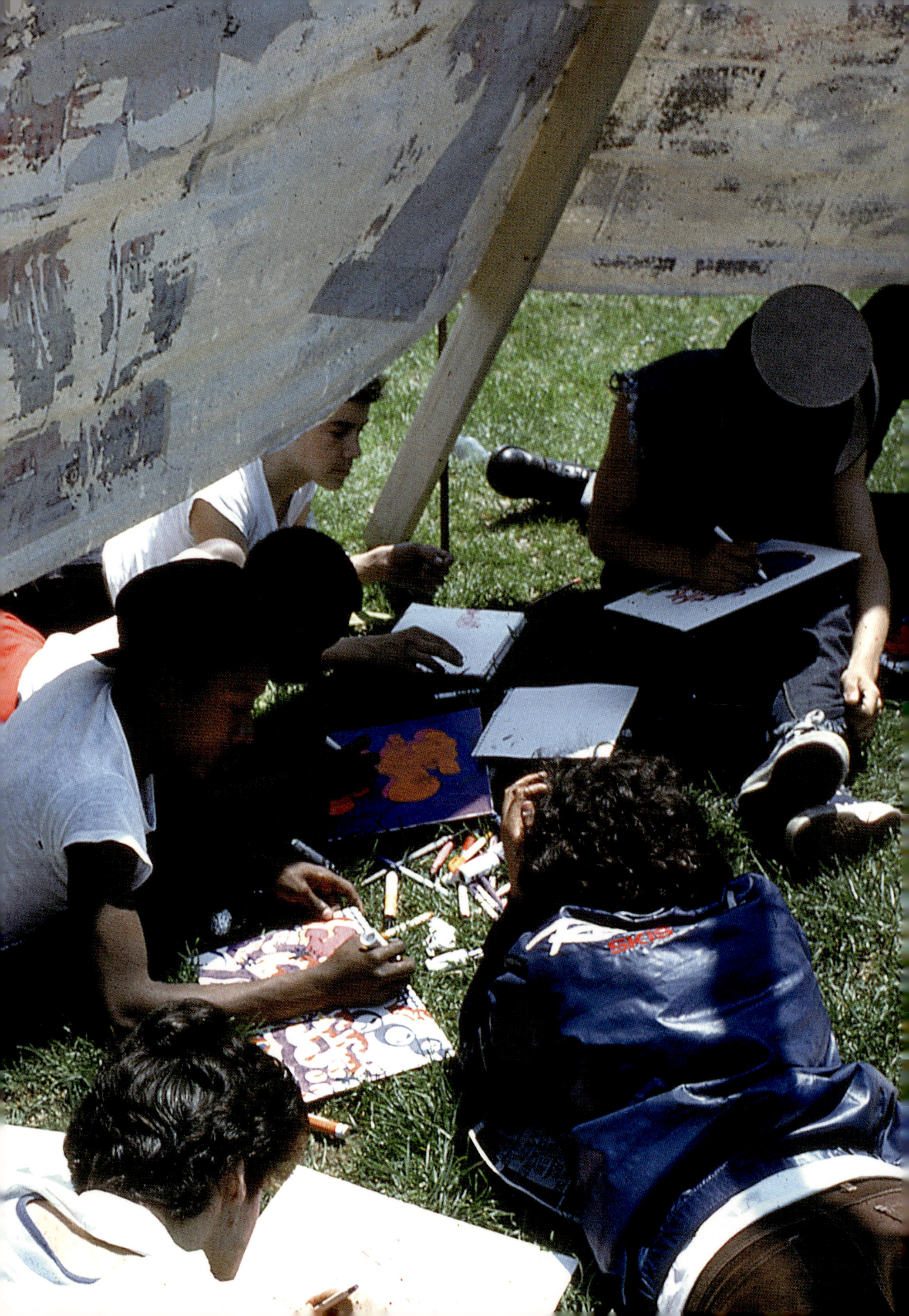

FOREWORD

Books always take longer than we want to make. Interviewing, editing, scanning and everyday interruptions all prolong the process. *Nation of Graffiti Artists, NYC* has been a long time coming.

Chris Pape introduced me to Michael Lawrence, who was an integral part of Nation of Graffiti Artists (NOGA), run by Jack Pelsinger. While UGA included and launched exceptional artists, NOGA leaned more community-based, producing murals and group projects for kids of all ages and abilities through the mid '70s, well before the early '80s public art boom. Michael not only photographed the five-ish-year experience in all its glory, but he wore many hats within the organization, as most people committed to nonprofits do. Above all, he championed NOGA's value by preserving a treasure trove of images and memories, which he so generously now shares with us.

As I was planning BEYOND THE STREETS New York, Chris Pape was writing this book, and while we considered it for the exhibit, things didn't get done in time — I could make a ton of excuses but there was just a lot going on. In the meantime, Michael unearthed even more photos and ephemera. Then, just as we thought we were done and ready for print, SAL 161 appeared out of nowhere with an incredible batch of photos and memories that helped fill in some missing links in the story. It was worth the wait. Some things can't be rushed.

I am honored to be able to tell the story of NOGA and present the photos — most never seen before. I thank all of the artists who are no longer with us who helped make it such a special place and those still with us who shared their memories.

—Roger Gastman

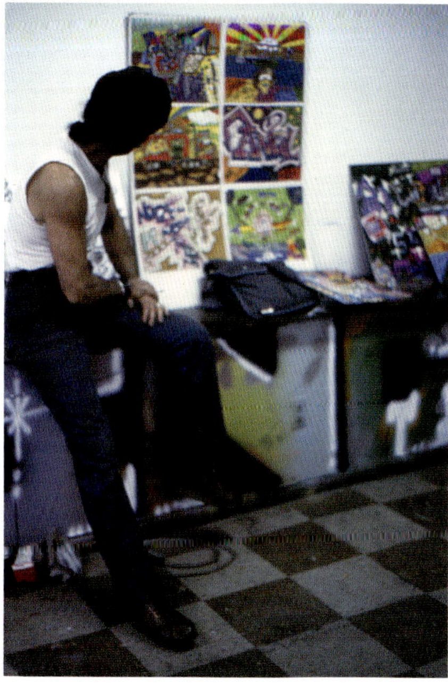

Jack Pelsinger takes a look at some newly painted
canvases by NOGA artists.
Photo by Michael Lawrence.

Opposite page:
CLIFF 159, BE3, BLOOD TEA and other
NOGA members drawing in Central Park, 1975.
Photo by Michael Lawrence.

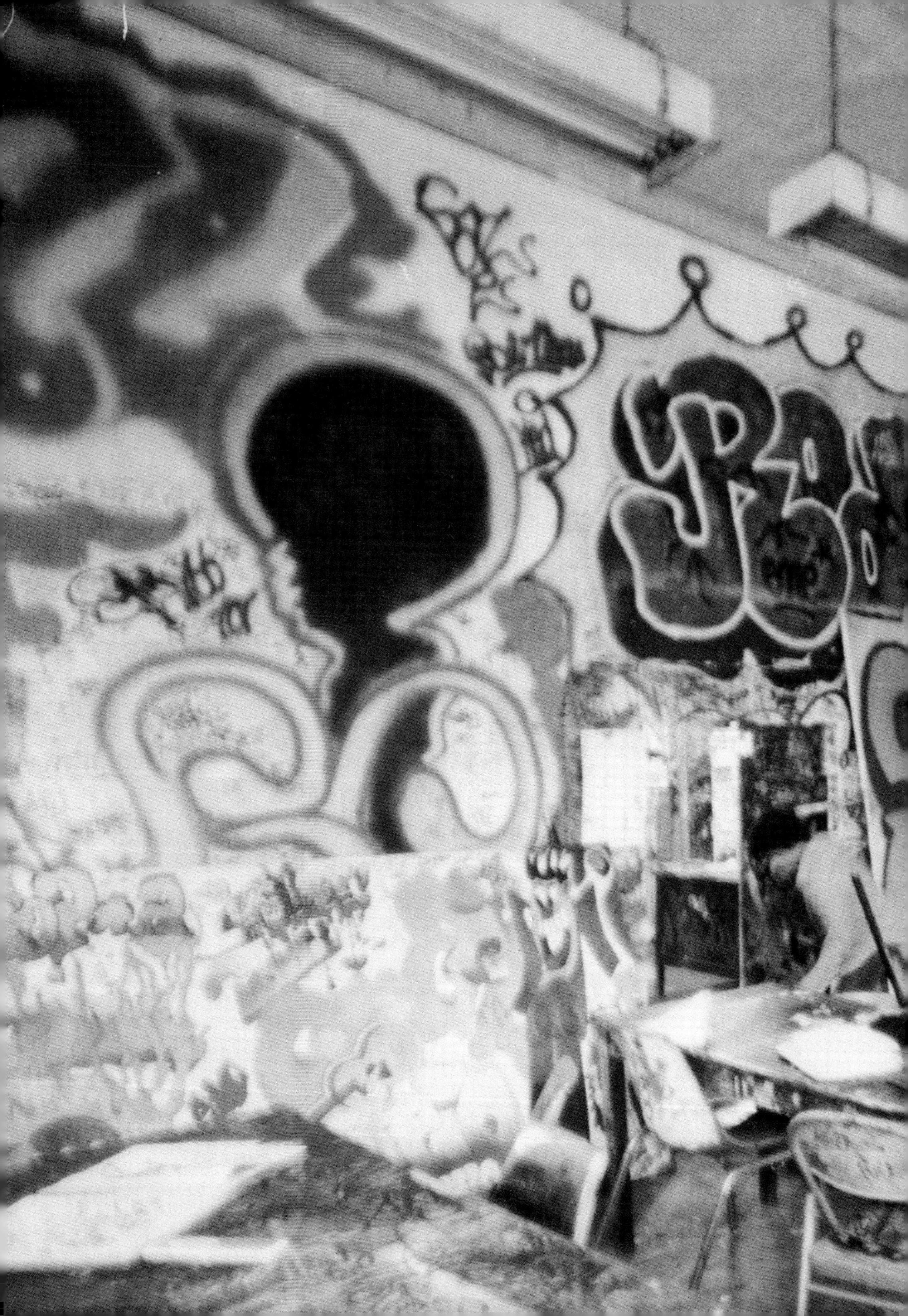

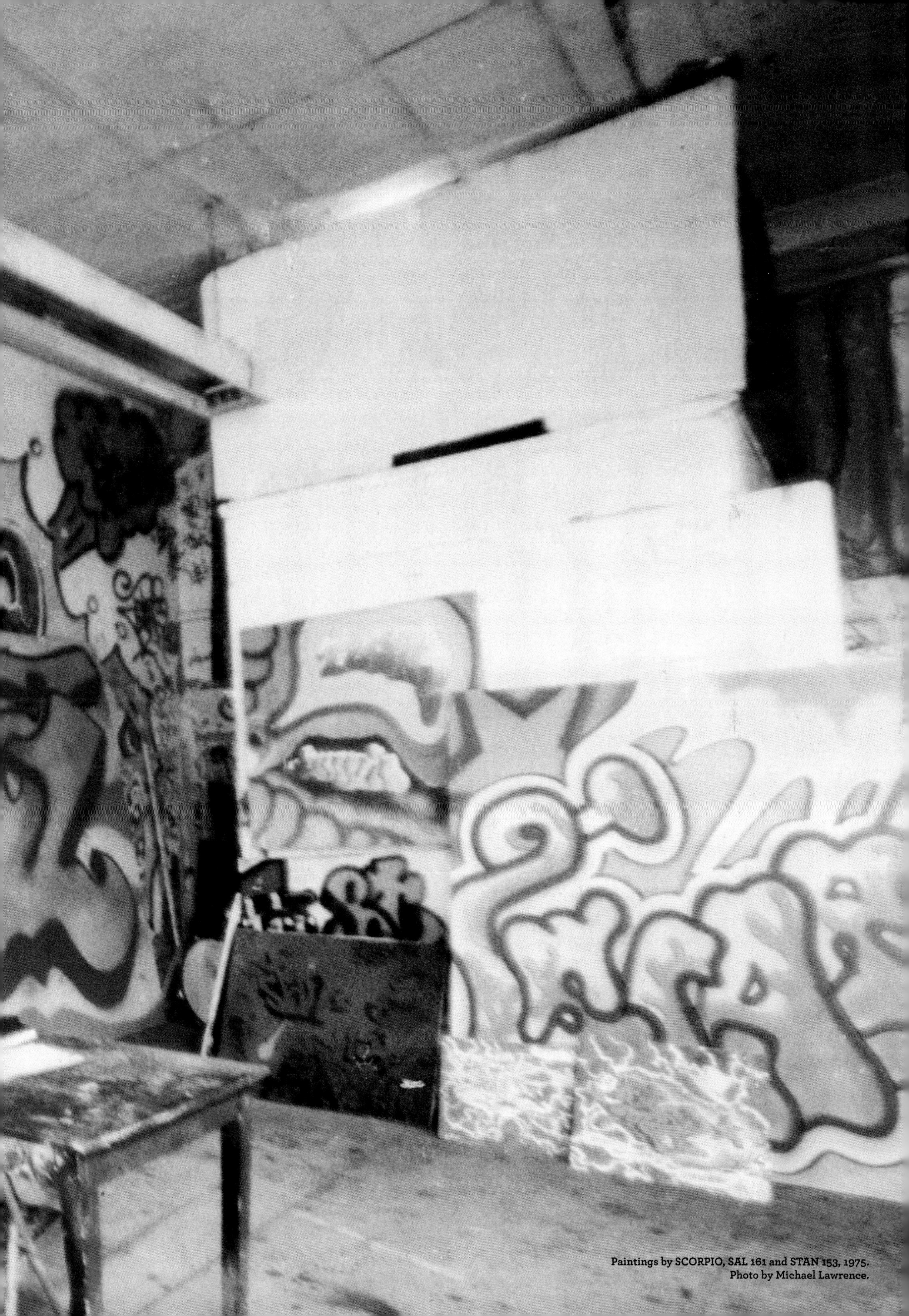

Paintings by SCORPIO, SAL 161 and STAN 153, 1975.
Photo by Michael Lawrence.

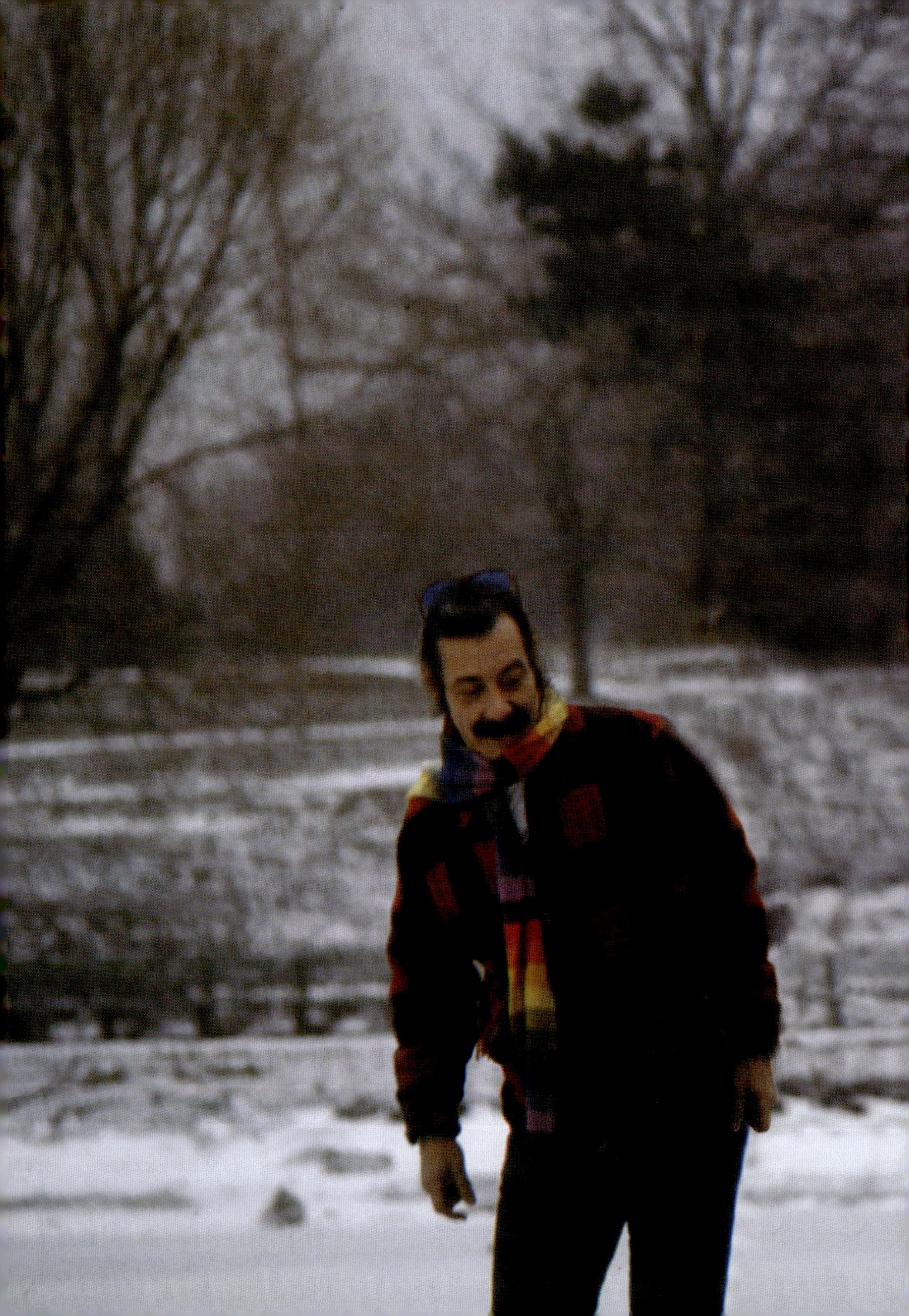

THE BEGINNING

In the 1970s, New York City had reached an all-time low. Jobs had all but disappeared in the two previous decades as factories moved from the city, and there was little money for keeping essential services open. Schools, mass transit, police, fire — they all took a hit. As the city crumbled, there was a certain sense of freedom on the streets. Almost anything went, good or bad. For many kids, graffiti provided an alternative to straight-up gang life. The more work you put into it, the higher up the food chain you went, and for kids in the inner-city, status was everything. As the media drew attention to the graffiti movement, a few interested parties stepped into the fray and helped shape the perception of what the kids were doing. Photographers Jack Stewart and Michael Lawrence documented the paintings on the trains, while advocates Hugo Martinez and Jack Pelsinger opened up workshops to shift the artists to canvas.

Martinez was an enterprising sociology major who saw legitimate artistic merit — as well as commercial potential — in the spray-paint and marker tags, where most saw only vandalism. In the fall of 1972, he recruited some of the best writers in town and organized them into a collective called the UNITED GRAFFITI ARTISTS (UGA). Soon after, he brought the group to City College and set them loose on a 10-by-40-foot wall for a first-of-its-kind gallery show that served as proof of concept.

One of the visitors to that show was Pelsinger, an entrepreneur of sorts who fell in love with the works and wanted to be involved. He reached out to Martinez and asked if the group needed studio space. The answer was yes, so Pelsinger scouted a loft in Chelsea and financed the rent, along with Michael Lawrence and arts photographer Herbert Migdoll. Lawrence was a young hippie at the time, experimenting with lots of things; when he met up with Migdoll he started to take photography seriously.

The artists began to meet and work at the loft. Of course, graffiti writers being what they are, they immediately started to tag the building, which led to a disagreement with the landlord and eventually the end of the studio arrangement. So Martinez began holding meetings at his home on 89th Street instead. Even in that cramped space, the artists thrived and continued to produce new works.

While UGA made important strides and got the writers some positive attention in the media and fine art circles, Pelsinger came to view the group as too elitist and too strictly focused on only the most skilled practitioners, so in 1974 he founded an alternative organization, the NATION OF GRAFFITI ARTISTS (NOGA), as an open workshop where kids of any age could come and learn to paint on canvas.

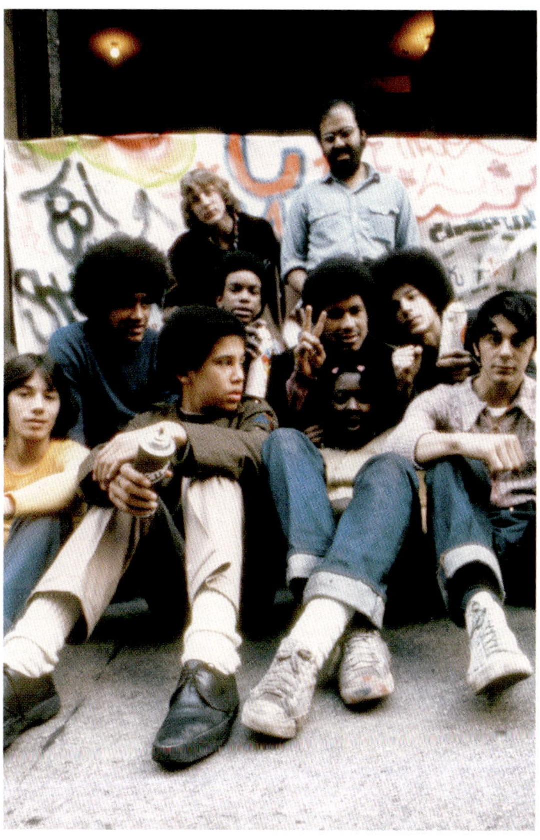

UGA, 1973. Photo by Herbert Migdoll.

NOGA had an unlikely leader in Pelsinger, an openly gay choreographer with bushy eyebrows and a handlebar mustache. He had toured the country as a modern dancer during the tumultuous 1960s. Most of his early days were spent in coffeehouses in Greenwich Village, where he developed a social conscience. In the early '70s, he taught dance, voice and acting in a space located on West 72nd Street. Pelsinger and Michael Lawrence remained friends after UGA; the young photographer even took some lessons from Pelsinger, who tried to recruit him for some of his off-Broadway musicals, most notably *Freak*, which ran in a church in Lower Manhattan.

Opposite page:
Jack Pelsinger in Central Park, 1976.
Photo by Michael Lawrence.

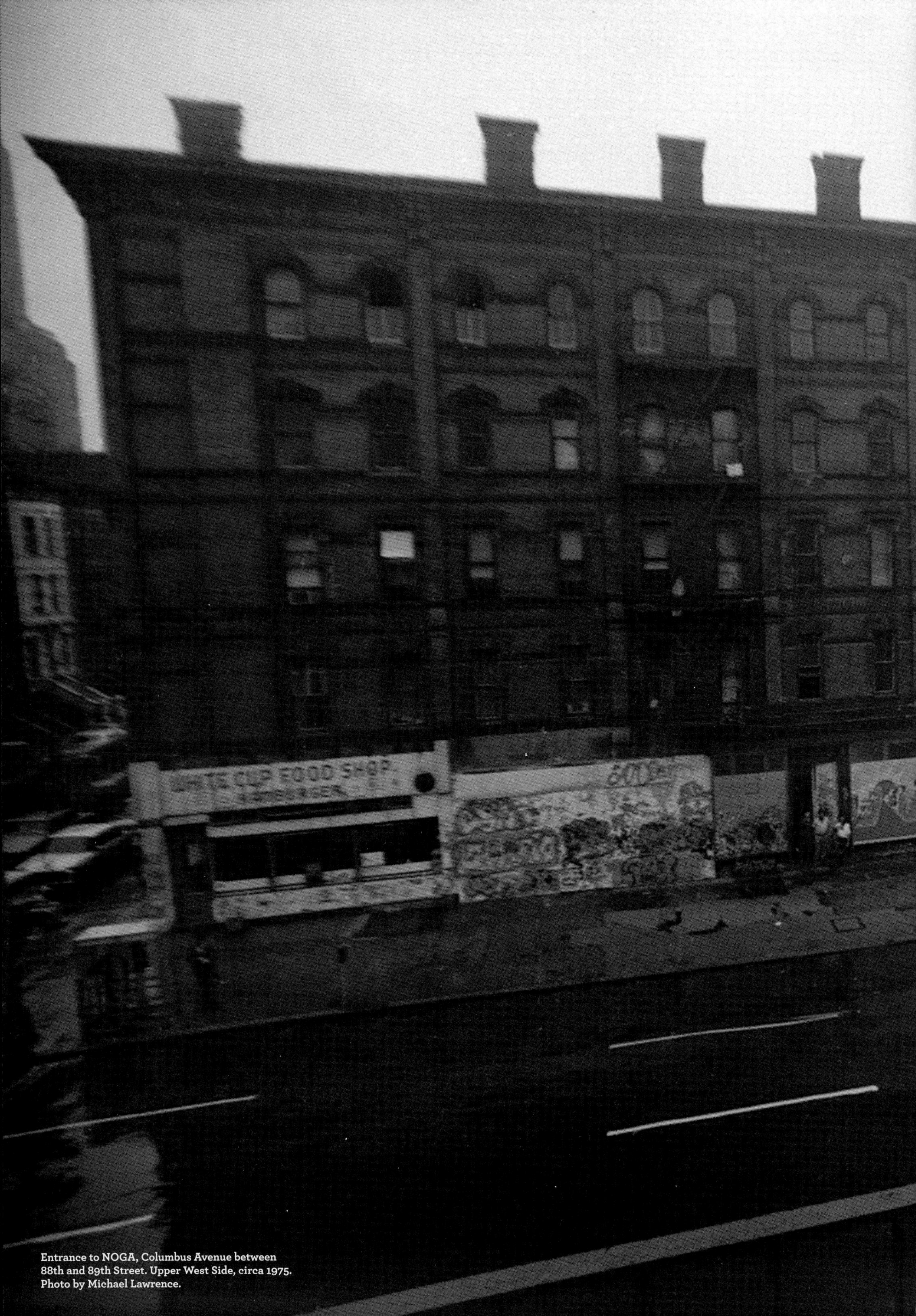

Entrance to NOGA, Columbus Avenue between
88th and 89th Street. Upper West Side, circa 1975.
Photo by Michael Lawrence.

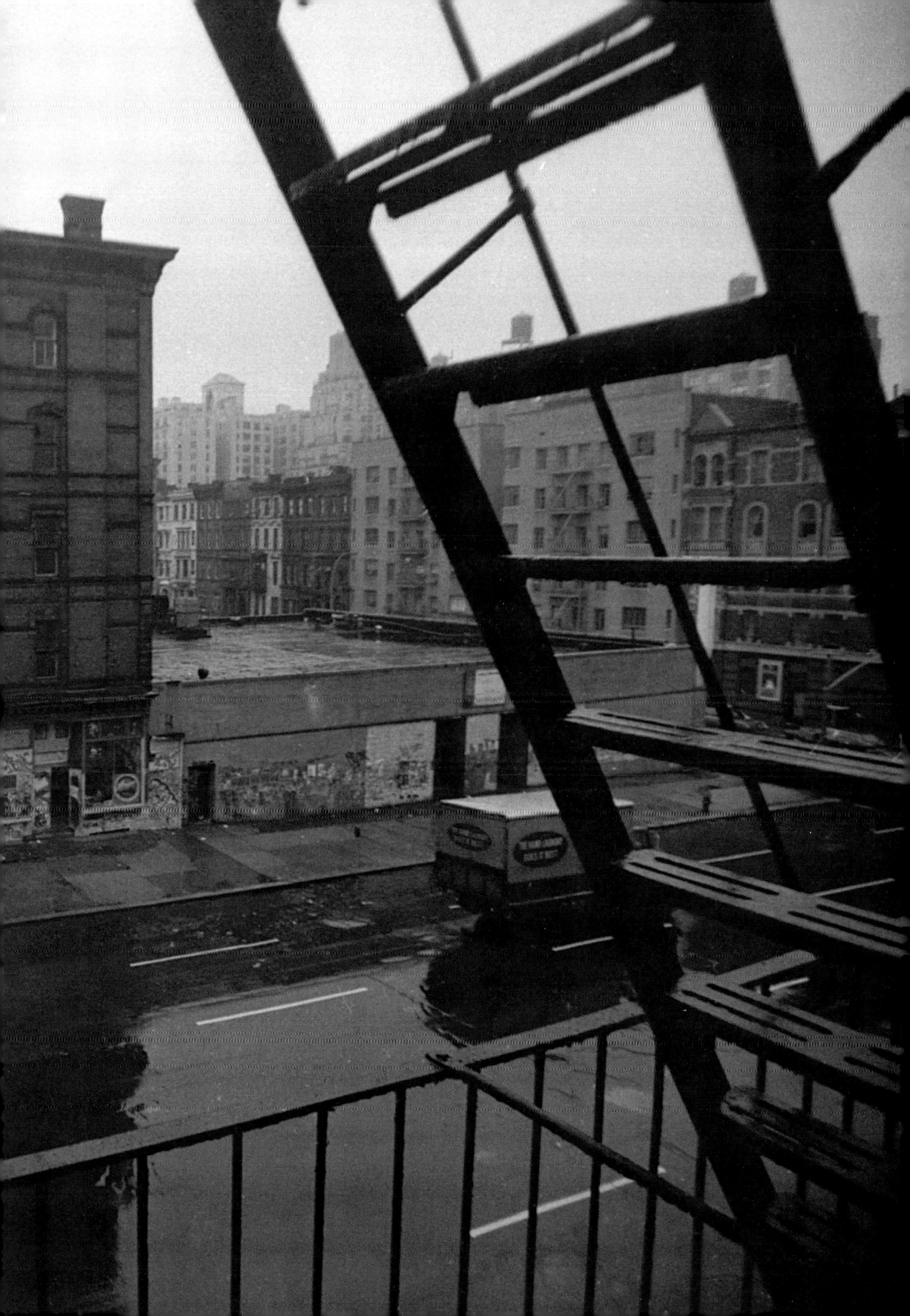

WHO'S IN CHARGE HERE?

In the summer of '74, Pelsinger was able to persuade the Mid West-Side Community Development Corporation to lease him a storefront on Columbus Avenue between 88th Street and 89th Street as a home for the NOGA workshop. He was charged a dollar a month and was given a small stipend for art supplies. The Upper West Side was a mess in the '60s, with crime running rampant and tenements falling into disrepair. The city responded in 1964 by bulldozing all buildings not in use from 84th Street to 96th Street and Columbus Avenue to Amsterdam Avenue, leaving large square patches of rubble and dirt dotting Columbus Avenue. Having kids indoors in a safe environment instead of playing in abandoned lots seemed like a great deal for the city. Over in Washington Heights, Hugo Martinez was given a large toy factory under the same terms, and UGA flourished.

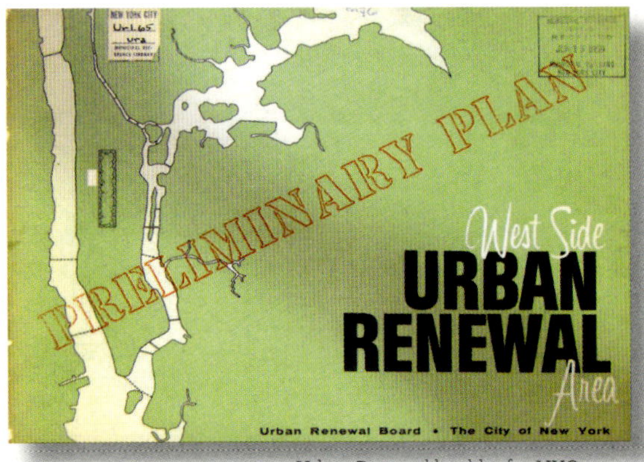

Urban Renewal booklet for NYC, 1959.

Both groups had the unenviable job of cleaning these places out and making them safe and usable. Martinez had a group of young artists who had already bonded over a number of successes; they were ambitious and worked hard to clean out the toy factory and turn it into a studio. Jack Pelsinger had no one. Unlike Martinez, who had worked on the streets and knew which writers were well respected, Pelsinger was informed only by what he had learned while at UGA. He could've pilfered some of the UGA roster but chose not to; he felt that if he built the right environment for writers, they would just show up. He would simply have to start from scratch and take all comers.

NOGA's first recruit was a neighborhood artist named Willie. Pelsinger happened to notice him because of the painted denim jacket he wore. NOGA was a perfect fit for the young artist because he was homeless at the time. Willie had grown up just a block away from the new NOGA HQ. The two struck up a conversation and discussed Pelsinger's plans for the group; both men seemed to need each other. Willie was 22 years old and could become the adult presence that was required at the workshop. In return, he'd get all the art supplies he needed. But first the place had to be built.

Willie would be the first to start hauling out all the garbage from the ground-floor storefront. As a reward, he built a loft bed for himself in the back, where he would live for two years. The artist adopted the name SCORPIO and set about mastering different mediums, including acrylic and oil paints. Pelsinger would drop by on a daily basis to leave art books around for the young painter, including a recently released book titled *Prop Art*, showing propaganda posters from around the world. The book was important, as it would help move the kids away from graffiti and into iconic imagery. Symbols would prove as important to the NOGA disciples as letters were to UGA artists.

Just weeks later, a neighborhood kid named Oscar walked through the door. He lived a block away in the projects on Amsterdam Avenue and was well liked in the neighborhood. For NOGA purposes, Oscar adopted the moniker BLOOD TEA. With his arrival the floodgates opened. Neighborhood kids turned up at all hours and pitched in to build out the workspace.

The third artist to take on a leadership role at NOGA was SAL 161, another neighborhood writer from 89th Street. As he tells it: "I was pretty much done with writing by 1974. I hit the Broadway line in 1972 and 1973, doing tags and pieces. One day in 1972 I was writing in a schoolyard with my partner MOUSEY 89. A man stood at the fence and asked me where he could find more writers. I told him to look uptown. That was Hugo Martinez. After UGA formed, Hugo told me he had enough writers, so that turned me off to UGA. When NOGA opened its doors, I was happy to do whatever I could to help. We were all from the neighborhood. Willie (SCORPIO) was from 88th Street — he was the oldest and a natural leader. Oscar (BLOOD TEA) was from my building on Amsterdam Avenue between 88th and 89th Street. He lived two floors below me. Between the three of us we knew most of the kids in the neighborhood. I think that helped get kids in there in the beginning. Some stayed, others didn't. There was a large community of writers on the Upper West Side, including a lot of first-generation writers like KING RAT, but they never showed up at NOGA. They were too old at that point."

Both SCORPIO and BLOOD TEA were natural leaders — as graffiti writers, though, they were no threat to any of the modern-day legends who walked through the door. In fact, both artists had only been to the train yards a few times. This was completely the opposite of UGA, where artists were voted in based on the impact they'd made on the trains.

Opposite page:
SCORPIO showing off his moves at NOGA, 1975.
Photo by Michael Lawrence.

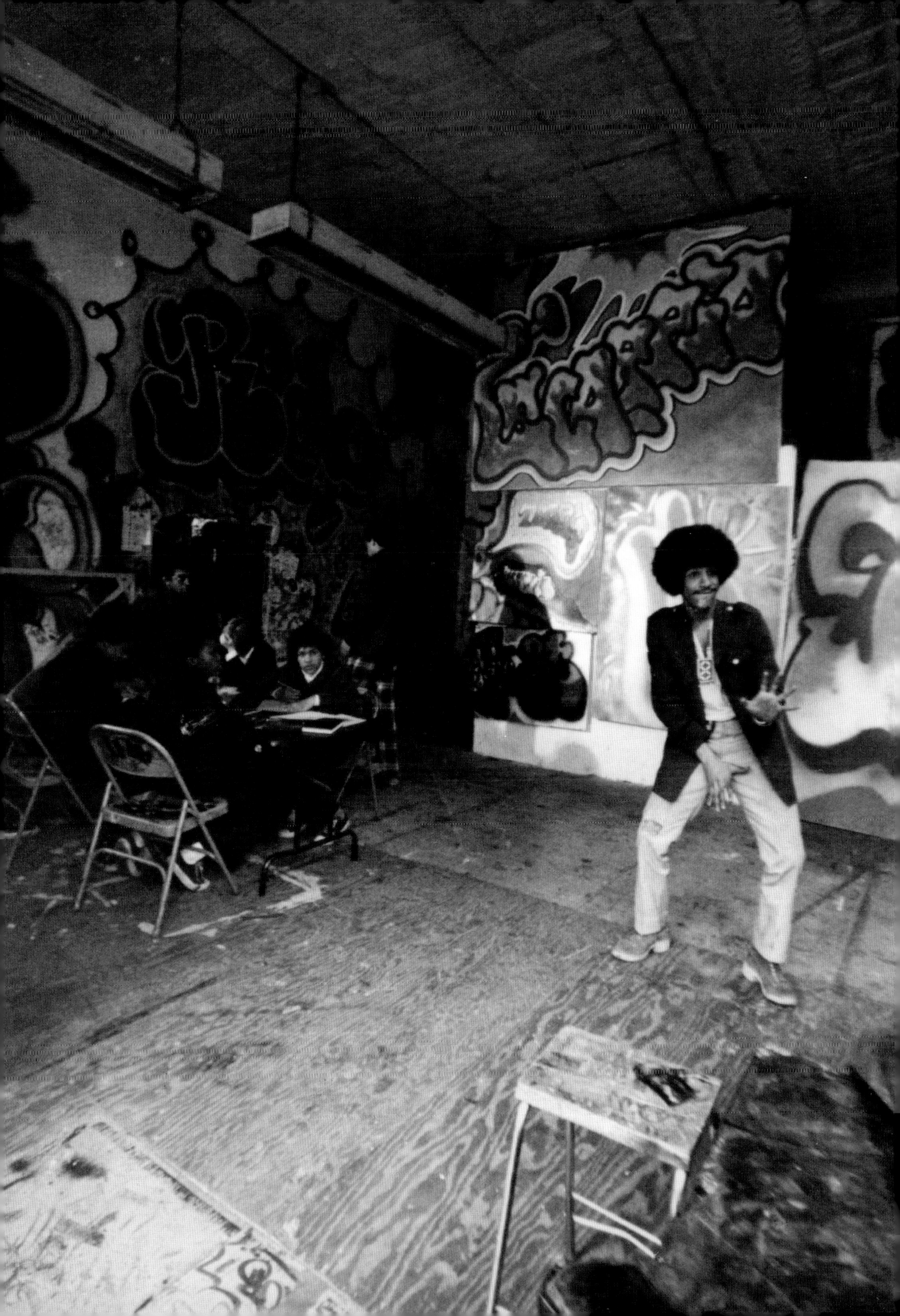

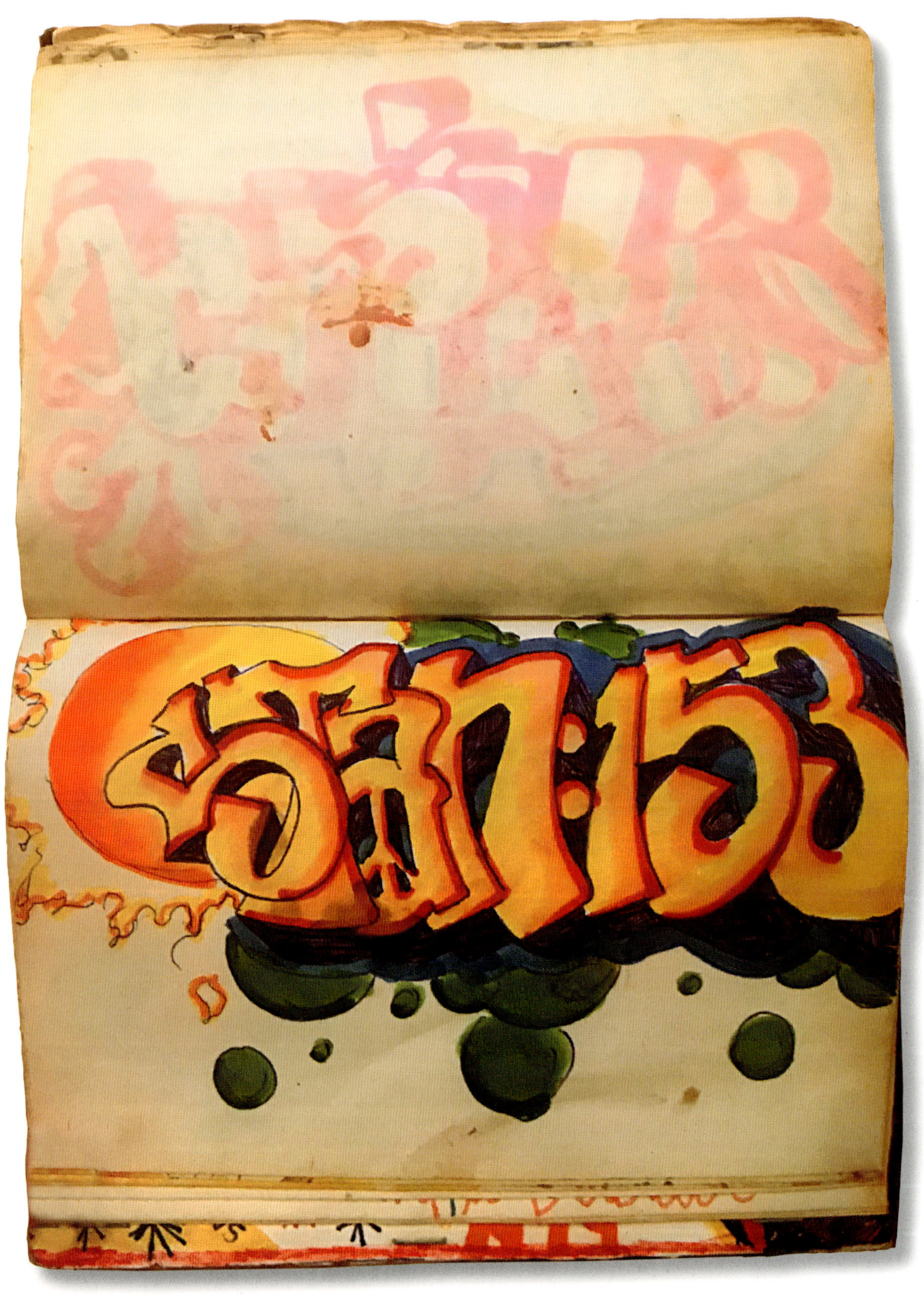

This page:
STAN 153's sketchbook, circa 1975.

Opposite page:
SCORPIO's sketchbook, 1975.

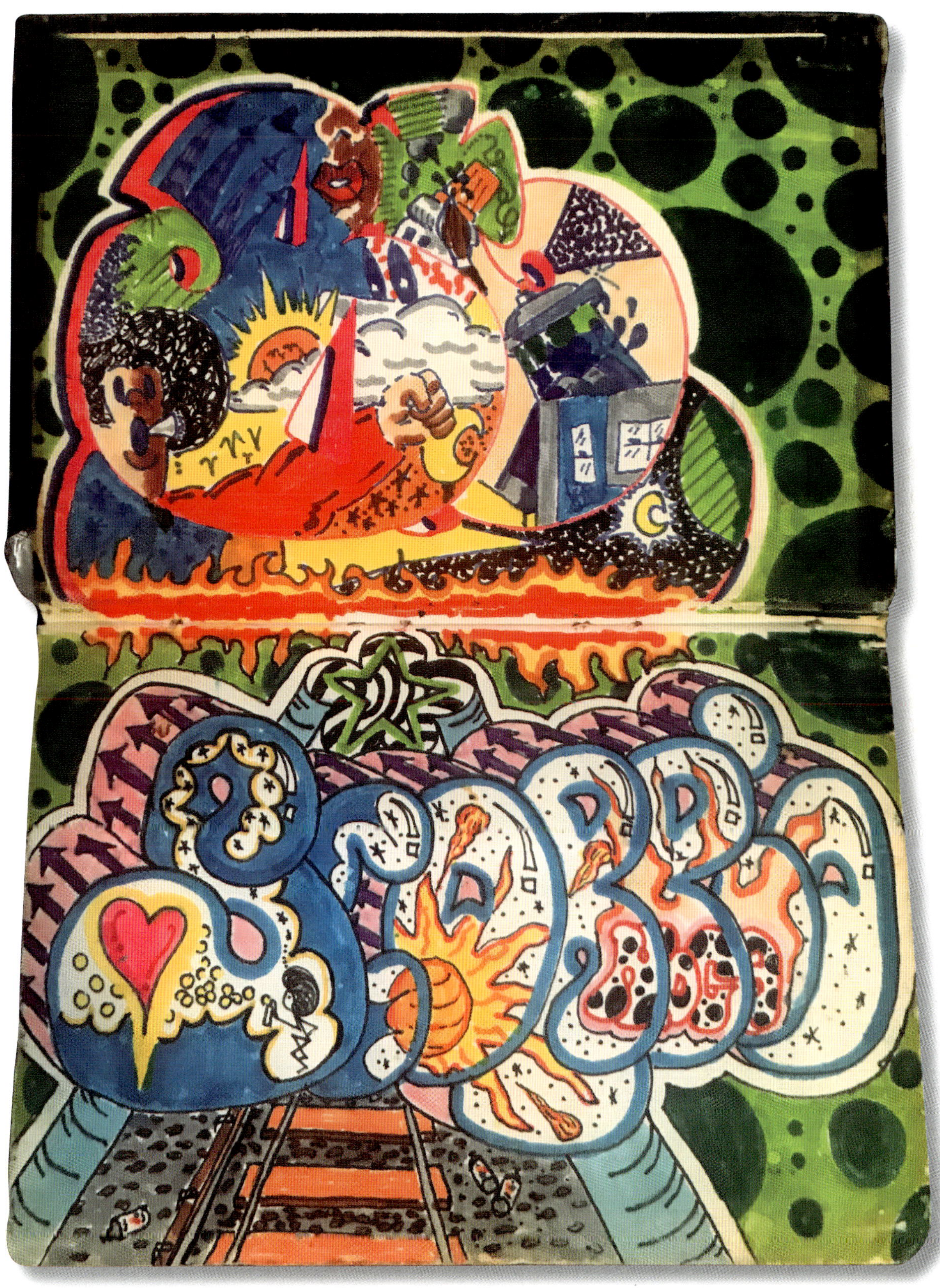

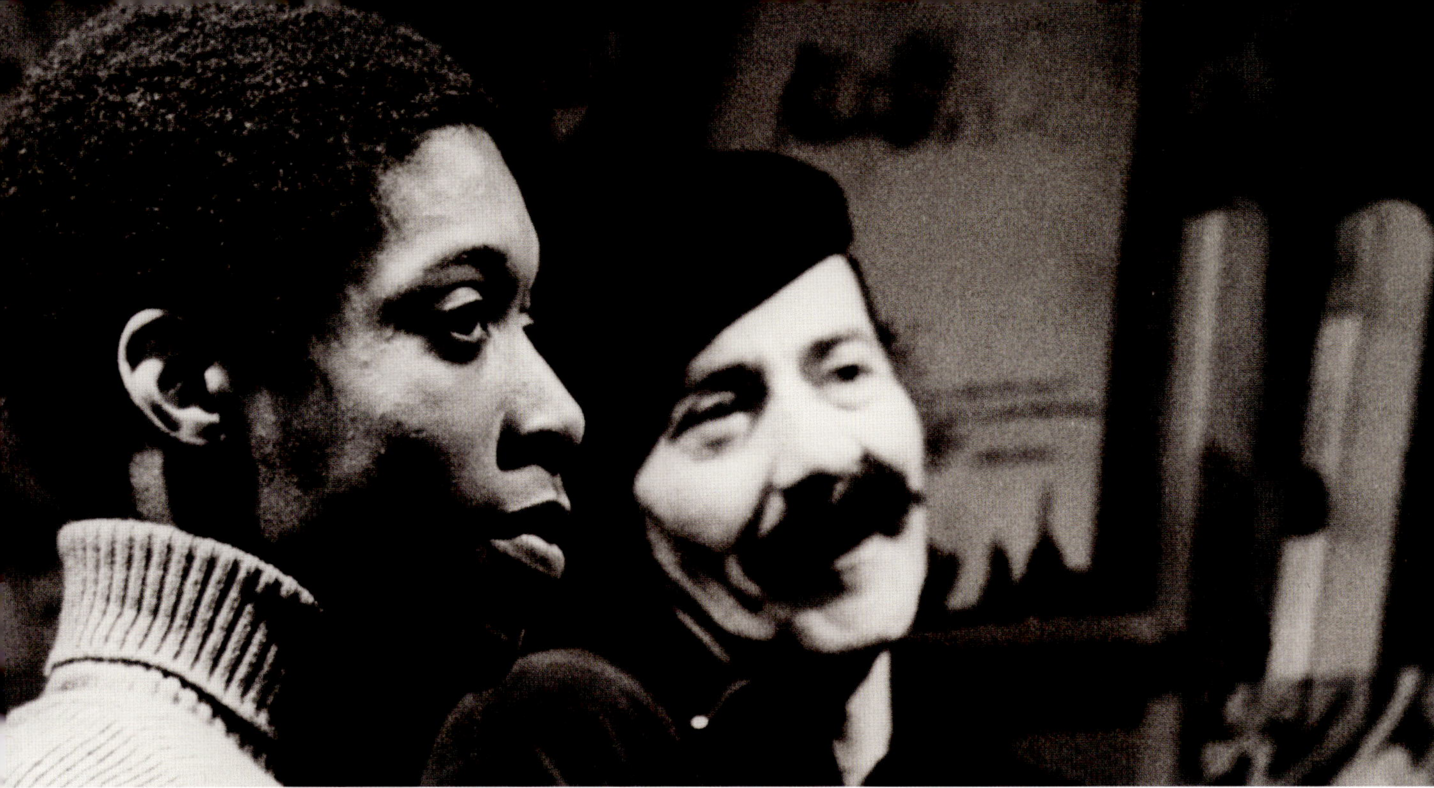

CLIFF 159

NOGA's existence spread quickly via word of mouth to the Writers Bench at 149th Street in the Bronx. It was just a quick trip on the 2 train from there to the 96th Street station; many writers took the ride just to check NOGA out.

One of the first big names to arrive at the workshop was CLIFF 159, the leader of the THREE YARD BOYS. CLIFF had started painting in 1970 as a kid writing on walls; he quickly became part of that first generation of writers to transition to hitting trains and did his first primitive pieces in 1972. Originally CLIFF was not known for having style, but that started to change in 1974 when he teamed up with TRACY 168. The two writers began painting cartoon imagery and TRACY helped CLIFF with his style and technique. In 1975 CLIFF pulled off a string of whole cars using comic book imagery, which helped push the painting of whole cars to a new level. As well as the whole cars, CLIFF's ubiquitous tags and pieces earned him the title of All-City King. His graffiti reputation was stellar, but he had a downside to him as well, as Michael Lawrence explains:

"My first time at NOGA was in early 1975. Jack and I had lost touch for a while. When I met him at his apartment, he told me all about the workshop and encouraged me to walk over there and take pictures, so I did. I walked through some abandoned lots down Columbus Avenue and found the place. I hung out for a while listening to Oscar play the conga drums. I watched SCORPIO working on a canvas. Kids would come in off the street and look around at the art. Some stayed, others ran off. I left after a few hours and started walking back to Jack's place. As I headed through one of the lots, I got jumped by two young guys with guns. I was scared, but I was also pissed off. I started to tell them where I was coming from and how I was a friend of Jack's. CLIFF 159 started laughing and put the gun away, saying the stickup was all a big joke. That's how I met CLIFF, and it was no joke."

Lawrence's assessment is spot on. NOGA was a two-room storefront with two glass windows that displayed canvases. The windows were shattered at one point and were eventually covered with sheetrock. As you entered the front door, the constant pulse of Oscar's conga drums carried through the room, in contrast to a lifeless piano that no one could figure out how to play. There were tags and pieces on every inch of the walls. Furniture had been scavenged from the street, and there were chairs and tables for people to work at.

There was a second room that you could enter on the left side of the space, but that room kept you out of the banter and shared experience of the first room — and NOGA was definitely intended to be a shared experience. Incense and marijuana mingled in the air, particularly in the late-night hours when the neighborhood kids were gone.

CLIFF 159 proved to be a wild card for the group. There were many late nights when CLIFF would walk Pelsinger home so he wouldn't get robbed, and that earned him a place of loyalty in his heart. That loyalty would one day be tested when CLIFF himself attempted to rob the older man. A number of writers heard of the incident and demanded CLIFF be thrown out, but Pelsinger wouldn't budge. CLIFF would stay for better or worse.

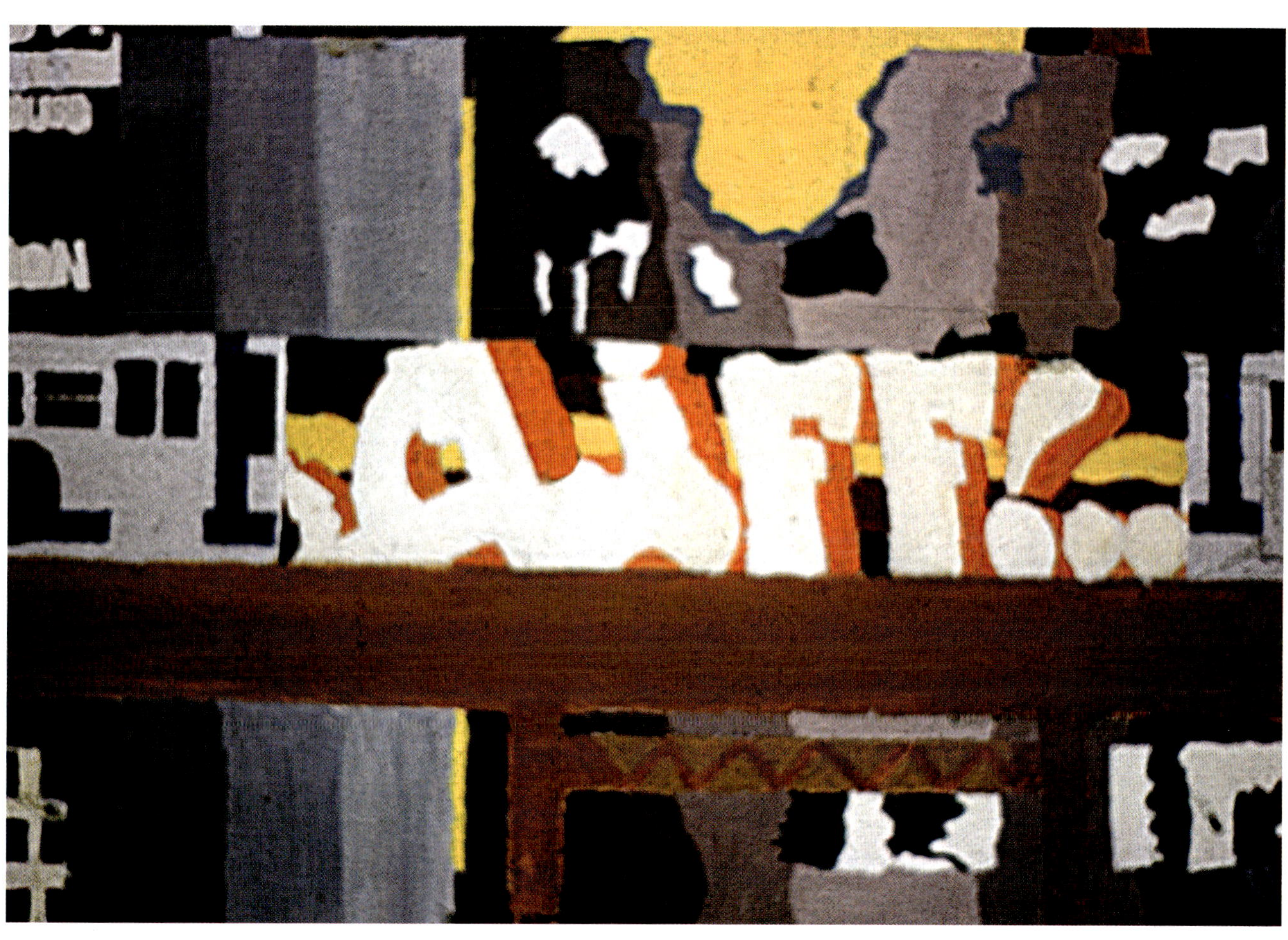

Opposite page:
CLIFF 159 and Jack Pelsinger, founder and organizer of NOGA, 1975.

This page:
CLIFF 159 was king of the city in 1975 when he
painted this canvas at NOGA. Photos by Michael Lawrence.

Graffiti finally gets welcome home

The West Sider 7/24-75

By STEVEN GREENHOUSE

Cliff 159 is only 17 years old, yet he has seen his best friend, Stim One, die and another close friend, Ali, burst into flames, almost burning to death.

The way Cliff tells it Stim One was spray painting graffiti inside a subway car when he was spotted by two undercover police officers. They gave chase and Stim One fled, hiding in between cars.

According to Cliff, Stim One either tried to jump off the moving train, which Cliff thinks his buddy was too smart to attempt, or was pushed by the police, which Cliff thinks is the more likely possibility. Whichever, Stim One spilled onto the tracks and was run over by the train.

Then there was Cliff's friend Ali. Several months ago, Ali, a gifted graffiti artist, was painting a "masterpiece" at the underground trainyard at 148th Street and Lenox Avenue. While painting, Ali stored his artist's materials—26 spray cans—in a shopping bag only a few feet from the third rail, which had its power off.

Around 5 a.m. Ali heard a train start up on a nearby track so he rushed over to move his aerosol arsenal before the electricity in his track was turned on. Just as he reached his shopping bag, a trainman flicked the power switch and his bag ignited into a mushrooming cloud.

Ali lunged away from the flames, but not soon enough; his clothes were ablaze. Today Ali's body is healed, but his hands remain scarred.

Cliff has also had his share of troubles, twice being arrested by

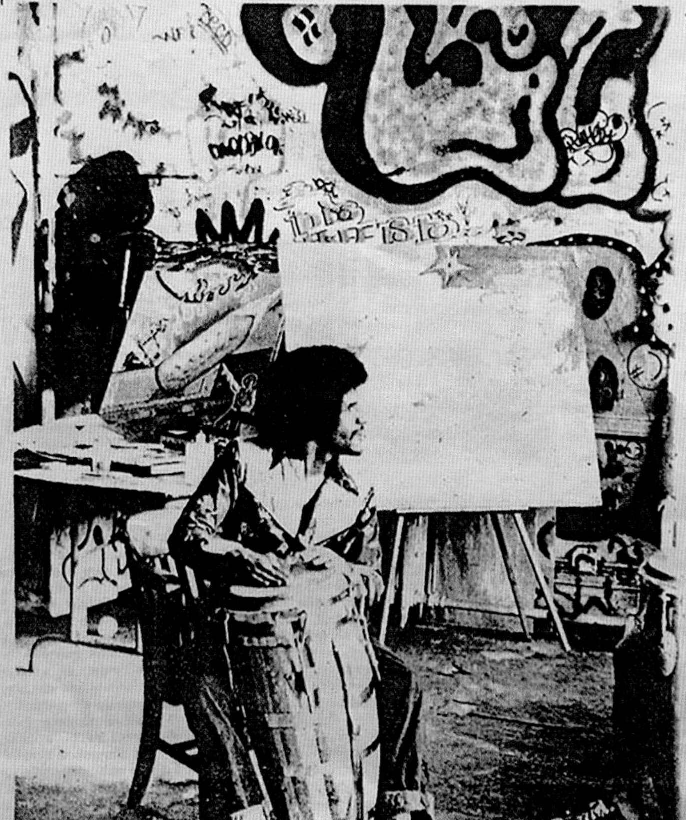

have been lack of space and lack of money. On some months as many as 1,500 youths from all over the city would drop into NOGA and at some moments the small makeshift center would be crowded with 75 youths. Many went back to painting trains because they were discouraged by the overcrowding.

Ultimately, NOGA would like a larger home—its members have their mind set on a deserted warehouse on West 90th Street. However, instead of a larger home, NOGA may end up with no home at all.

Pelsinger and company say the city's rent increase and subsequent eviction notice typify its callous attitude towards NOGA and graffiti artists in general. Pelsinger says that NOGA, which relies on contributions and the sale of its members' paintings, can't possibly afford to pay the rent increase.

Explaining why the city raised NOGA's rent, Philip Furman, the Housing and Development Administration's chief of management, said, "The city is broke and in need of money, so we've been reviewing the rents of some tenants. We're landlords and we have to get money from our buildings."

Furman said that groups threatened by rent increases can come to the HDA to negotiate. He said that NOGA never came down to a hearing to state why it couldn't pay a rent hike.

Pelsinger denies ever having received a notice about any hearing and added that if evicted, NOGA's artists would squat somewhere and set up shop.

Blood Tea, a thin, energetic 16-year-old who spends his days at

to worry about police dogs, personal danger and public disapproval.

Cliff has moved his workshop 60 blocks downtown from the 148th Street Yard to a kaleidoscopically colorful, cluttered storefront at 88th Street and Columbus Avenue, the Nation of Graffiti Artists.

Cliff is one of 200 graffiti artists, ranging from 12 to 25 years of age, who paint regularly at NOGA, which celebrates its first birthday in August.

"Celebrate" may be the wrong word since by August NOGA may be evicted from its storefront for not paying the city its rent, which was raised from $1 a month to $55 a month in June. So Cliff and his 200 brothers-in-graffiti may soon be back on the street or in the subway tunnels.

Cliff shudders at the thought of NOGA's closing. NOGA has been good to him since he came here four months ago, providing him with oil paints, acrylics, canvases, friends, guidance, reinforcement, a taste of social respectability and a market for his art.

Cliff fears that if NOGA closes he'll return to his old, perilous routine—cutting school, stealing spray cans during the day and painting at night.

Jack Pelsinger fears this also. Pelsinger, a 40-year-old former dancer, actor, artist and filmmaker was the Prometheus who provided the spark to establish NOGA.

For two years before opening NOGA, Pelsinger worked on a film about graffiti, which in his opinion deserves public appreciation rather than condemnation.

His vision was to establish a center where graffiti artists could work with pride, without danger, with materials provided for them, with the opportunity to work with and learn from one another, and with the possibility of directing their energies and talents to more socially acceptable and profitable channels.

Pelsinger's vision took a long step towards fruition in early 1974 when he first introduced himself to Scorpio, a 22-year-old graffiti artist, who was drunk on the corner of 88th and Columbus. For weeks, Pelsinger had admired Scorpio's brilliantly painted denim jacket and finally stopped to chat with Scorpio.

A bushy-haired, friendly youth who immigrated from the Dominican Republic when he was 12, Scorpio first thought Pelsinger was an undercover policeman. He later grew to trust Pelsinger and under Pelsinger's guidance swore off the bottle and swore to start taking his painting seriously.

"If it weren't for NOGA, I'd still be a bum on the street," Scorpio said the other day, while about 20 people painted, played

congas, blared music, danced, sketched and chatted at NOGA. Scorpio, NOGA's most prolific artist, has sold about ten of his paintings, several of them for more than $300. His successes have inspired many NOGA artists.

Scorpio keeps half the money for himself and the other half goes back to NOGA, which operates on a tattered shoestring of a budget—between $100 and $200 monthly, according to Pelsinger.

Ever since NOGA was founded, its principal problems

train so let's book him. We're not hurting anyone. We're not mugging anyone."

Blood Tea would like to see NOGA "become a city-wide thing for ghetto people." He'd like to see it grow into a center for music and theater also—indeed NOGA is trying to set up a band. "It's not just an art place," says Blood Tea. "It's a place for people to relate, to get to know they're people."

To suggestions that artists go down to NOGA and teach art, Pelsinger says, "In time we'd like to learn new forms, but for now art teachers would undoubtedly take away from the originality and charm of their work. What's so good about it now is that you just give them a canvas and they go out and do it."

Scorpio, for instance, dots his paintings with transparent domes symbolizing the world of harmony and wholeness he'd like to see. One night he did a painting entitled "Afro-Liberty" of a black Statue of Liberty in chains and a question mark on her face. Scorpio wrote his signature in lightning letters shattering Liberty's chains.

A french gallery purchased "Afro-Liberty" for $300. This winter several NOGA artists are scheduled to go to Paris to show and try to sell some of their works at a Left Bank gallery. Not bad for a group of youths who rarely leave the inner city.

In addition to going to France, NOGA's artists would like to see the city give them 10 subway cars to paint. "A lot of graffiti is a mess," says Cliff. "We'd organize ourselves and work together and show people what we're capable of doing. They'd be amazed."

Scorpio, graffiti artist par excellence, plays a conga in NOGA's colorful headquarters.

Photos: Steven Greenhouse

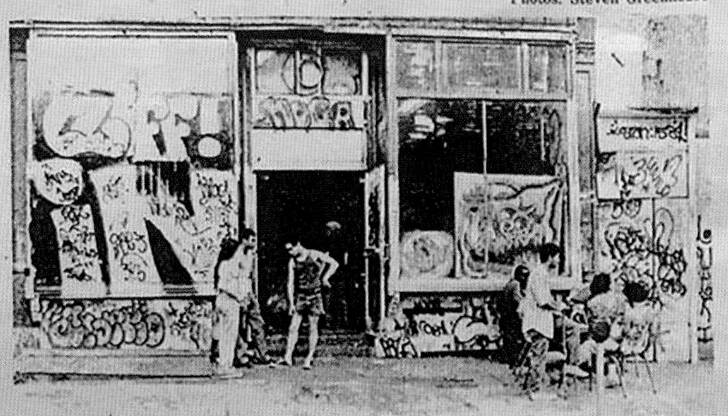

A typical scene of NOGA's storefront on a sweltering summer afternoon.

"

"CLIFF FEARS THAT IF NOGA CLOSES HE'LL RETURN TO HIS OLD, PERILOUS ROUTINE– CUTTING SCHOOL, STEALING SPRAY CANS DURING THE DAY AND PAINTING AT NIGHT."

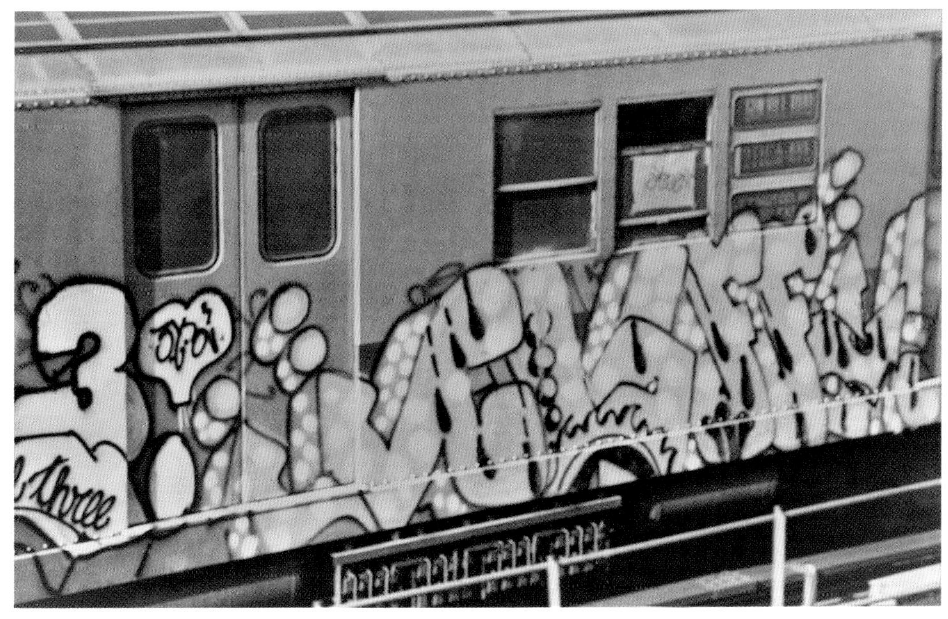

Opposite page:
Article from *The West Sider*, July 1975.

This page:
CLIFF 159 piece done at the height of his fame, 1975.
Photo by Michael Lawrence.

For.Them Graffiti Is No Longer An Underground Movement

By SANDY SATTERWHITE

Oscar Acevedo, better known to his peers as "P̶ ̶ ̶ Tel." (and more re- ̶ ̶ ̶ Nigger") ̶ ̶ "name" in bold ̶ ̶ ̶ most graffiti

̶ ̶ y hitting the trains once in ̶ days. ̶ ̶ as joined the ̶ Graffiti Artists, a ̶ ̶ ̶ ed workshop, where he paints on canvas.

Gesturing to indicate a depth of expression, he said, "To me, my art is my name, I put my feeling into my art, I make my name into the mood I'm in, I do it differ- ently, in acrylics, oils..."

He's a 15-year-old fresh- man at Brandeis HS. The other day he stood before a mural which the teenagers were in the process of paint- ing on the walls in a hallway of WARM UP, a musical re- hearsal studio at 315 W. 36th St.

"Going to the workshop keeps me out of trouble (he was never busted for "writ- ing"), my mind is more at ease," he said.

Pointing to the "Goo-Goo" eyeballs which overlooked every piece of his work on the mural, Acevedo explain- ed, "It's me watching what I do. Since I can't be there, my 'eyes' are looking over it, making sure that nothing happens to it."

The Nation of Graffiti Artists was founded less than a year ago by Jack Pel- singer, a 40ish one-time pain- ter, dancer, theater director who arranged for the studio mural painting and for an exhibit now on display at the Central Savings Bank branch at Broadway and 73d St.

Pelsinger believes that graffiti, known for its adornment or defacement — depending on your point of view—of the city's subways, has been accepted within the last year as an art form in New York City. "Art critics have called it an art form," he said. "They just don't understand it outside the city." Then, after a pause, "I think Chicago does."

He had thought it was "wonderful, watching the trains go by with color and form." But he had also re-

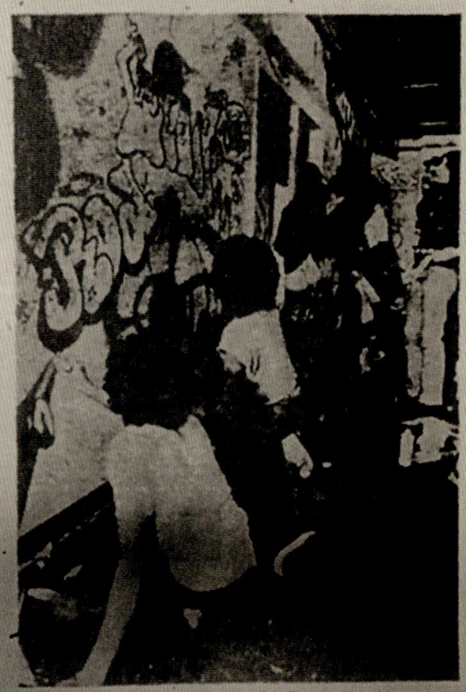

Post Photo by Nury Hernandez

Young members of Nation of Graffiti Artists Workshop do their thing legally.

engaged in graffiti "were screaming out to be wanted, accepted, needed, helped, all of these things."

Pelsinger, who refers to these teenagers as "graffiti people," said he's trying to rechannel their energies. "Hopefully, I'm trying to show them how to use their art to make a living because some of these people are not only interested in graf- fiti, but also other forms of art."

With his dark-brown hair pulled back with an elastic band under a denim paint- er's cap, he was at the musical rehearsal studio the other day keeping a watch- ful eye on operations. The owners, Mark Abramson, a record producer, and his wife, Janet Young, an actress, are converting the garment cent- er loft into a modern studio for use by professional musicians.

"I think it's [graffiti] beautiful, it's indigenous to this city," Janet Young said. "There's a lot of energy in their work, they do a lot of primary colors, it seems musical to me as well."

Contact:

Jack Pelsinger
580-9760

Livi French
737-9358

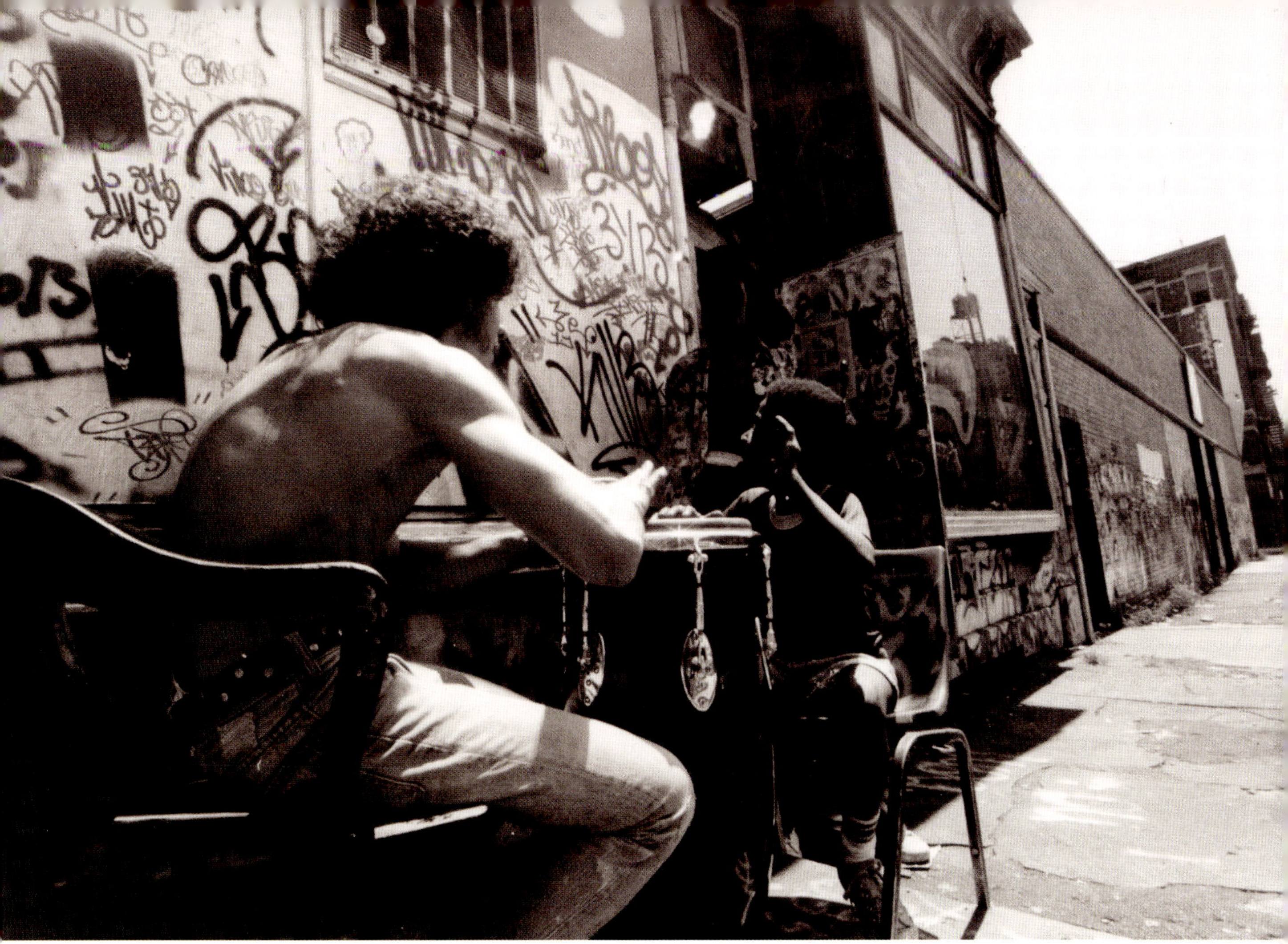

THE CAST OF CHARACTERS

By the time Michael Lawrence arrived to take photos of the workshop, a pecking order had developed among the artists. They were divided into three groups on a list on the wall. Group A were the heavy hitters in the graffiti community, as well as neighborhood writers who had helped build the place. Among them were SCORPIO and BLOOD TEA; ALI, the founder of the SOUL ARTISTS; STAN 153, a newly retired writer whose name appeared in Norman Mailer's book *The Faith of Graffiti*; SAL 161; and CLIFF 159, one of the top writers of his generation. There were others in the A column, including BAMA, the leader of UGA, who arrived at NOGA to help teach painting in 1975. In a recent interview he described the experience:

"NOGA was very free flowing — it was like a party with kids of all ages hanging out. I always thought that what we were doing was art, even when I was tagging trains. When UGA started, I began working on canvas and became a painter, so when I arrived at NOGA that was how I identified myself. I was the guy who had had gallery success, who knew how to stretch canvases and who worked in different mediums, and I was glad to pass on what I knew."

STAN 153 had this to say about the NOGA/UGA comparison in a 2019 interview: "The writers from UGA were considered the A team in 1975, the best there was, while NOGA was viewed as the B team. But the NOGA guys were younger and still painting trains, and by 1976 the NOGA writers had become the A team."

The neighborhood's reputation for lawlessness was captured in 1975, when the movie *Taxi Driver* was filmed across the street from the workshop. Travis Bickle's apartment (of "You talkin' to me?" fame) was set up in an abandoned building on the other side of Columbus Avenue. *Deadly Hero*, a gritty crime drama featuring James Earl Jones and a young Treat Williams, was shooting just around the corner at the same time. Lawrence spent six weeks working on that film with other members from NOGA, a deal brokered by Pelsinger. During those weeks the photographer was given valuable excess film to shoot with. The exterior of NOGA can be seen during a chase scene in the film.

Opposite page:
New York Post article from the NOGA press kit assembled by Livi French, 1974.

This page:
NOGA provides the backdrop for two conga players on Columbus Avenue, 1975. Photo by Michael Lawrence.

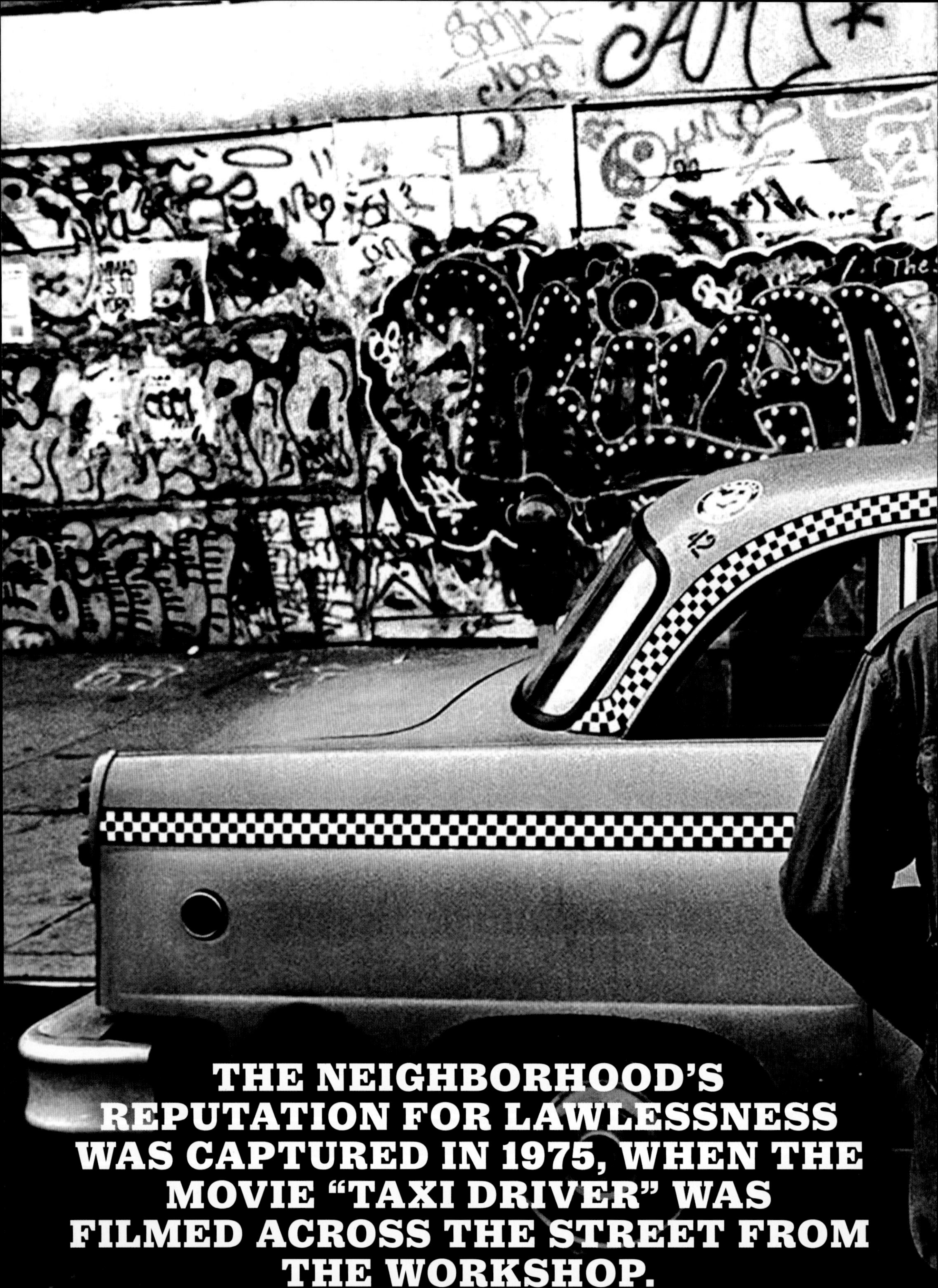

THE NEIGHBORHOOD'S
REPUTATION FOR LAWLESSNESS
WAS CAPTURED IN 1975, WHEN THE
MOVIE "TAXI DRIVER" WAS
FILMED ACROSS THE STREET FROM
THE WORKSHOP.

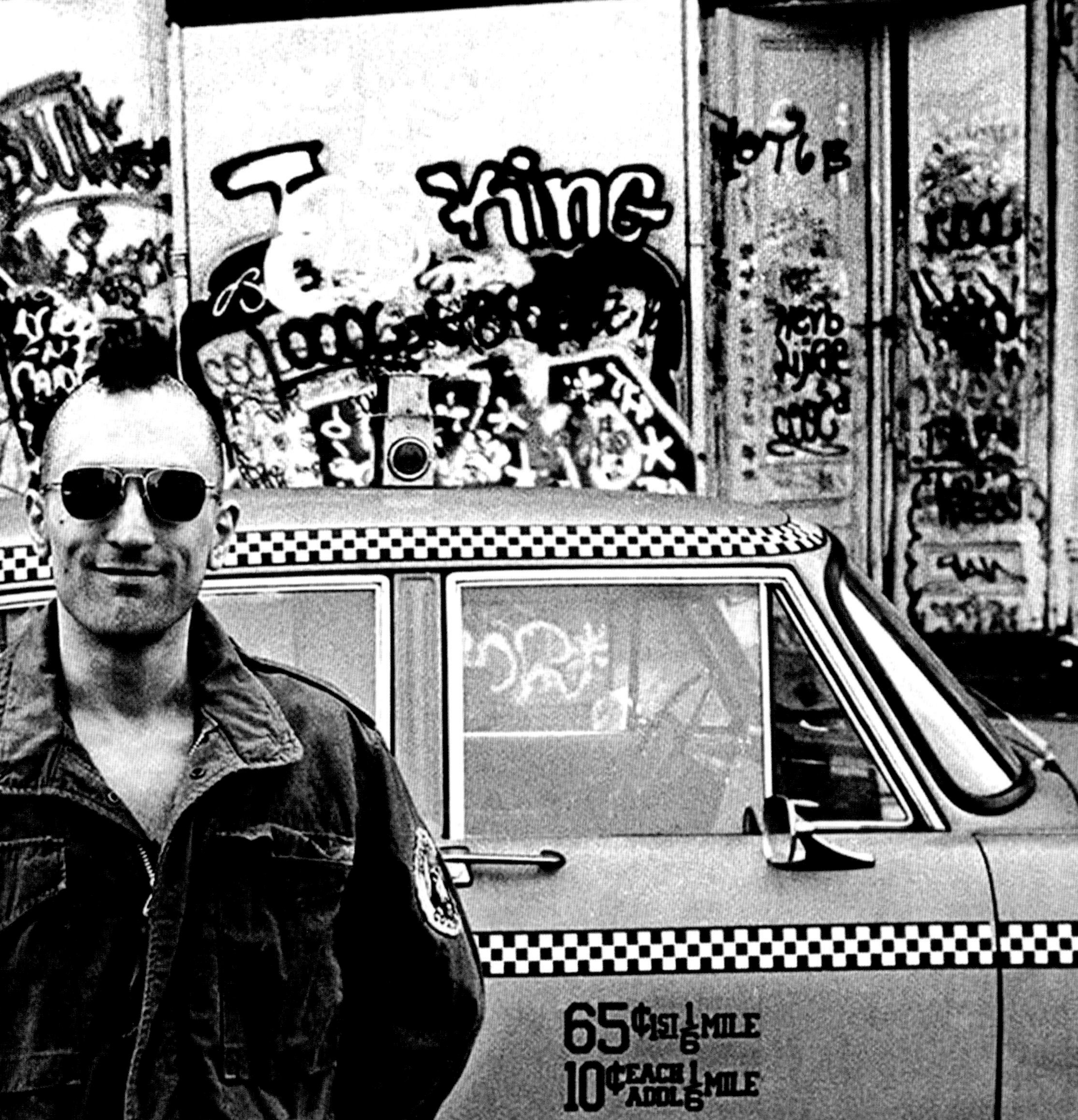
KING
65¢ 1ST 1/6 MILE
10¢ EACH ADDL 1/6 MILE

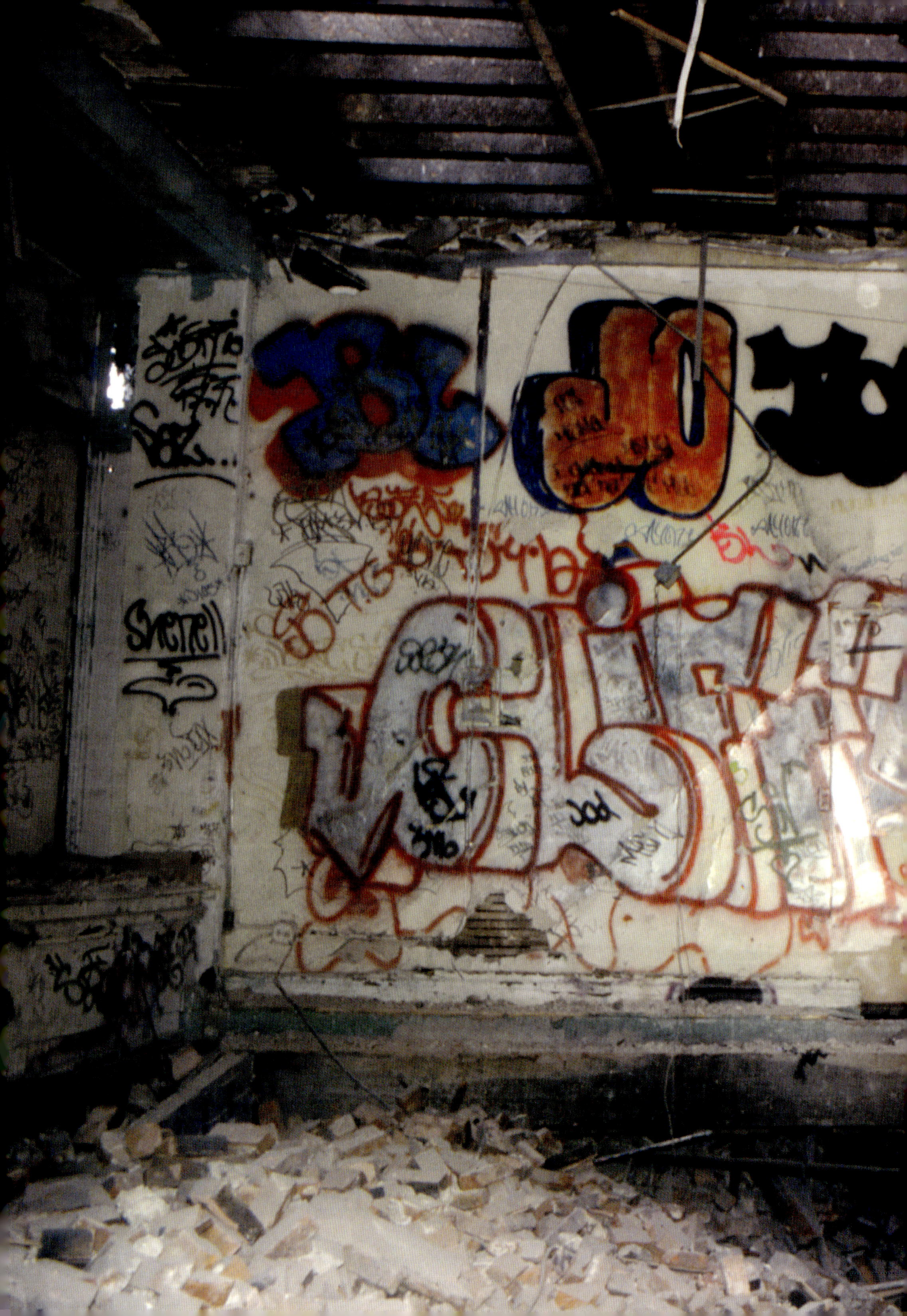

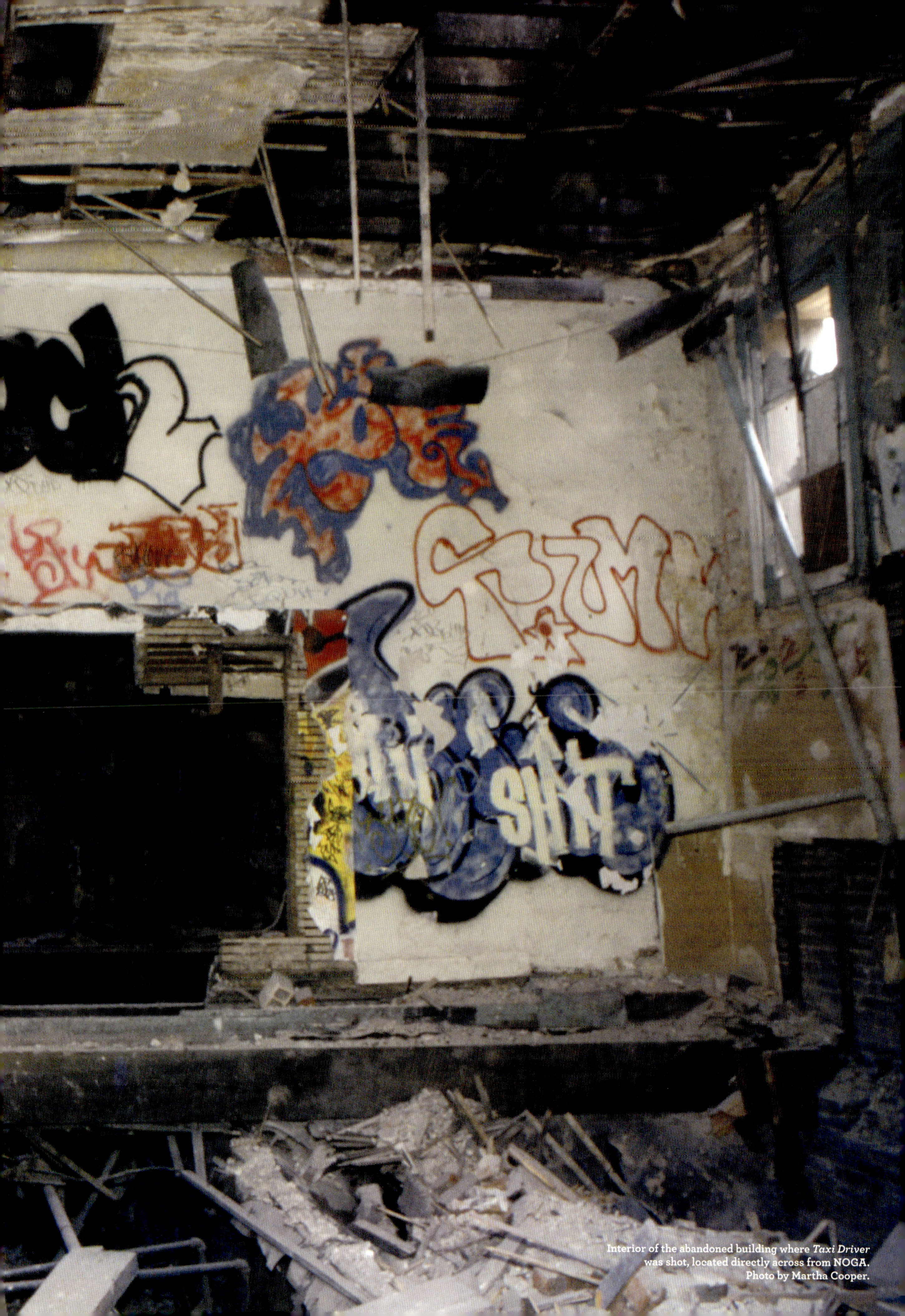

Interior of the abandoned building where *Taxi Driver* was shot, located directly across from NOGA. Photo by Martha Cooper.

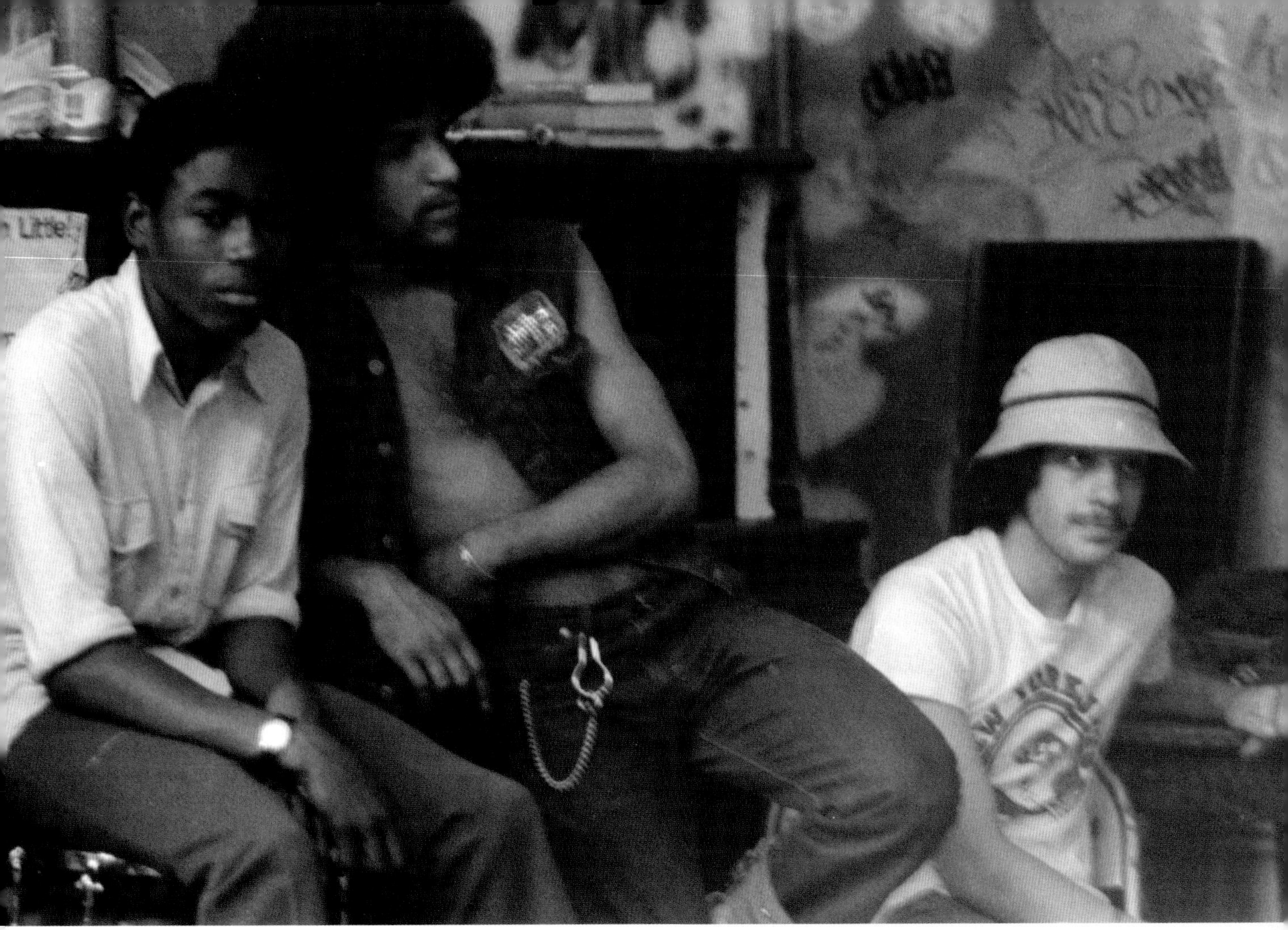

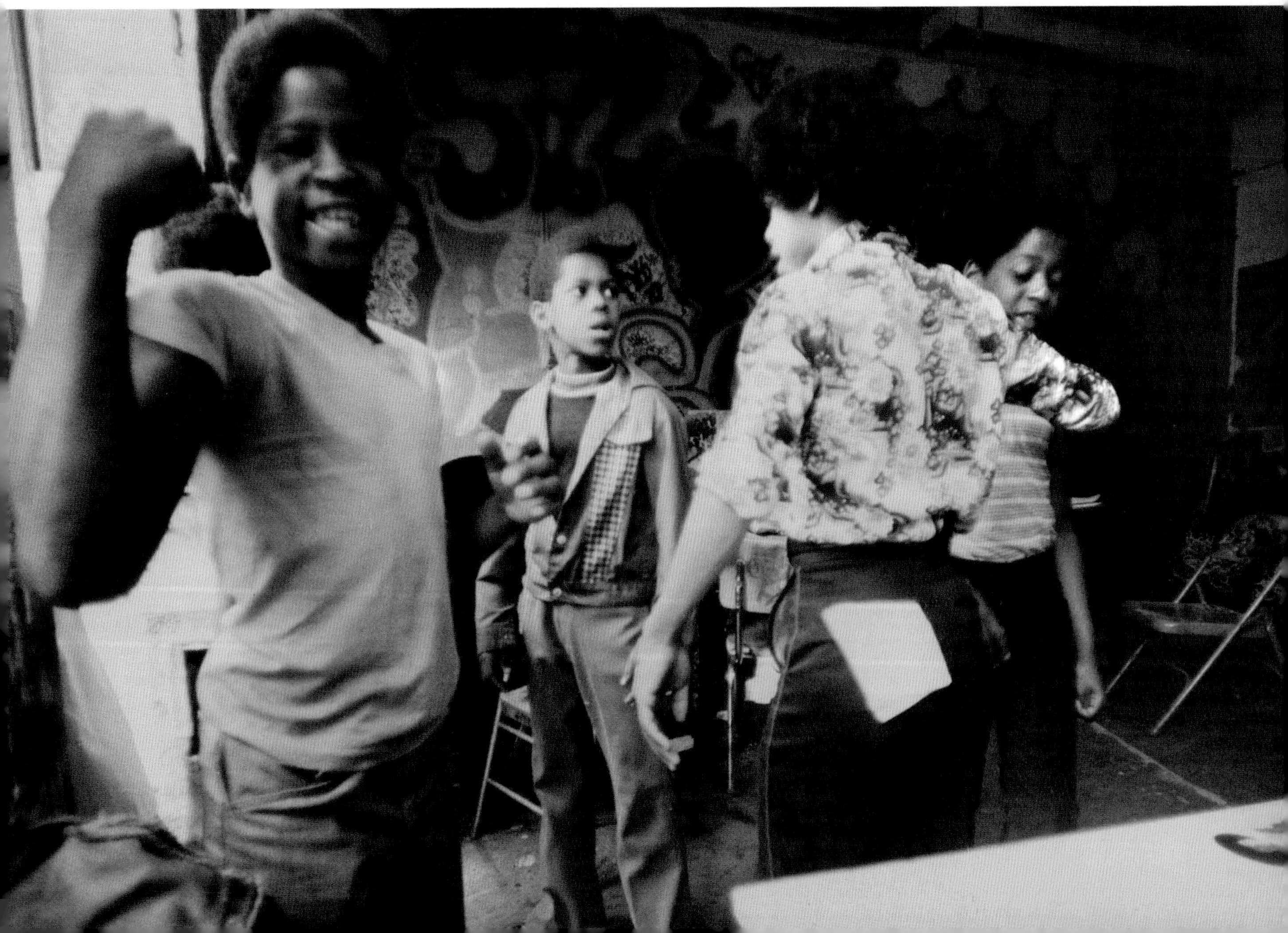

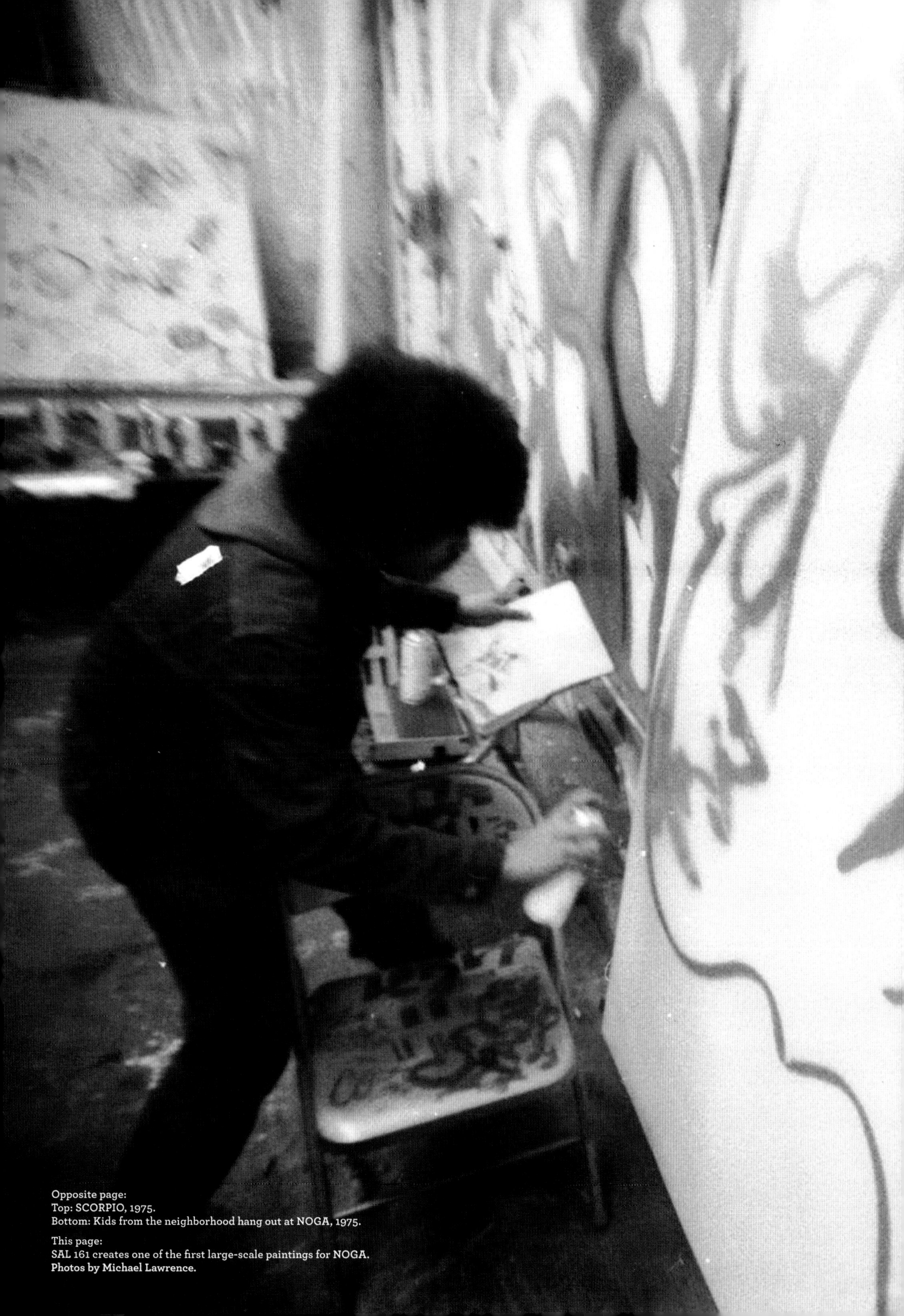

Opposite page:
Top: SCORPIO, 1975.
Bottom: Kids from the neighborhood hang out at NOGA, 1975.

This page:
SAL 161 creates one of the first large-scale paintings for NOGA.
Photos by Michael Lawrence.

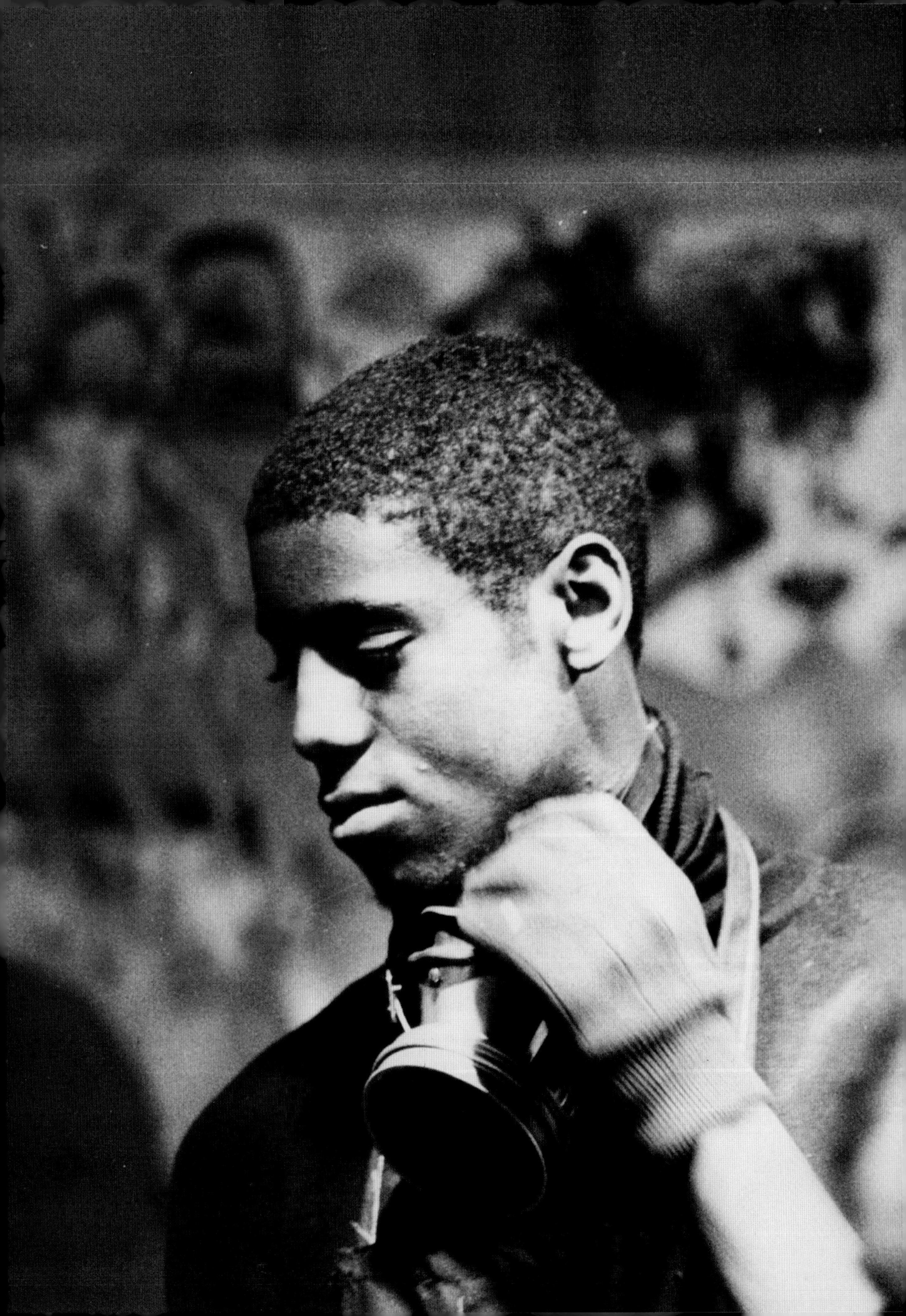

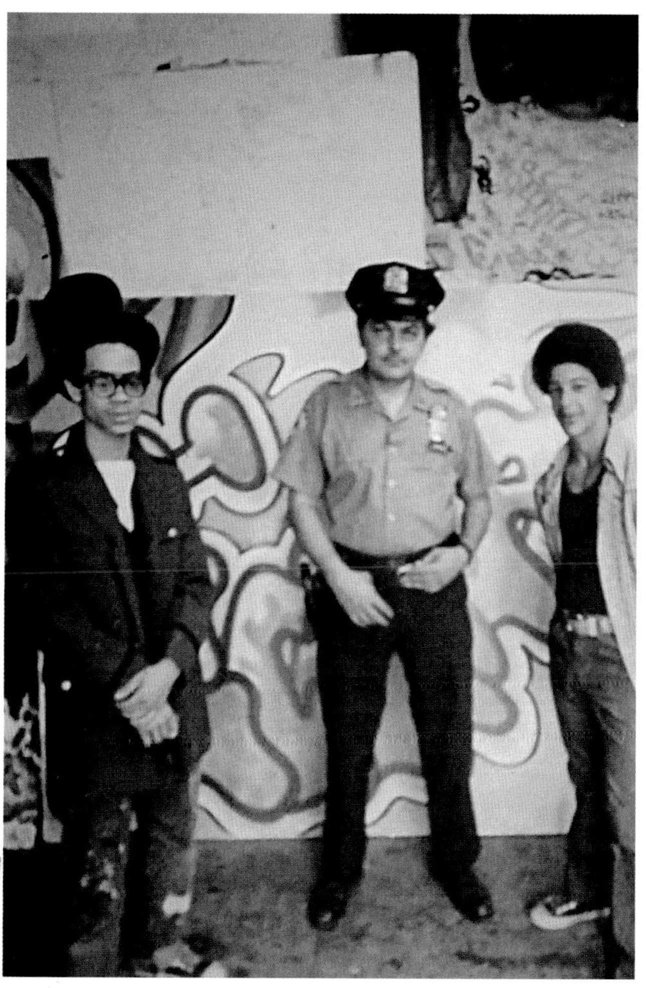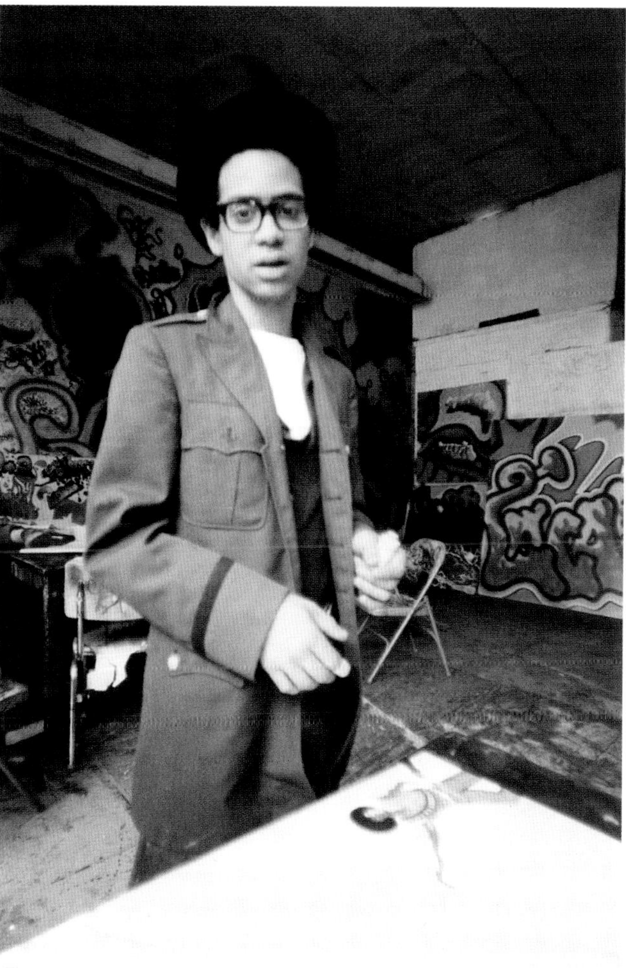

Opposite page:
SCAR 36, 1975.

This page:
BLOOD TEA with local police officer and fellow NOGA artist, 1975.
BLOOD TEA, 1975.
Photos by Michael Lawrence.

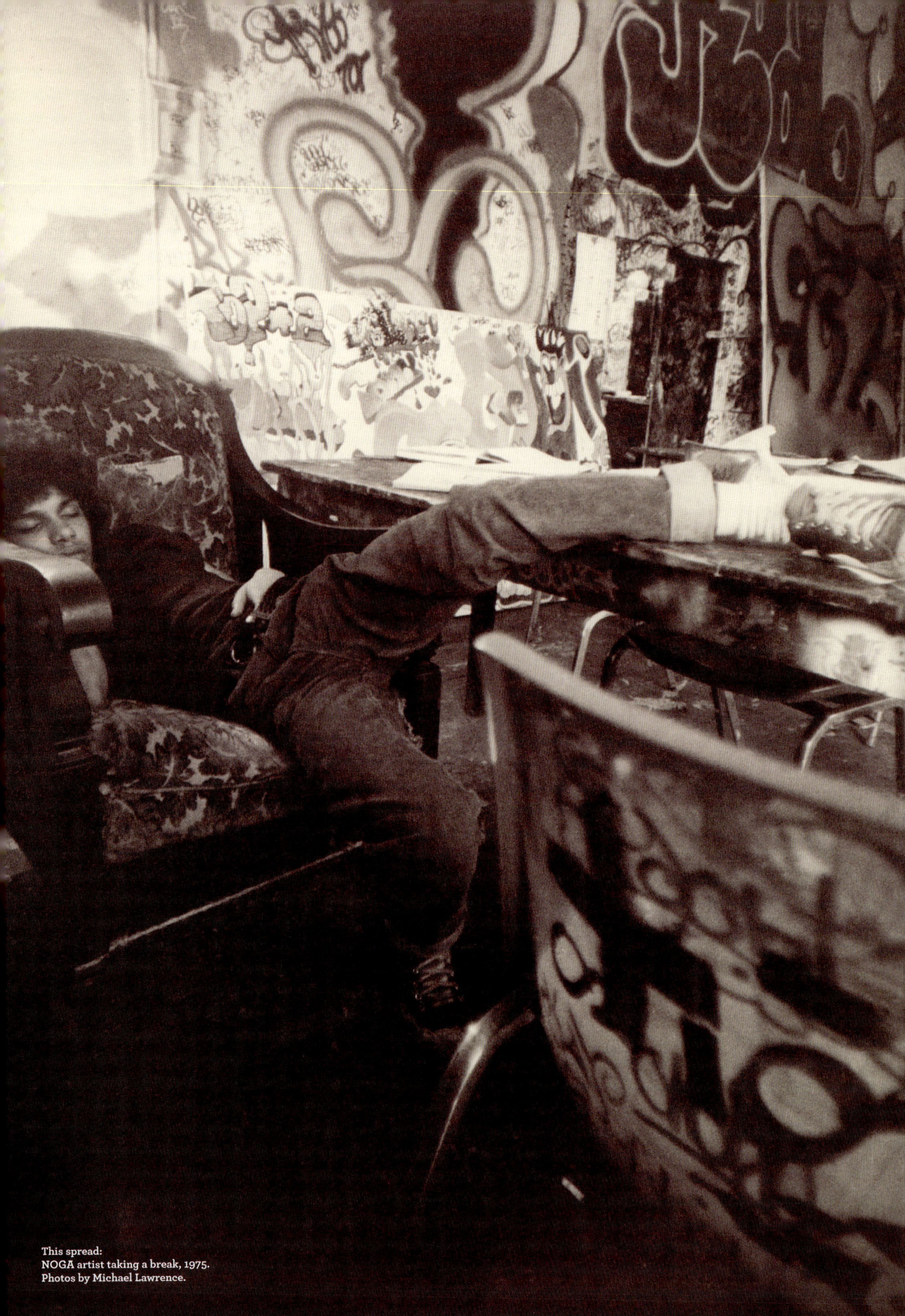

This spread:
NOGA artist taking a break, 1975.
Photos by Michael Lawrence.

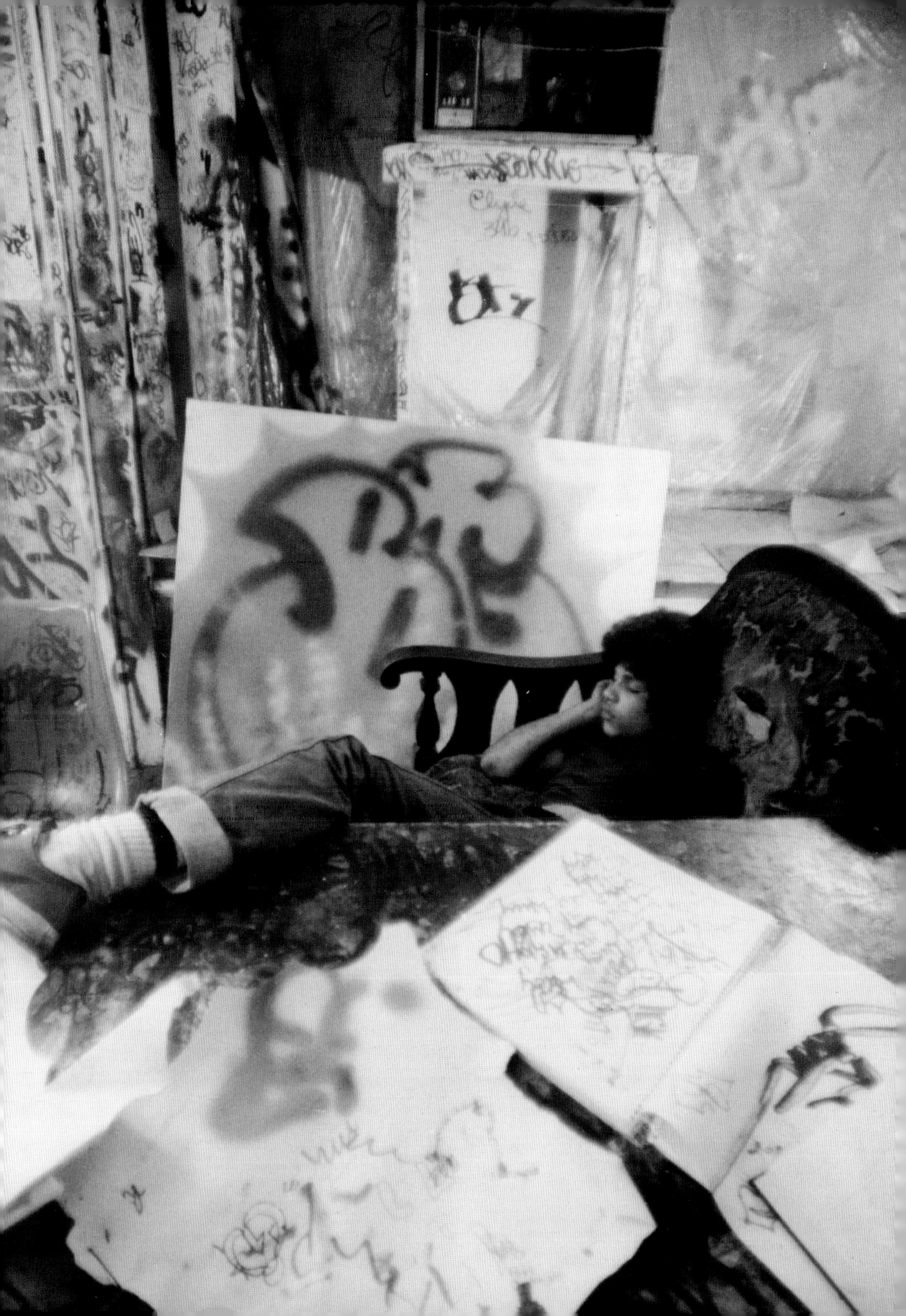

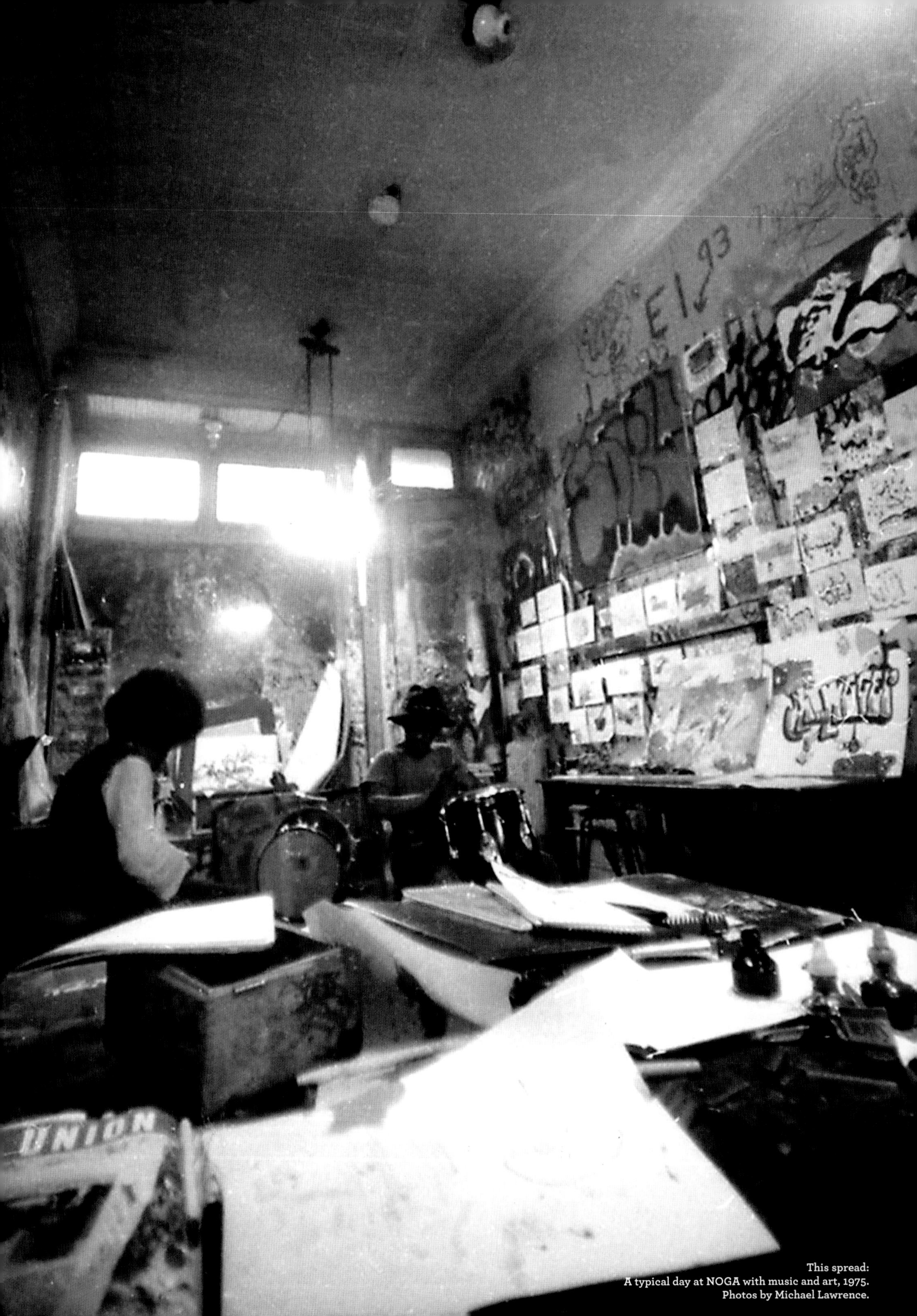

This spread:
A typical day at NOGA with music and art, 1975.
Photos by Michael Lawrence.

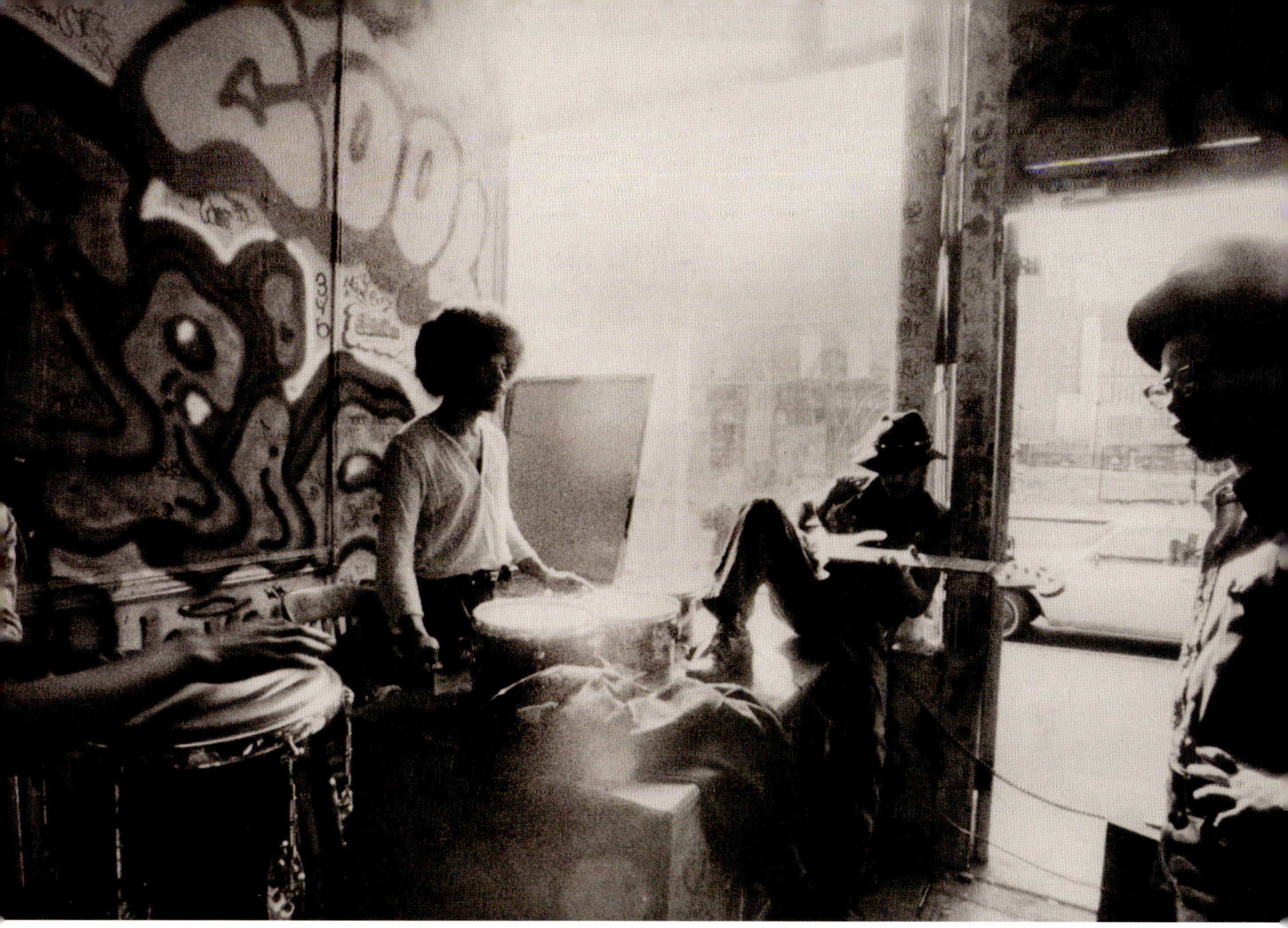

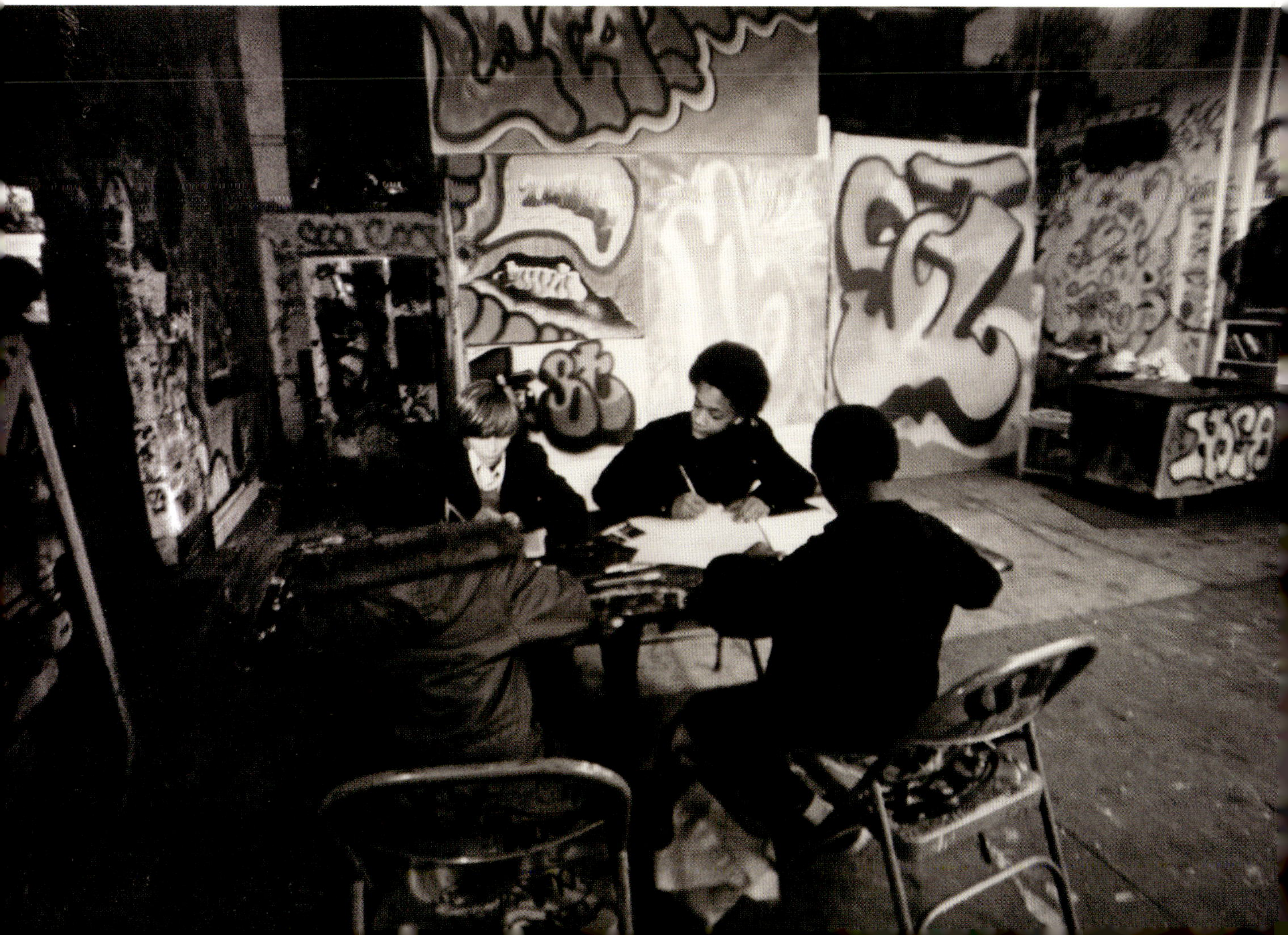

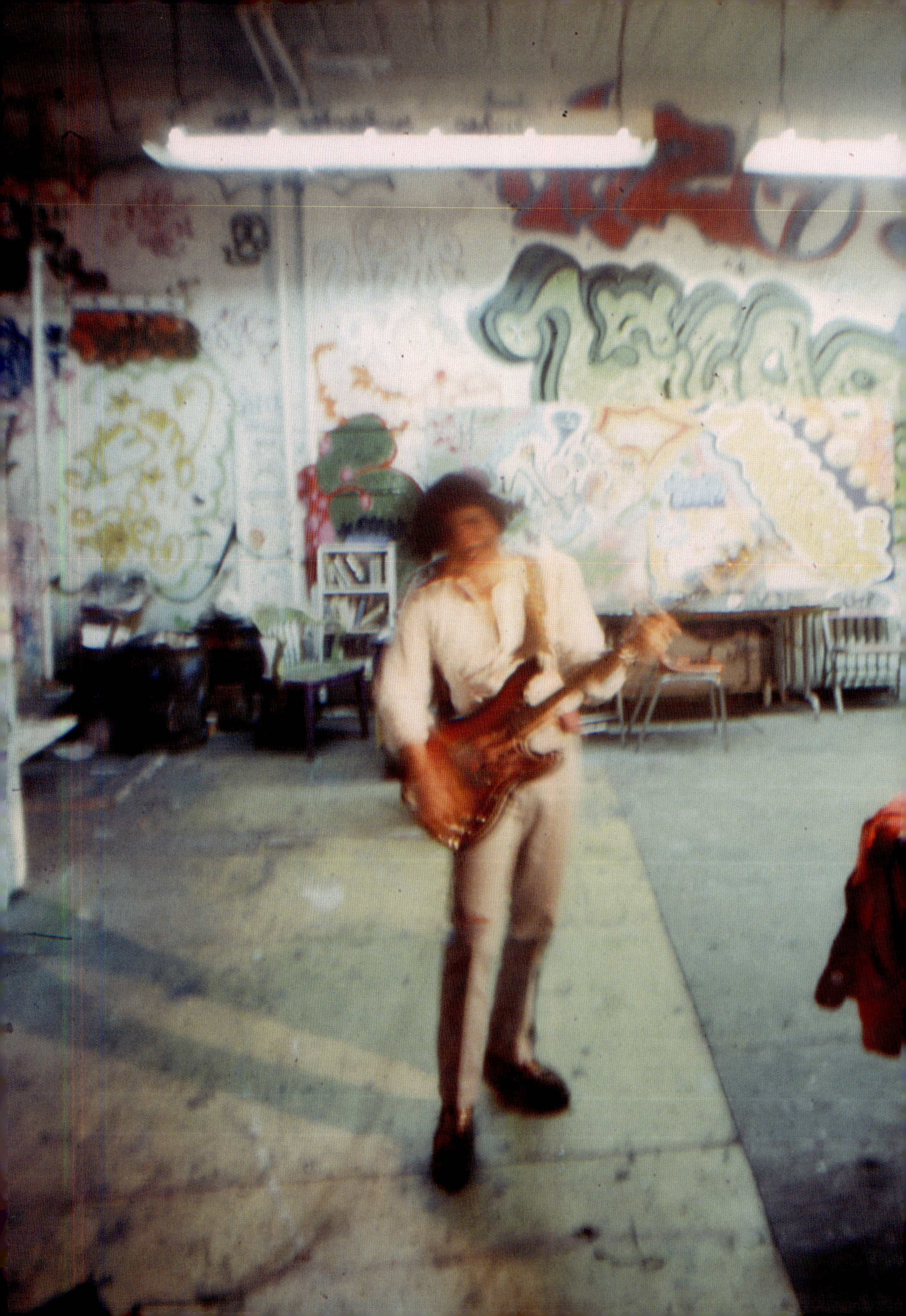

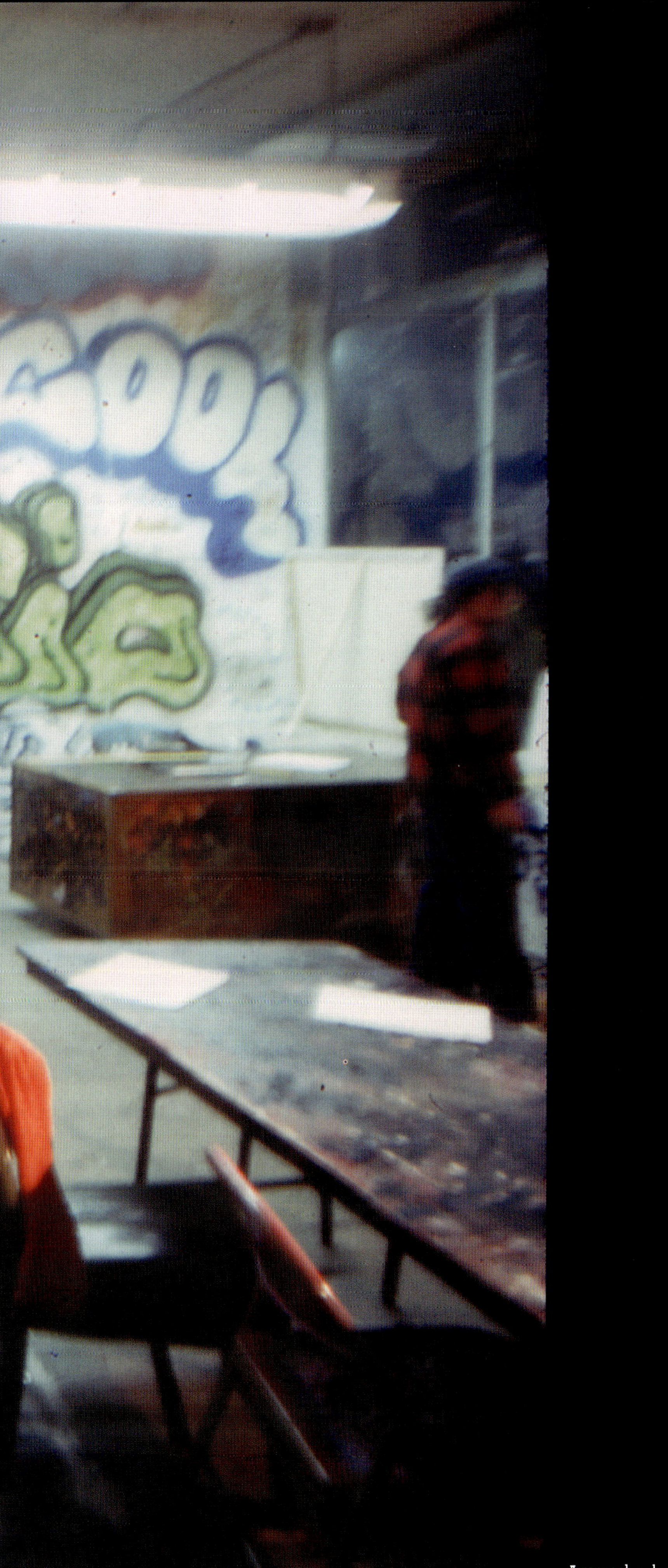

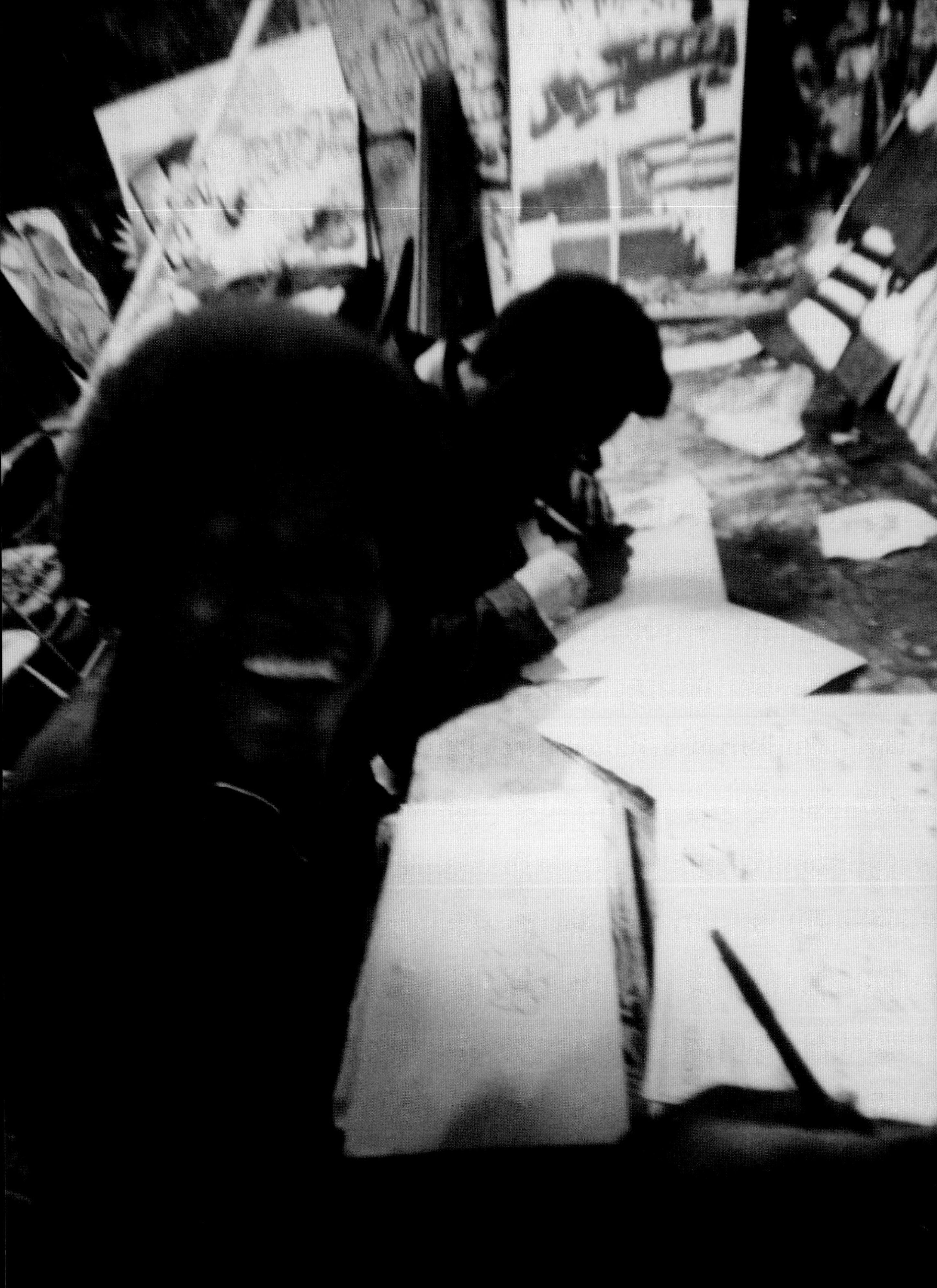

NOGA artists, 1975.
Photo by Michael Lawrence.

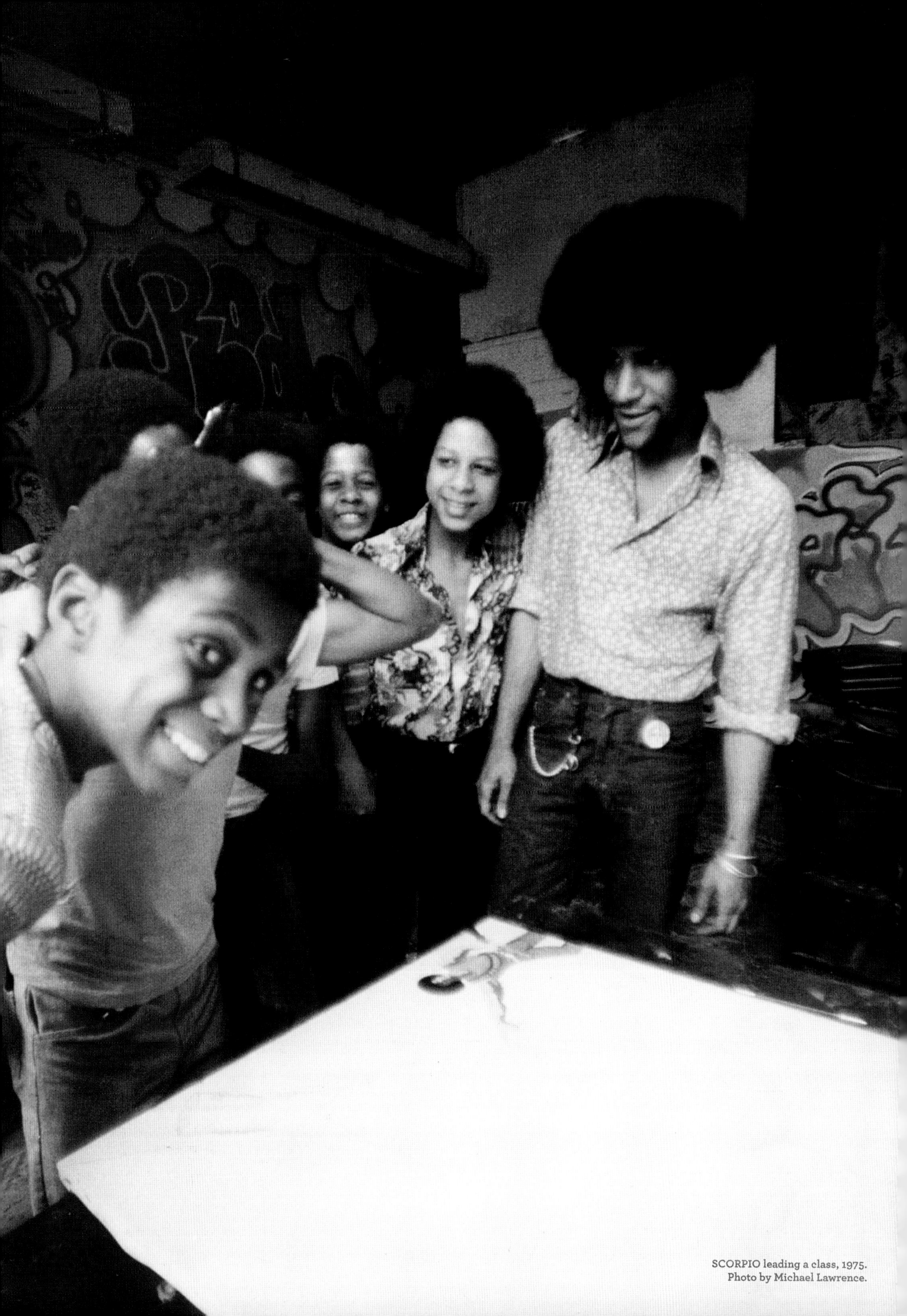

SCORPIO leading a class, 1975.
Photo by Michael Lawrence.

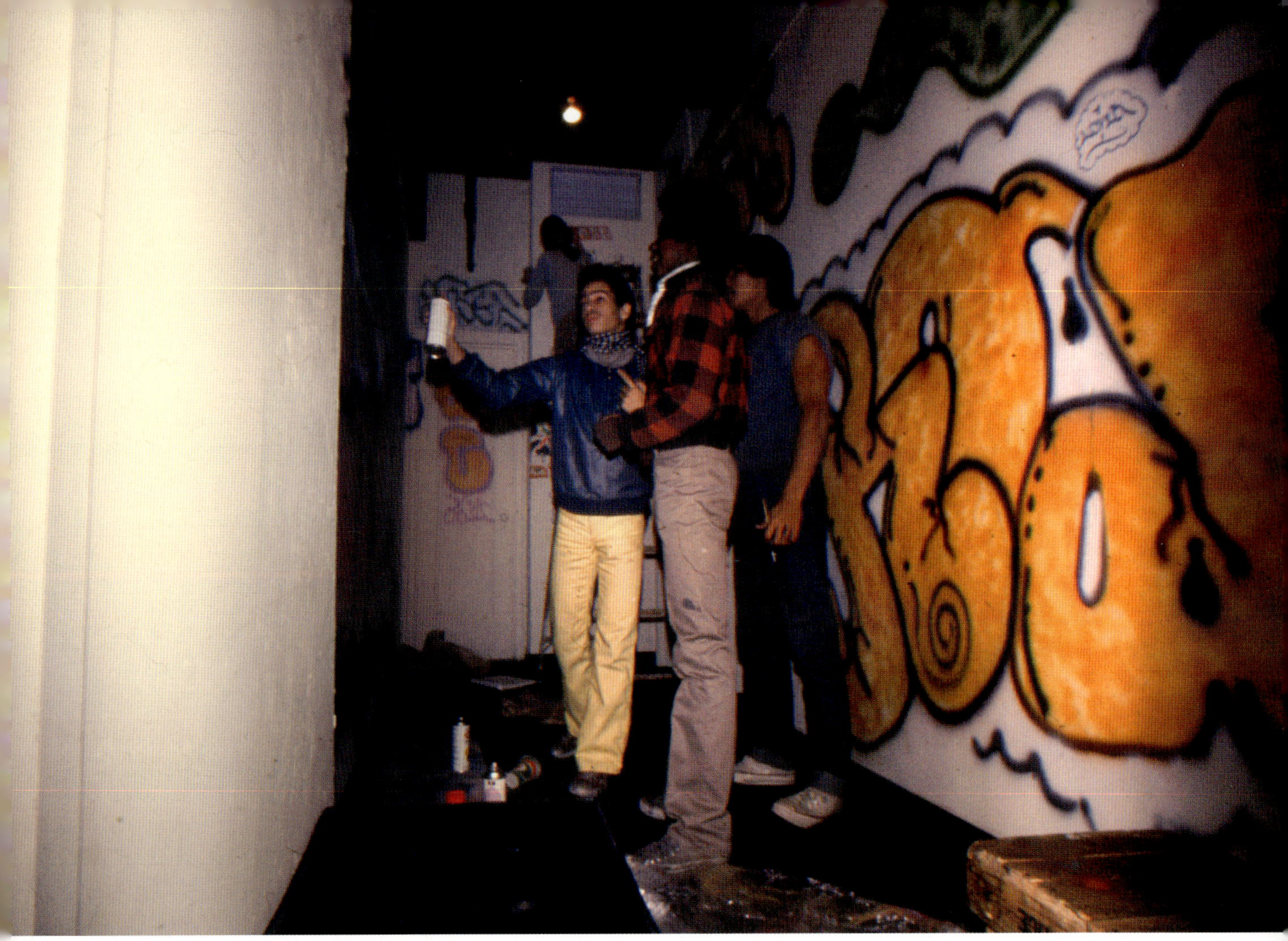

JOB #1

Pelsinger could be found in and out of the workshop on a daily basis. He couldn't teach the technical side of painting, but he could be a cheerleader. As a social activist he moved the kids directly into protests, usually held in Central Park. The actual causes didn't seem to matter — it could be boycotting lettuce one day and the Vietnam War the next. What mattered to Pelsinger was that the kids learned how to fight for what they believed in. In an ironic twist, most of the older writers didn't show up, leaving Pelsinger with a group of hippie teenagers.

As a person who saw that NOGA needed money to continue, he taught the kids how to sell their works, usually at street fairs on the Upper West Side. If UGA represented the elite, fine art world, then NOGA subsisted by selling at least some of their canvases as graffiti souvenirs.

The first job Pelsinger was able to get for the group was painting the exterior of a recording studio downtown named Warm Up Music Studio. This was done with marker and spray paint applied directly to the walls. Some of the writers used the mural to expand their vocabulary with paint; for example, a subway train was rendered on the wall. Other writers used the wall to put up tags and pieces. The sum total was exuberant chaos, not unlike the MTA trains themselves. The experience was a positive one for the group: They had faced a challenge and succeeded.

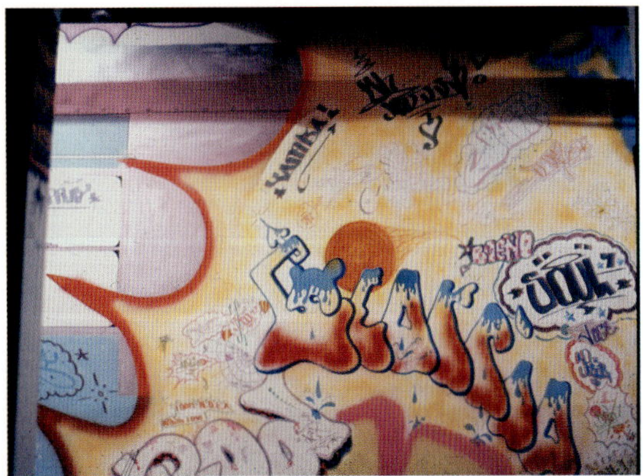

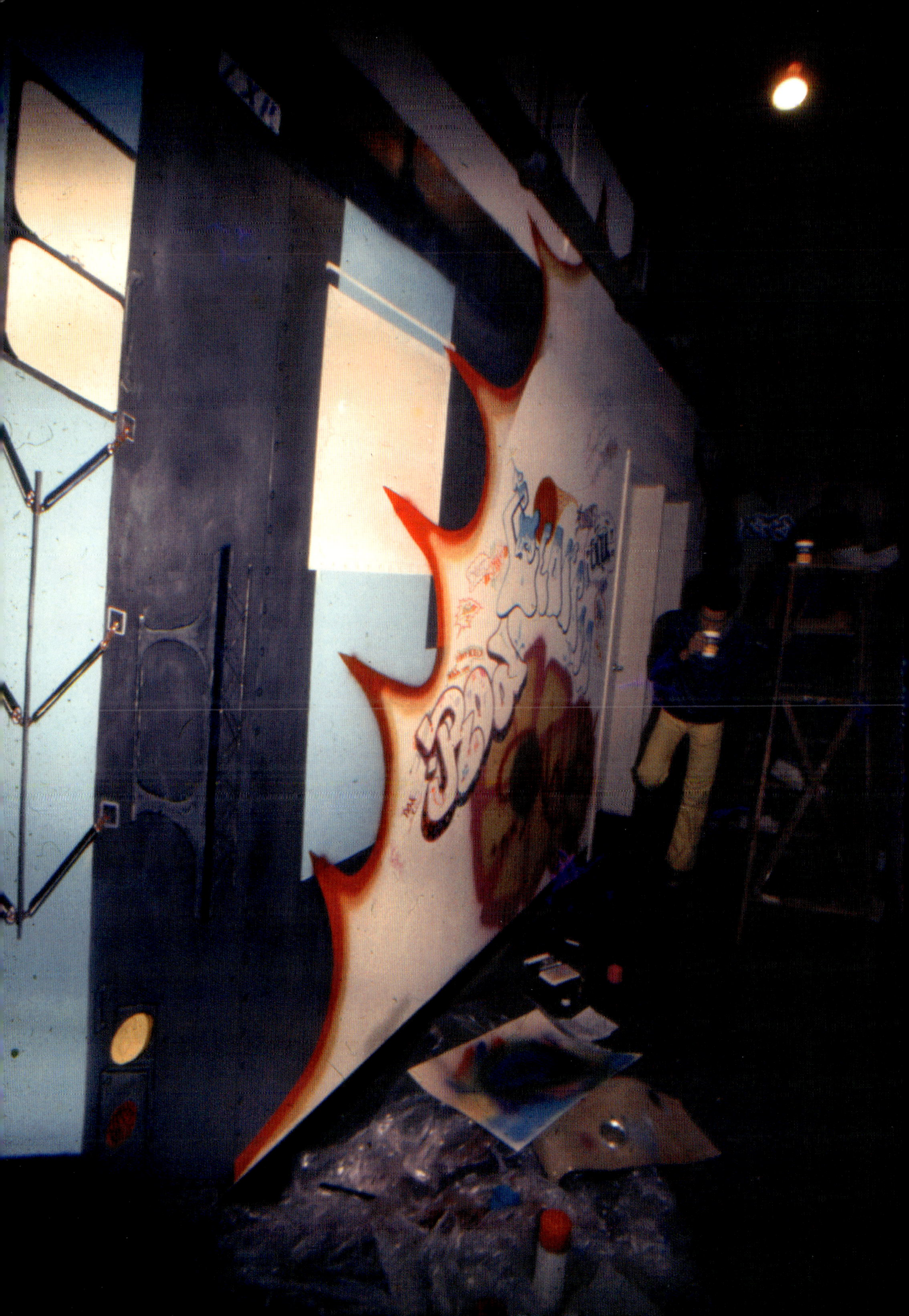

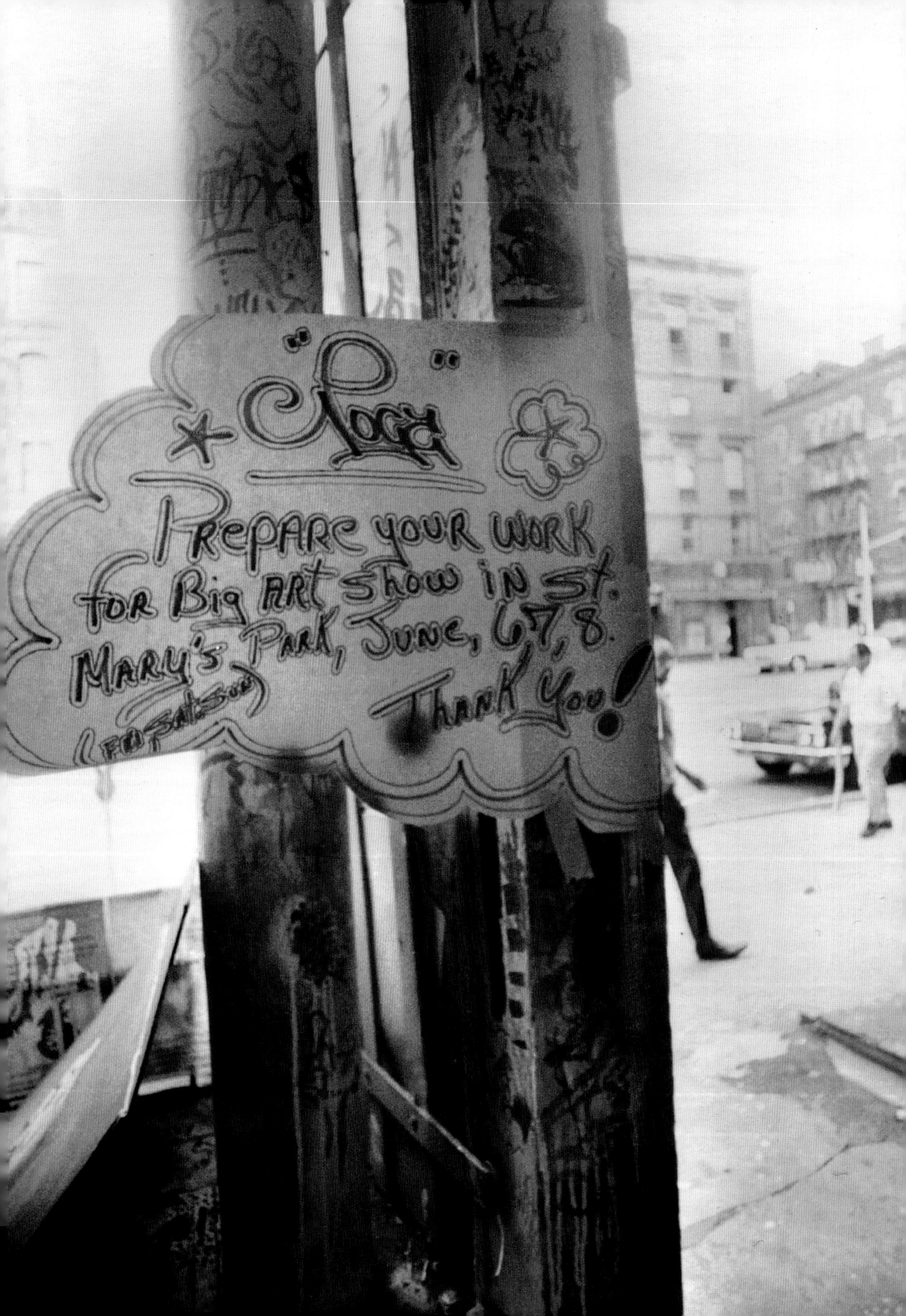
Roger
Prepare your work
for big art show in St.
Mary's Park, June, 6, 7, 8.
(Leo Batson)
Thank You!

GETTING OUT

Shortly after the studio painting, NOGA held its first exhibition, at Central Savings Bank on 73rd Street and Broadway. The show was modest, as were the canvases themselves. On any given day you could find a number of the writers hanging out in the bank showing off their works. This is where NOGA received its first media exposure with an article in the *New York Post*. A few of the pieces sold and spirits remained high, but for the rest of 1975, the group primarily hawked their wares at street fairs.

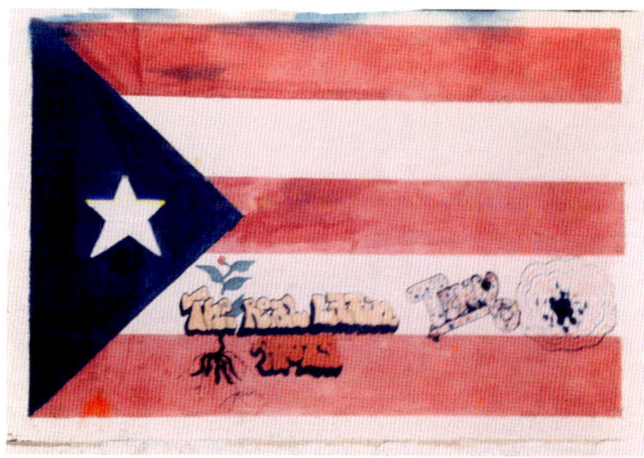

SAL 161 gives this account of the street fairs on the Upper West Side: "In the early '70s there were a lot of street fairs in the neighborhood. Middle-class people were moving into the neighborhood and they had young kids, so they held these street fairs where you could buy food, run around and buy things from local artists. The good thing about street fairs is that we had a lot of space, which meant painting large canvases. I did my first large spray-painted canvas for the 88th Street Fair, and it sold for $300. To this day I couldn't even break down what happened to the money — I know I got some and the workshop got some. The money wasn't important; having someone buy a painting from you, that was the thing that had meaning."

A new member of NOGA emerged around this time. An artist and student of fabric design, Livi French had tried and failed to catch on with UGA. She loved the art and attended the meetings, but Hugo Martinez really had no use for her. Pelsinger, however, needed someone like Livi, and she was more than happy to help. If there was one thing that Jack Pelsinger couldn't stand it was bureaucracy. He was passionate and wanted so many things for the kids, but typing up proposals in triplicate form was not his style. If you go through the various correspondence signed by Pelsinger from that period, most of it was fine-tuned and typed up by Livi French.

One of French's duties was coordinating an outreach program to the elementary schools in the area, demystifying the new medium for local art classes. (For many people in the neighborhood the interior of NOGA was foreboding. If you looked through the cracked-open front door, you might see teenagers hanging out and smoking weed.) SCORPIO would give a quick tour and explain his canvases, which had taken on a psychedelic look. The school visits helped to pull back the curtain and show that positive change could happen from a grassroots effort spearheaded by kids.

Opposite page:
Sign on NOGA's door for an art show, 1975.

This page:
THE REAL LATIN ROOTS by TONY, 1975.
Photos by Michael Lawrence.

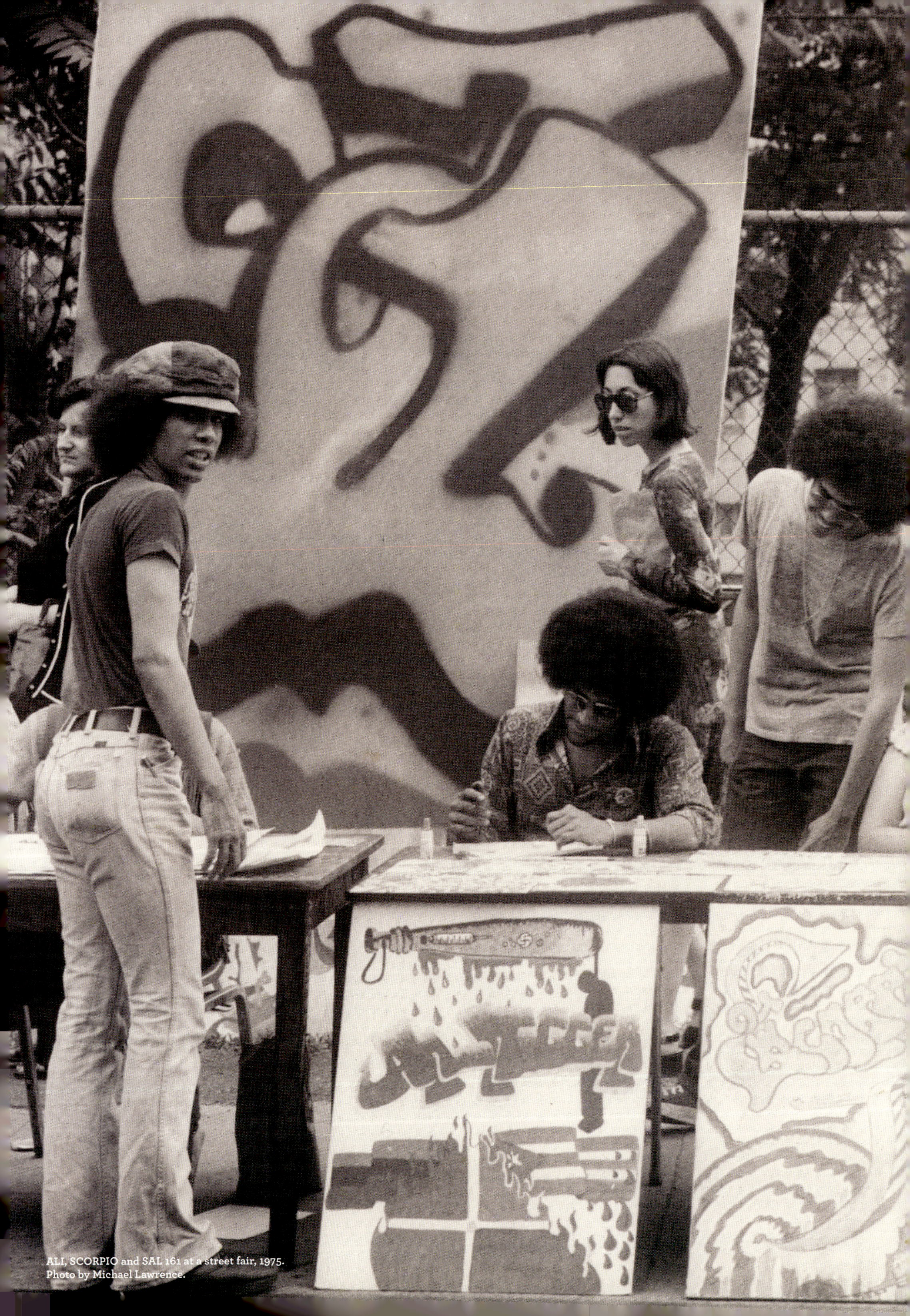

ALI, SCORPIO and SAL 161 at a street fair, 1975.
Photo by Michael Lawrence.

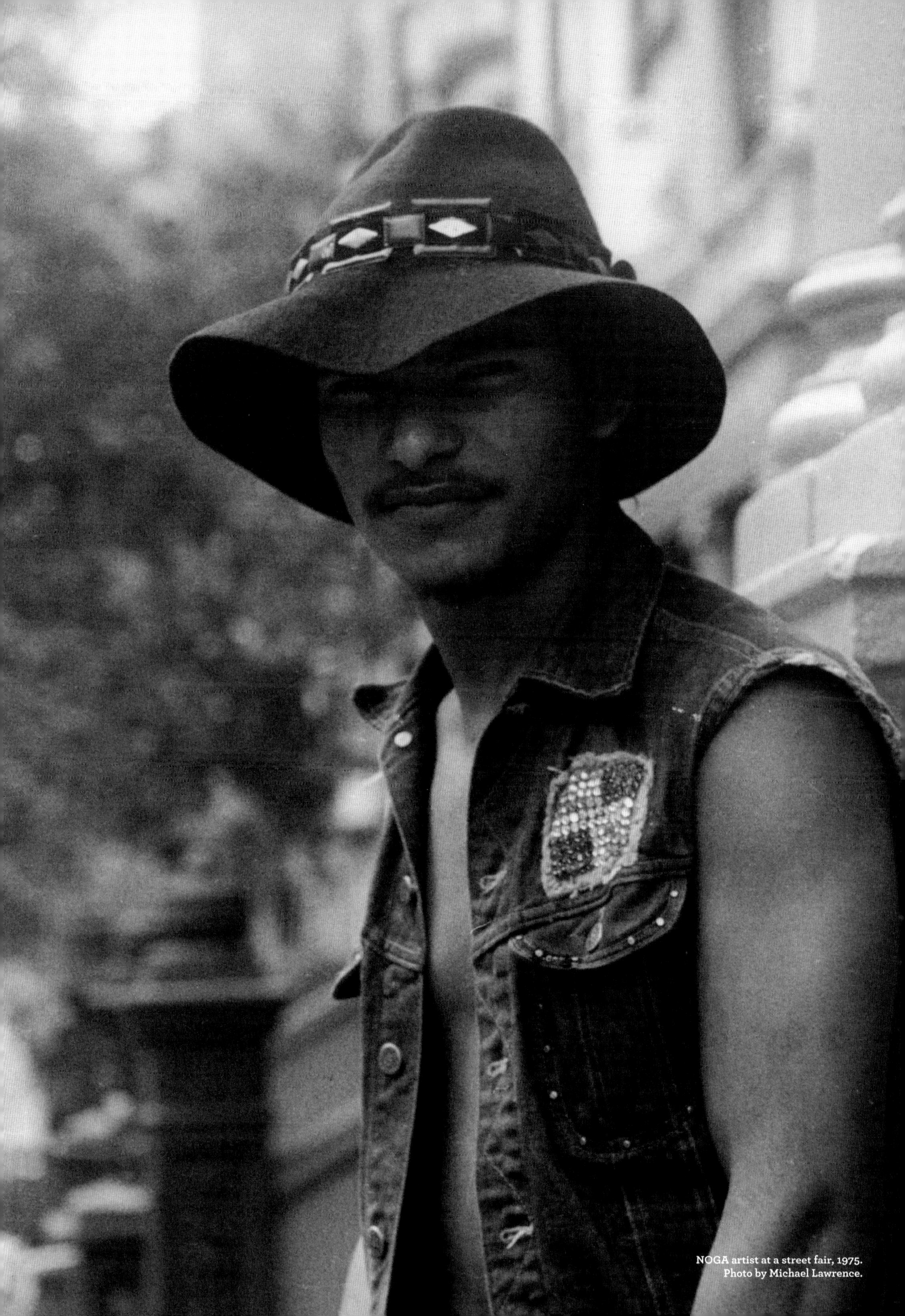

NOGA artist at a street fair, 1975.
Photo by Michael Lawrence.

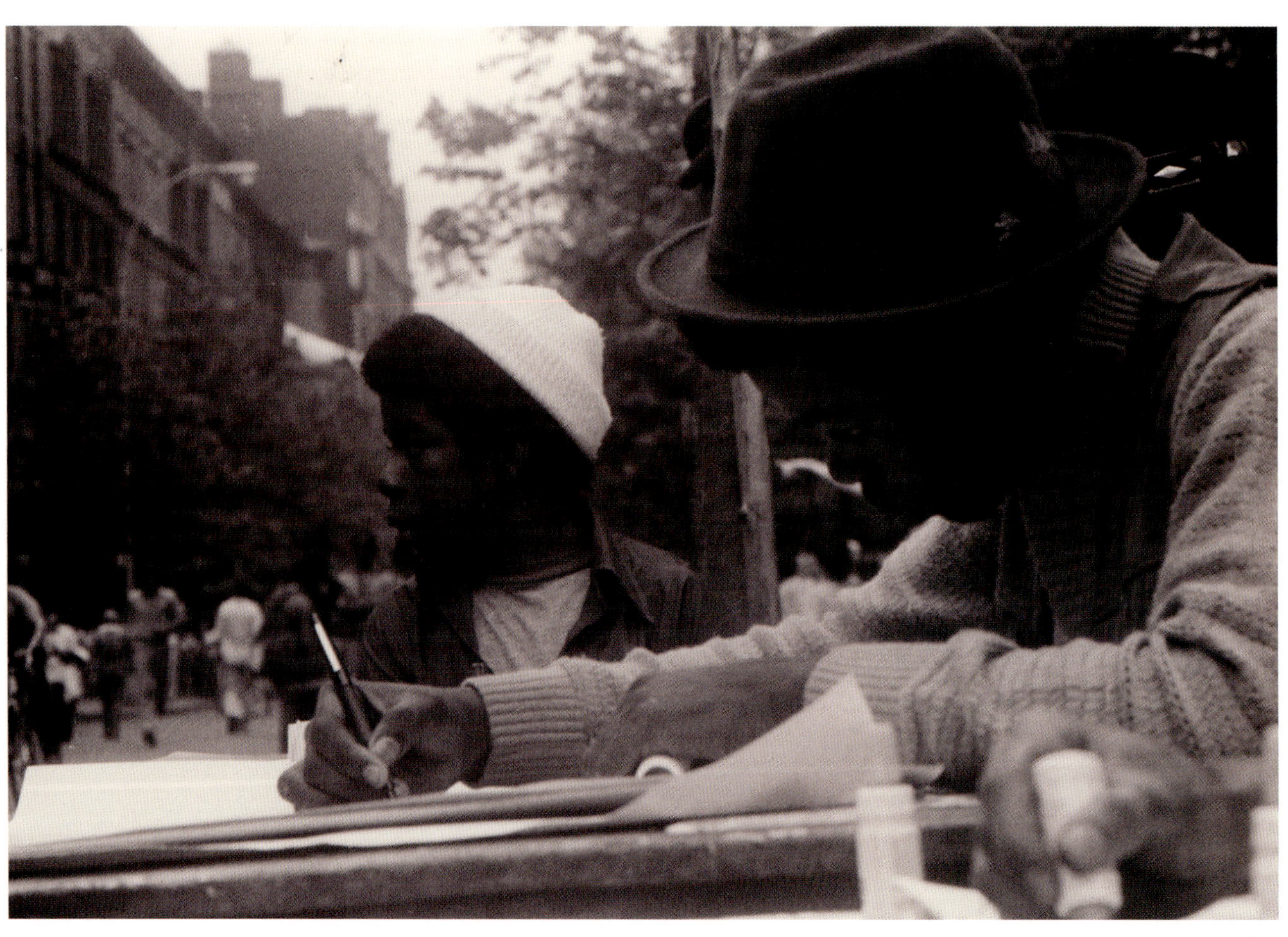

NOGA artists at the 88th Street Fair, 1975.
Photo by Michael Lawrence.

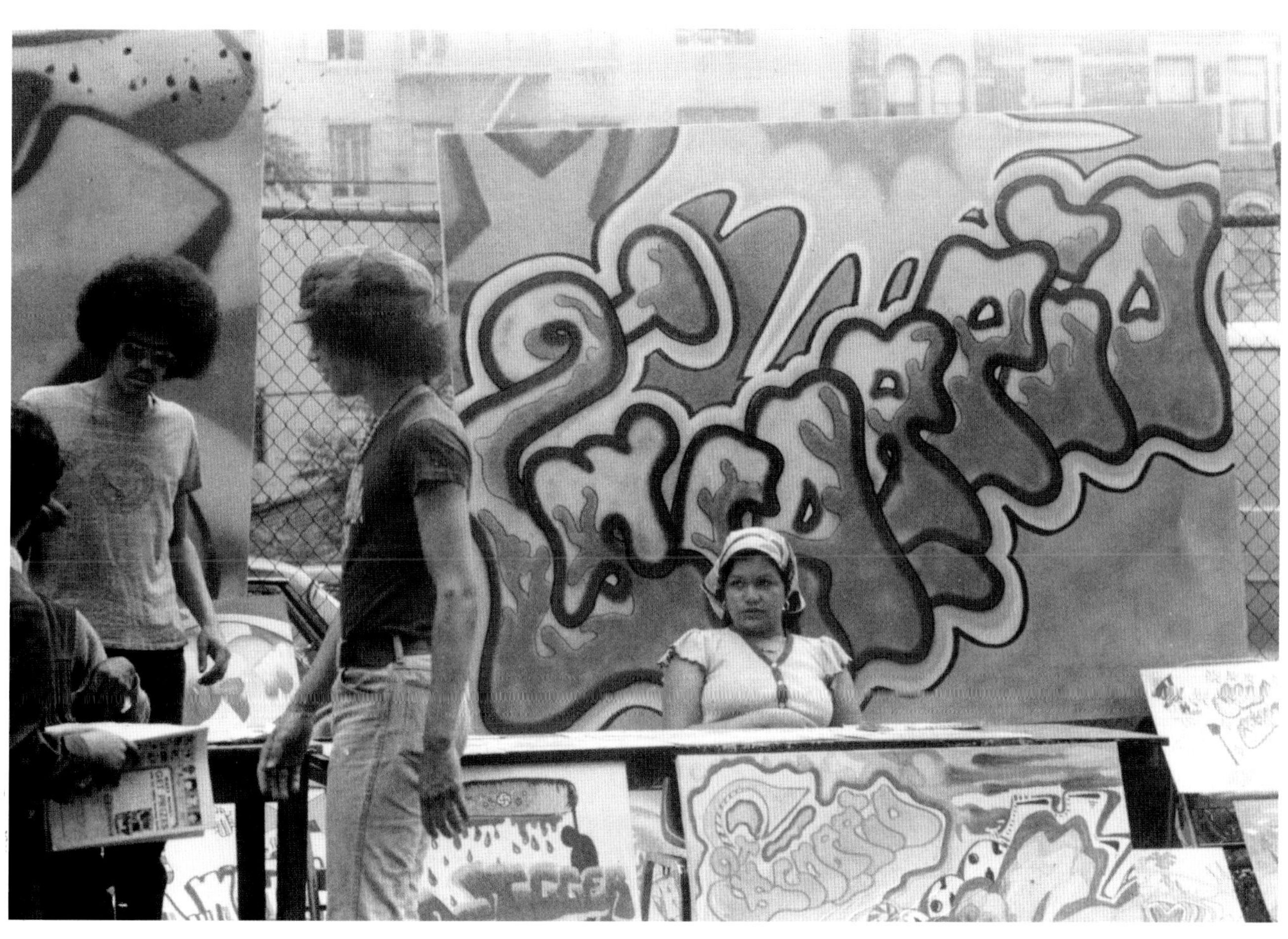

ALI and SAL 161 stand in front of a SCORPIO
painting at the 88th Street Fair, 1975.
Photo by Michael Lawrence.

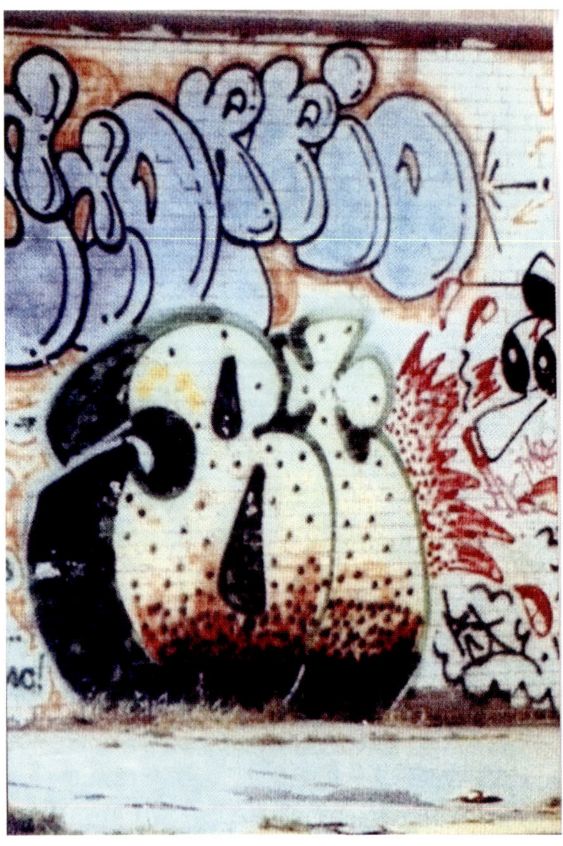

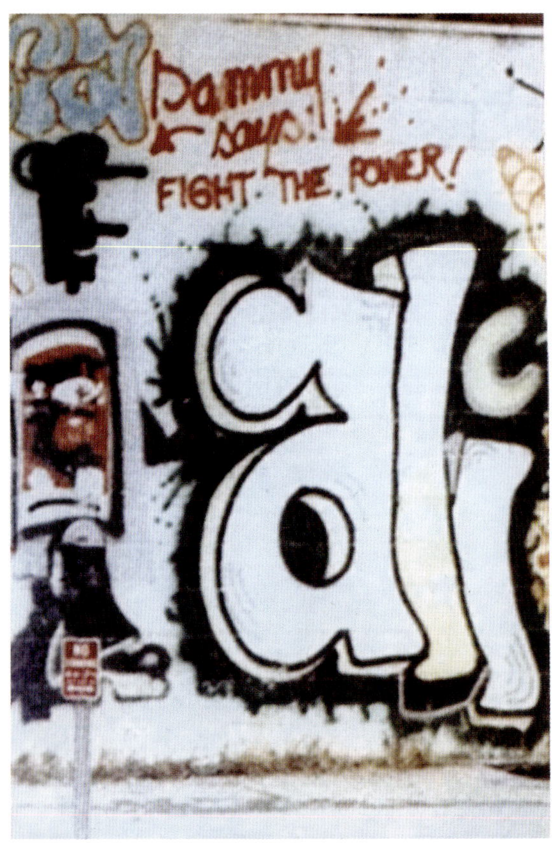

STIM 1

The exterior of NOGA had been tagged since the day it opened, but in the spring of 1975 it would get a facelift. Earlier in the year, STIM 1 from Brooklyn had fallen under a train and was crushed to death. STIM was the first graffiti death that could be linked directly to the crime itself. He had been hanging out at the Atlantic Avenue station when he and some other kids decided to do some motion tagging. The boys entered the last car of the train and began writing when two Transit cops confronted them. STIM knew that if he had one more bust he would be sent away, so he made a break for it. He scrambled for the door to the train and jumped out in between cars, mistiming the jump. He was run over by the subway car at just fourteen years old.

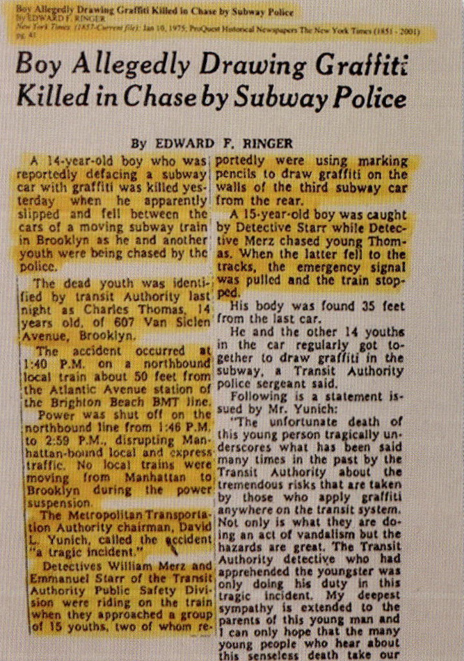

Boy Allegedly Drawing Graffiti Killed in Chase by Subway Police

New York Times (1857-Current file); Jan 10, 1975; ProQuest Historical Newspapers The New York Times (1851 - 2001) pg. 41

Boy Allegedly Drawing Graffiti Killed in Chase by Subway Police

By EDWARD F. RINGER

A 14-year-old boy who was reportedly defacing a subway car with graffiti was killed yesterday when he apparently slipped and fell between the cars of a moving subway train in Brooklyn as he and another youth were being chased by the police.

The dead youth was identified by transit Authority last night as Charles Thomas, 14 years old, of 607 Van Siclen Avenue, Brooklyn.

The accident occurred at 1:40 P.M. on a northbound local train about 50 feet from the Atlantic Avenue station of the Brighton Beach BMT line.

Power was shut off on the northbound line from 1:46 P.M. to 2:59 P.M., disrupting Manhattan-bound local and express traffic. No local trains were moving from Manhattan to Brooklyn during the power suspension.

The Metropolitan Transportation Authority chairman, David L. Yunich, called the accident "a tragic incident."

Detectives William Merz and Emmanuel Starr of the Transit Authority Public Safety Division were riding on the train when they approached a group of 15 youths, two of whom re-portedly were using marking pencils to draw graffiti on the walls of the third subway car from the rear.

A 15-year-old boy was caught by Detective Starr while Detective Merz chased young Thomas. When the latter fell to the tracks, the emergency signal was pulled and the train stopped.

His body was found 35 feet from the last car.

He and the other 14 youths in the car regularly got together to draw graffiti in the subway, a Transit Authority police sergeant said.

Following is a statement issued by Mr. Yunich:

"The unfortunate death of this young person tragically underscores what has been said many times in the past by the Transit Authority about the tremendous risks that are taken by those who apply graffiti anywhere on the transit system. Not only is what they are doing an act of vandalism but the hazards are great. The Transit Authority detective who had apprehended the youngster was only doing his duty in this tragic incident. My deepest sympathy is extended to the parents of this young man and I can only hope that the many young people who hear about this senseless death take our cautionary words to heart."

STIM was a partner of CLIFF 159 and a leading member in his crew, the THREE YARD BOYS. As the first warm days of spring arrived, a large-scale graffiti mural was painted in his honor next to the workshop. The artists involved were NOGA stalwarts: IN, ALI, CLIFF 159, SCORPIO, BLOOD TEA and a few others. It's the first known legal graffiti wall painted in New York City. The pieces were done the same way they would've been done on a subway train, only a bit cleaner. IN's contribution was a top-to-bottom western-style piece; the CLIFF 159 that was adjacent to it had more of a wild-style feel to it with arrows pointing in different directions. The ALI piece was another bubble-style work with a spray-can character painted next to it. Above the piece was the phrase "Sammy Says Fight the Power!" SCORPIO's piece seemed to float along the wall, starting in the middle and rising toward its final letters. BLOOD TEA also went with tall bubble letters; he then painted two wide-open cartoon eyes staring at the piece. High above all the names was the inscription "In Memory of Charles Thomas, STIM 1 3YB." STIM 1 had never set foot inside of NOGA, yet his name was immortalized on the outside wall.

IT'S THE FIRST KNOWN LEGAL GRAFFITI WALL PAINTED IN NEW YORK CITY.

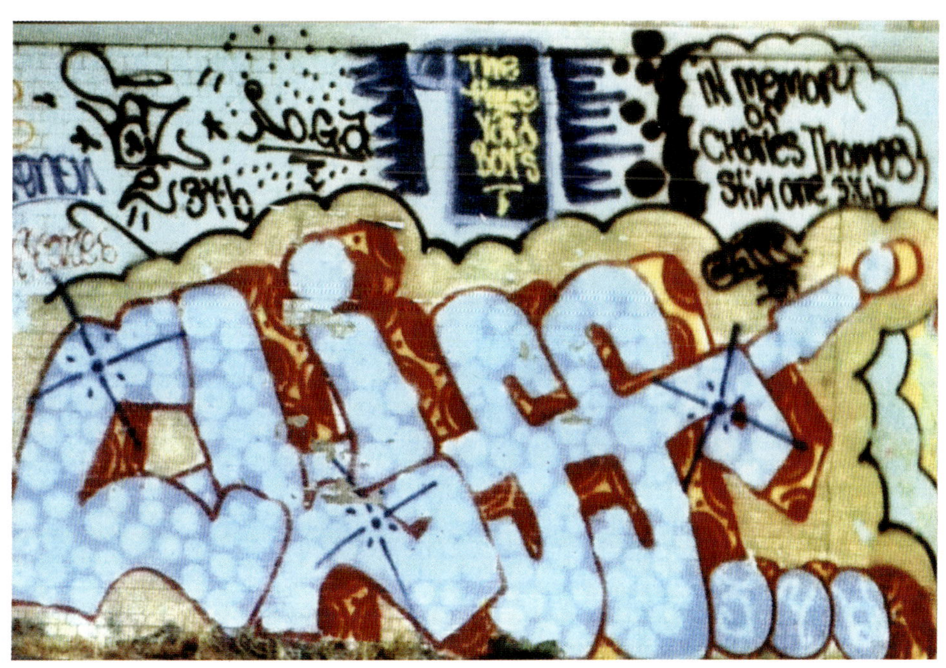

Inset:
Article on STIM's passing, *New York Times*, January 1975.
Courtesy of AZ.

This spread:
NOGA exterior on Columbus Avenue featuring pieces by SCORPIO,
BLOOD TEA and ALI, leader of the SOUL ARTISTS, CLIFF 159, 1975.
Photos by Michael Lawrence.

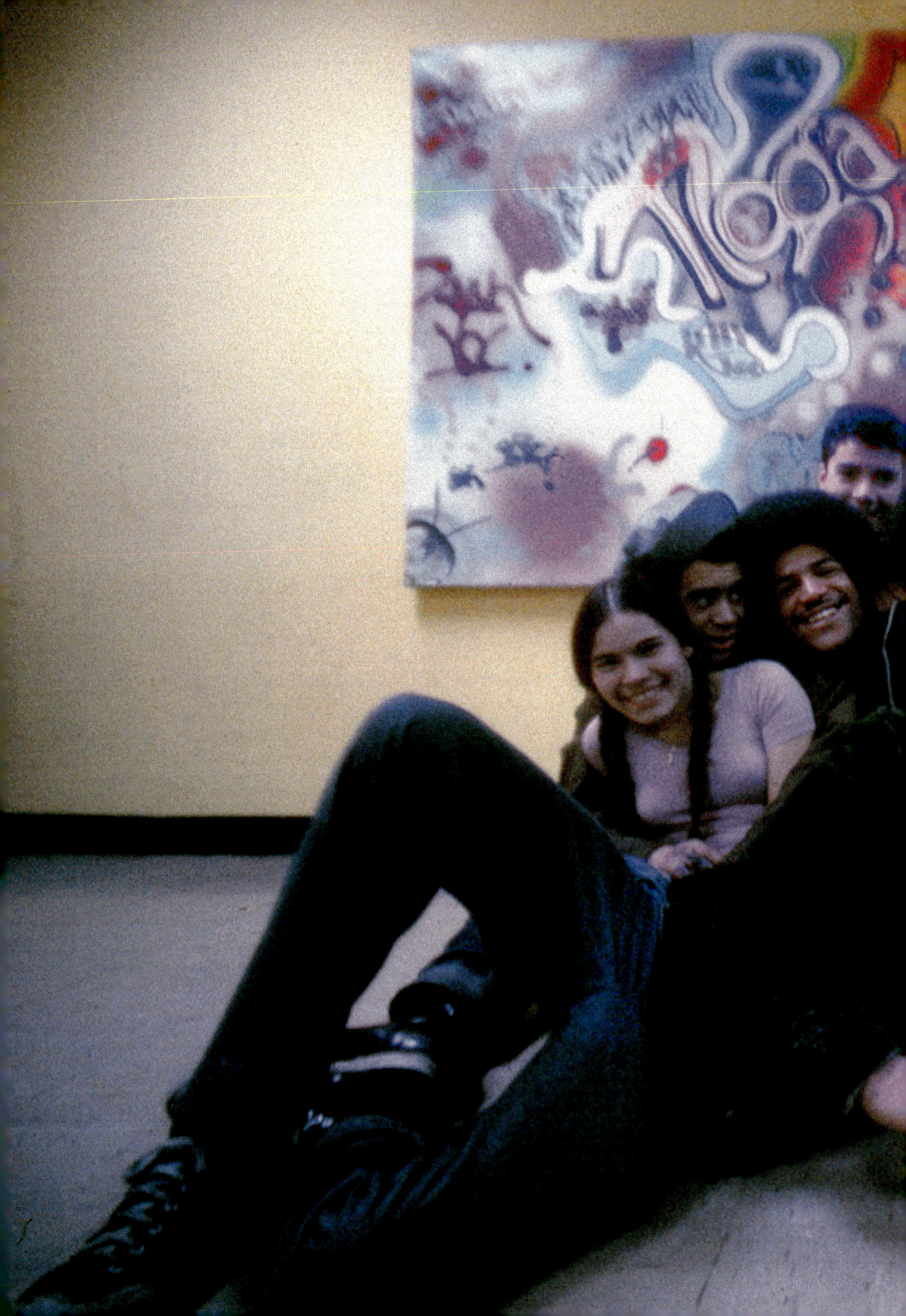

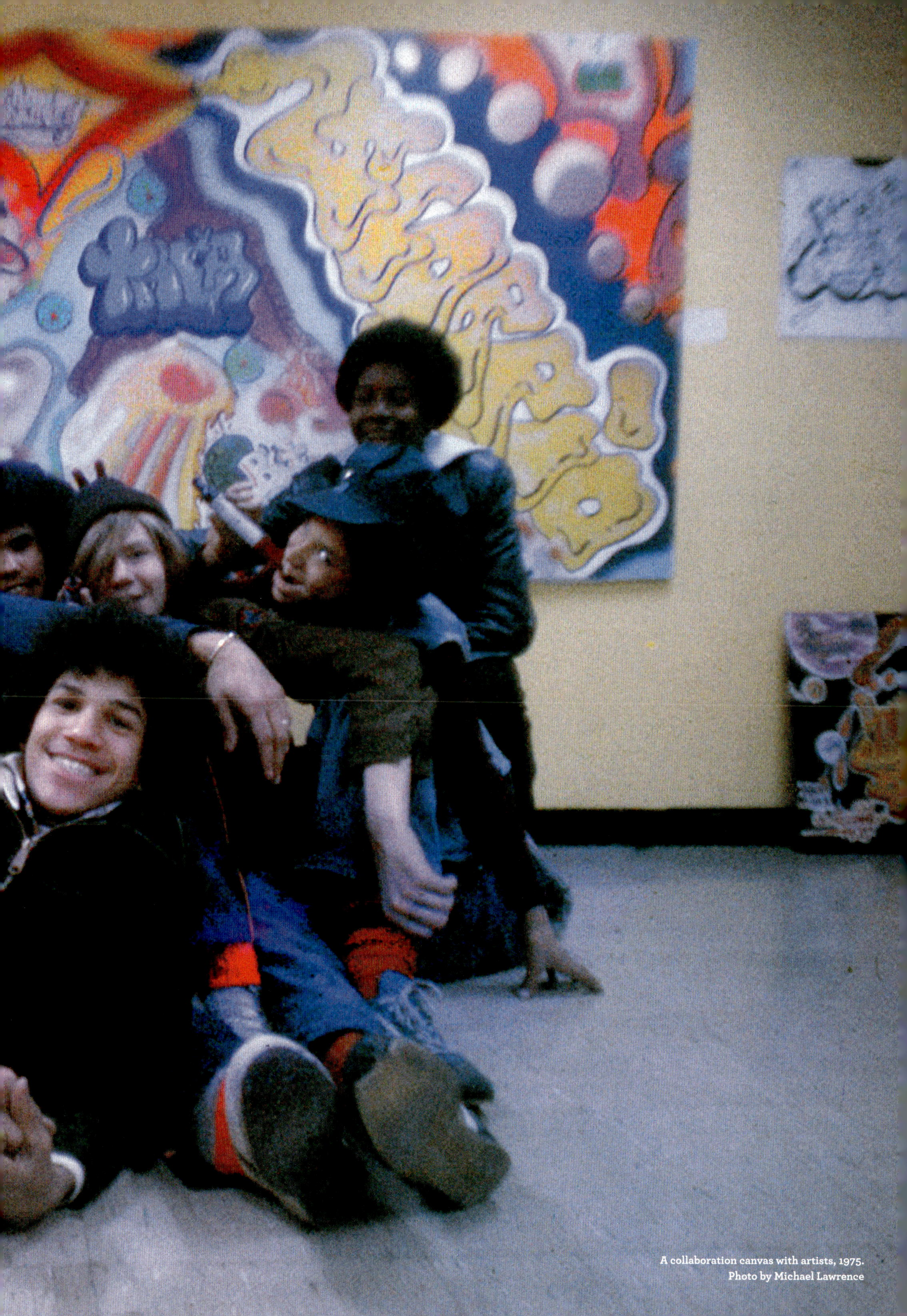

A collaboration canvas with artists, 1975.
Photo by Michael Lawrence

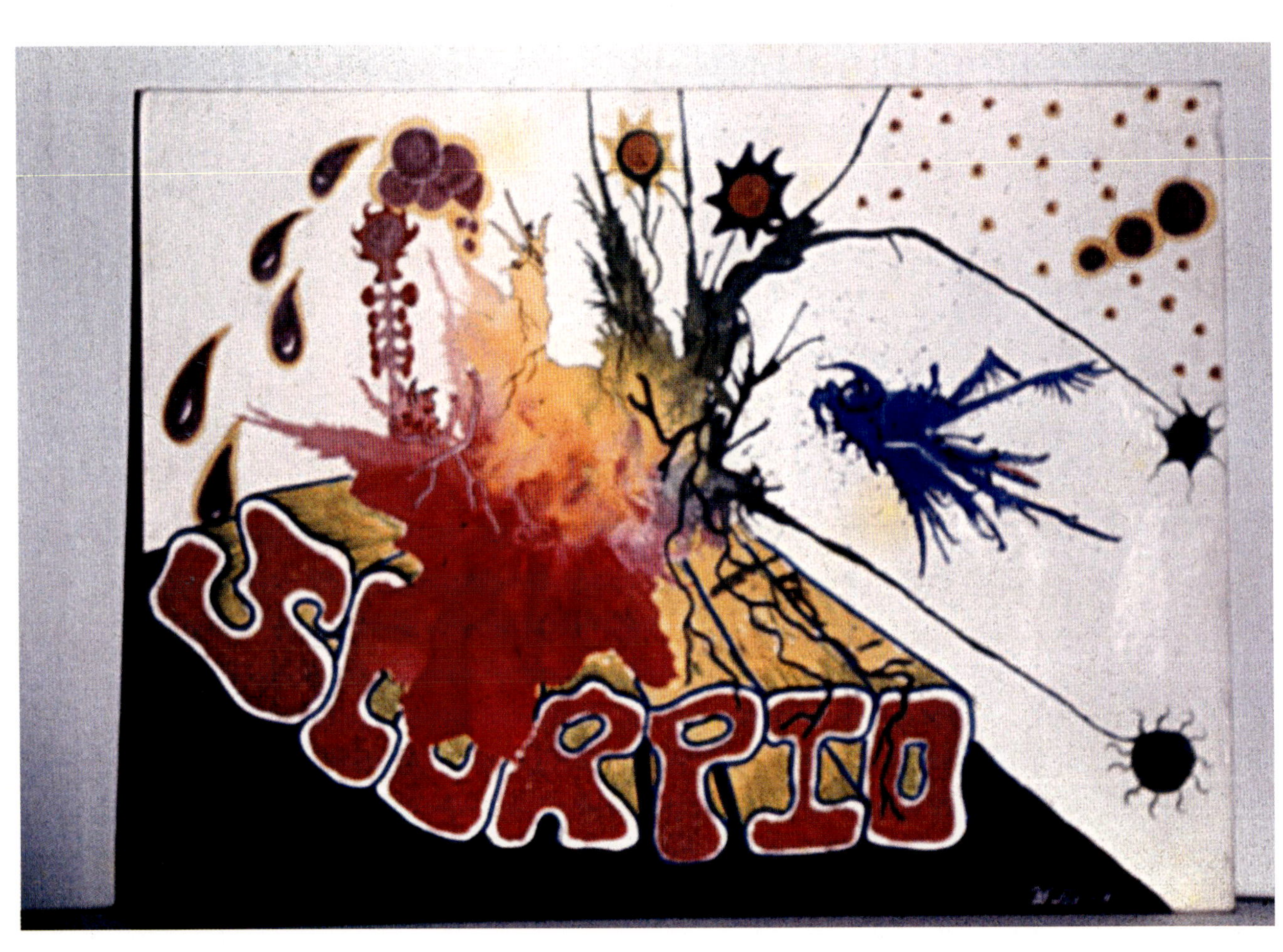

SCORPIO canvas, 1975.
Photo by Michael Lawrence.

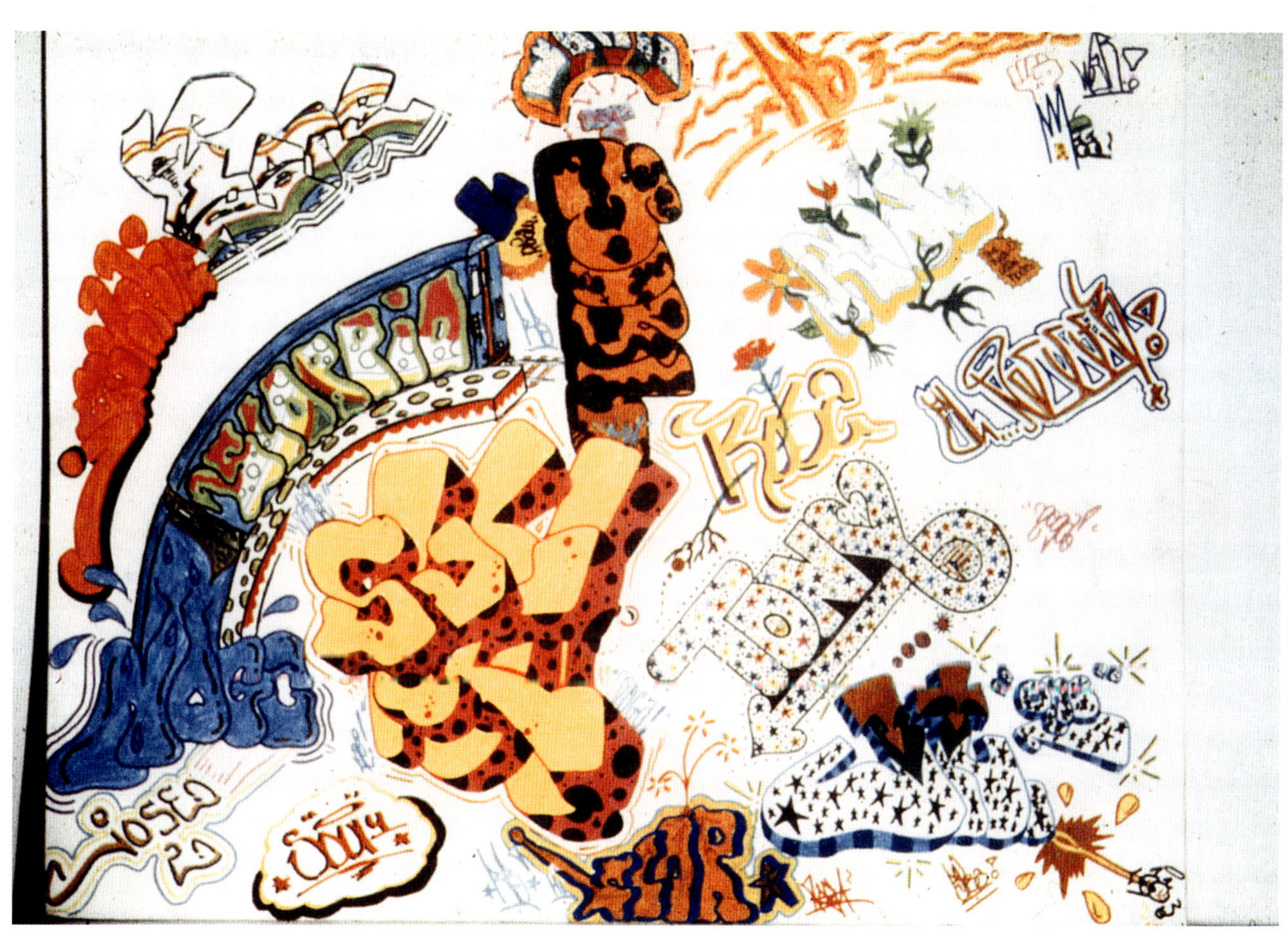

Collaboration on a canvas by NOGA artists, 1975.
Photo by Michael Lawrence.

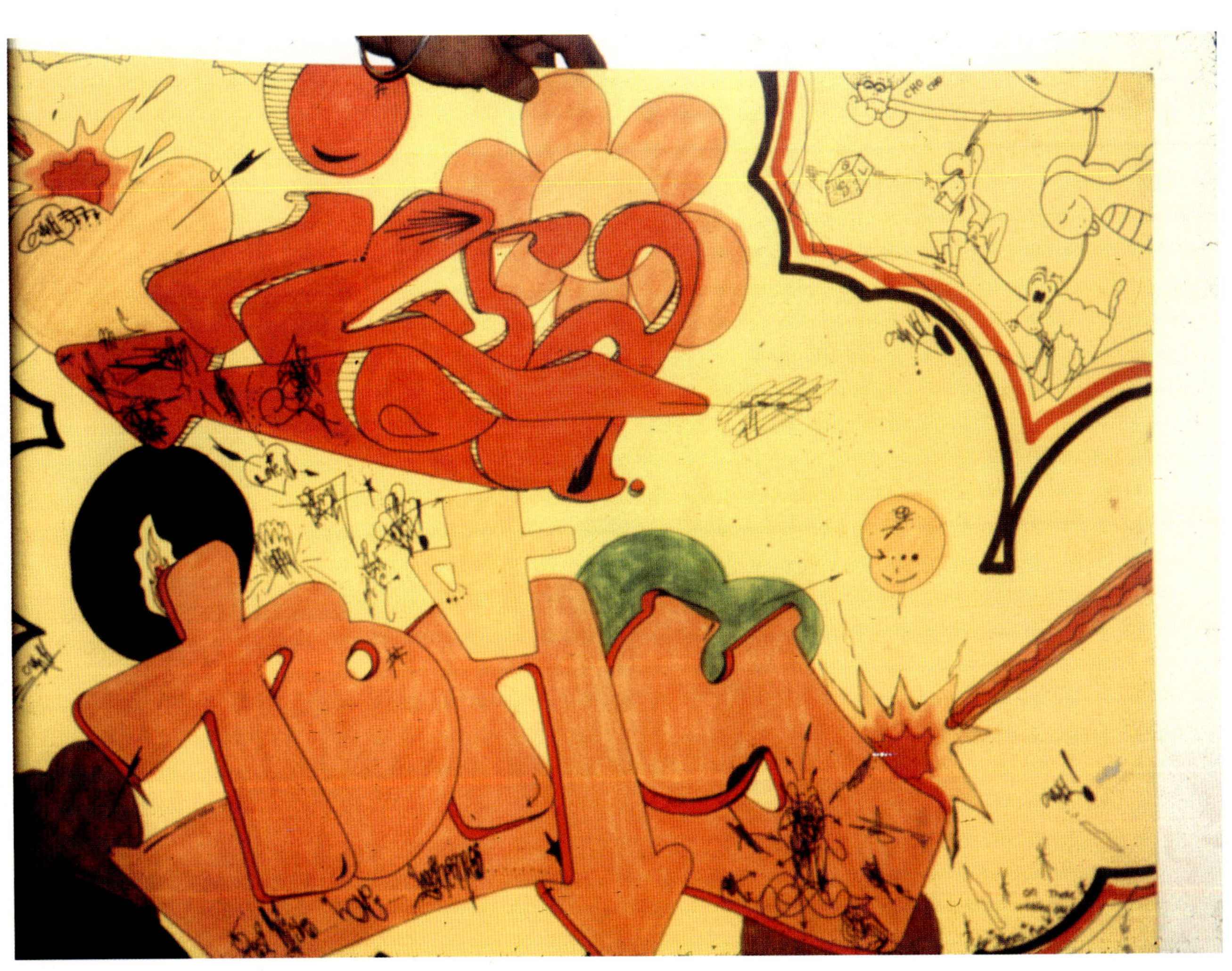

Various canvases by TONY and BLOOD TEA, 1975.
Photos by Michael Lawrence.

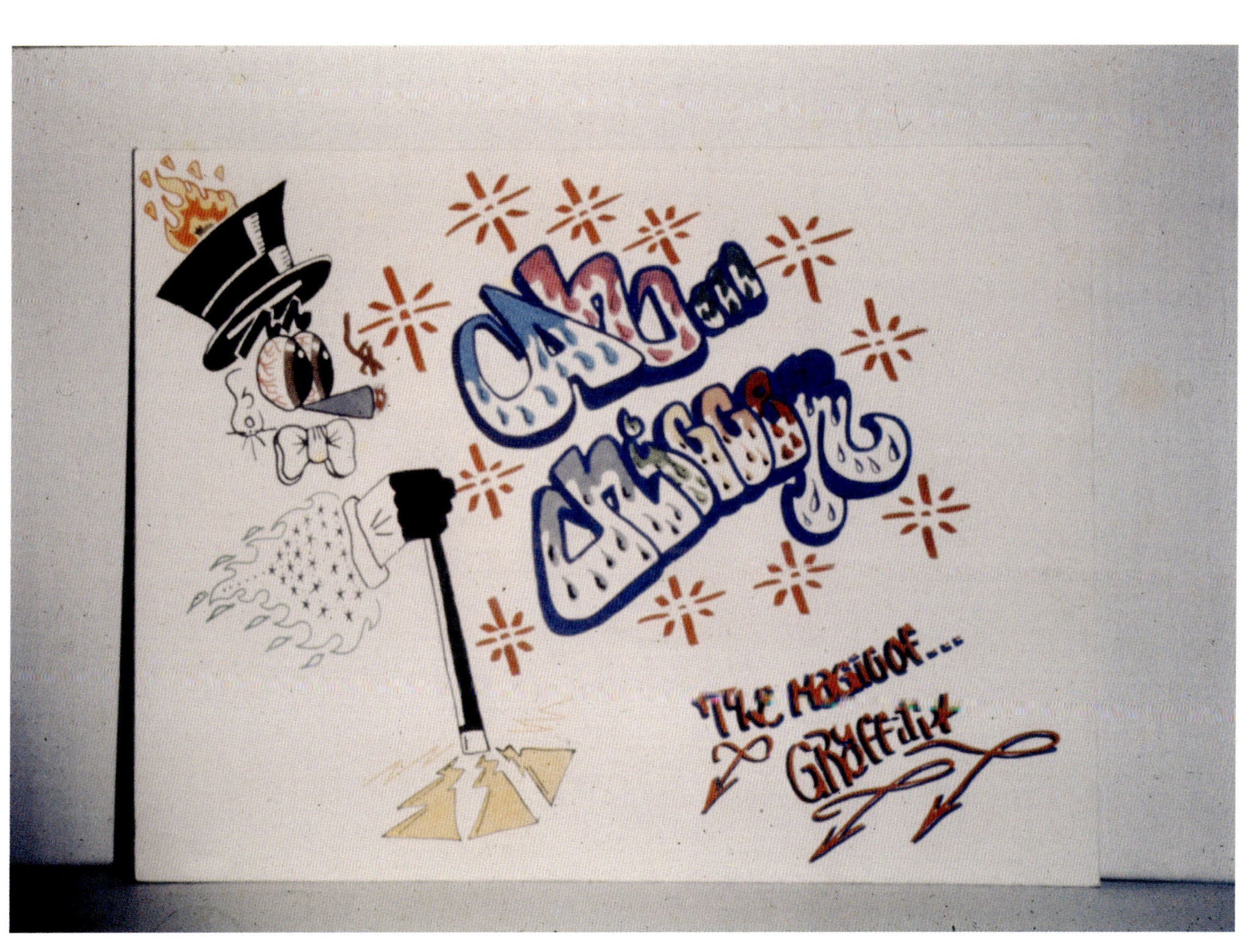
THE MAGIC OF...
GRAFFITI

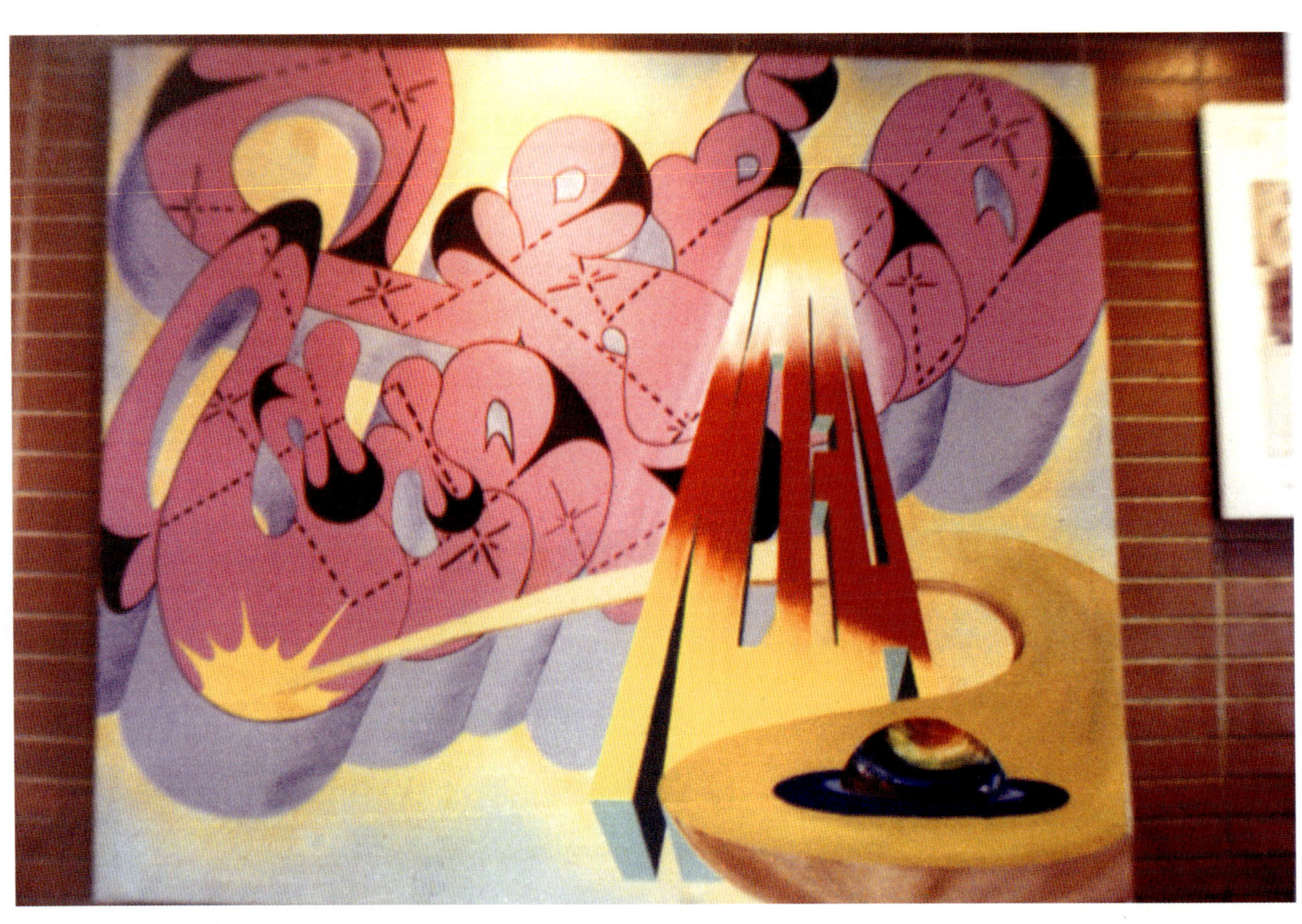

SCORPIO canvas and a STAN 153 canvas paying homage
to fallen writers RC 162, STIM 1 and SOLID 1, 1976.
Photos by Moses Ros/SAL 161.

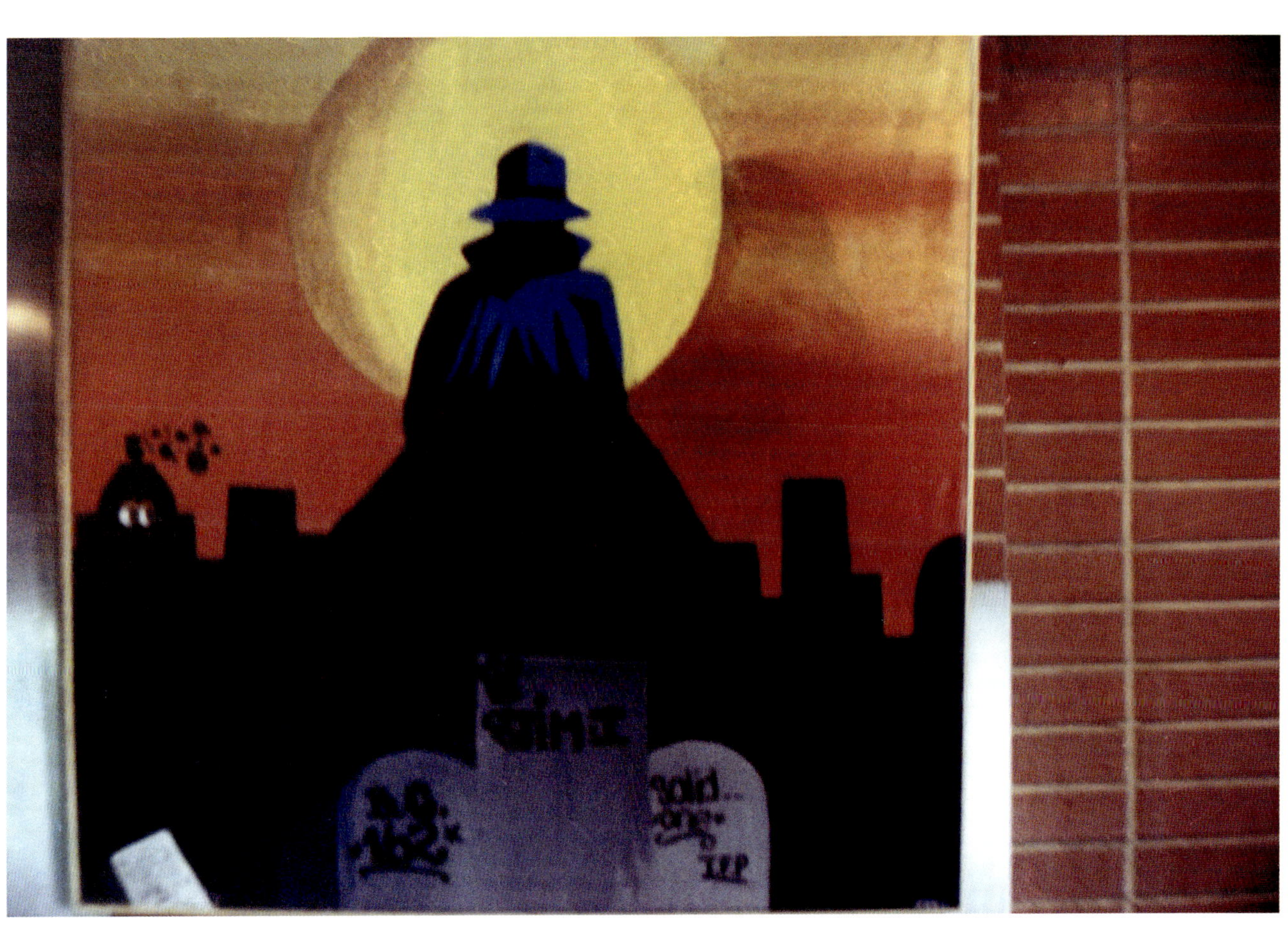

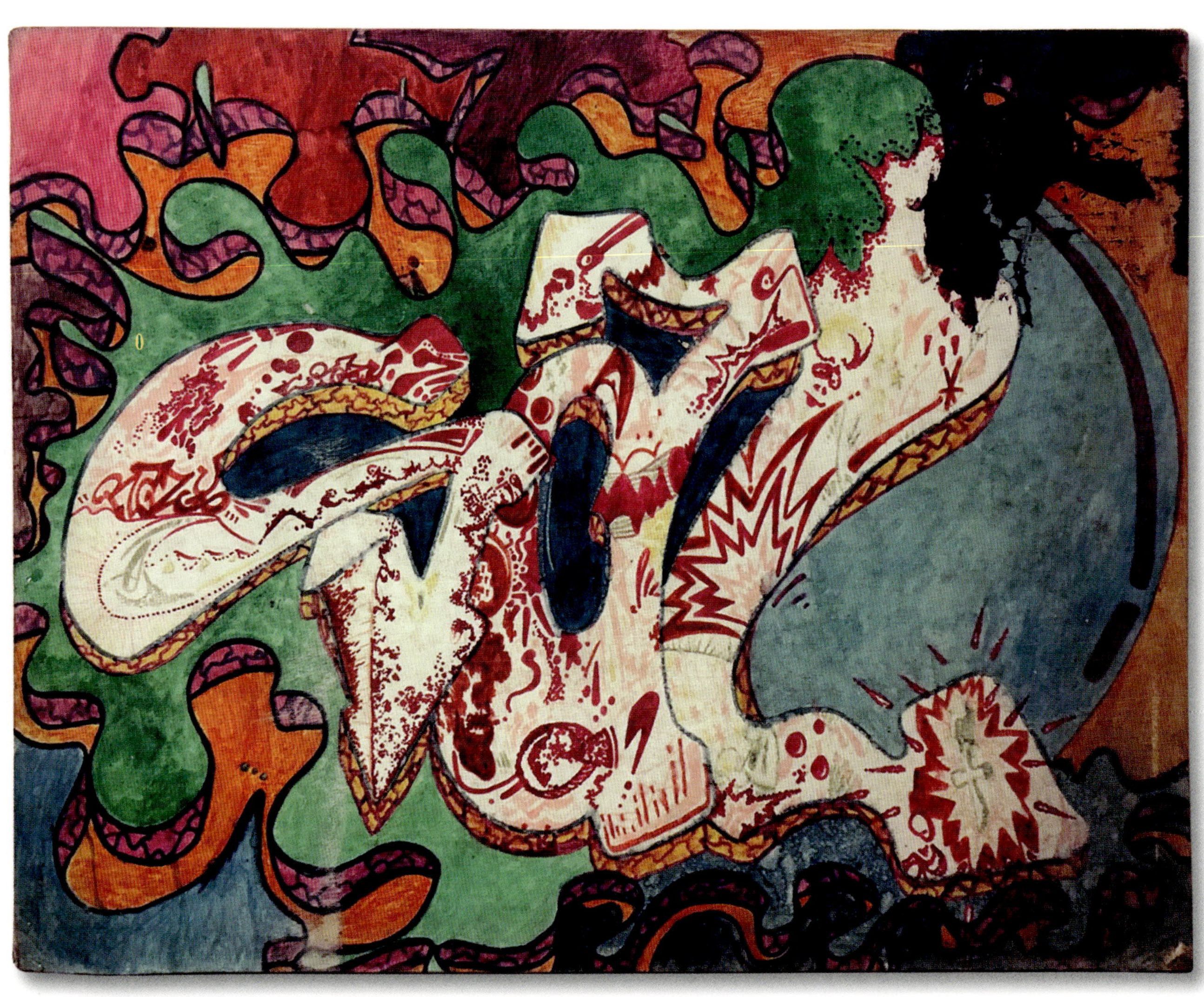

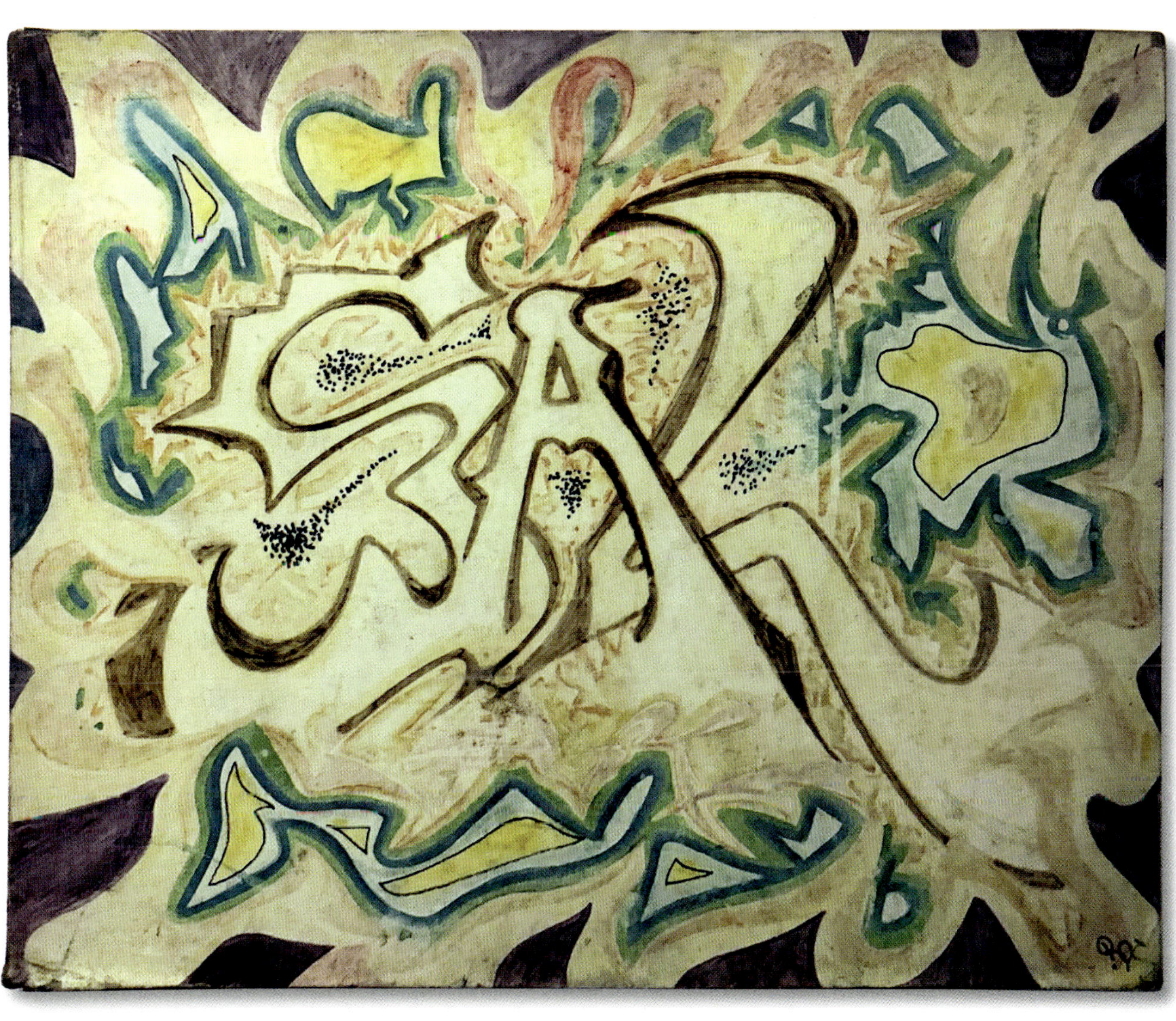

This spread:
SAL 161 canvases, 1975.
Photos by Moses Ros/SAL 161.

33-60 21 Street
L.I.C., New York 11106
March 4, 1975

Mr. Jack Pelsinger, Director
Nation of Graffiti Artists
c/o 261 West 93 Street, Apt. 2
New York, N. Y. 10025

Dear Jack:

I was happy to have visited the "NOGA" Workshop because, professionally, I wanted to observe these deprived teenagers, many of whom, I understand, are school drop-outs. As you know, I am a Supervising Probation Officer and have worked with teenagers and young adults in trouble for the past 39 years, at the New York State Training School for Boys, Rikers Island Penitentiary, New York State Division of Parole, and the New York State Supreme Court Probation Department.

The adolescents and young adults at "NOGA" were very outgoing and friendly, and anxious to show me their works. The graffiti, which I abhor on and in the subway cars, here was channeled in a positive direction of artistic sketches and murals. Such art demands public recognition instead of scorn.

The youngsters seemed enthusiastic, happy and disciplined to work freely within the limits you have set. They worked with no disciplinary problems and seem to respect you very much.

The Nation of Graffiti Artists workshop seems to me to be an excellent example of how the city can solve the problem of subway graffiti in a positive way. Unfortunately, however, the working space was cramped, and when I was there the premises uncomfortably cold on a freezing day. I noticed too that there was a serious shortage or lack of art supplies, such as canvases, sketch books, paints, brushes, pens, easels.

Your organization is an excellent community resource which I plan to have my department use for anyone with an interest or ability in art. I have some reservations about doing this, however, because the inadequate working facilities and materials shortage would deprive those already in your program, should others request admission through me.

I sincerely hope that you will be successful in getting your program adequately funded, so that the underprivileged and poor can continue to profit from it. It offers them positive pursuits, relief of boredom from their colorless homes, perilous streets, and tempting subway yards.

Respectfully,

Simon Tropp
MSW, CSW, ACSW

21 June 1975

Mr. Jack Pelsinger, Director
"Nation of Graffiti Artists"
261 West 93 St.
New York, N.Y. 10024

Dear Mr. Pelsinger:

We have heard that you and your "Nation of Graffiti Artists" face a "vacate Notice" at your storefront studio on Columbus Ave., and thus the possibility of ending your unique contribution to our Community. We believe that if this were to happen it would be an unfortunate and tragic loss to us, and, indeed all of New York City. When one considers that you have taken a group of young, misguided people who were defacing subways and public property with their graffiti, and provided them with a normal, natural, responsible outlet for their talent, the value of what you are doing is obvious. With some 200 youngsters now sworn off pointless public graffiti, and painting on boards and canvas, you have shown that one can sucessfully re-channel this creative talent and energy into positive values for all concerned.

Certainly what "Nation of Graffiti Artists" does for young people is most highly commendable;--we want very much for it to continue. We stand ready to help you in any possible way in your efforts to continue in your storefront studio.

With good wishes for future success,

Jerry Clark

PRESIDENT

d/
cc:Percy Sutton,Pres.Man.Borough
   Edward Schwarzer, Fed.of Citywide
       Block Assns.
   Robert Kagen,Chm.,Comm. Bd.7

This spread:
Various letters responding to fundraising pleas by Pelsinger, 1975.

BROADWAY AND 73rd STREET   NEW YORK, N.Y. 10023   (212) 787-4500

EVELYN C. WALSH
Vice President

**CENTRAL
SAVINGS
BANK**

July 8, 1975

Mr. Jack Pelsinger
Nation of Graffiti Artists
589 Columbus Avenue
New York, New York 10024

Dear Mr. Pelsinger:

We appreciated very much the opportunity to participate
in the program of the Nation of Graffiti Artists through an exhibit
at the main office of the Bank. Certainly we received more feed-
back from the staff, depositors, and public than for that of any
other exhibit we have shown, evidence once again of the stimulating
role of the arts in our every day lives.

As corporate citizens and individuals, we thank you for
your dedicated effort with these creative young people and trust
you will receive the practical support needed to continue the work.

Sincerely,

Evelyn C. Walsh

ECW:hs

CHARLES B. RANGEL
19TH CONGRESSIONAL DISTRICT
NEW YORK

107 CANNON HOUSE OFFICE BUILDING
WASHINGTON, D.C. 20515
TELEPHONE: 202-225-4365

GEORGE A. DALLEY
ADMINISTRATIVE ASSISTANT

COMMITTEE:
WAYS AND MEANS

DISTRICT OFFICE:
55 WEST 125TH STREET
NEW YORK, NEW YORK 10027
TELEPHONE: 212-348-1600

MRS. VIRGINIA L. BELL
DISTRICT ADMINISTRATOR

Congress of the United States
House of Representatives
Washington, D.C. 20515

July 15, 1975

PLEASE RESPOND TO
OFFICE CHECKED:
☐ WASHINGTON
☐ NEW YORK

PLEASE RESPOND TO
720 Columbus Avenue
New York, New York
10025

Mr. Jack Pelsinger, Director
Nation of Graffiti Artists
589 Columbus Avenue
New York, New York 10024

Dear Mr. Pelsinger:

    I would like to commend the Nation of Graffiti Artists for its effort in providing new cultural opportunities to the youth of New York. At a time when the City and State are cutting back on programs for young people, it is encouraging that neighborhood and community efforts are not giving up.

    I believe that it is crucial that we fully develop the talent, creativity and energy of youth to enrich both their own lives and society. This is the mission of the Nation of Graffiti Artists and I am hoping for your continued successes.

Sincerely,

CHARLES B. RANGEL
Member of Congress

CBR:e

This page:
A letter from Congressman Charles Rangel thanking NOGA for its efforts, 1975.

Congress of the United States
House of Representatives
Washington, D.C. 20515

August 6, 1975

Mr. Jack Pelsinger, Director
Nation of Graffiti Artists
261 West 93 Street - Apt. 2
New York, N. Y. 10025

Dear Mr. Pelsinger:

I want to congratulate the Nation of Graffiti Artists, its directors and staff for the highly original work all of you have been doing in the community, rechanneling some of the unharnessed creative energy that -- if not for NOGA -- would still be undiscovered and unappreciated today.

I am glad that many of our young artists who'd previously limited the application of their talent to the somewhat controversial "canvas" of the subway, have now joined you in an effort to refine their gifts and bring them, literally, to the surface.

I especially appreciate the vitality of their work, and I believe, thanks in good measure to NOGA, that many will now be motivated to pursue their art so that all of us can enjoy it properly.

I wish you many more years of success.

Sincerely,

Bella S. Abzug
Member of Congress

BSA/as

This page:
Letter from Congresswoman Bella Abzug praising the workshop, 1975.

State of New York

David L. Yunich
Chairman and
Chief Executive Officer

**Metropolitan
Transportation
Authority**

December 11, 1975

Dear Mr. Pelsinger:

As you have been informed, the Metropolitan Transportation Authority has been required to delay, for a short time, our plans to work with your organization on a "graffiti art show" and subsequent projects. This delay, although unfortunate, is necessary to insure maximum opportunity to obtain a substantial grant from John Jay College to aid our existing and future graffiti programs.

This temporary delay should not be construed as a change in MTA's policy regarding your organization and its fine work. We are committed to working closely with N.O.G.A. and Western Electric in undertaking the "graffiti art show" and future projects.

Sincerely,

David L. Yunich

Mr. Jack Pelsinger
Nation of Graffiti Artists
102 West 73rd Street
New York, NY 10023

1700 Broadway   New York, New York 10019

This page:
Letter responding to fundraising pleas by Pelsinger, 1975.

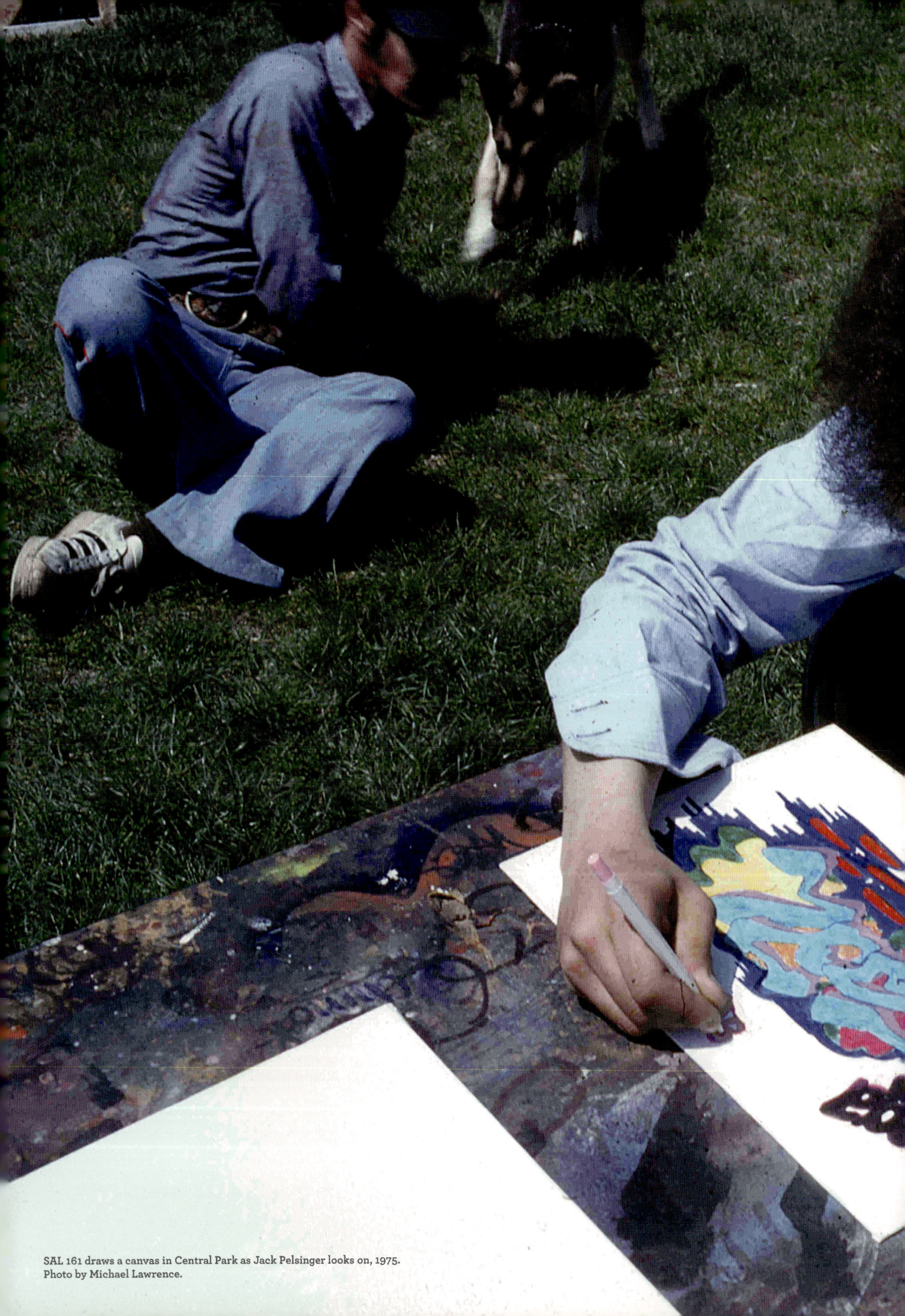
SAL 161 draws a canvas in Central Park as Jack Pelsinger looks on, 1975.
Photo by Michael Lawrence.

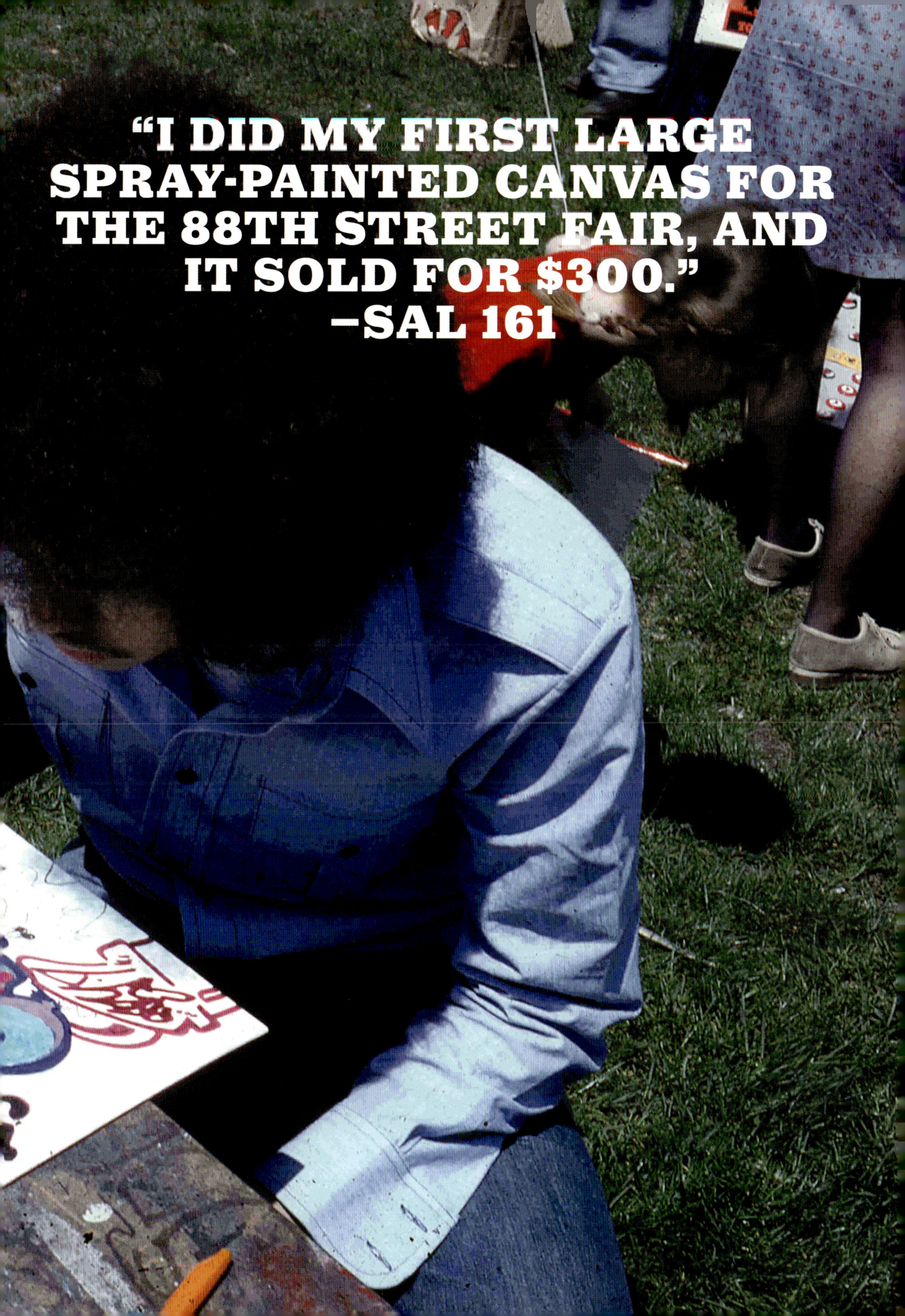
"I DID MY FIRST LARGE SPRAY-PAINTED CANVAS FOR THE 88TH STREET FAIR, AND IT SOLD FOR $300."
—SAL 161

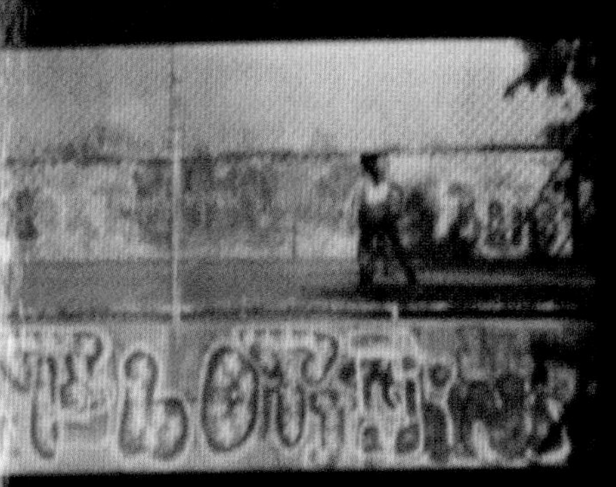
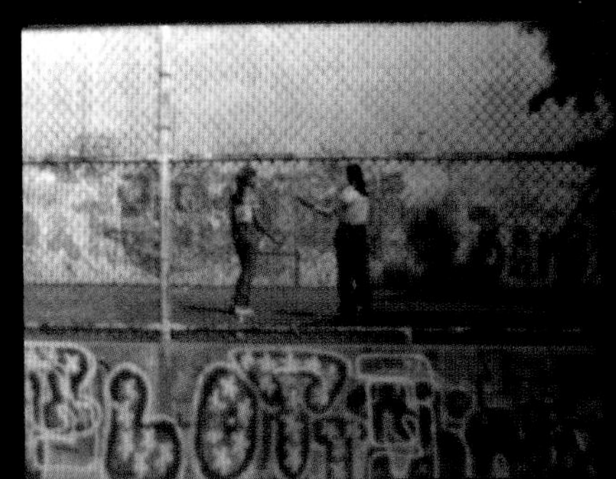
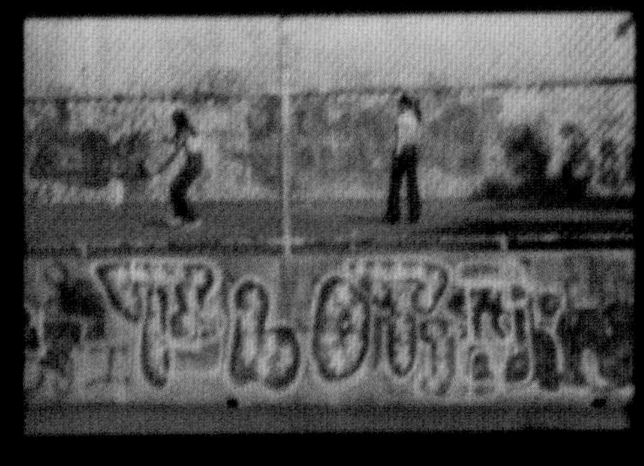
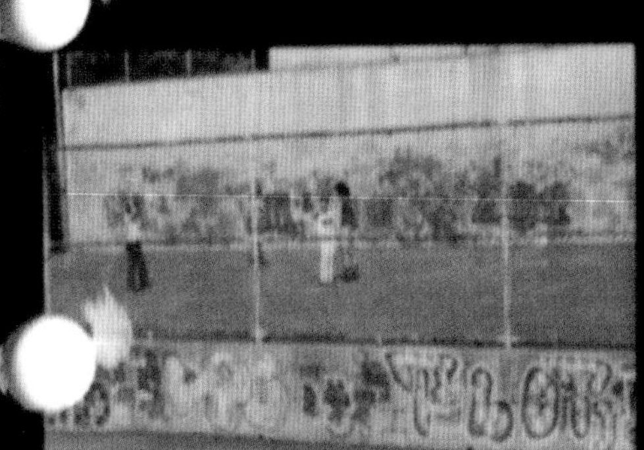
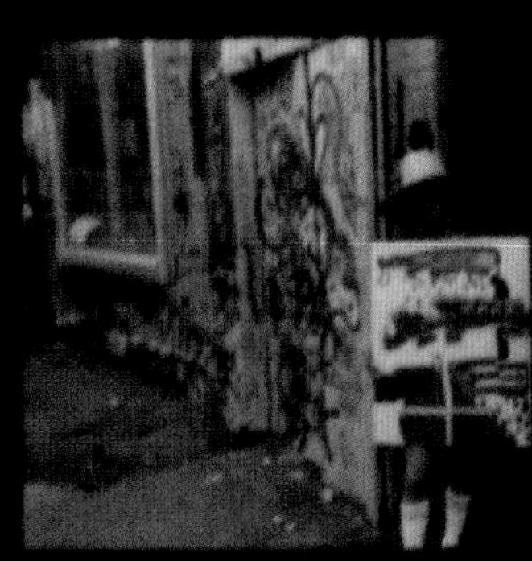
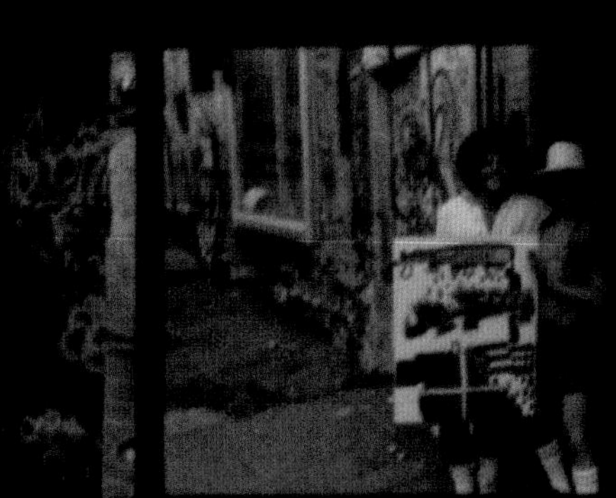
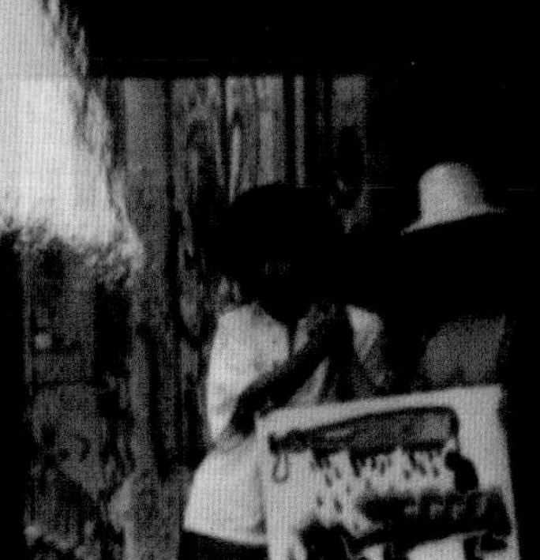
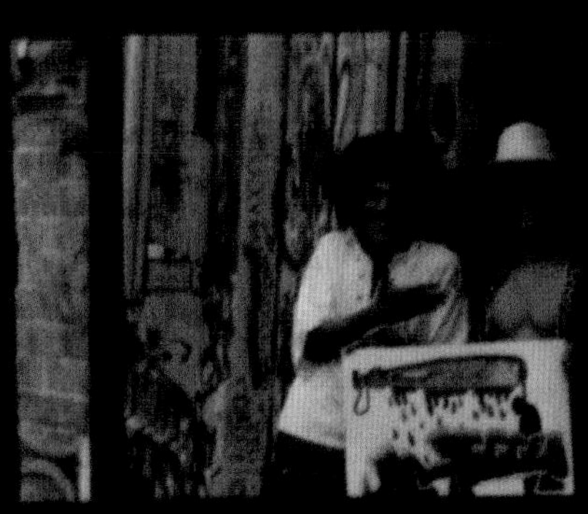
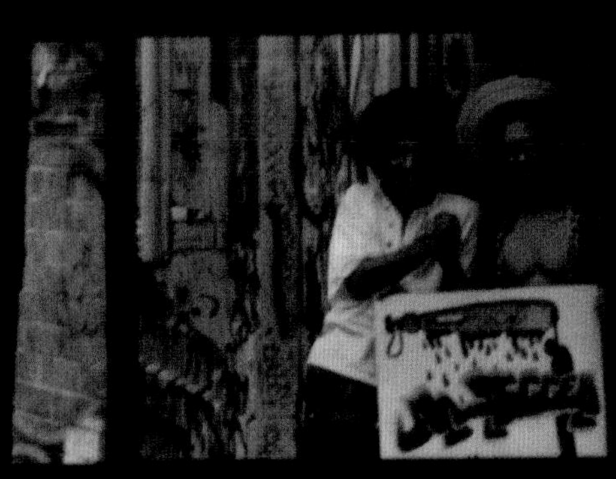
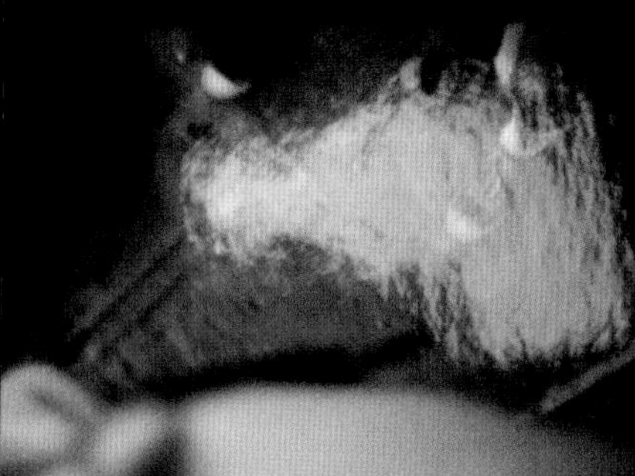
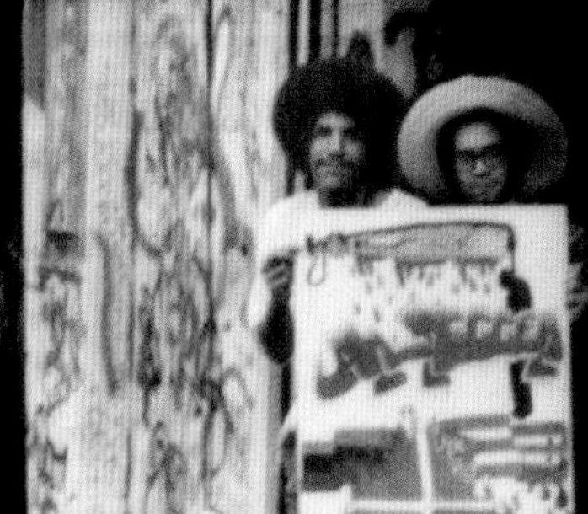
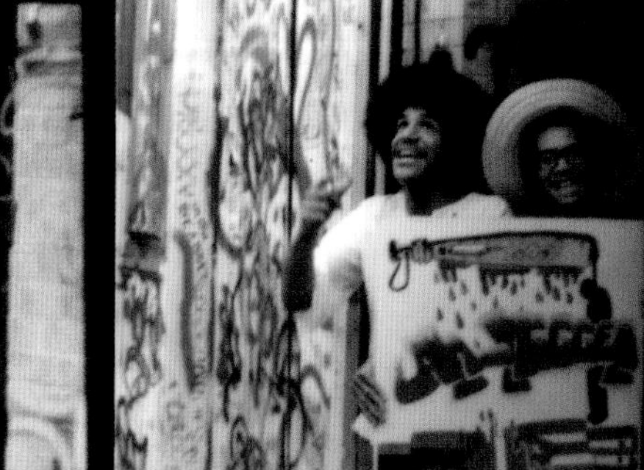

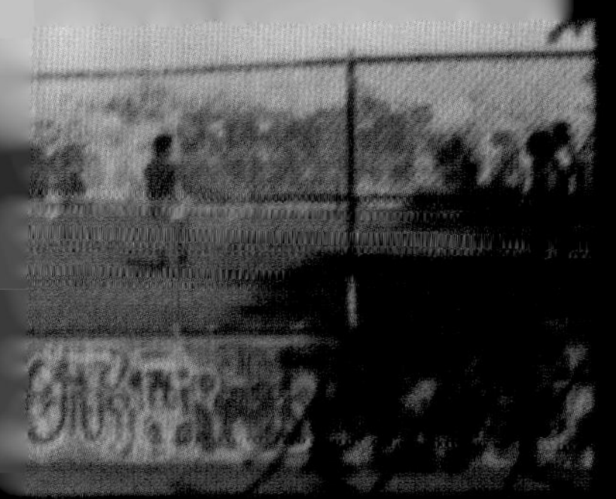
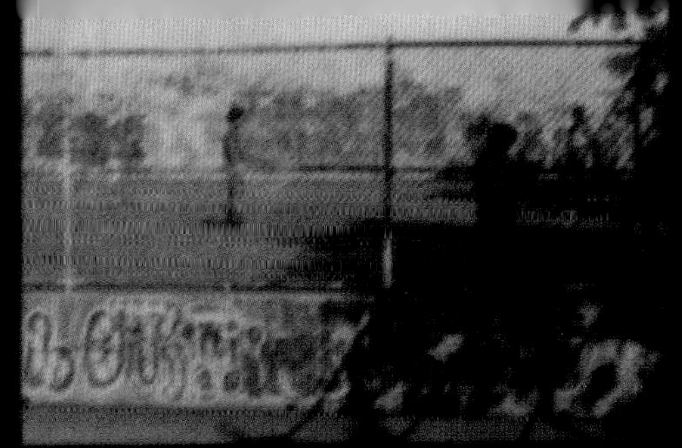
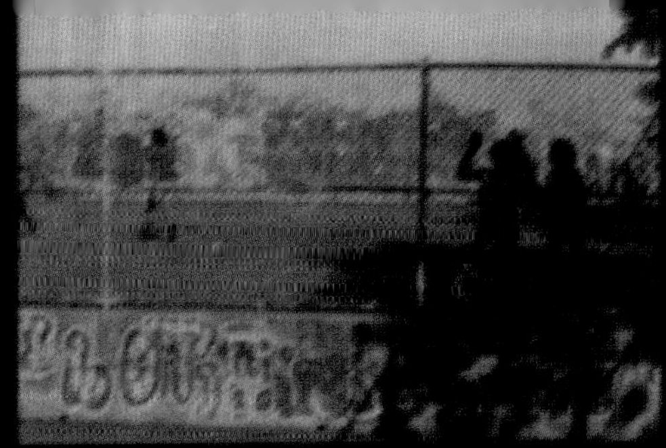
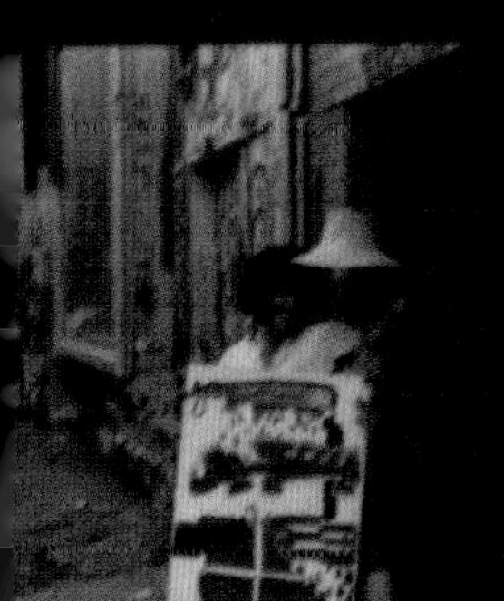
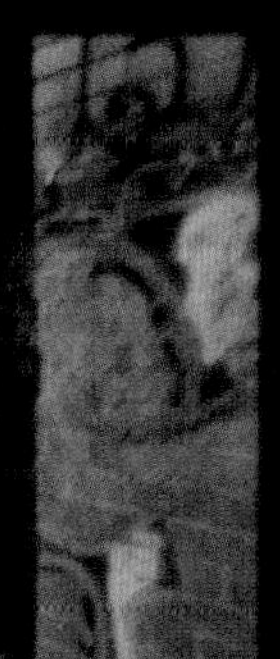
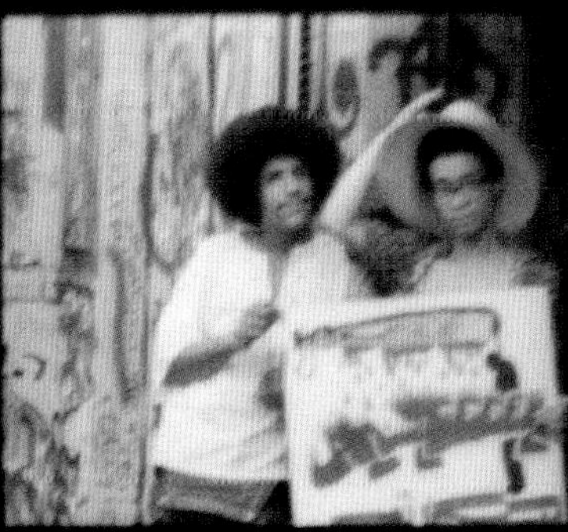
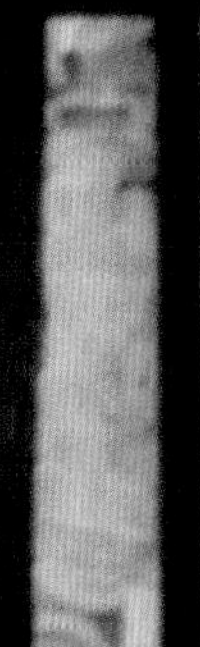
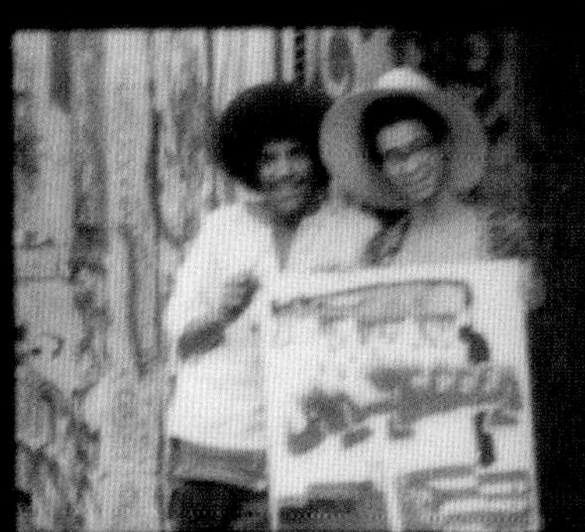
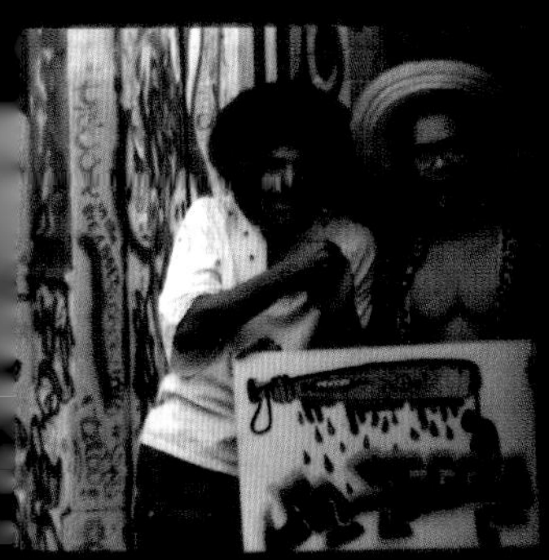
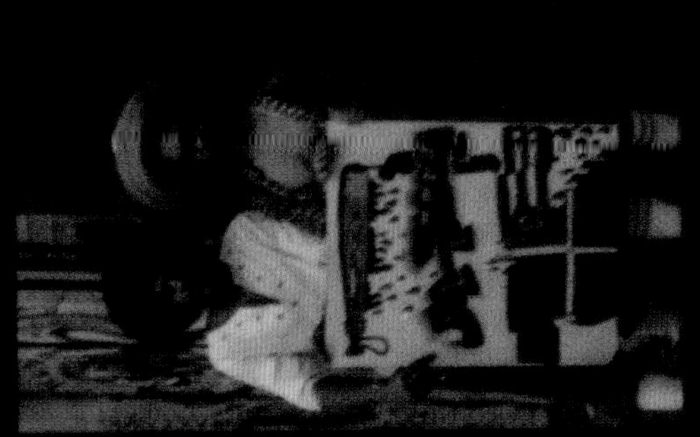
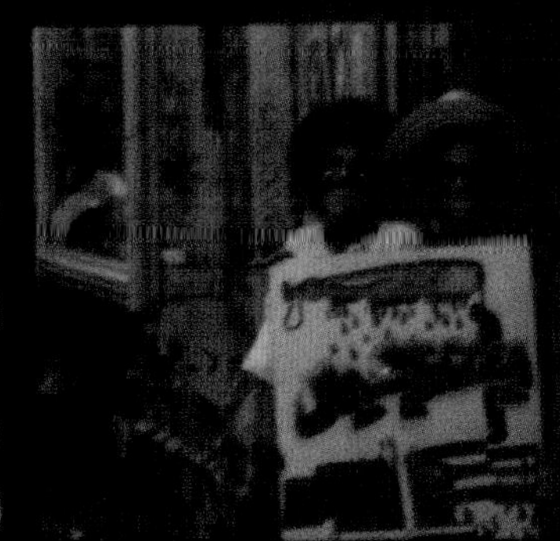
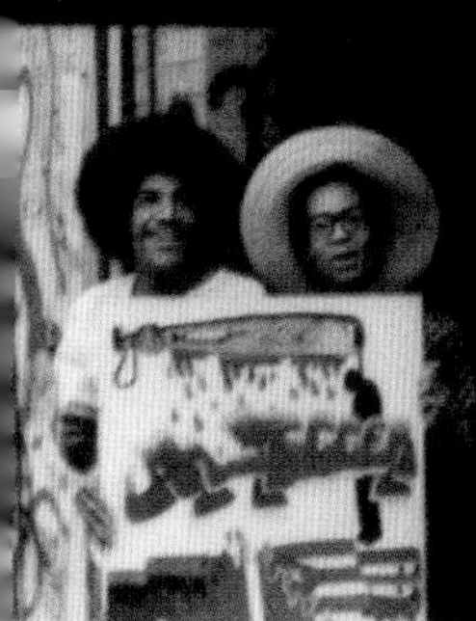
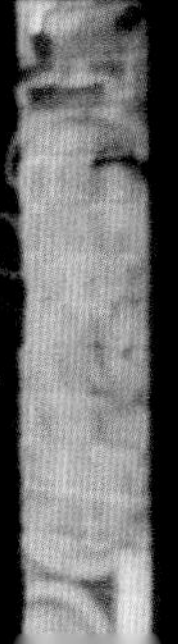
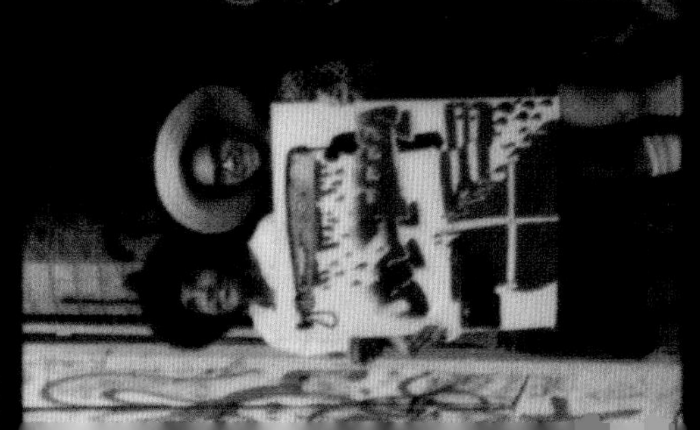
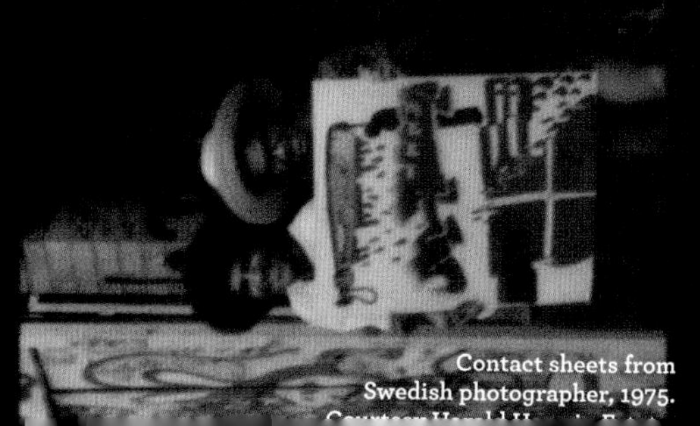

Contact sheets from
Swedish photographer, 1975.
Courtesy Harold Haizen Foto

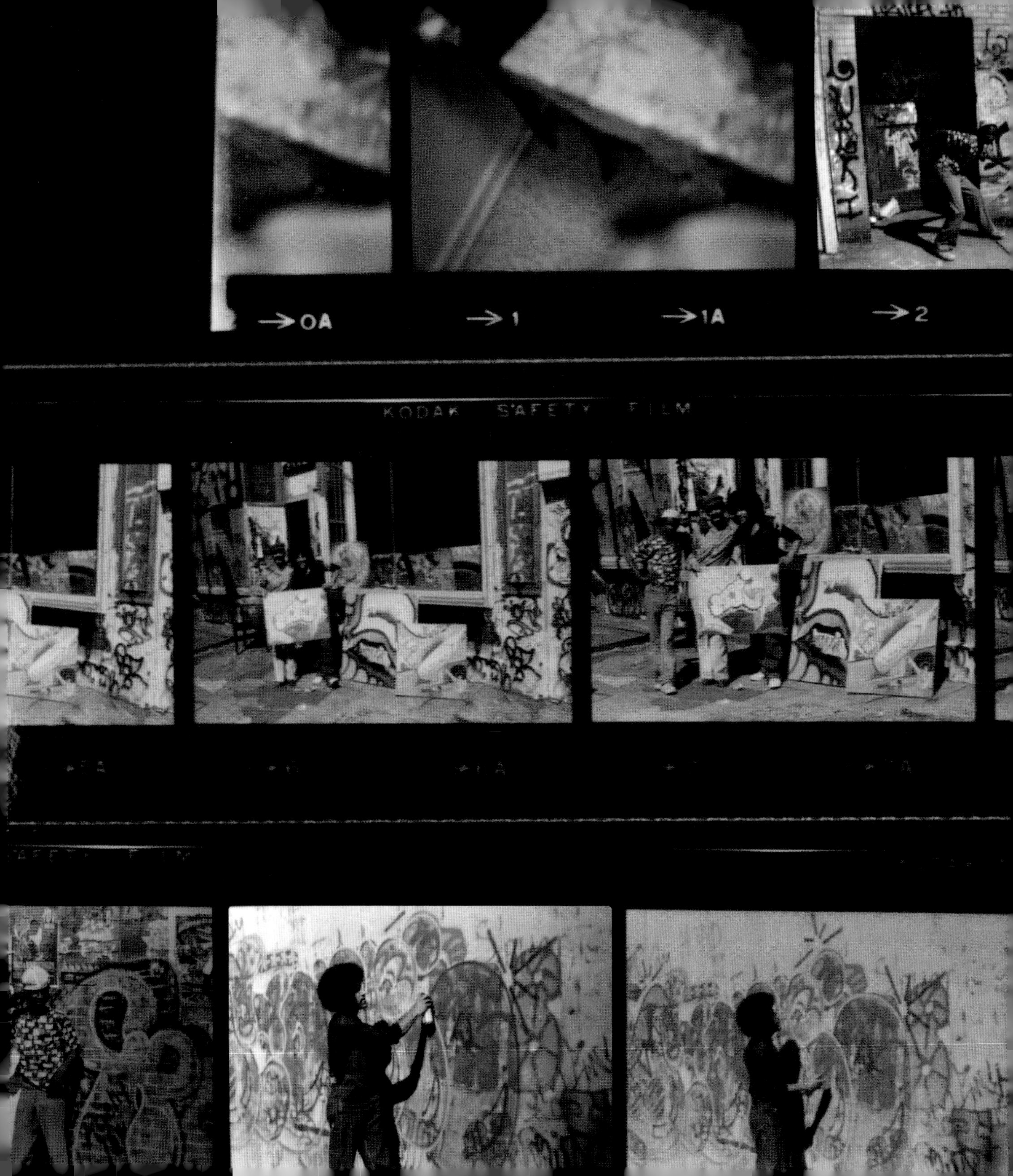

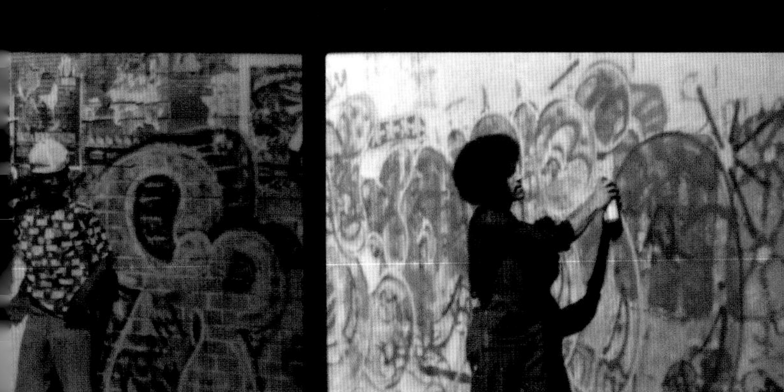
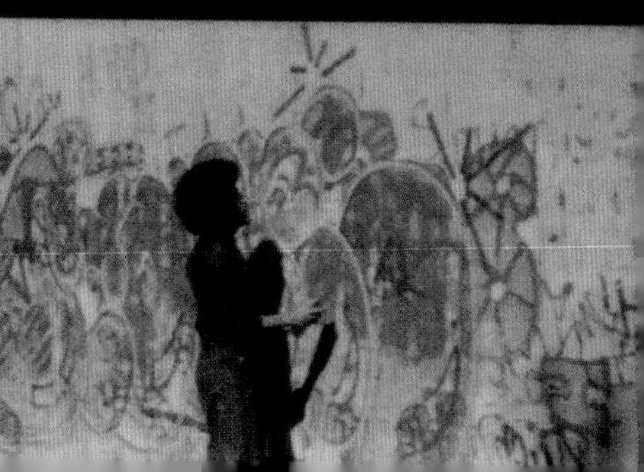

→ OA
→ 1
→ 1A
→ 2
KODAK SAFETY FILM

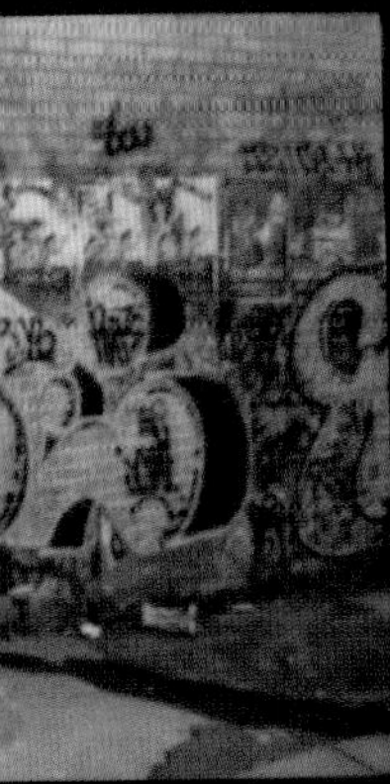
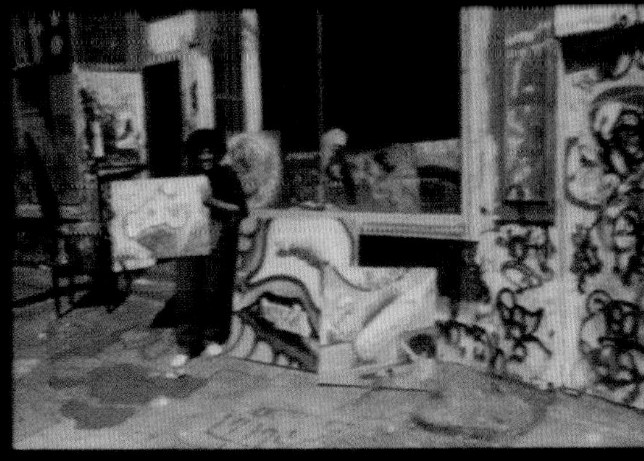
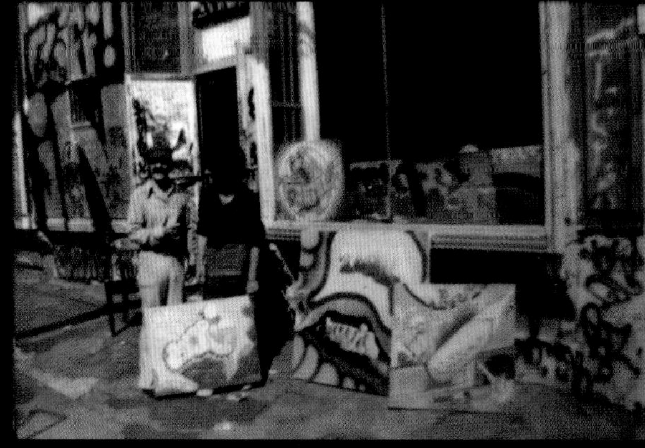

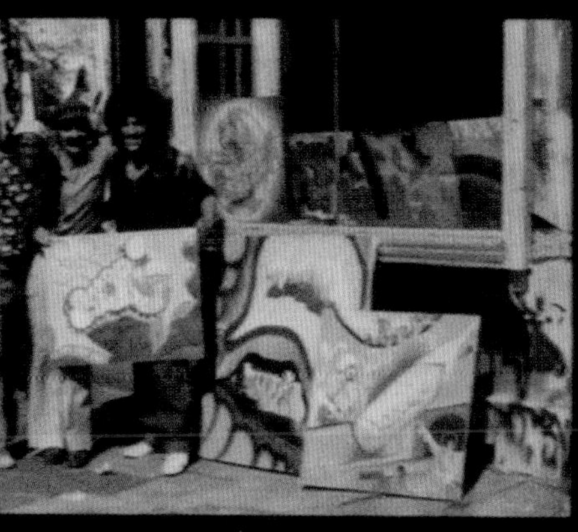
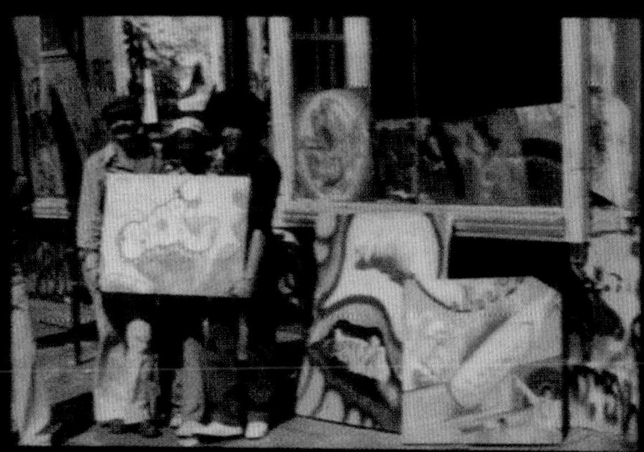
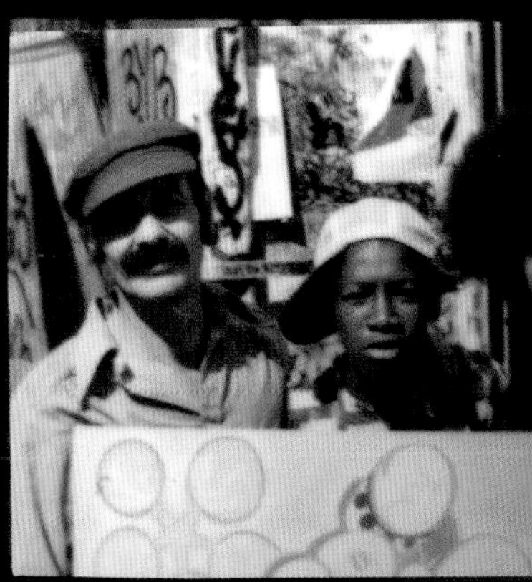

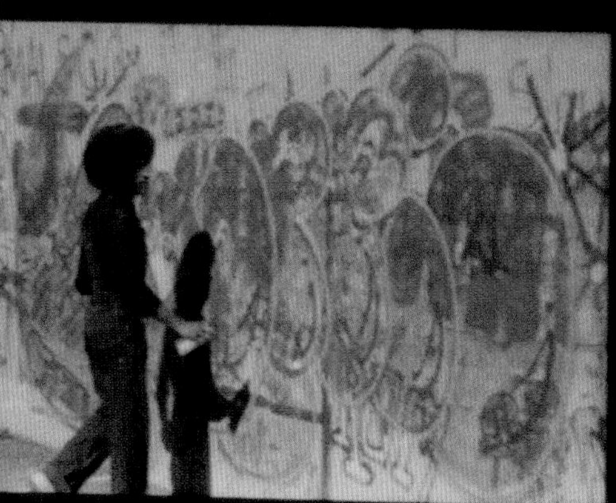
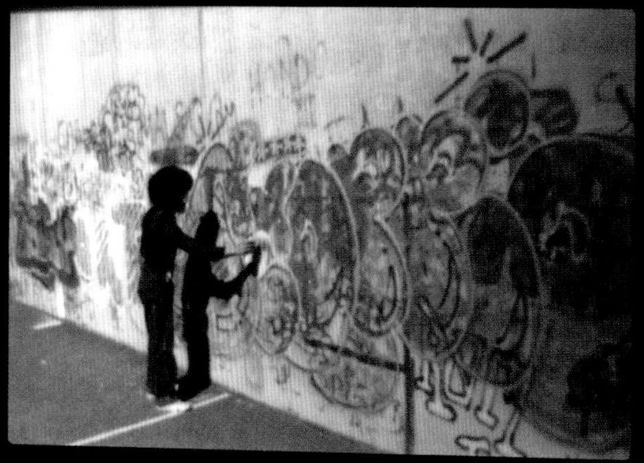
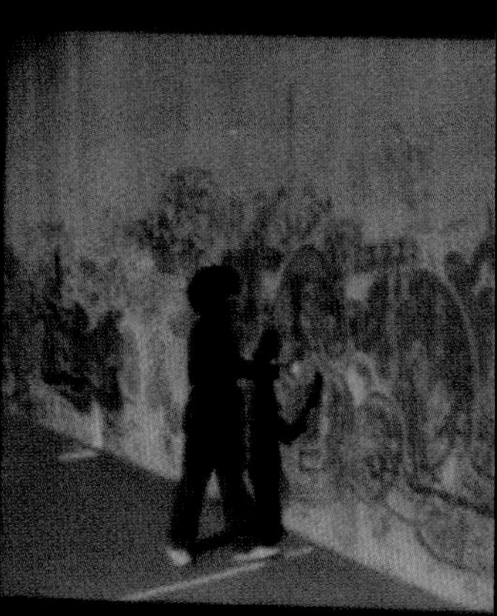

Contact sheets from
Swedish photographer, 1975.
Courtesy Harald Hamrin Estate.

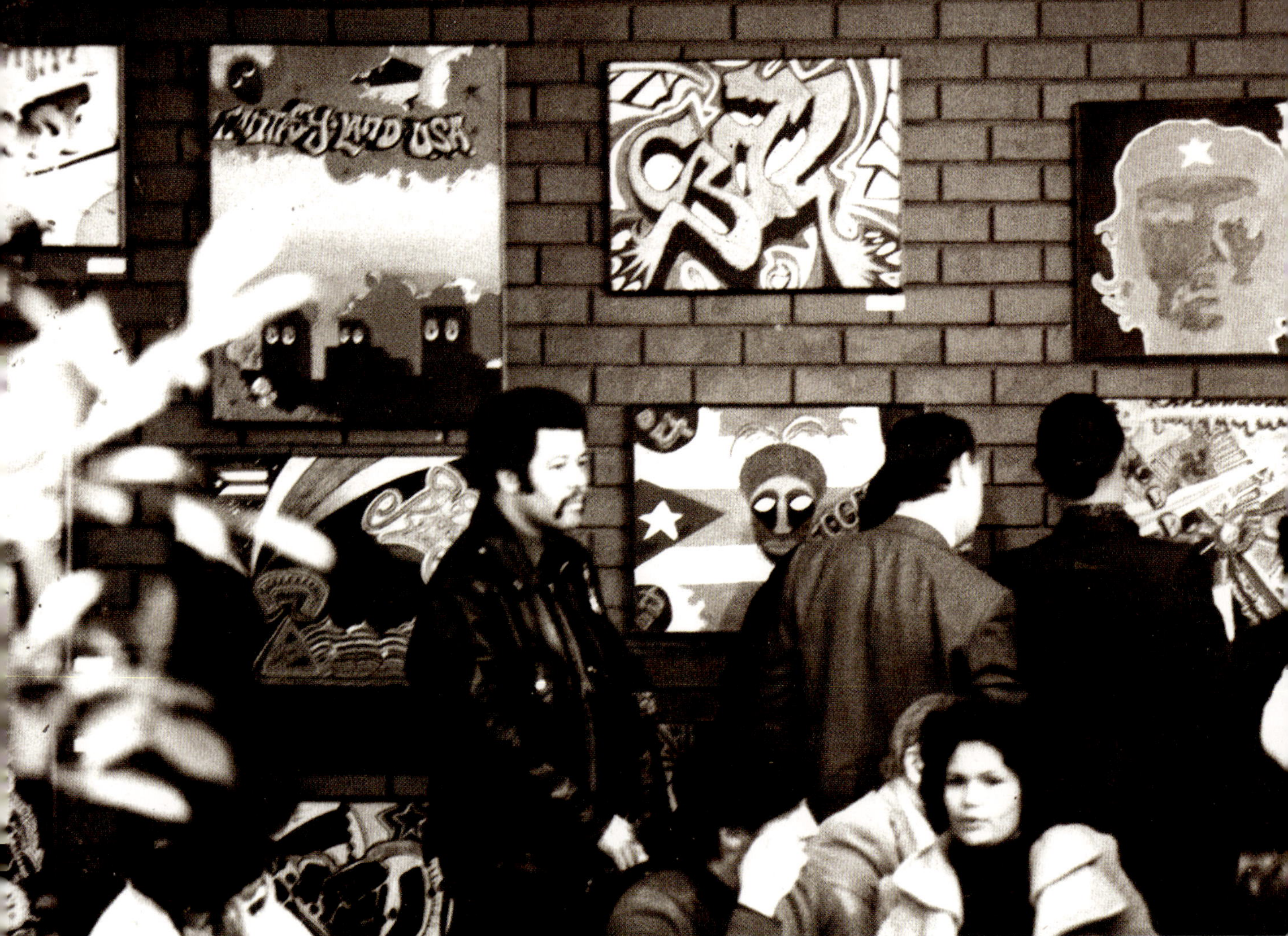

GROWTH

When NOGA did get another show — in March 1976 at Bank Street College on 112th Street and Broadway — the writers continued to present smaller works done on inexpensive canvas boards. The quality of the art was much better, with several of the writers working in acrylic with brush. While some writers used their tags, others did paintings of political slogans, many of them based on posters they'd seen in a book Pelsinger had brought in. During the run of the show, NOGA writers were willing to do a bubble-letter piece of your name in Magic Marker for five dollars. Those same five dollars kept the NOGA doors open but held them back from consideration as fine artists.

SAL 161 explains the show this way: "I had been away for most of 1975. I was in the Dominican Republic. I came back around the time of the Bank Street show, which I exhibited in. A number of writers started to display more ability working on canvas, and the show looked good, more professional. That may have been the highlight of NOGA. I started going to Brandeis High School, where I designed the entire yearbook. I was spending a lot more time at school, and when I looked around, NOGA was gone. I worked up a portfolio and applied for Pratt Institute and made it in. I was on my way to being an architect."

In September of 1976, the NOGA artists were asked to paint a mural for Prospect Hospital in the Bronx. The group arrived on a Saturday and set up in the parking lot. BLOOD TEA performed on the conga drums as each writer added his name on a long vertical canvas that the hospital had provided. It was an enjoyable experience for all involved — until it was time to get paid. The hospital balked at first but finally came up with $100 for the group. The photographs of that day are important because they show off a roster of talent that would soon take over the trains, including NOC 167, KASE 2, BUTCH 2 and CHAIN 3 — all members of NOGA who had previously been overshadowed by CLIFF 159, SCORPIO and BLOOD TEA. It was the beginning of a changing of the guard. As STAN 153 explains:

"I don't remember if there was even a workshop in 1976. I got a call from Jack to be at the hospital and I went over there and we painted. Most of the writers were from the Bronx, like BUTCH and KASE. That was different than the NOGA on Columbus Avenue, where everyone was from the neighborhood."

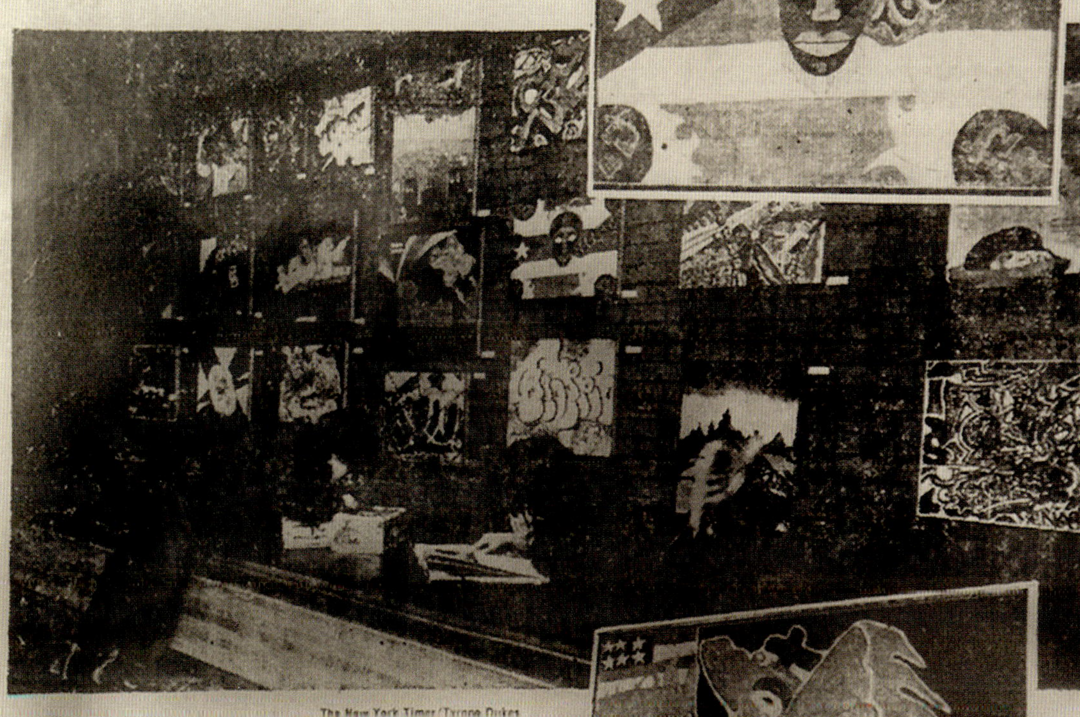

Some Artful Dodgers Find a Different Line

The New York Times/Tyrone Dukes

Part of the exhibit by the Nation of Graffiti Artists at Bank Street College of Education on West 112th Street.

For disadvantaged youths like Scar-36, the defiant graffiti that can annoy or puzzle riders on New York City's subway system is merely a creative quest for identity.

But stricter law enforcement has caused Scar-36 and thousands of other "underground artists" to give up their trade or readjust their style.

Many of them have joined the Nation of Graffiti Artists, a graffiti workshop that was formed to help youths from depressed areas of the city develop as artists. The group staged an exhibition of graffiti recently at the Bank Street College of Education on West 112th Street.

The scrawling of graffiti is a misdemeanor in New York. Youths under 16 who are caught often spend a week on cleanup details. Older violators have spent a week or more at the Spofford House of Detention.

Jack Pelsinger, the director of the graffiti workshop, has been working with officials at the Metropolitan Transportation Authority to have the laws changed or to hire the most prolific graffiti drawers to create attractive designs on the trains. But until an agreement between both parties has been reached, many of the underground artists say they will continue their designs and work mostly in the yards, where the trains are parked at night.

"One night I worked from 10 o'clock to 6:30 in the morning on one design," said 16-year-old C.D. of Brooklyn.

C.D. and many of his comrades say that they feel lost in the city and that graffiti is their way of gaining recognition. His goal, like many of the others, is to become king of a line—by having his identity placed on as many trains of a given subway line as possible.

The graffiti workshop furnishes supplies to its artists with the partial financing the workshop receives from the New York Telephone and Western Electric Companies and has also helped to encourage its artists to spend less time on their ventures and more time in school.

"Why should I waste time putting my design on the trains, when people will pay me to put it on canvas," said Sal 161, who has sold two of his works since joining the workshop six months ago.

"When you have it on canvas, you don't risk getting

Opposite page:
Bank Street College graffiti art show, 1976.

This page:
New York Times review of the Bank Street College show in 1976.

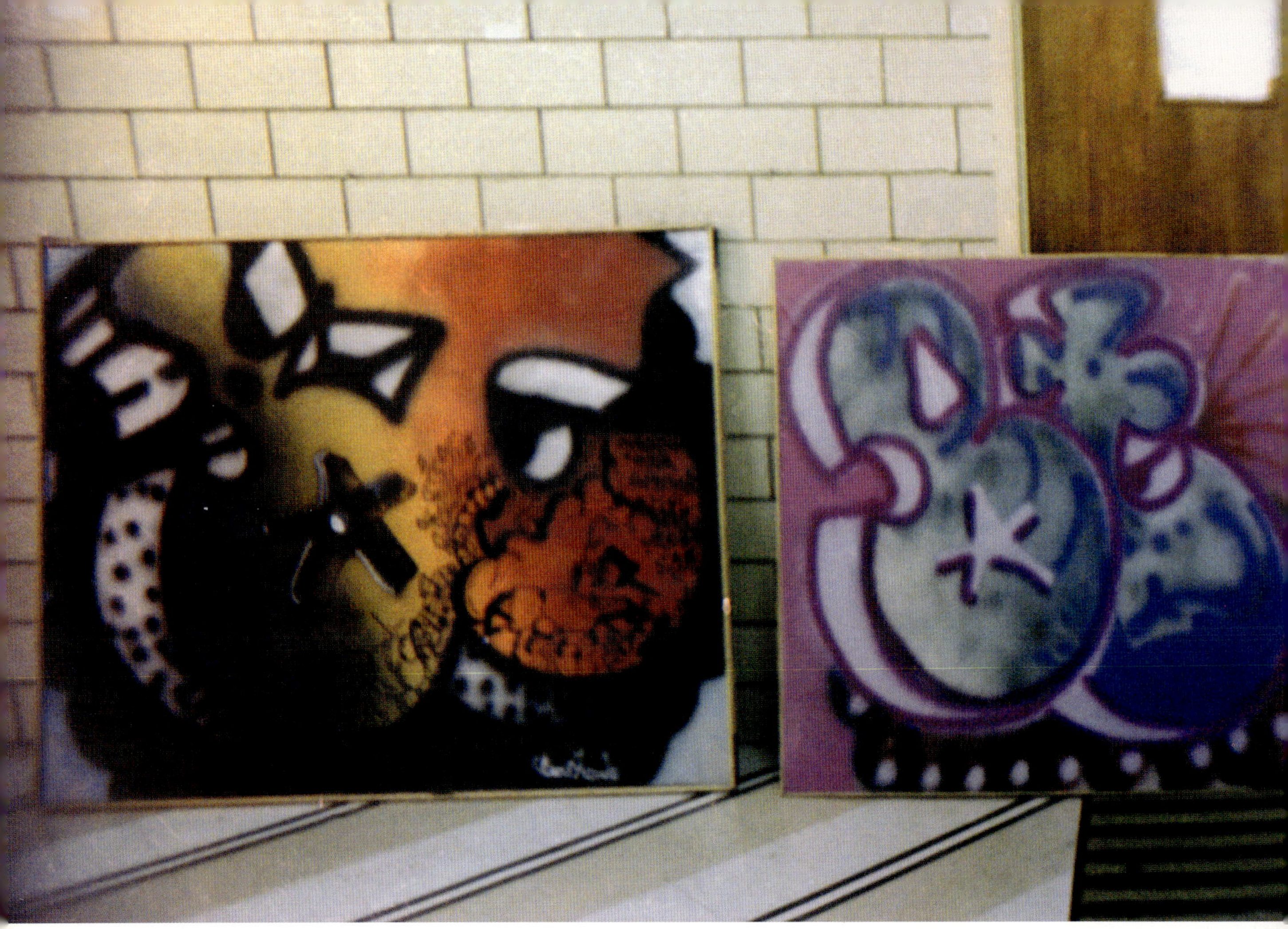

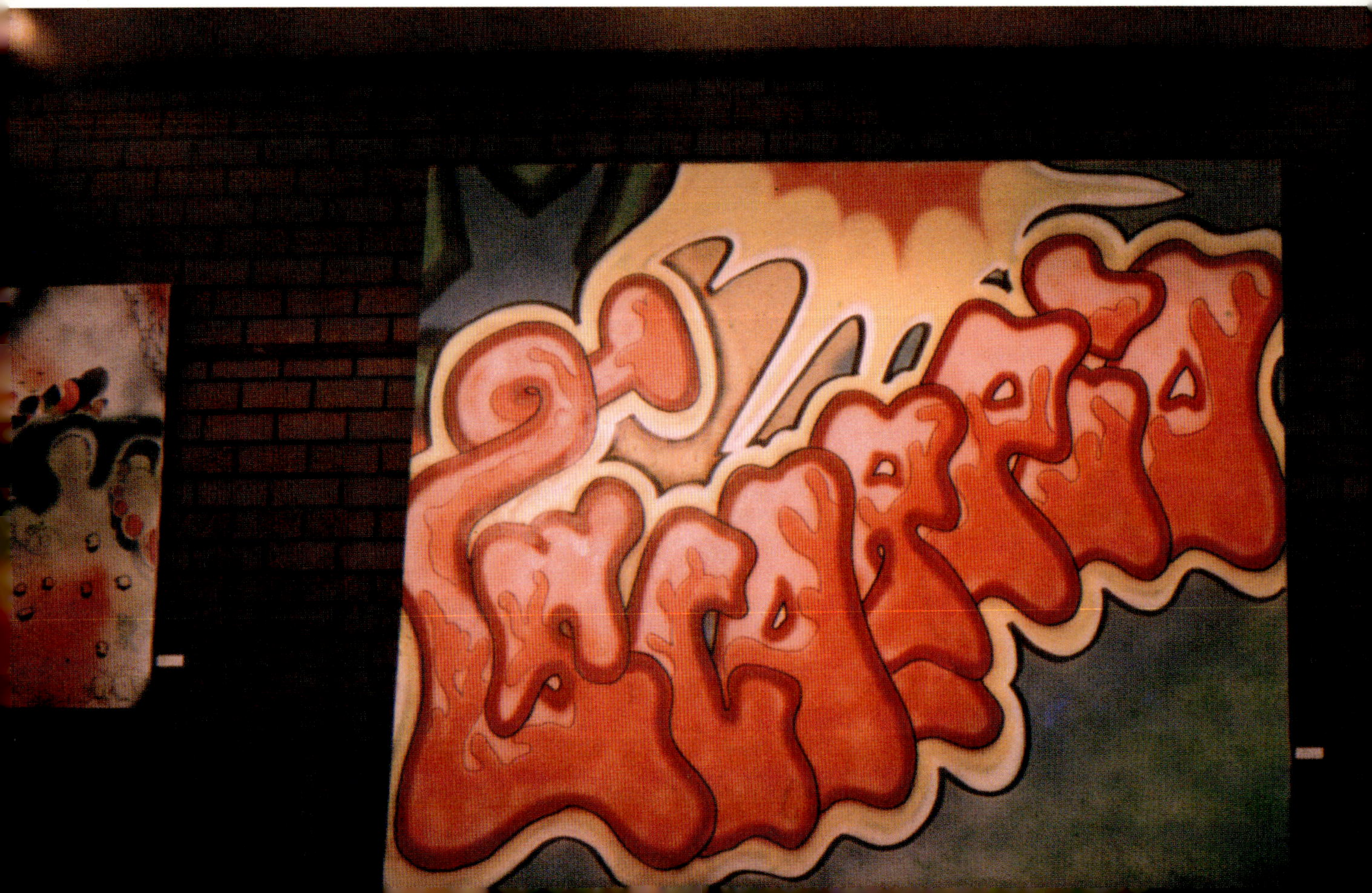

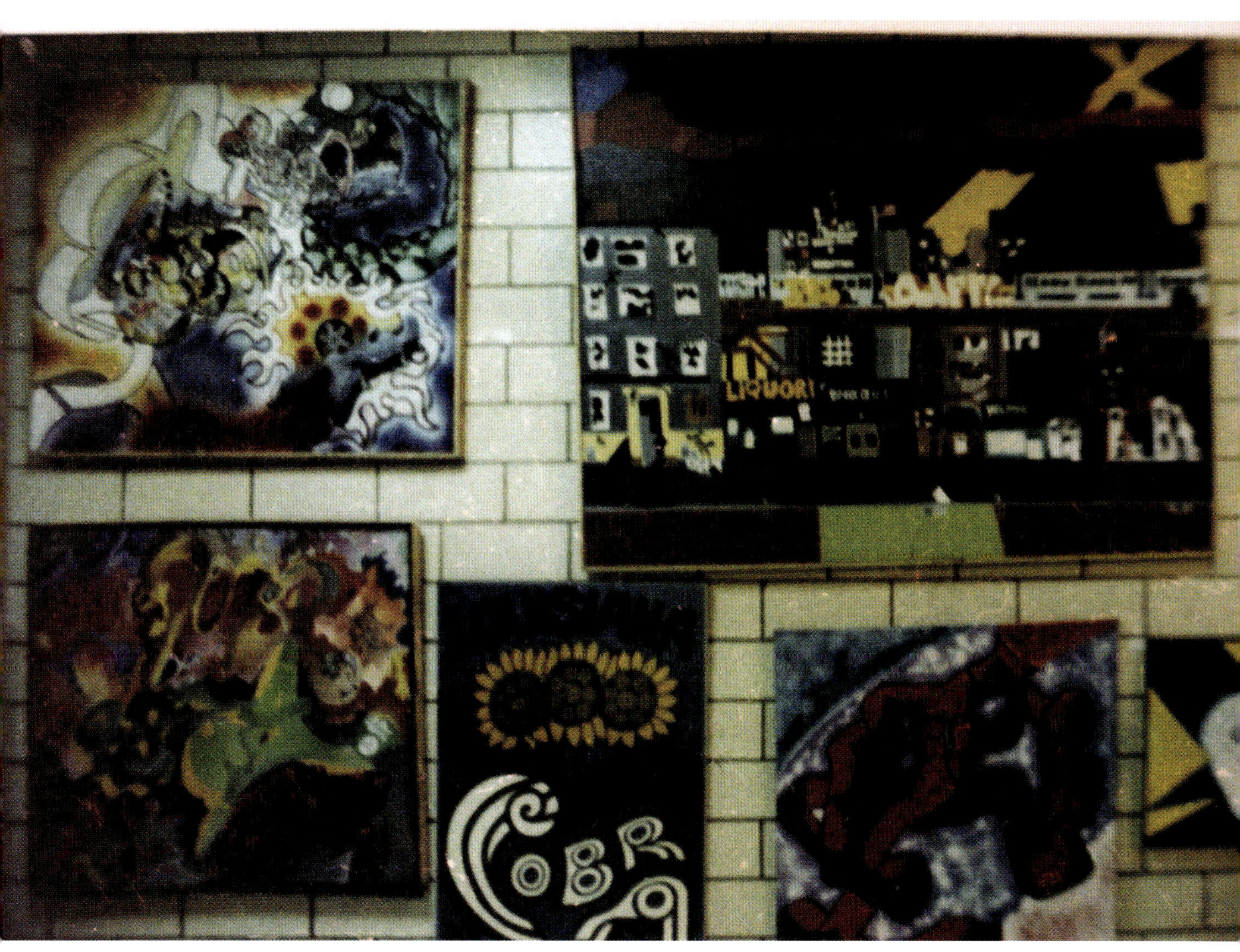

This spread:
Bank Street College show, 1976.
Photos by Michael Lawrence and Moses Ros/SAL 161.

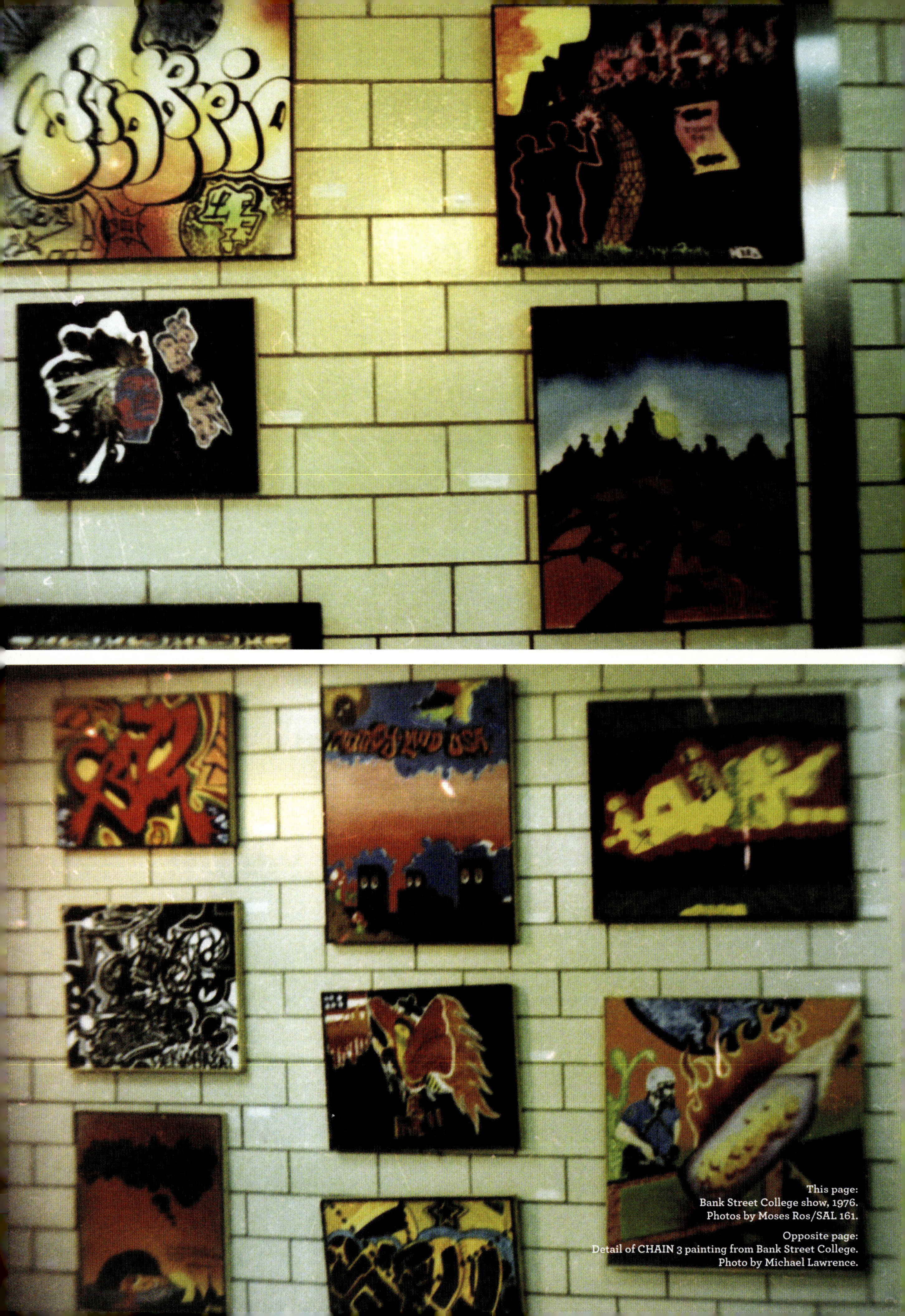

This page:
Bank Street College show, 1976.
Photos by Moses Ros/SAL 161.

Opposite page:
Detail of CHAIN 3 painting from Bank Street College.
Photo by Michael Lawrence.

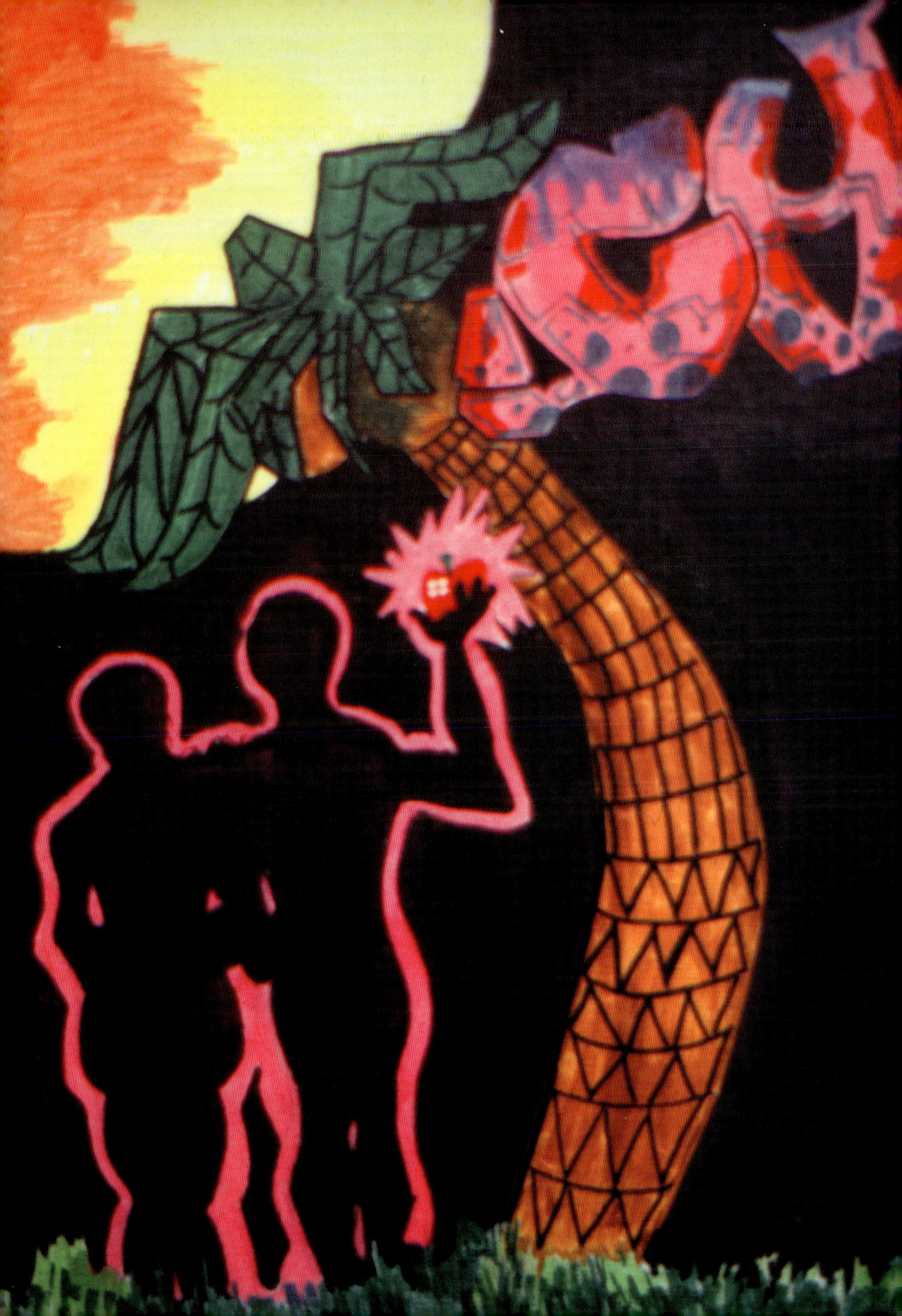

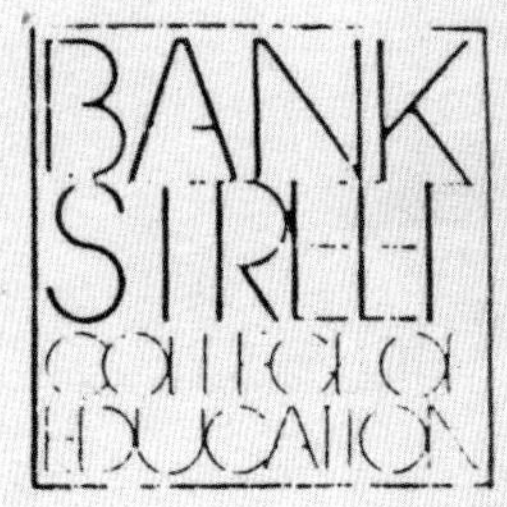

610 WEST 112TH STREET
NEW YORK, N.Y. 10025
PHONE (212) 663 7200

January 26, 1976

Mr. Jack Pelsinger
Nation of Graffiti Artists
102 West 73 Street
New York, New York 10023

Dear Mr. Pelsinger,

Let me take this opportunity to thank you for the opportunity of seeing the work of the artists who have joined Nation of Graffiti Artists.

I was impressed with the craftsmanship and technical skill evident in the paintings. The paintings are vivid expressions of a vital community art form, of interest to everyone who is concerned about the creative arts.

My recent viewing of the artists' work brought home to me the constant question which all too often has been ignored: Are there not adequate ways to support the creativity of young American artists?

I commend the artists for their tenacity in pursuing their work in the face of many obstacles. It is my hope that the exhibit of the Nation of Graffiti Artists scheduled to open at Bank Street College will, in a variety of ways, support N.O.G.A.'s efforts.

Sincerely,

Gordon Klopf
Provost-Dean
Bank Street College of
Education

This spread:
Correspondence regarding the Bank Street College show, 1976.

Dr. Jacob B. Freedman
Executive Director

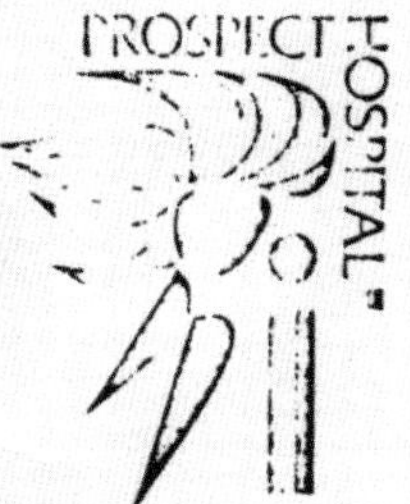

December 27, 1977

Mr. Jack Pelsinger, Director
Nation of Graffiti Artists
P.O. Box 119
New York, New York 10028

Dear Mr. Pelsinger:

Just a short note to tell you how delighted I was to see you
on the Felipe Luciano show the other evening. It certainly
brought back some very fond memories, especially our Graffiti
Concert in the parking lot.

I was happy to learn that you were finally able to locate permanent quarters for your group, and regret we were not able
to reach a mutual understanding in this regard. You are to
be highly commended for the excellent work you've been doing,
and I wish you the very best of luck in all your future en-
deavors.

Please extend to everyone my best wishes for a health and
happy New Year.

Sincerely yours,

DR. JACOB B. FREEDMAN

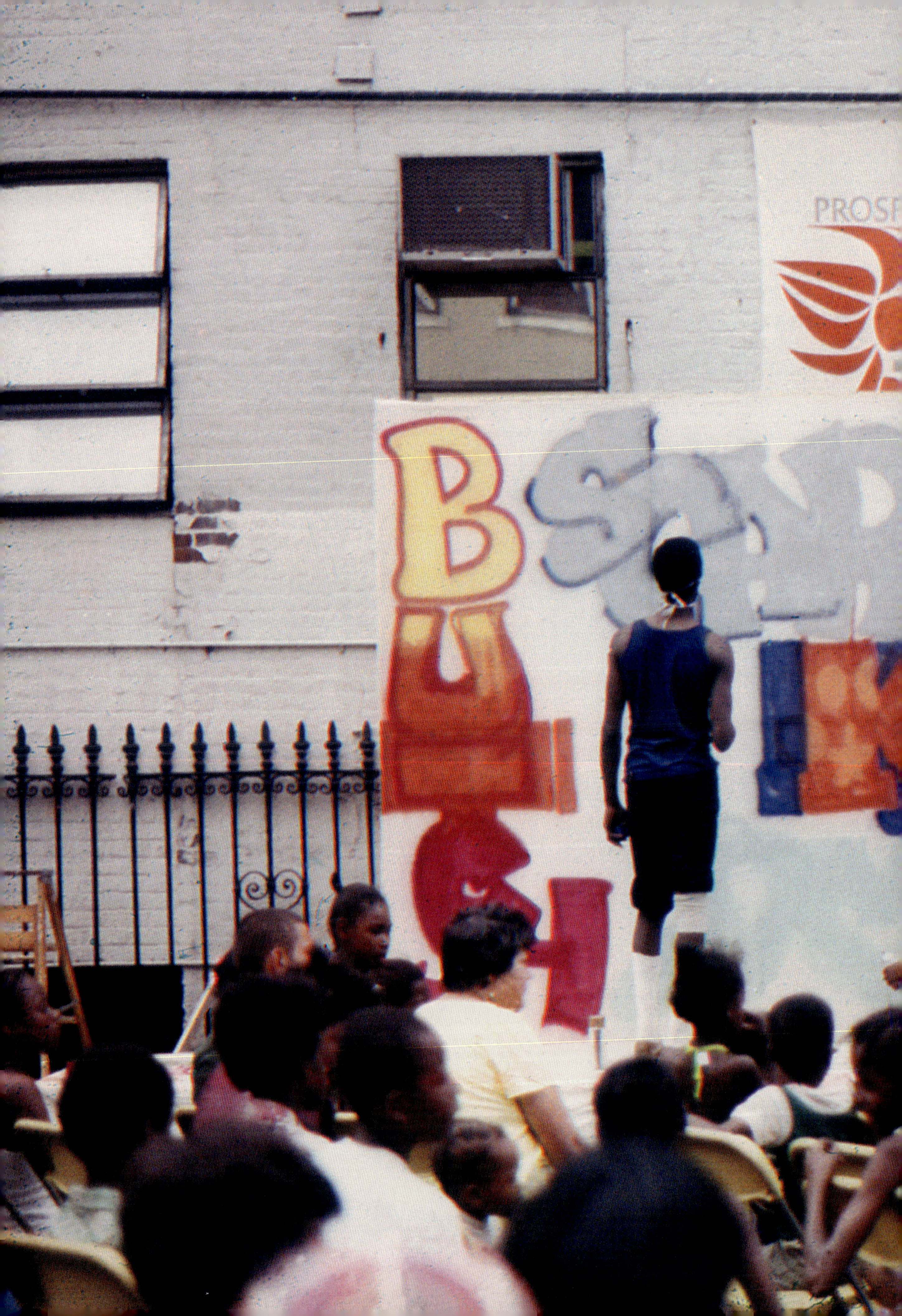
PROSP
B

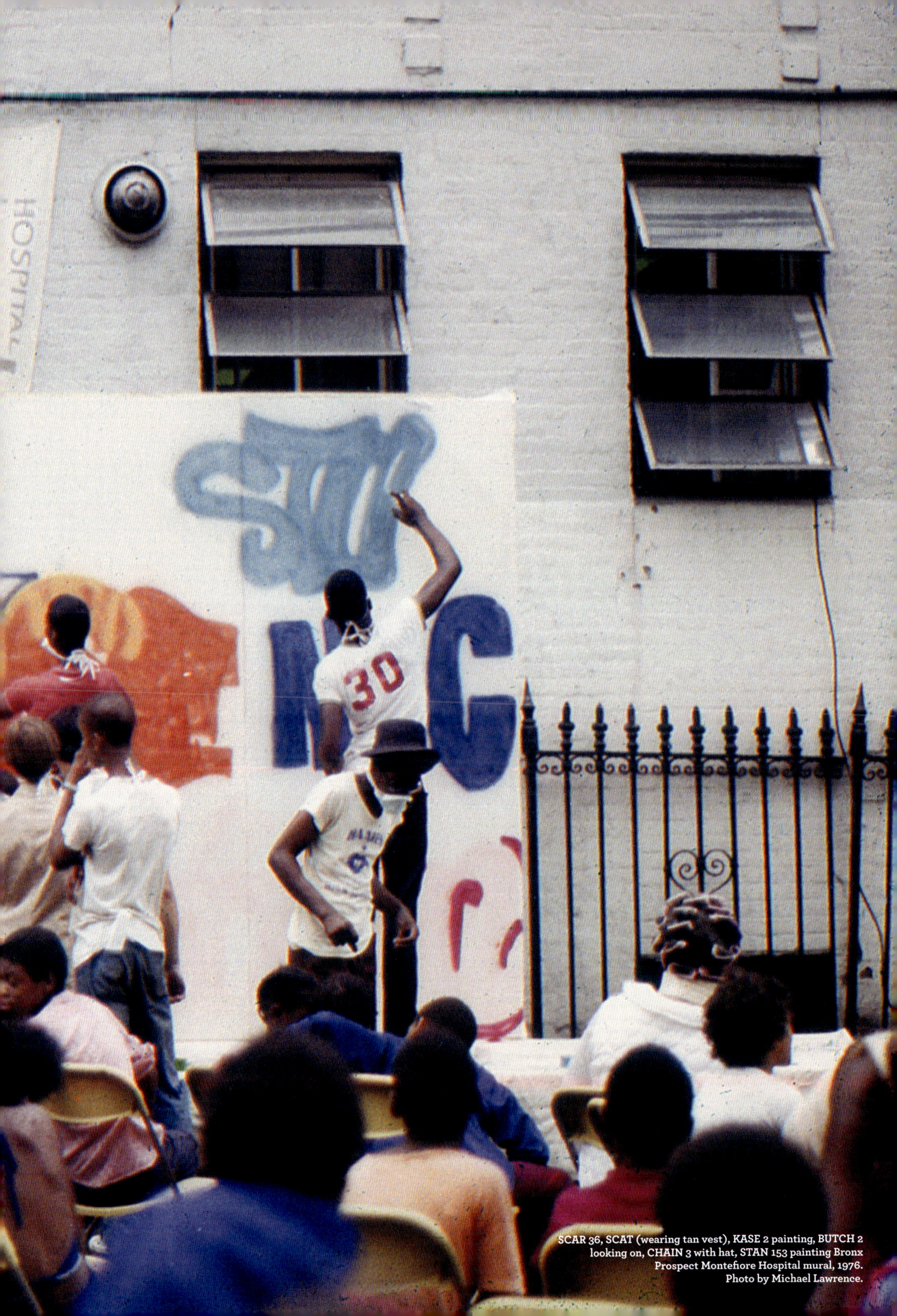

SCAR 36, SCAT (wearing tan vest), KASE 2 painting, BUTCH 2 looking on, CHAIN 3 with hat, STAN 153 painting Bronx Prospect Montefiore Hospital mural, 1976. Photo by Michael Lawrence.

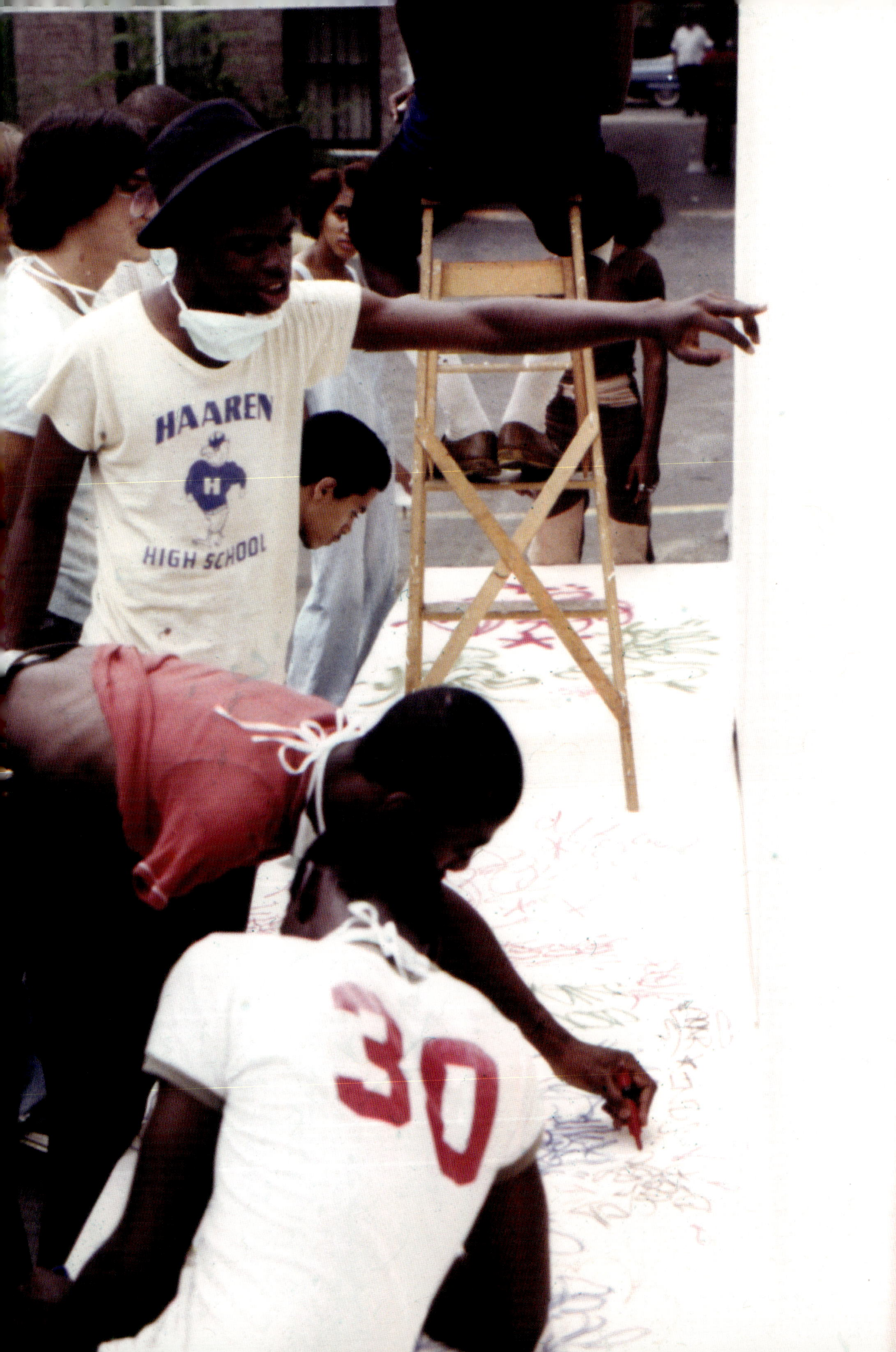
HAAREN
H
HIGH SCHOOL
30

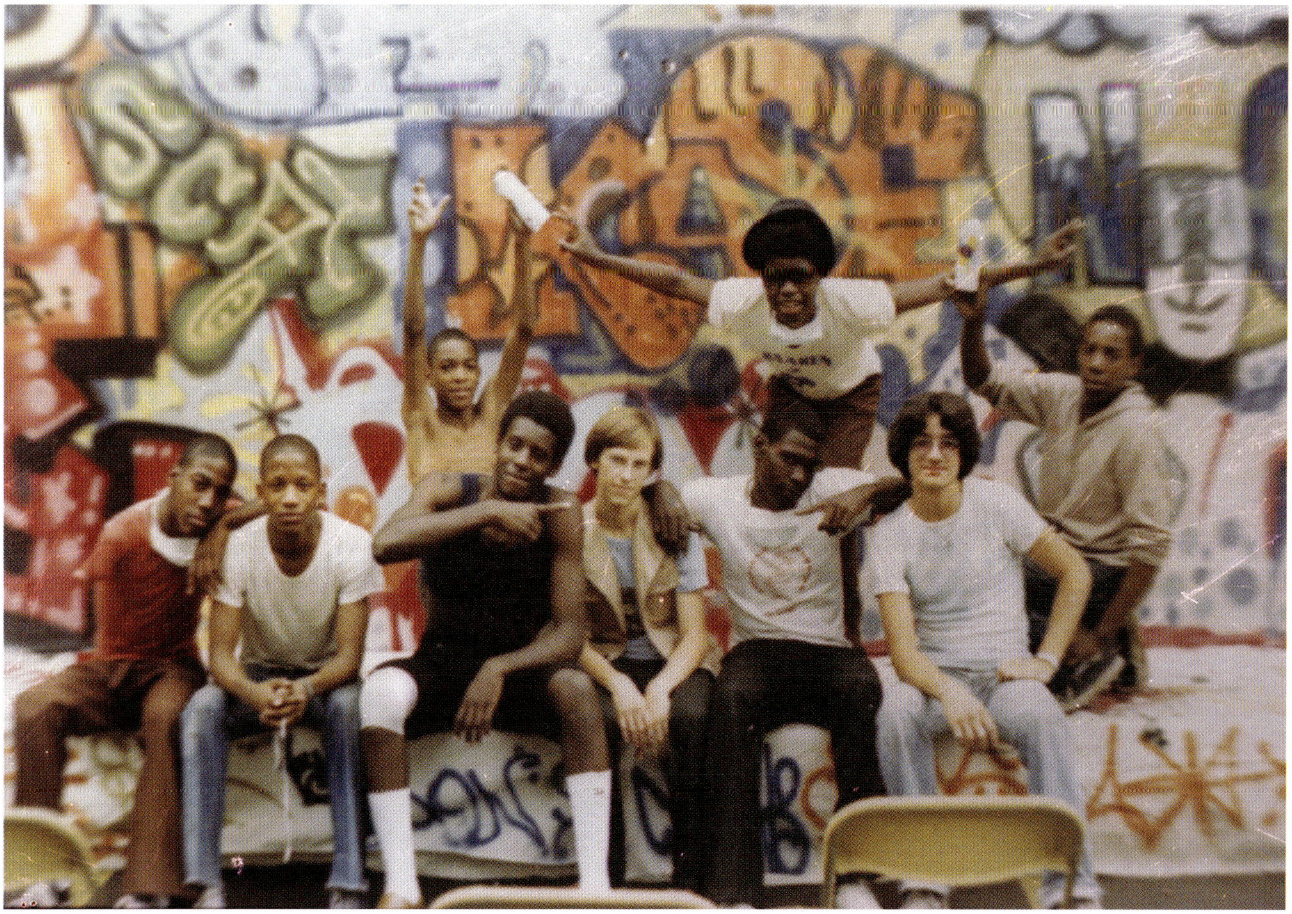

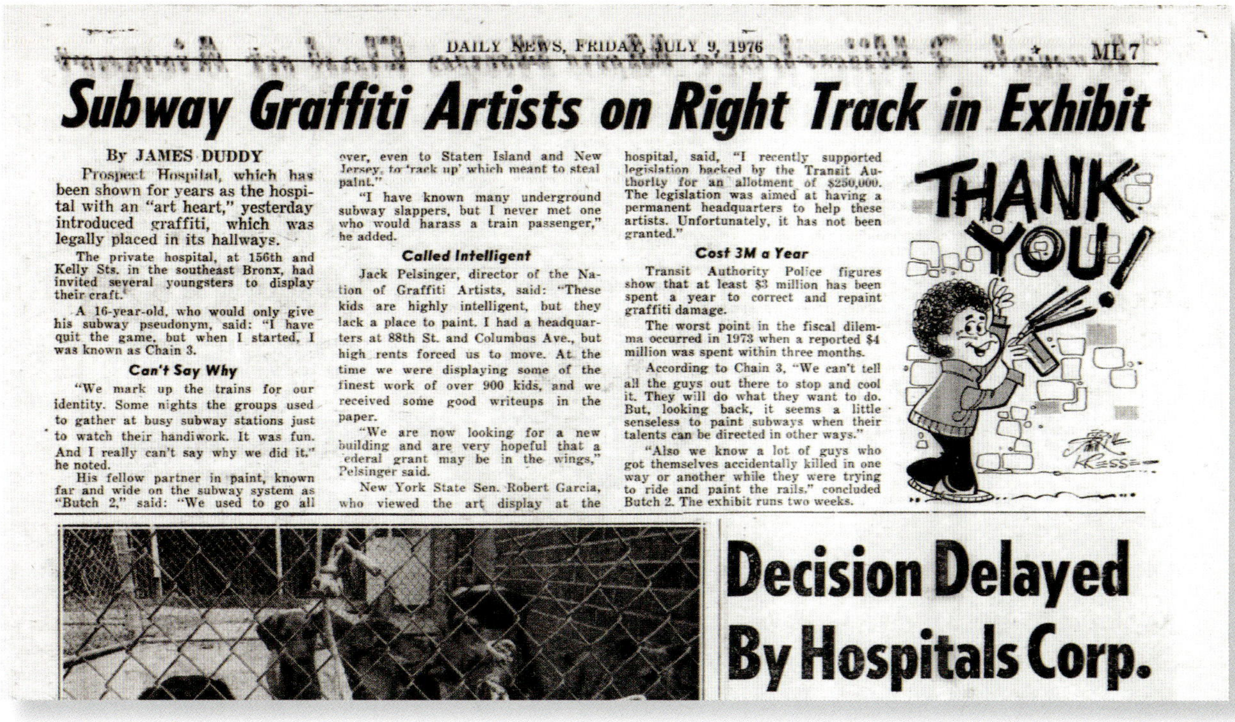

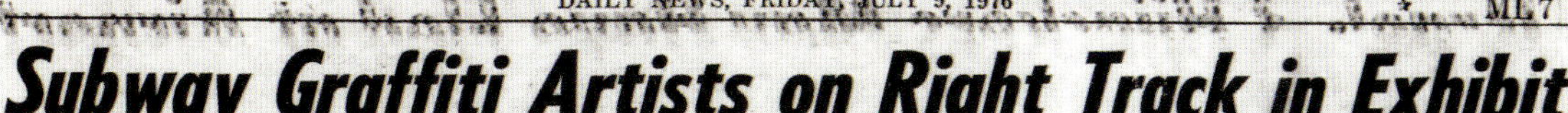

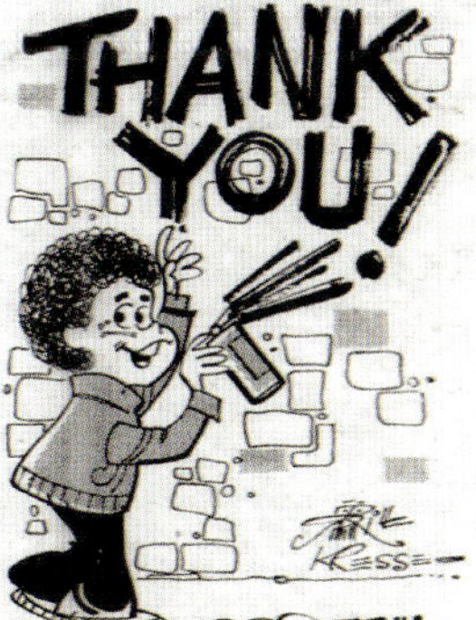

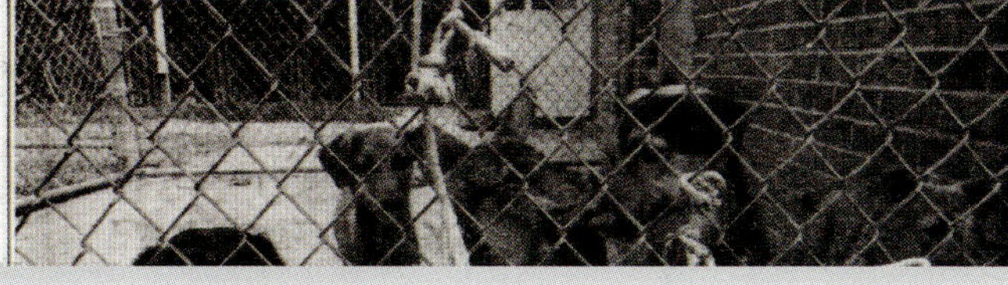

Subway Graffiti Artists on Right Track in Exhibit

By JAMES DUDDY

Prospect Hospital, which has been shown for years as the hospital with an "art heart," yesterday introduced graffiti, which was legally placed in its hallways.

The private hospital, at 156th and Kelly Sts. in the southeast Bronx, had invited several youngsters to display their craft.

A 16-year-old, who would only give his subway pseudonym, said: "I have quit the game, but when I started, I was known as Chain 3."

Can't Say Why

"We mark up the trains for our identity. Some nights the groups used to gather at busy subway stations just to watch their handiwork. It was fun. And I really can't say why we did it," he noted.

His fellow partner in paint, known far and wide on the subway system as "Butch 2," said: "We used to go all over, even to Staten Island and New Jersey, to 'track up' which meant to steal paint."

"I have known many underground subway slappers, but I never met one who would harass a train passenger," he added.

Called Intelligent

Jack Pelsinger, director of the Nation of Graffiti Artists, said: "These kids are highly intelligent, but they lack a place to paint. I had a headquarters at 88th St. and Columbus Ave., but high rents forced us to move. At the time we were displaying some of the finest work of over 900 kids, and we received some good writeups in the paper.

"We are now looking for a new building and are very hopeful that a federal grant may be in the wings," Pelsinger said.

New York State Sen. Robert Garcia, who viewed the art display at the hospital, said, "I recently supported legislation backed by the Transit Authority for an allotment of $250,000. The legislation was aimed at having a permanent headquarters to help these artists. Unfortunately, it has not been granted."

Cost 3M a Year

Transit Authority Police figures show that at least $3 million has been spent a year to correct and repaint graffiti damage.

The worst point in the fiscal dilemma occurred in 1973 when a reported $4 million was spent within three months.

According to Chain 3, "We can't tell all the guys out there to stop and cool it. They will do what they want to do. But, looking back, it seems a little senseless to paint subways when their talents can be directed in other ways."

"Also we know a lot of guys who got themselves accidentally killed in one way or another while they were trying to ride and paint the rails," concluded Butch 2. The exhibit runs two weeks.

Decision Delayed By Hospitals Corp.

Opposite page:
DON 1 in profile, CHAIN 3 pointing, KASE 2 tagging, STAN 153, SCAR
36 on ladder. Bronx Prospect Montefiore Hospital mural, 1976.

This page:
Top: From left to right, sitting: KASE 2, BUTCH 2, SCAR 36, SCAT,
STAN 153, DON 1. Standing: NOC 167, CHAIN 3, SEK 170, 1976.
Photo by Yolanda Rodriguez.
Bottom: *Daily News* article on the NOGA mural at Montefiore
Hospital, 1976.

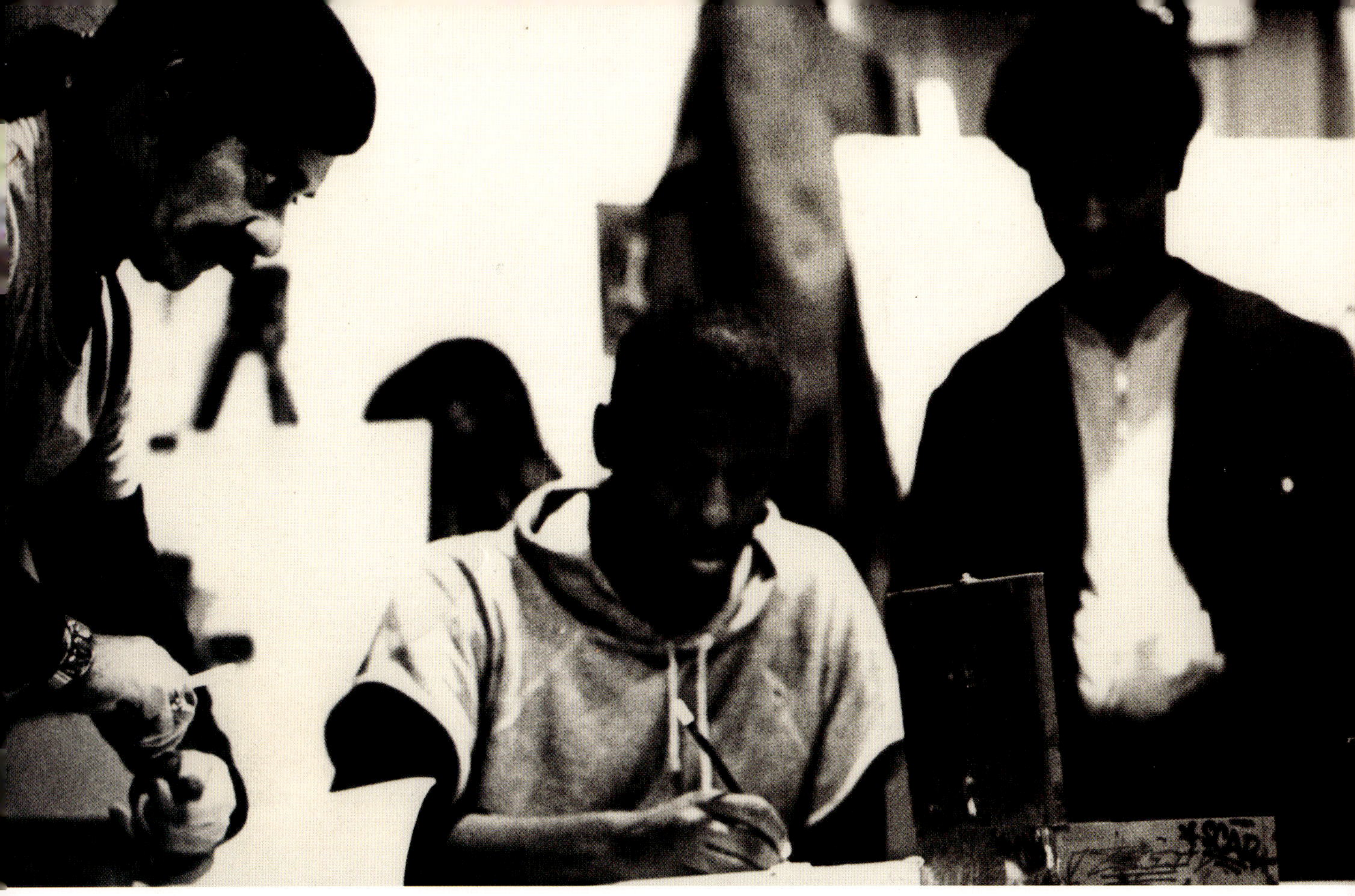

EXODUS FROM THE UPPER WEST SIDE

In 1976, as the bicentennial swept the nation, Pelsinger had to close the doors on the Columbus Avenue workshop after the city bumped up the rent on the location. BLOOD TEA took home the conga drums, and the canvases and art supplies wound up at Pelsinger's home. During the fall of 1976 a number of writers continued to work on projects in the small apartment. MTA blueprints had been found and reprinted on glossy paper. From there, SCORPIO, BLOOD TEA and CLIFF 159 sketched designs on the train cars for an upcoming proposal to the city. Pelsinger and the artists had a meeting with the MTA and asked for $1,500 to paint the designs on the trains. The MTA didn't take the bait, and the writers were left dejected.

In a July 1976 article in the *Daily News*, Pelsinger seemed to make a plea to the paper's readers: "These kids are highly intelligent, but they lack a place to paint. I had a headquarters at 88th Street and Columbus Avenue, but high rents forced us to move. At the time we were displaying some of the finest work of over 900 kids, and we received some good write-ups in the paper. We are now looking for a new building and are very hopeful that a federal grant may be in the wings."

The *Daily News* quote reflected Pelsinger's view of the situation for public consumption, but privately he felt there were more sinister forces at work. One of his drama students, a young poet named Bushka, was from the Ukraine, which was still a communist country in the 1970s. Bushka's green card was running out, which prompted a sham marriage between the two in order to keep her in the country. When the rent suddenly went up on the workshop, a number of backers, including AT&T and Western Electric, stopped taking Pelsinger's calls. He believed he was being blacklisted. Pelsinger filed a Freedom of Information request with the FBI and received a 30-page folder of redacted material on his life. Over the years, the former dancer, singer, activist and teacher had met many people of interest to the FBI, but he concluded that the reason they shut him down was that he was married to a woman from a communist country. As NOGA continued, its leader never once wavered in his belief.

As the year came to a close, NOGA was given access to a space in the West Village. The space was temporary and how Pelsinger got the space is a mystery. The look of the studio was much cleaner than the Columbus Avenue location — white walls with framed paintings on them, easels, and the desktops featured no graffiti anywhere. The paintings and the artists standing before them all seemed much more mature. There was at least one airbrush in use at the new location, a sophisticated tool that probably would've been stolen in the old location. The space was only available for a short while before NOGA was out on the street again.

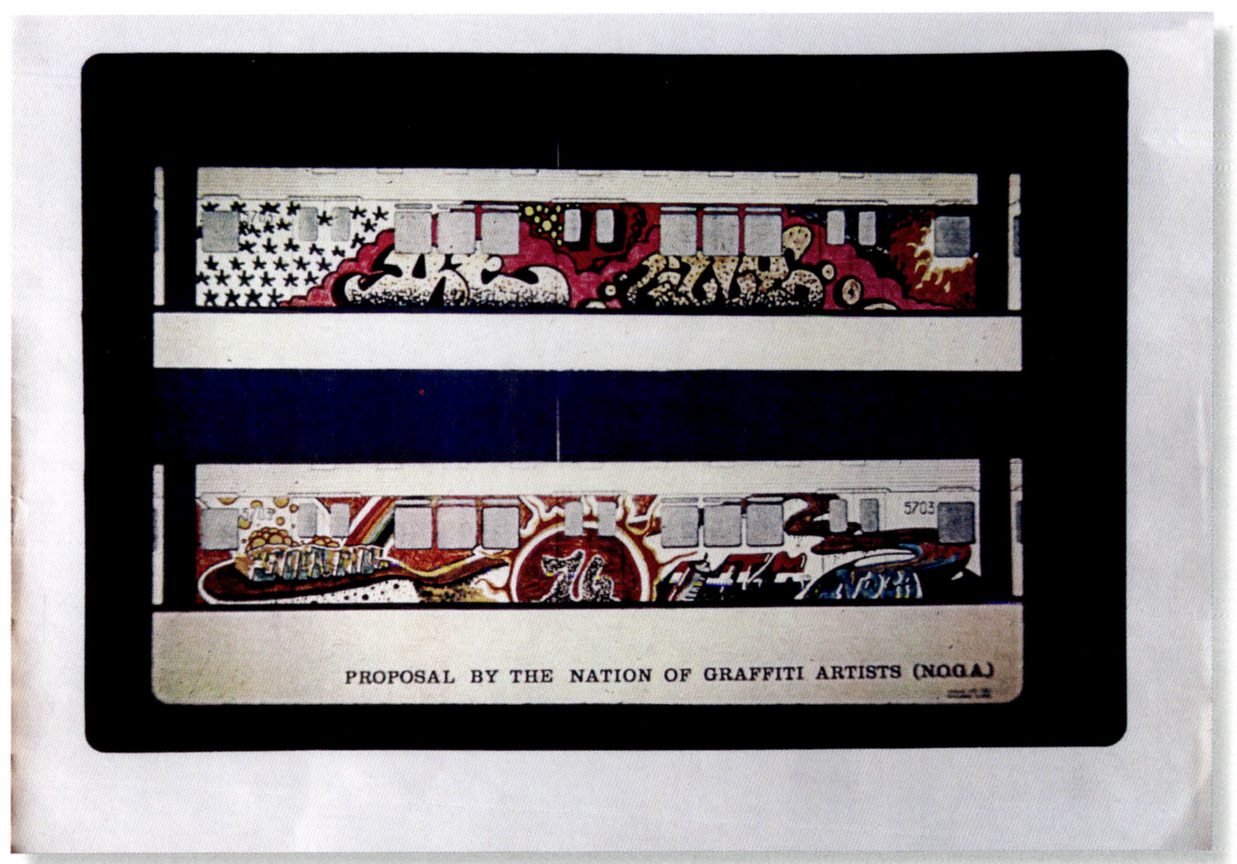

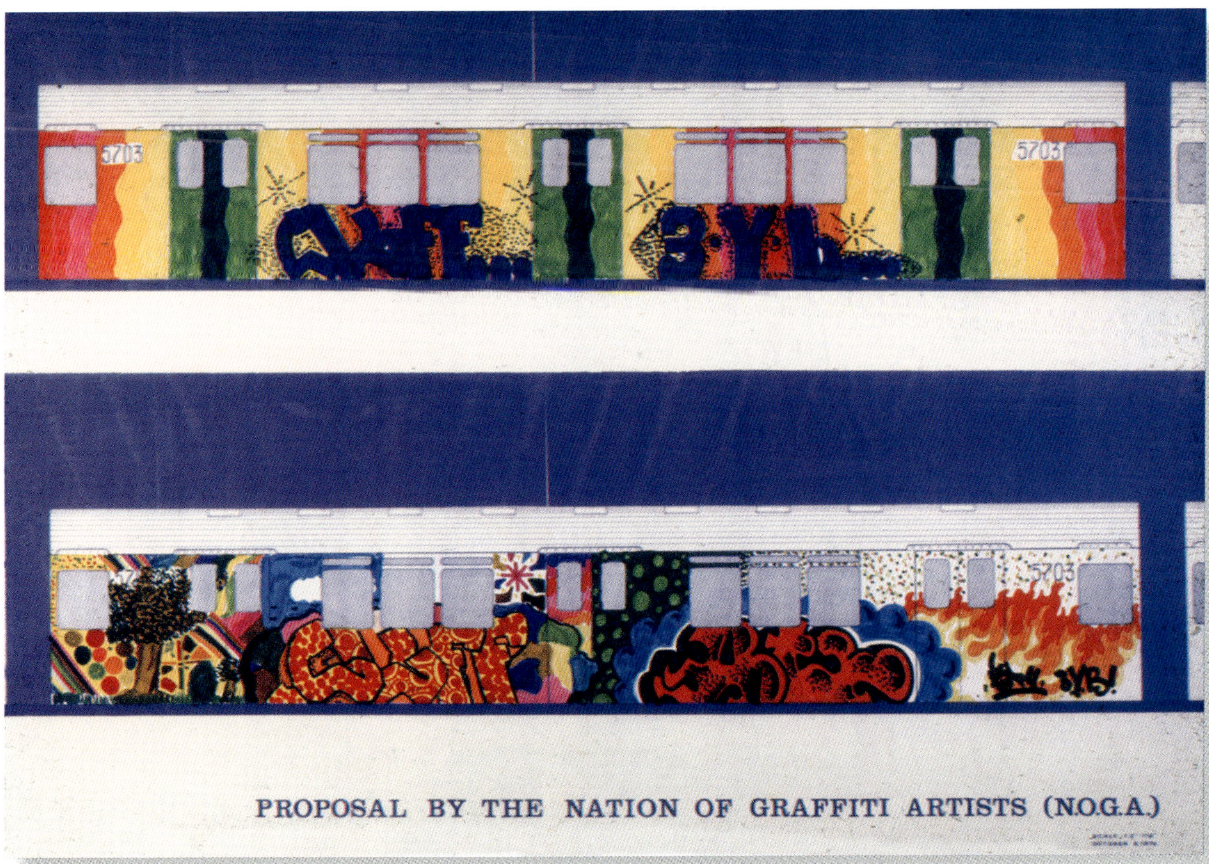

Opposite page:
Jack Pelsinger looks on as SCAR 36 works on a drawing, 1976.
Photo by Michael Lawrence.

This page:
NOGA proposals for MTA featuring drawings by CLIFF 159,
BLOOD TEA and SCORPIO, 1975, 1976.

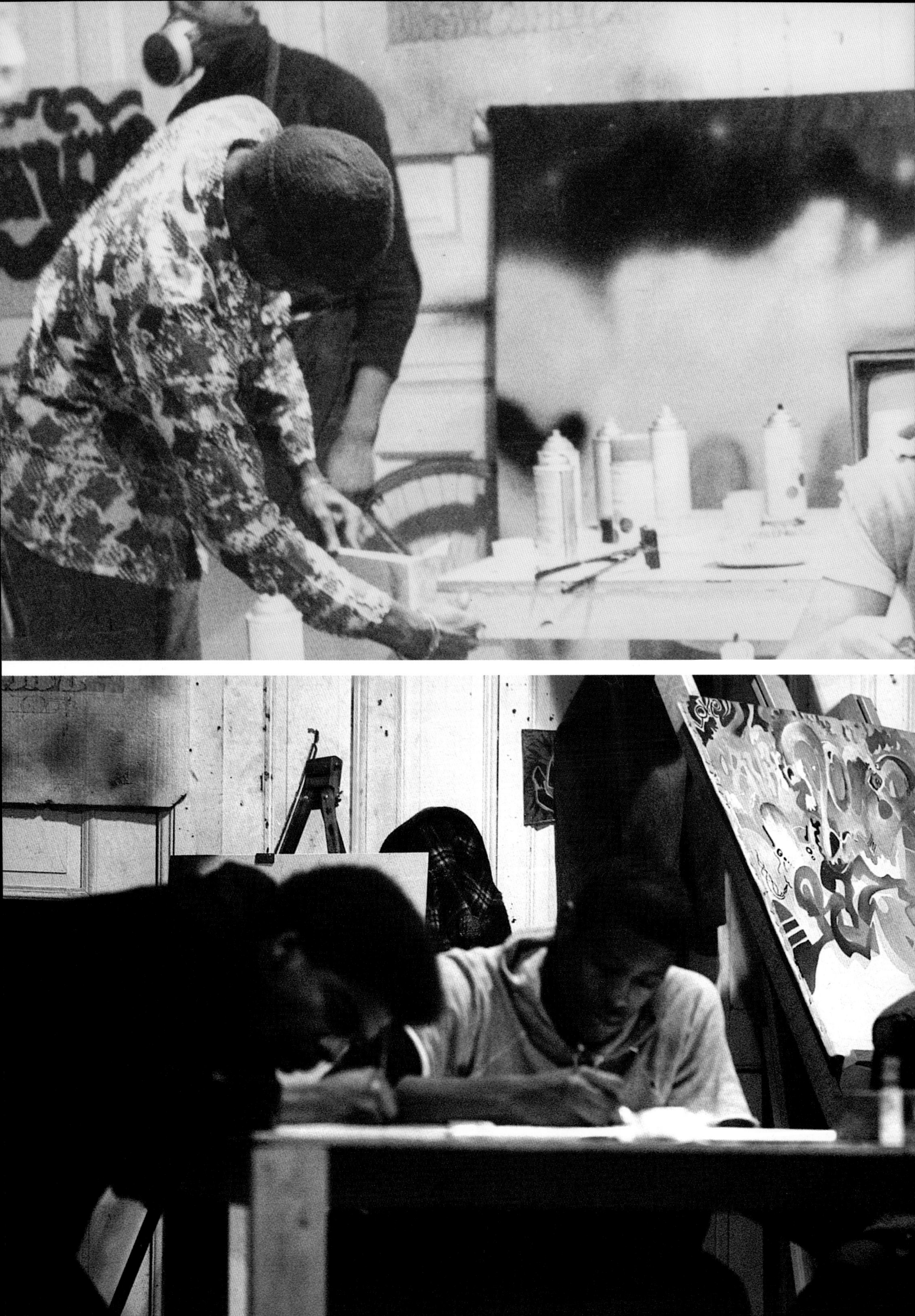

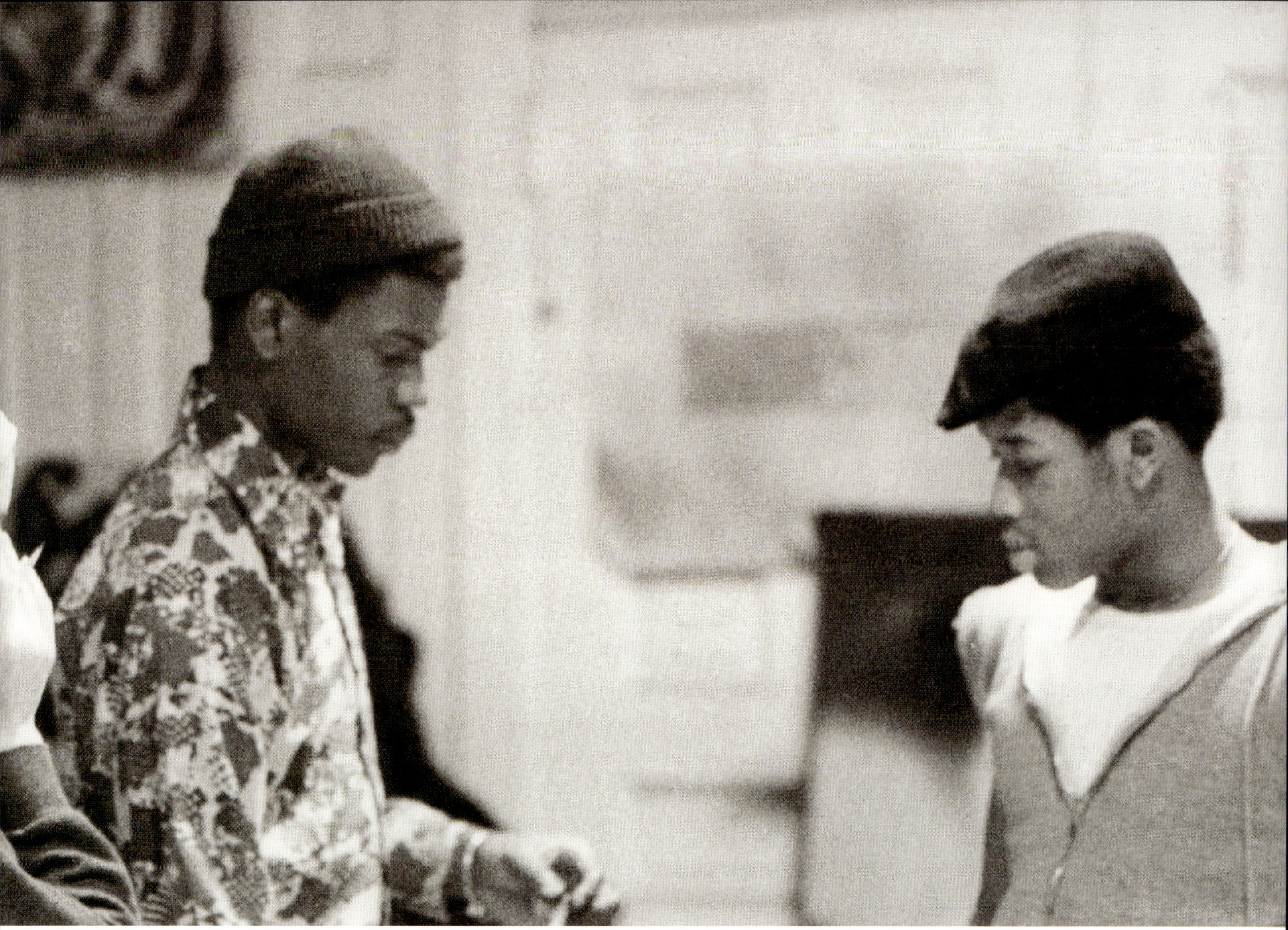

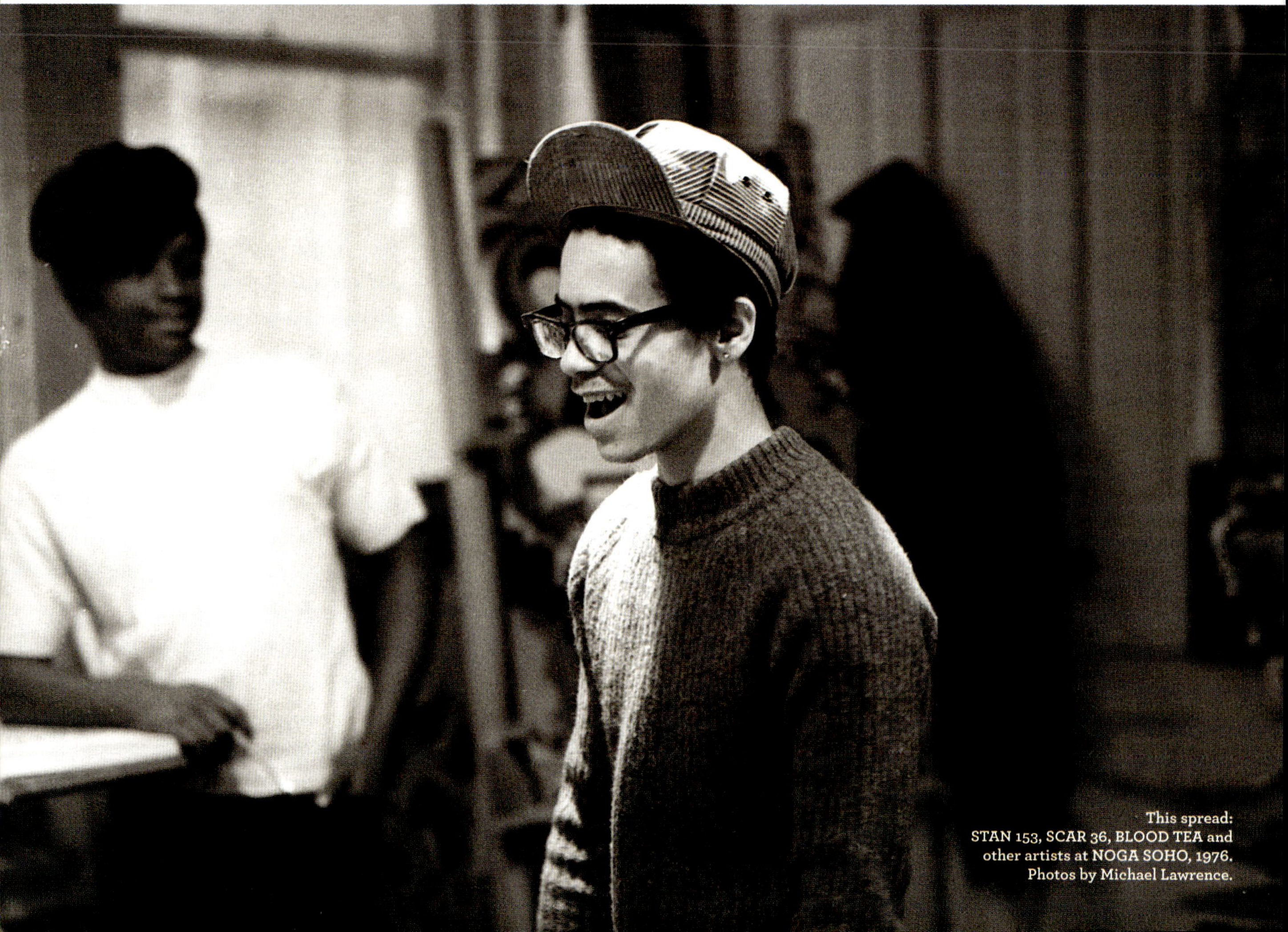

This spread:
STAN 153, SCAR 36, BLOOD TEA and
other artists at NOGA SOHO, 1976.
Photos by Michael Lawrence.

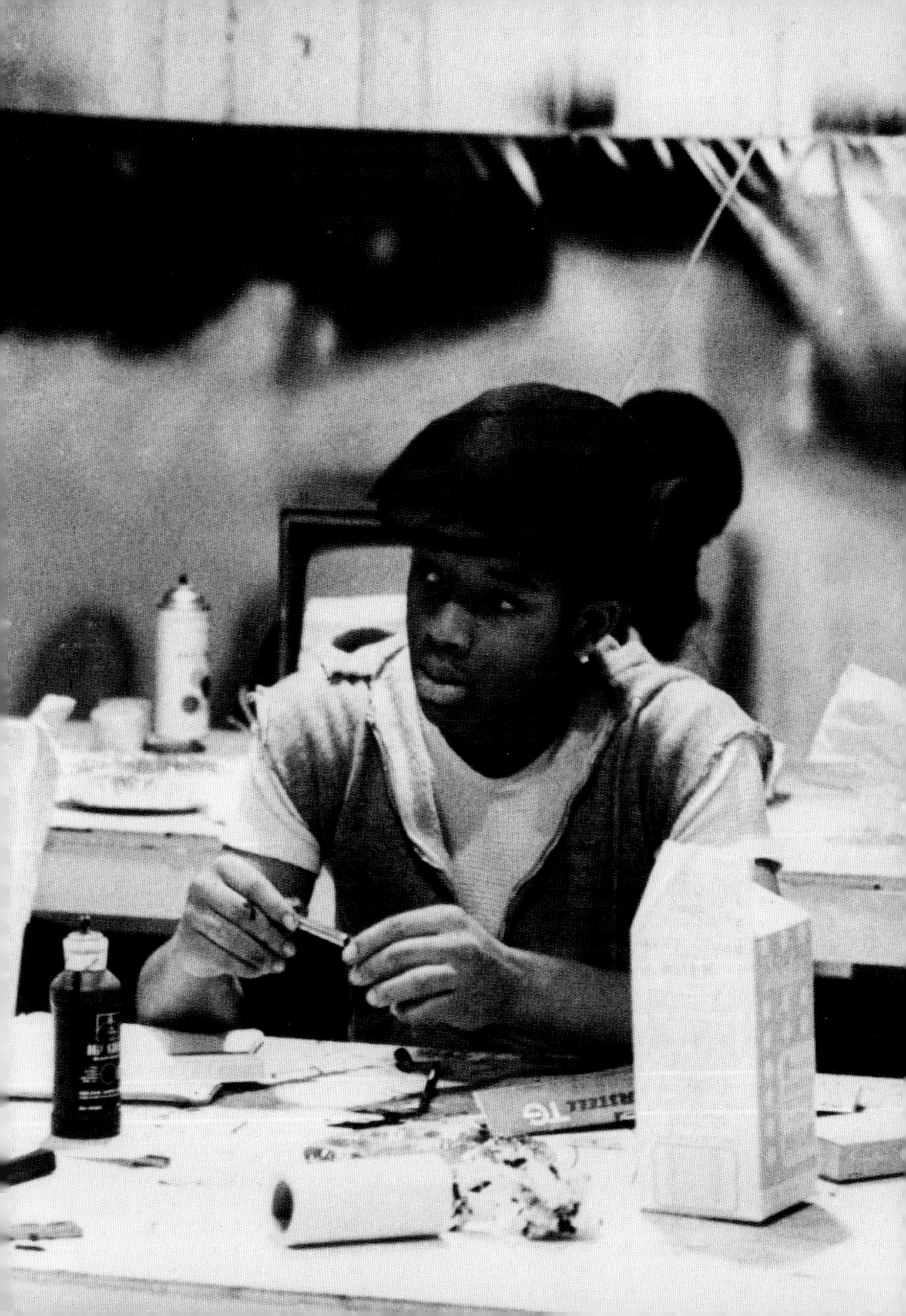

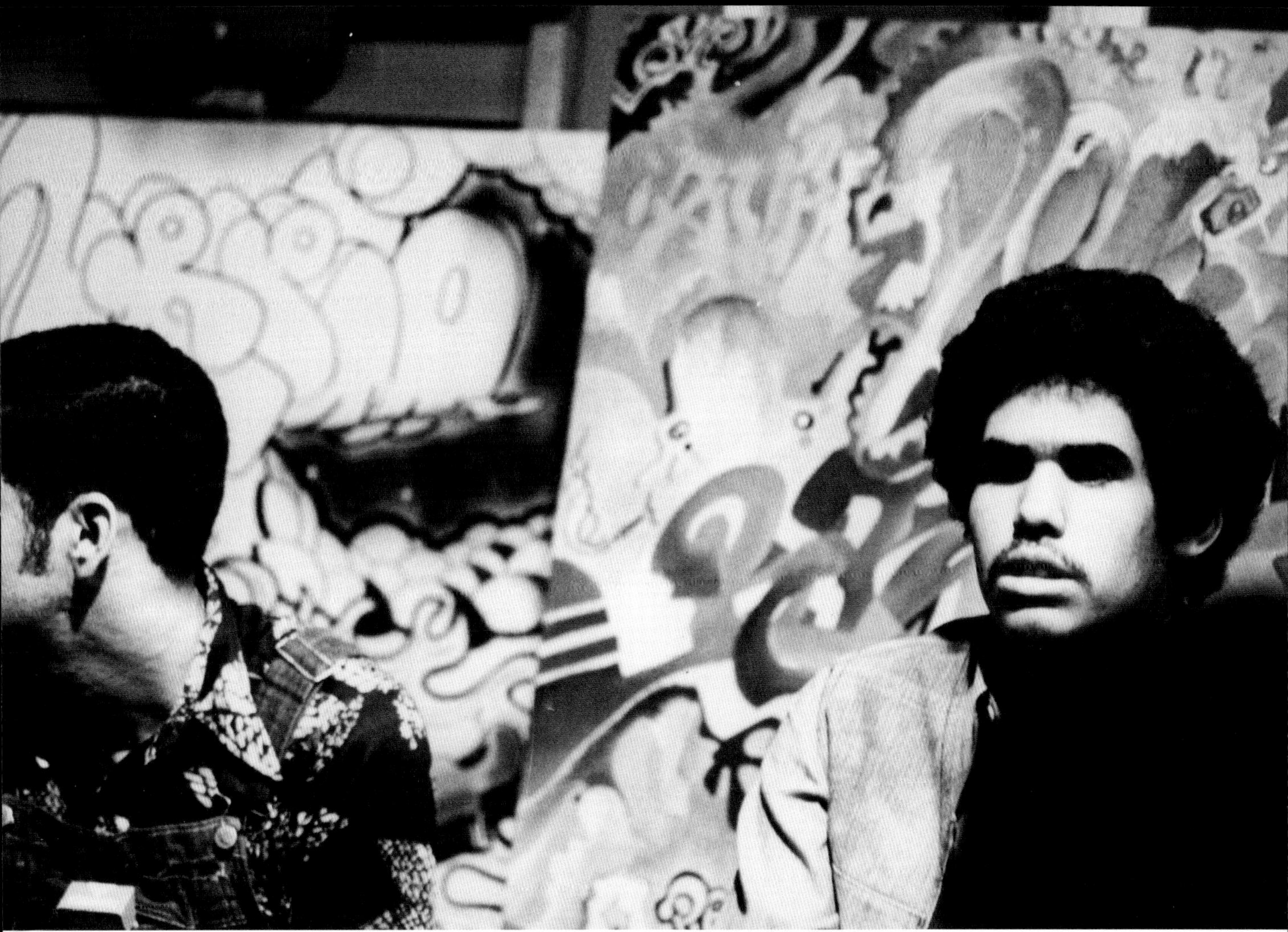

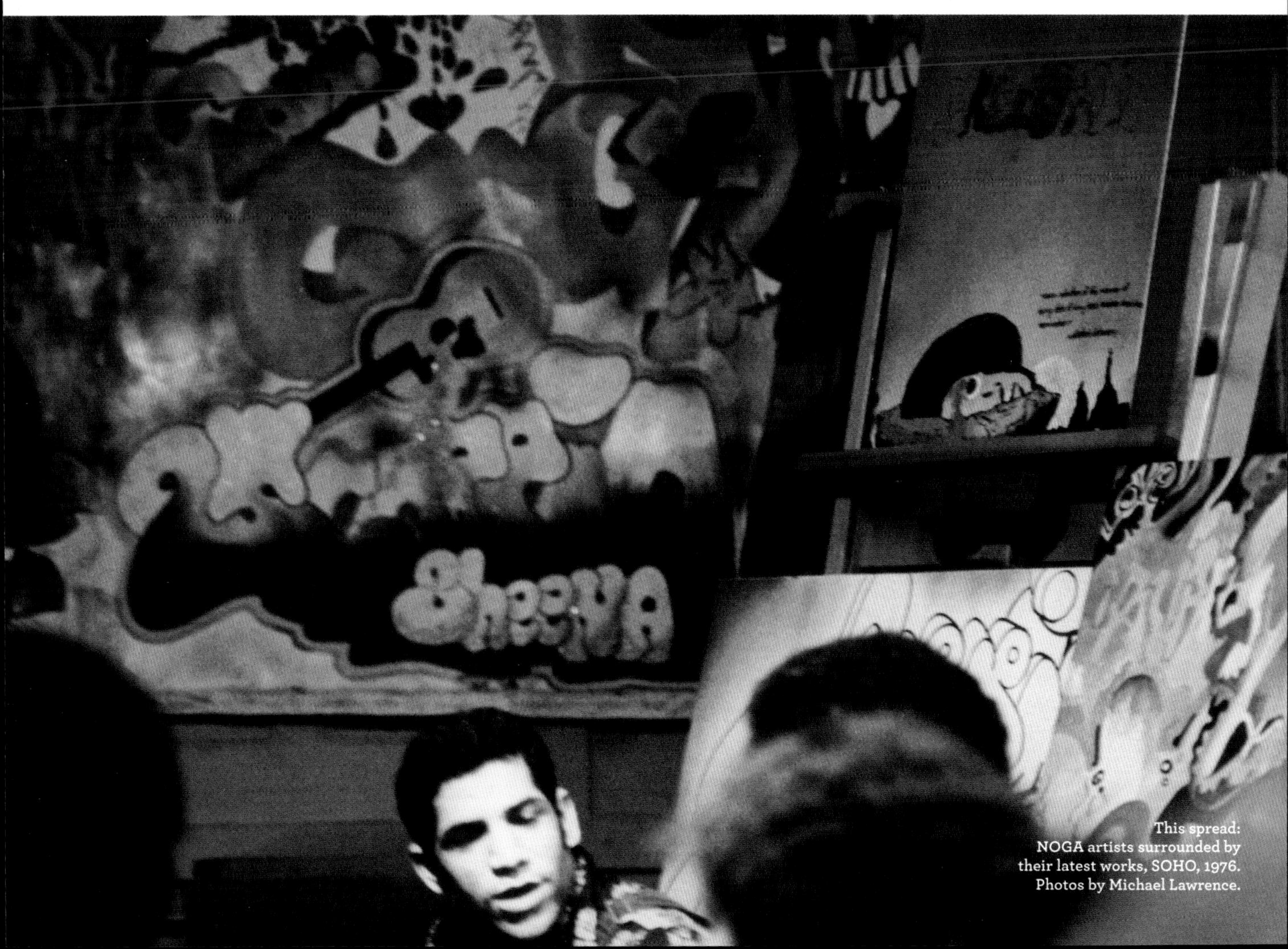

This spread:
NOGA artists surrounded by
their latest works, SOHO, 1976.
Photos by Michael Lawrence.

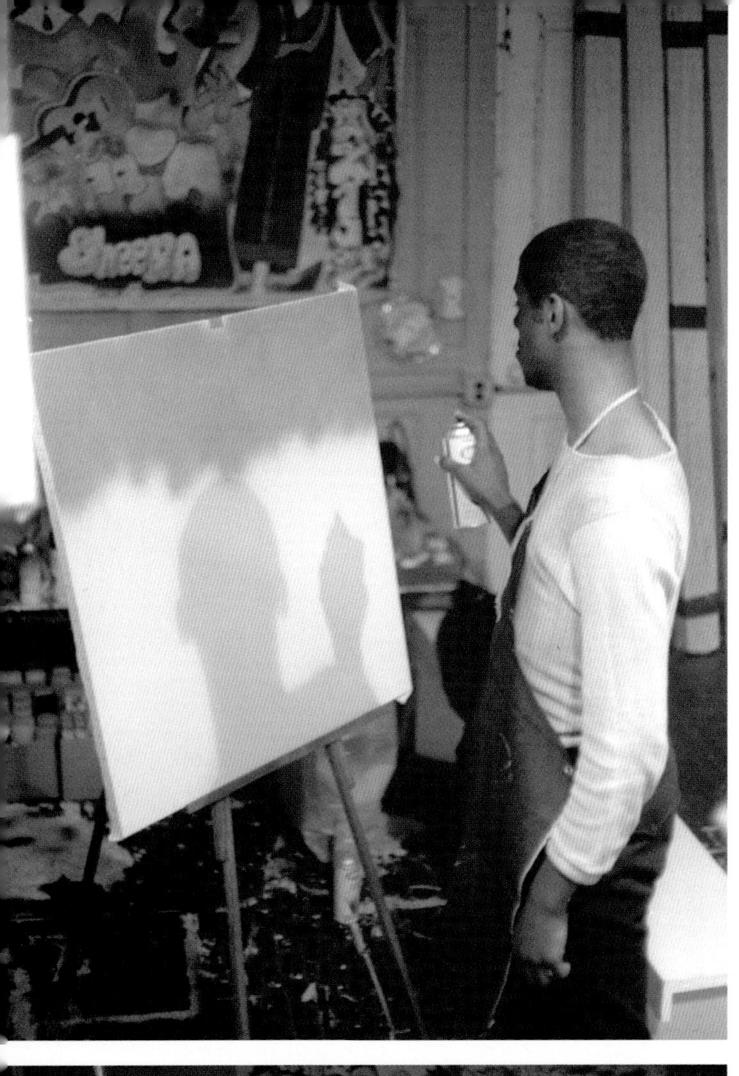
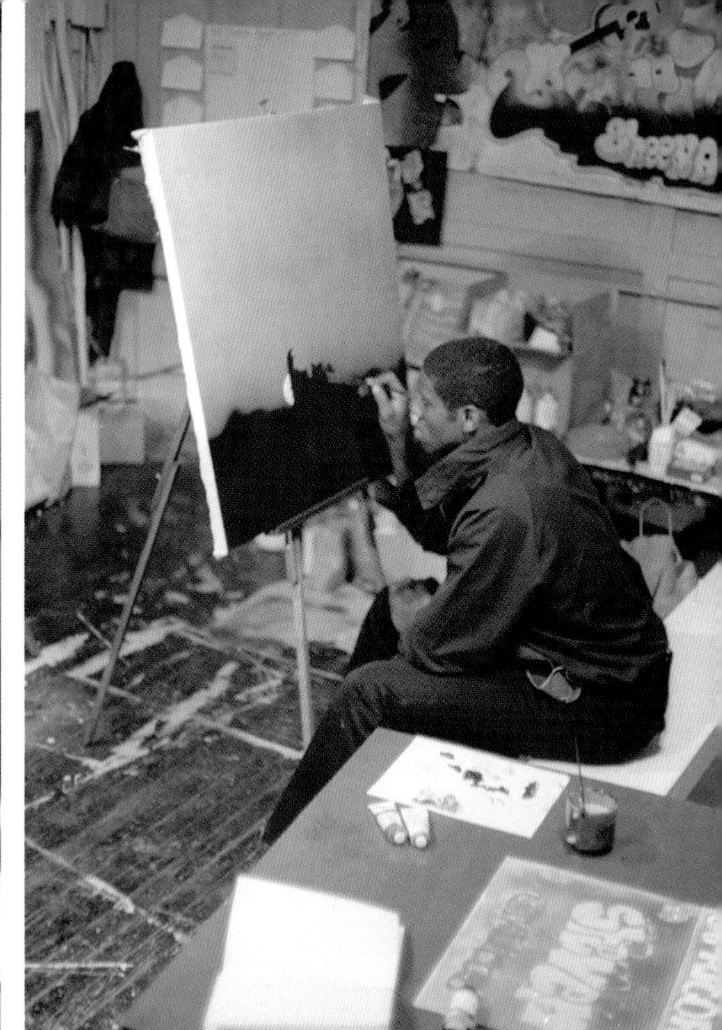
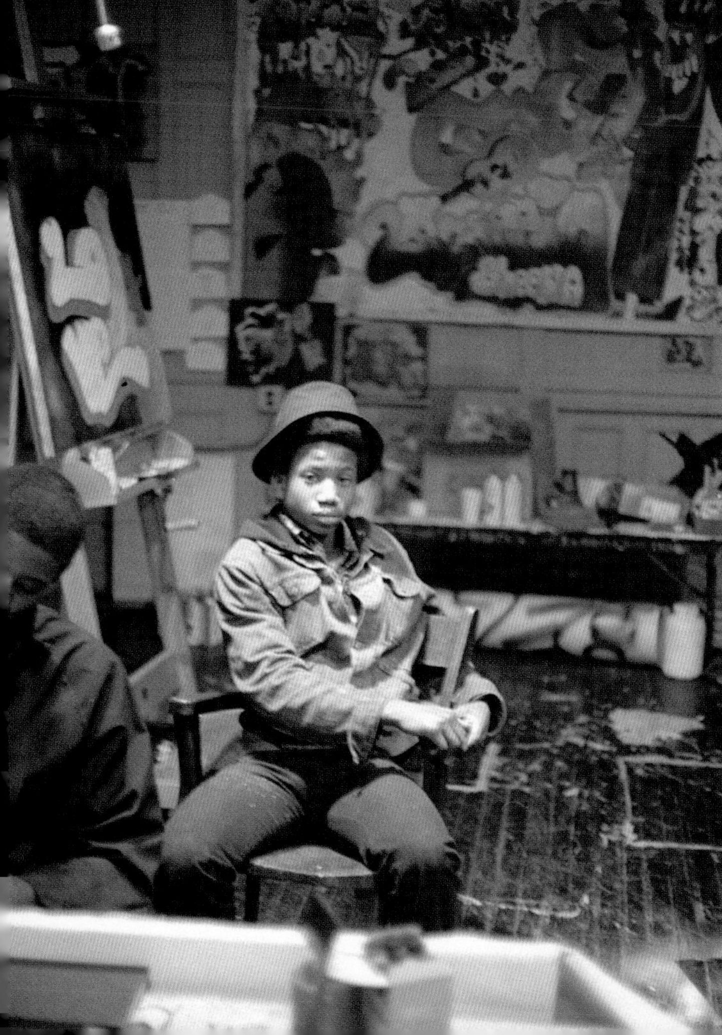
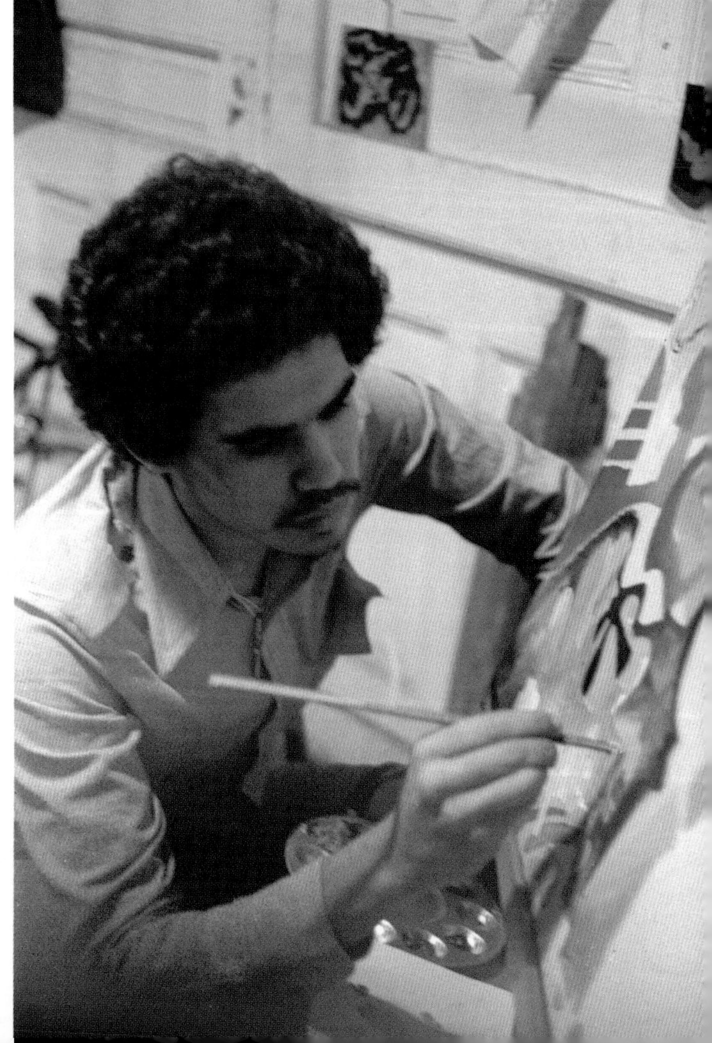

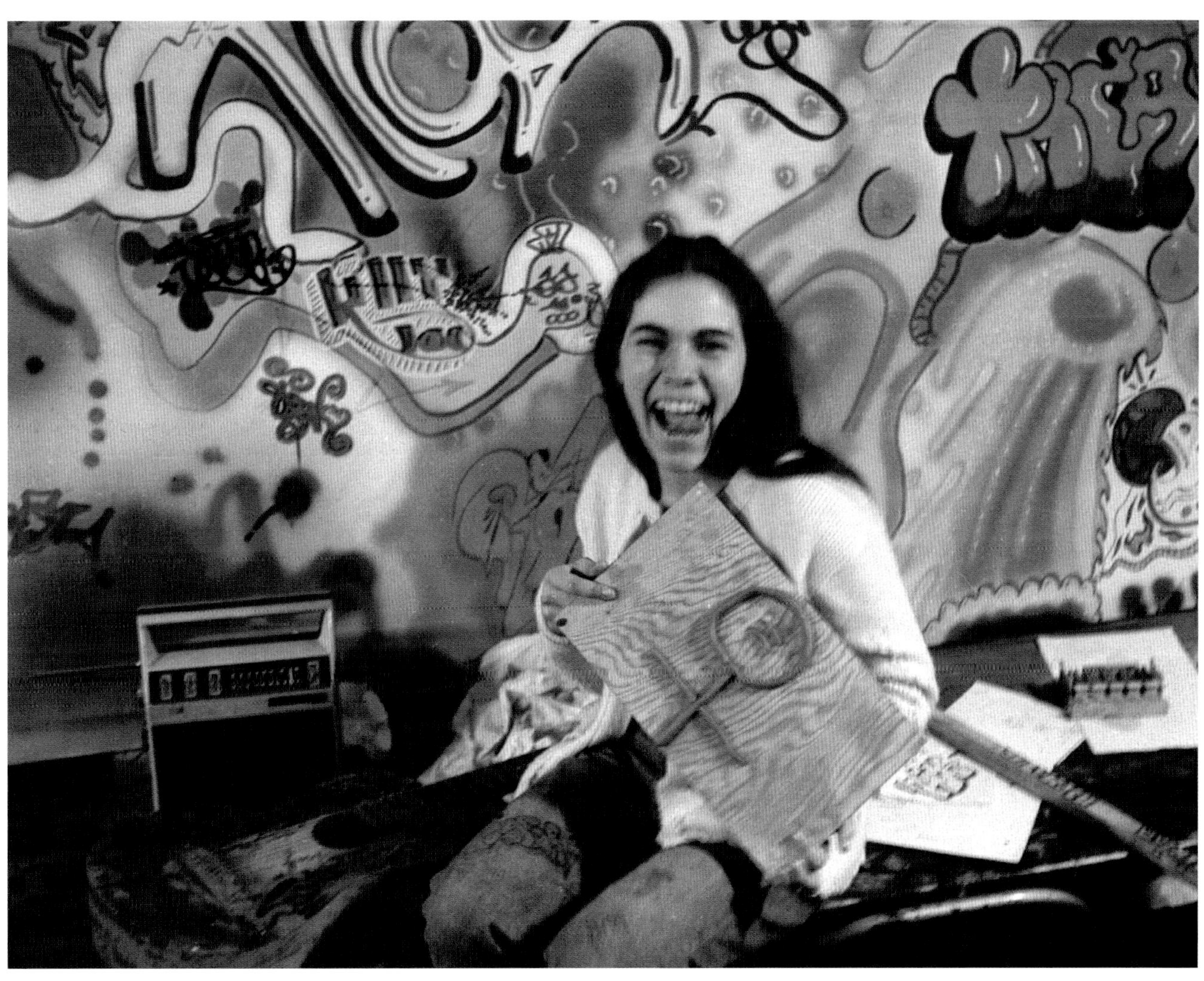

Opposite page:
SCAR 36 and SAL 161 add finishing touches to their
paintings at the NOGA studio, 1976.

This page:
LILLY 101 shows off her art at the studio, 1976.
Photos by Moses Ros/SAL 161.

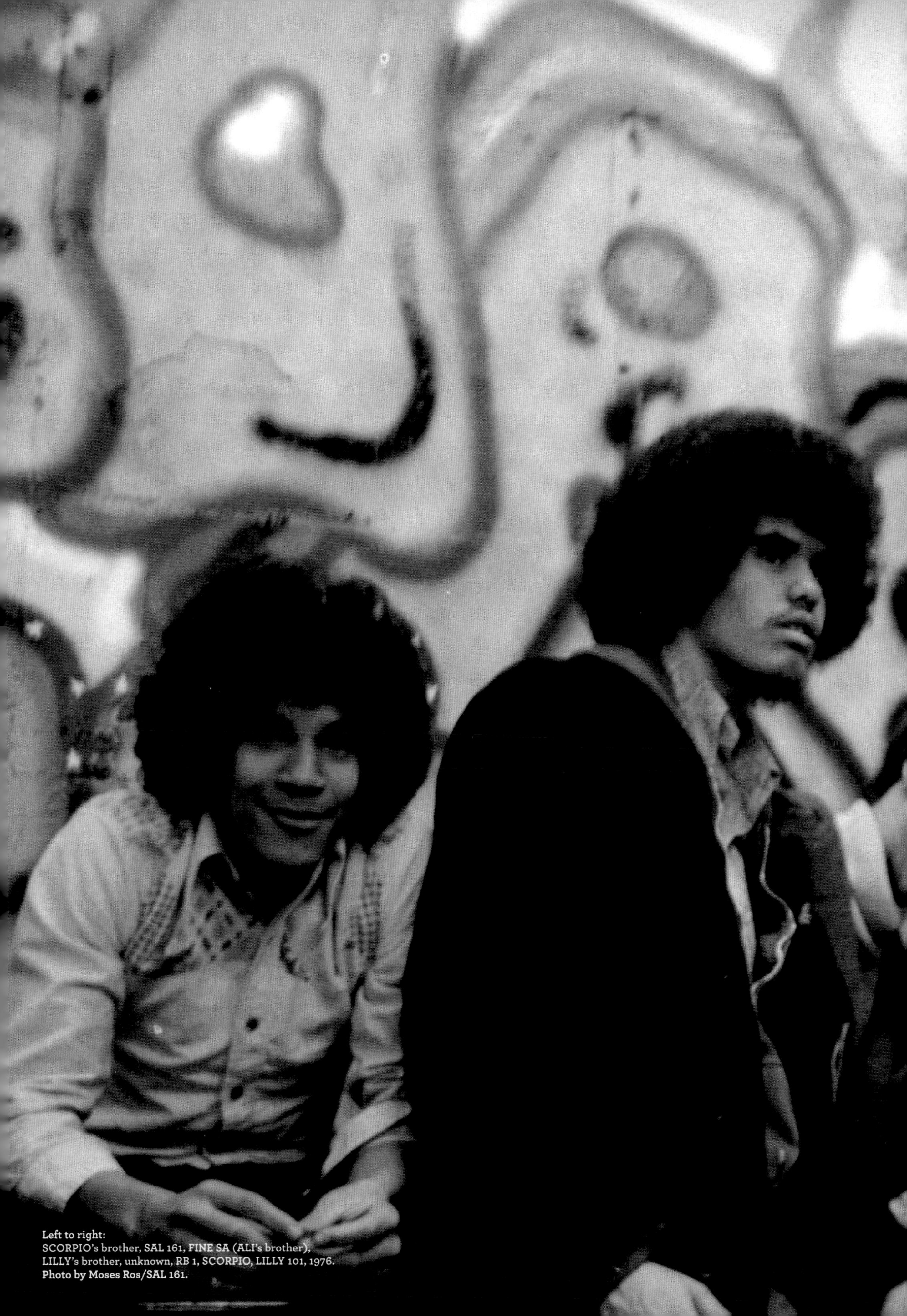

Left to right:
SCORPIO's brother, SAL 161, FINE SA (ALI's brother),
LILLY's brother, unknown, RB 1, SCORPIO, LILLY 101, 1976.
Photo by Moses Ros/SAL 161.

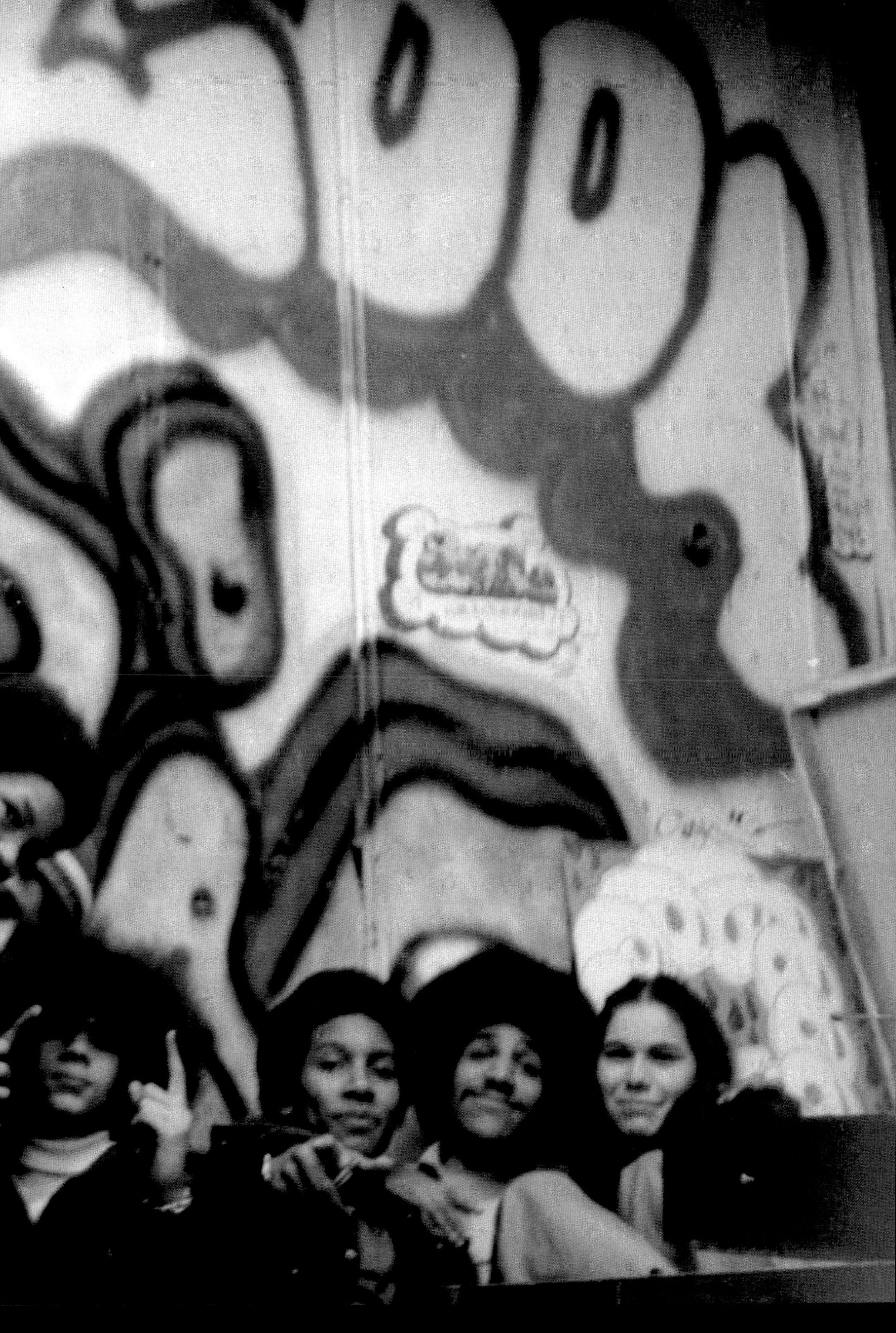

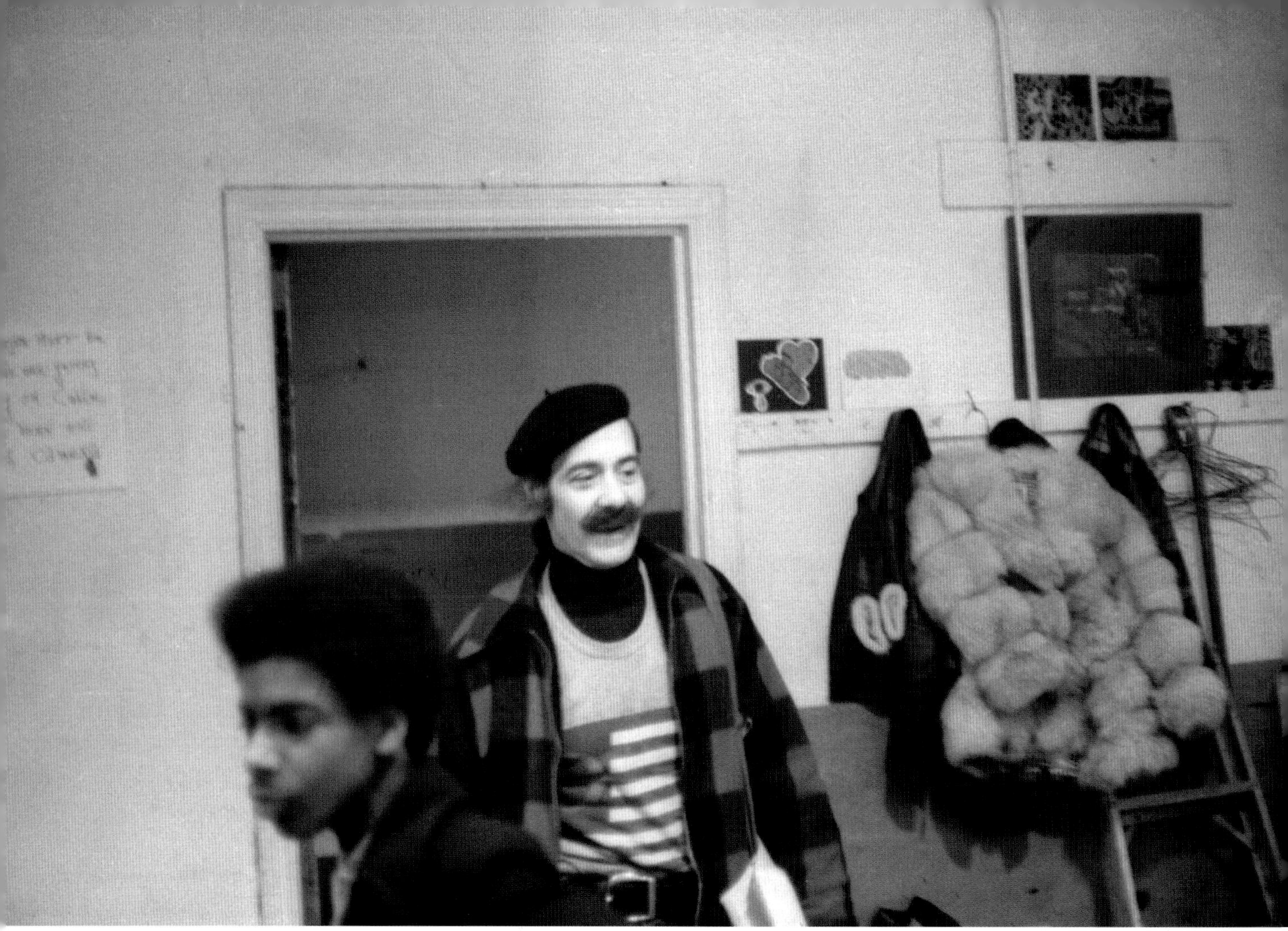

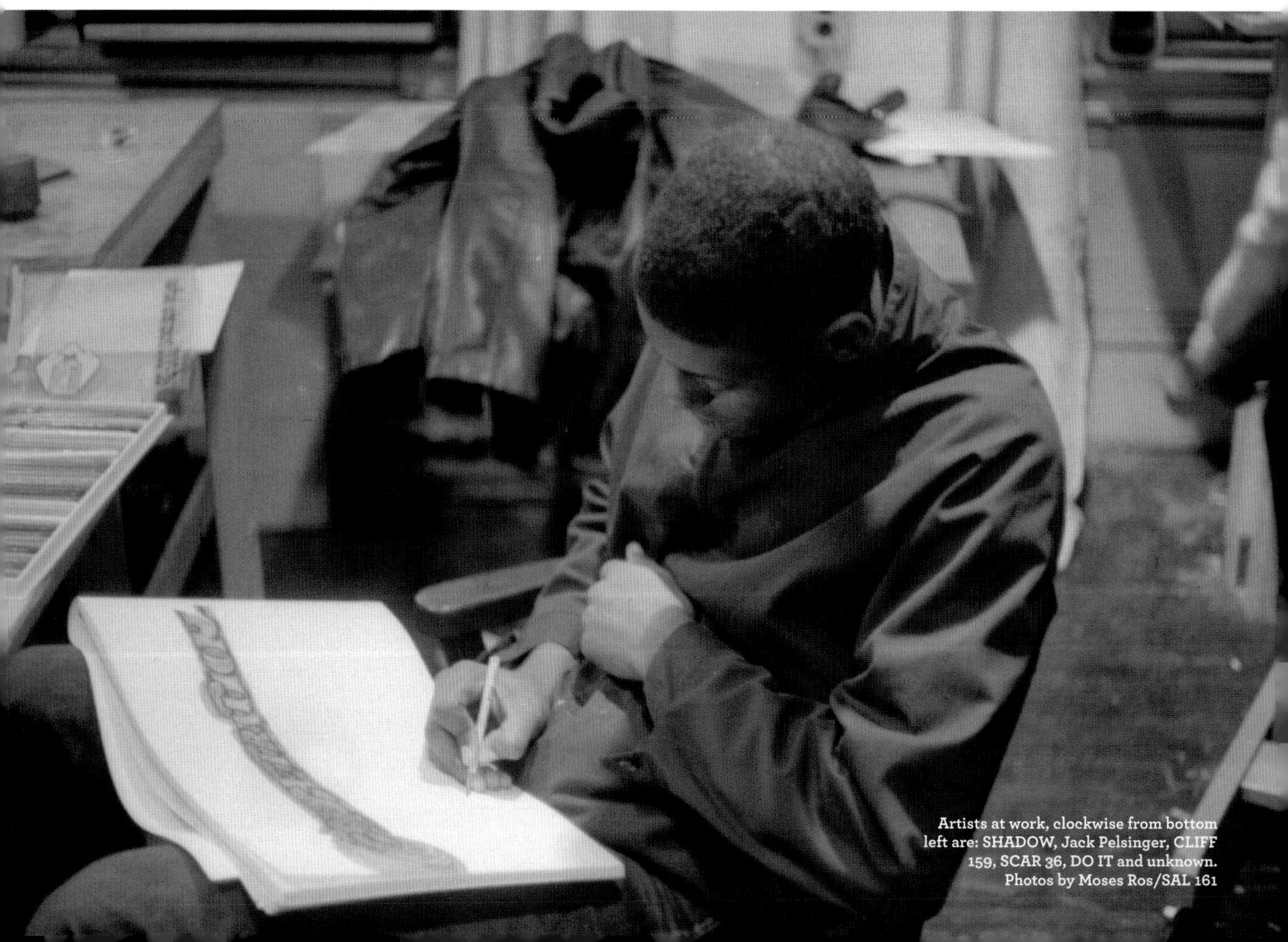

Artists at work, clockwise from bottom left are: SHADOW, Jack Pelsinger, CLIFF 159, SCAR 36, DO IT and unknown.
Photos by Moses Ros/SAL 161

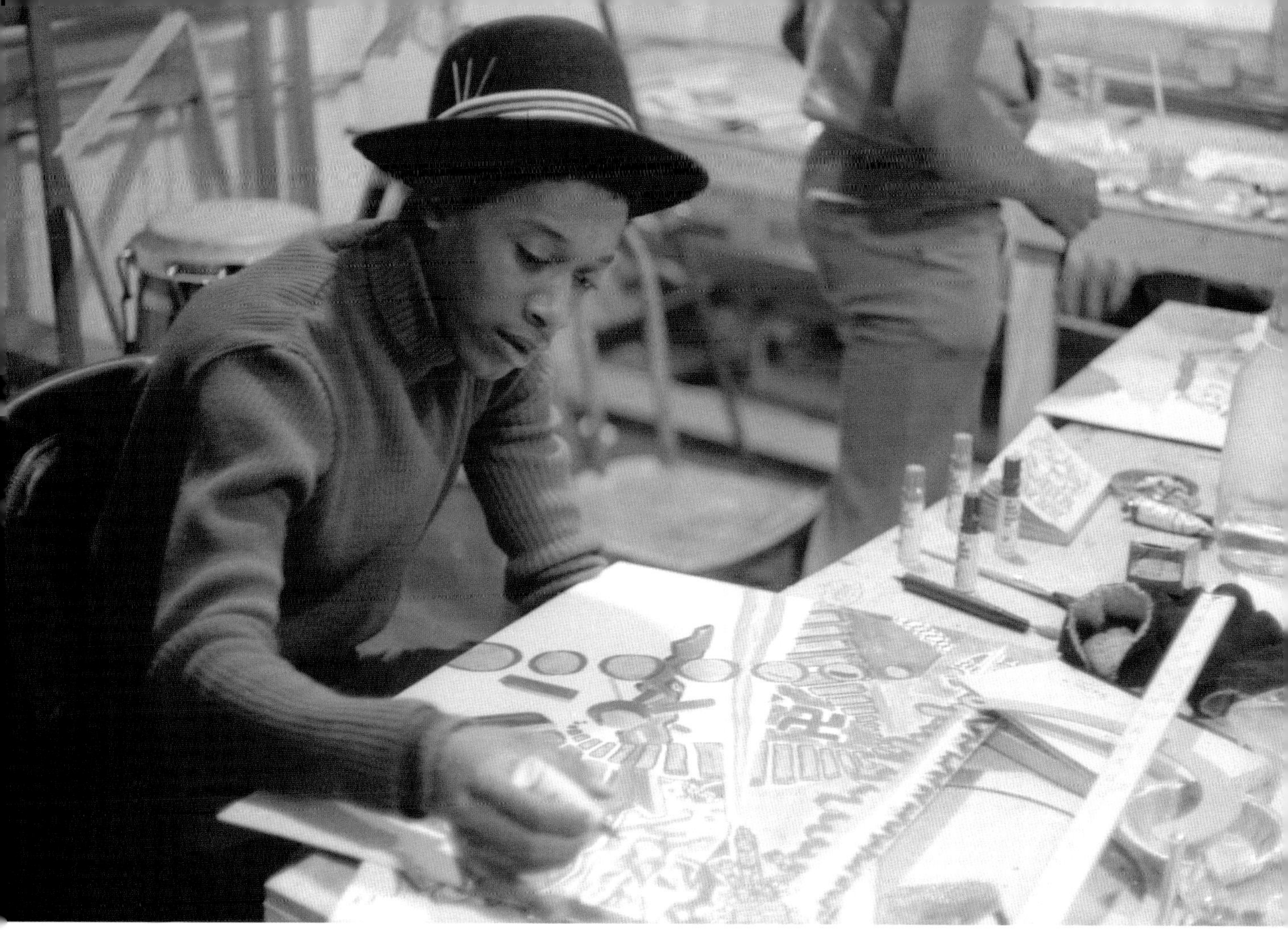

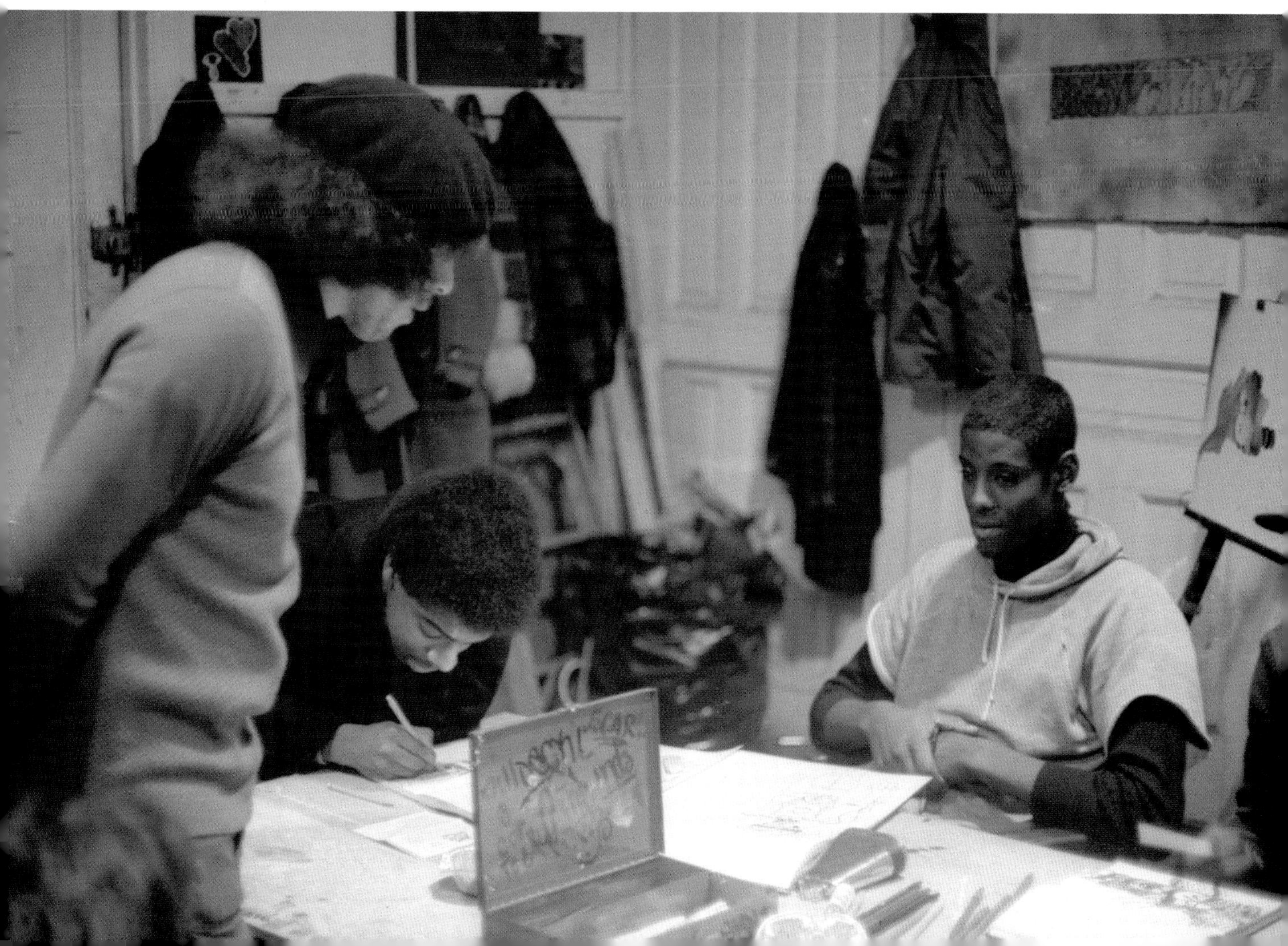

991-5763 — Day Care Center
323-1815 — Senior Citizen Center

ALIANZA CIVICA TROPICAL
DAY CARE AND SENIOR CITIZEN CENTER, INC.
910 EAST 172nd STREET
BRONX, N. Y. 10460

PAUL A. MUSCILLO
Board Chairman

OFFICERS

HARRY KAEFITZ
1stt Vice Chairman

RABBI HAILU PARIS
Recording Secretary

ELOISE SEALY
Corresponding Secretary

REV. RAMON MAISONET
Treasurer

PAUL GONZALEZ
Assistant Treasurer

January 25, 1977

Mr. Jack Pelsinger
Director
Nation of Graffiti Artista (NOGA)
P.O. Box 119
New York, New York 10028

Dear Mr. Pelsinger:

This letter is in the nature of a response to your request of December 10, 1976, wherein you wish to temporarily locate your project in three rooms of our second floor.

Permission has been granted to you to do so for a renewable six month period. We welcome useful and needed projects like yours in our Community. We feel your project will have a decided effect on diverting the youths from aberrant behavior.

Moreover we expect that you project will be mutually supportive to our Agency and its long term goals.

Sincerely yours,

Paul A. Muscillo
Chairman of the Board

PAM/lg.

BOARD OF EDUCATION OF THE CITY OF NEW YORK

C.S. 61	Bronx, New York 10460	1550 Crotona Park East	329-7975
SCHOOL	BOROUGH ZONE	ADDRESS	TELEPHONE

OFFICE OF THE PRINCIPAL

October 25, 1977

Jack Pelsinger, Director
Nation of Graffiti Artists
149 West 80 Street
New York, New York 10024

Dear Mr. Pelsinger:

I hav e read about the fine work your organization has accomplished over
the past three years. In addition to providing creative and aesthetic experiences for the young artists in your program and their large audience of New
Yorkers, NOGA is providing guidance and giving positive educational and voca-
tional training to its members. We are very anxious to become the benefici-
aries of your inspiring work.

At C.S. 61 we have been involved over the past two years in a program called
Arts in General Education sponsored by the Central Board. As members of this
project we seek opportunities to involve our children in art experiences that
will sharpen their powers of observation, critical thinking, problem solving,
self-expression, written expression, logic, verbalization. etc. I am convinced
that NOGA can provide such a learning experience for our children through the
planning and execution of a mural that is relevant to their school, home and
community life.

We have approximately 600 children at C.S. 61 in kindergarten to Grade 6.
Almost 100 of these children are in Special Education classes. All our children
will benefit from an activity that emphasizes the constructive aspects of the
paintbrush rather than the destructive aspects and that finally results in a positive,
self-satsifying educational experience.

I am anxious to learn if you are able to help us with a project for C.S. 61.

Sincerely,

Sherman Tufel
Principal

MOVE TO THE BRONX

In February of 1977 there was another move, this time to the Bronx. Pelsinger and French had managed to get a free studio located on the second floor of a senior living facility. PART, a leading writer from the DEATH SQUAD, had this to say about the Bronx studio. "The Senior Home was where I first started to hang out. There was a whole group of us: NOC 167, BUTCH 2, STAN 153, KASE 2, a lot of the writers that painted the Montefiore Hospital mural. We liked the space because you could look out the windows at the 2s and the 5s and check out the pieces. Some people were doing paintings there, and some just hung out. I think it was different from the spot on Columbus Avenue because you didn't have kids running in and out. It seemed like a more mature spot. It lasted for a while."

Freedom's NOGA card from 1979. Courtesy of Chris Pape.

There's no telling why NOGA moved again, although the theory is that the old folks they shared the space with may have had a problem with the noise and spray paint. In 1977, Pelsinger was able to secure a temporary home for NOGA in the South Bronx, in the basement of a Methodist church. The old guard at NOGA was changing: CLIFF 159 was no longer the talk of the city, and SCORPIO and BLOOD TEA mostly stayed on the Upper West Side. One of the best writers hanging out at NOGA in 1976 was REE 2; he was widely liked and had already done everything a major writer had to do. His résumé included whole cars as REE 2 and his alternate moniker, OPEL. He did window-down burners as REE 2, OPEL

and RUB. In 1977, REE 2 lived just a few blocks away from NOGA's new home, and he quickly took on the role of leader.

REE's original crew, MTA, had morphed into a new crew called TMT. It was the TMT members who benefited the most from REE's new position. Several important stylists from the crew — KADE, TEAN, TYBU, CHAIN 3 and KRANE — were all doing canvases. These paintings were larger and more sophisticated than what had been done at NOGA previously, reflecting the advancement in style that played out on the trains in '76 and '77. Other writers who took advantage of the space were BAMA, DAZE, NOC 167, STAN 153 and BUTCH 2. They were all members of NOGA and passed through the workshop in a transient way, sometimes hanging out and drawing in piece books but staying away from canvas.

Both UGA and NOGA members were supposed to tell the media that they were giving up their illegal ways to work on canvas. REE saw firsthand that this was Pelsinger's goal: "In 1977 I was with some of the TMT guys on Broadway and we were going to paint a train. We bumped into Jack and he asked us what we were doing. I told him and he looked at me, trying to figure out a way to get us to stop. After a few minutes he said, 'Why don't you guys just come up and paint my apartment, we'll have a party.' And we did. We painted everything, even his shower curtain. Jack was trying to get people off the trains."

One of the highlights from that year was when some of the members painted a handball court nearby. REE recounts how it came about:

"BLOOD TEA had asked me if there was a wall where we could paint. I told him I had a practice wall nearby in the elementary school I had gone to. He didn't really like the idea at first because it was illegal, but I assured him it was a safe spot to paint, and that I had pieces on the wall dating back to 1974. We all walked over there and they started to paint. I even let them paint over one of my OPEL pieces. I chose not to paint because I was still an active writer. It all went fine, and Michael Lawrence was there to document it."

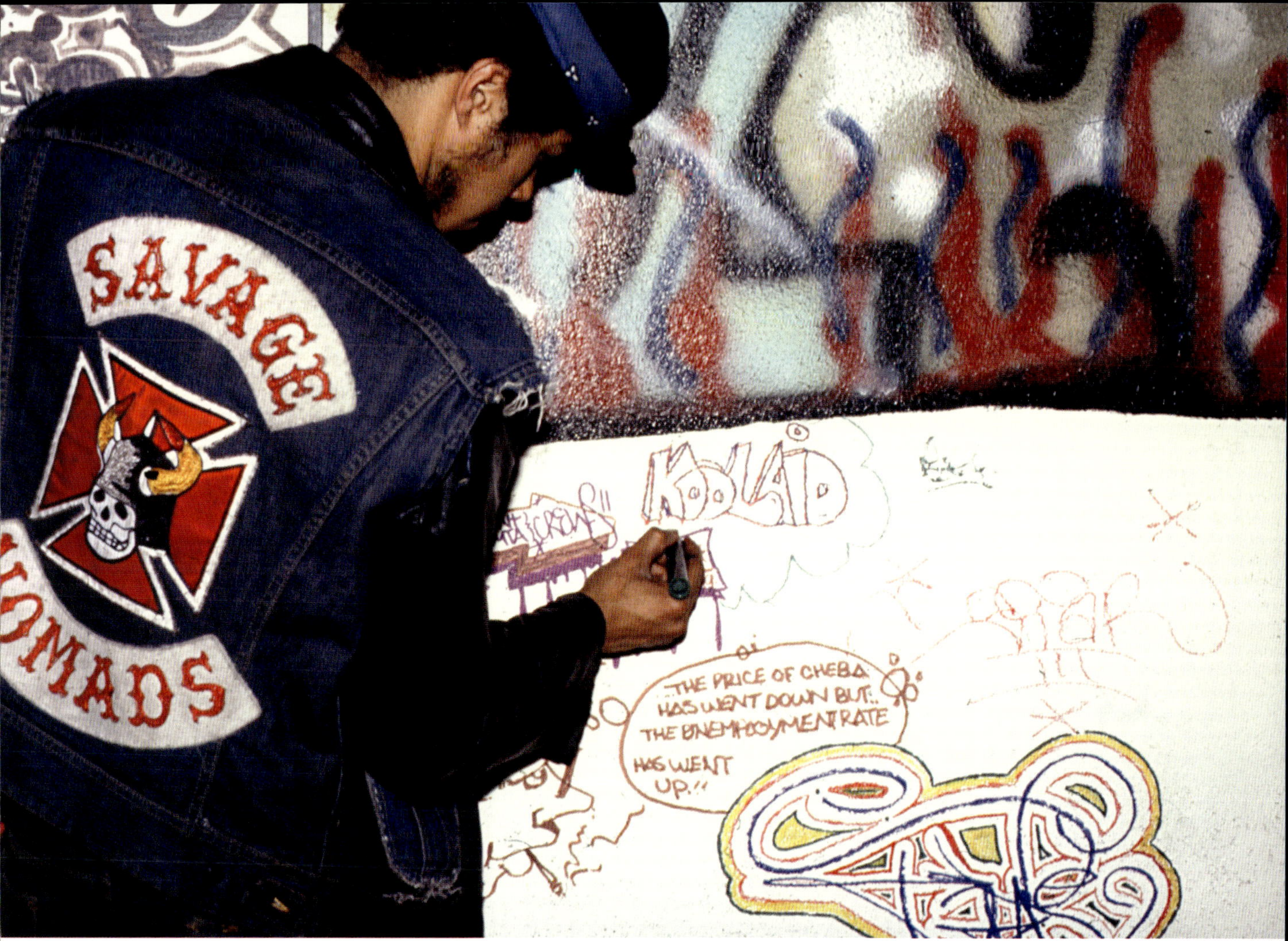

SAVAGE
NOMADS
KOOL AID
..THE PRICE OF CHEBA
HAS WENT DOWN BUT..
THE UNEMPLOYMENT RATE
HAS WENT UP.!!

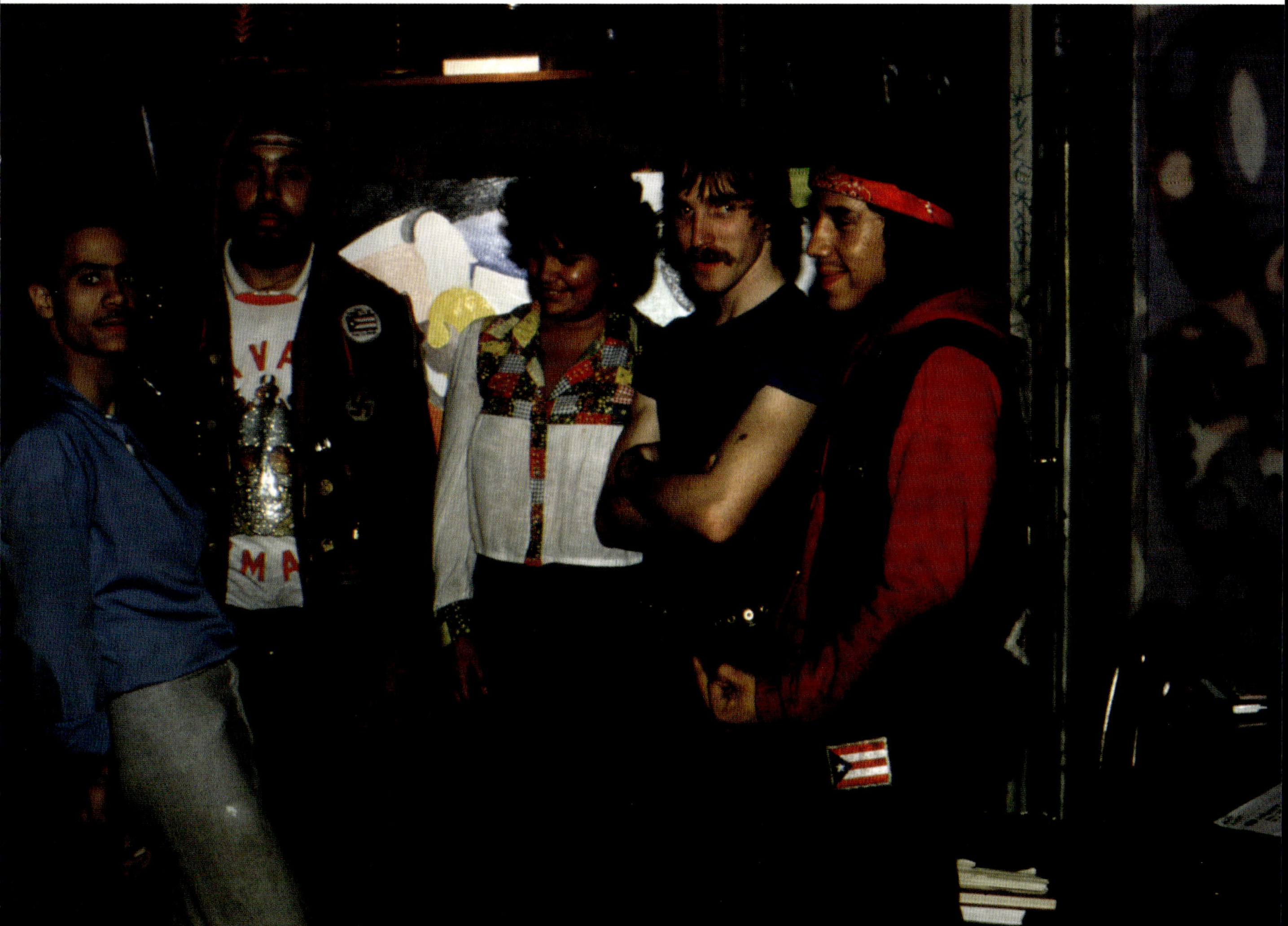

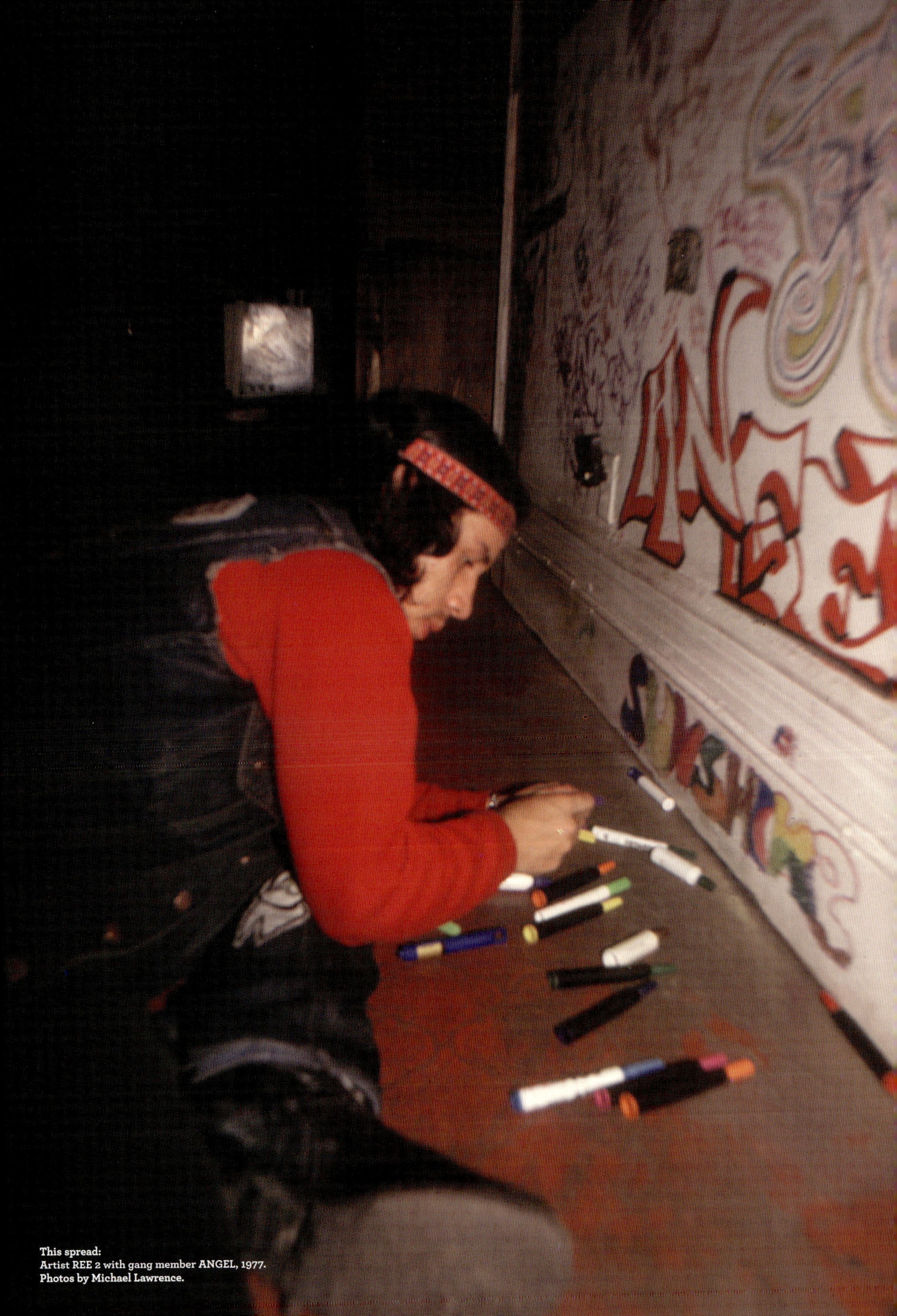

This spread:
Artist REE 2 with gang member ANGEL, 1977.
Photos by Michael Lawrence.

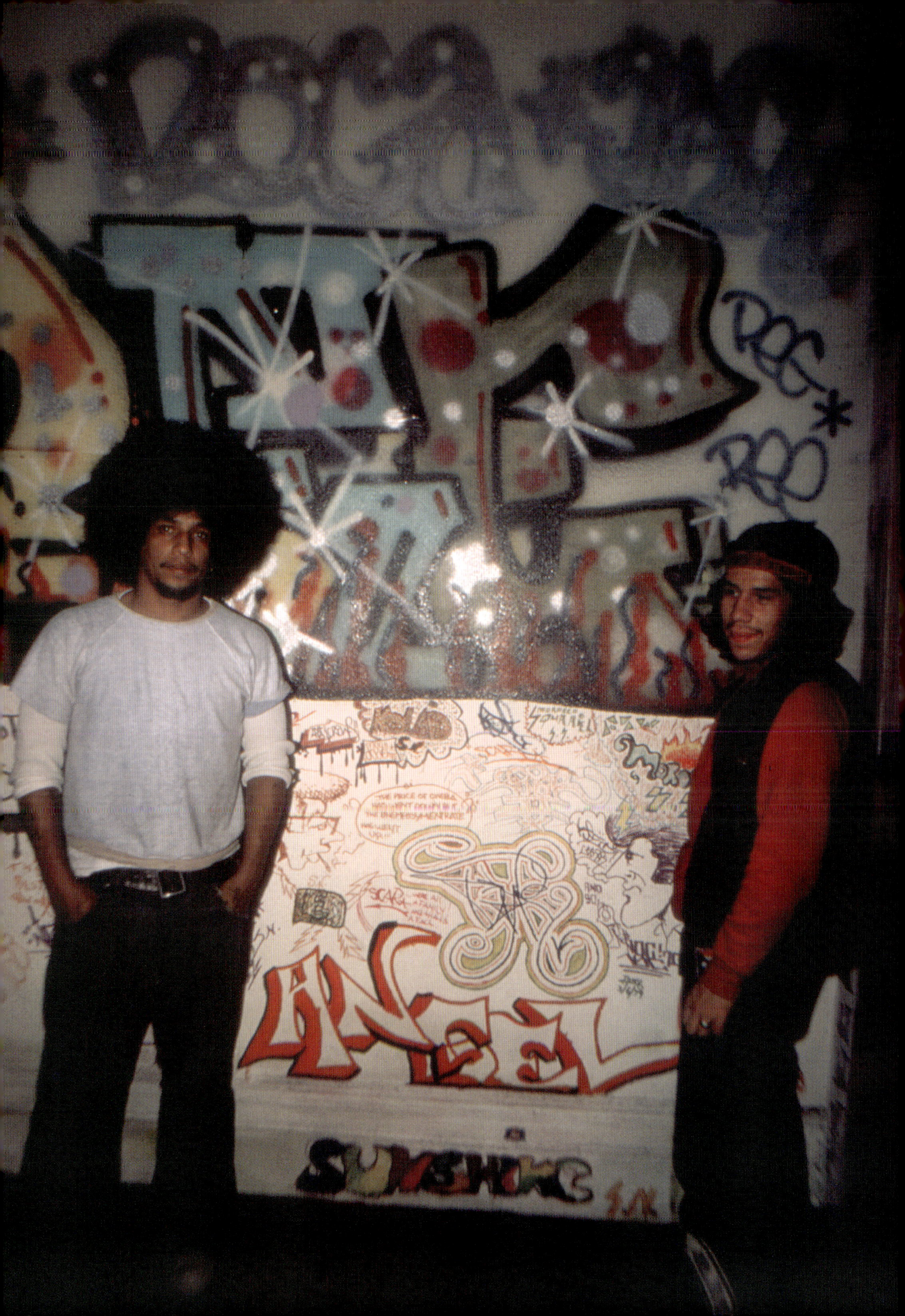

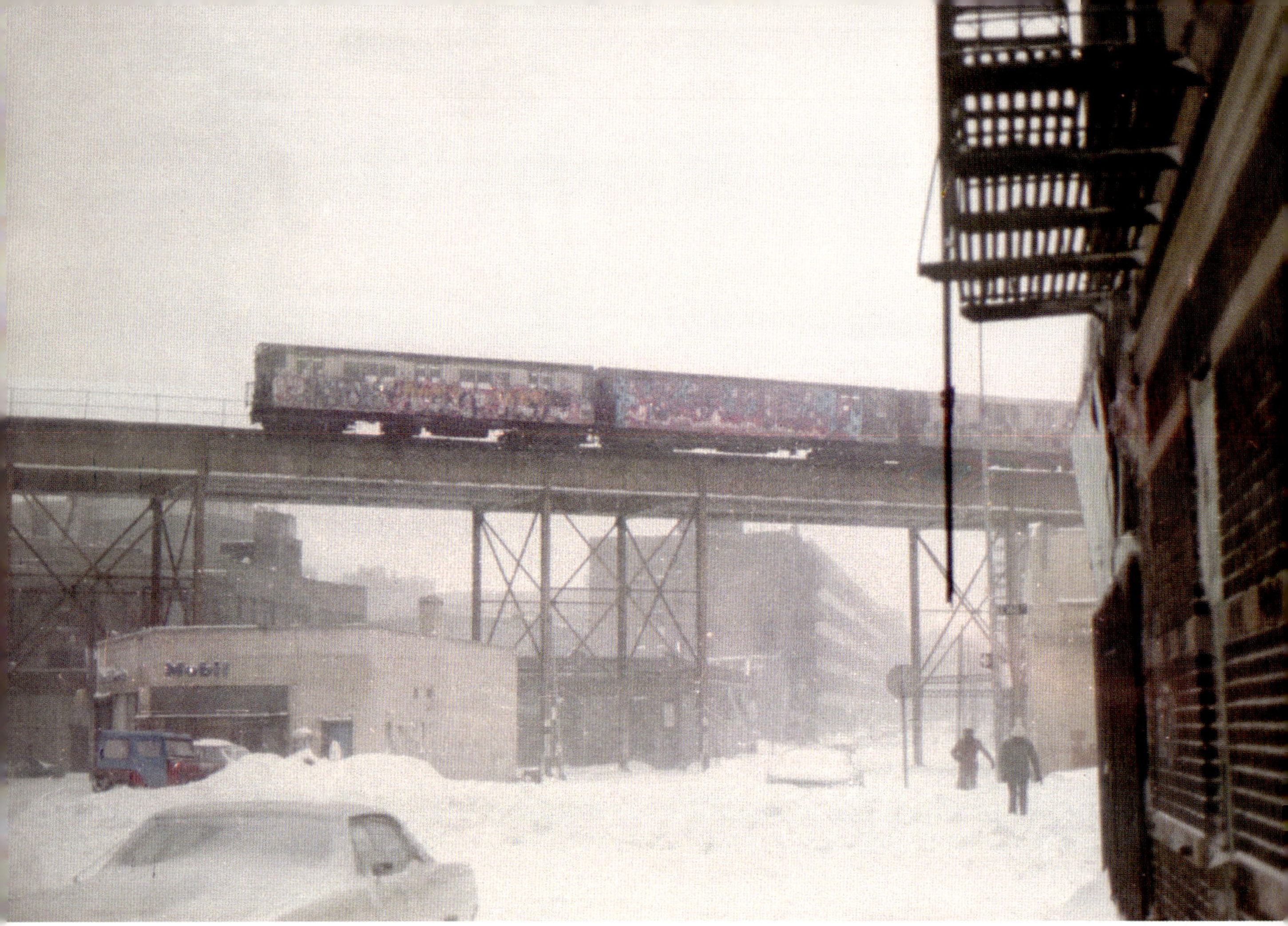

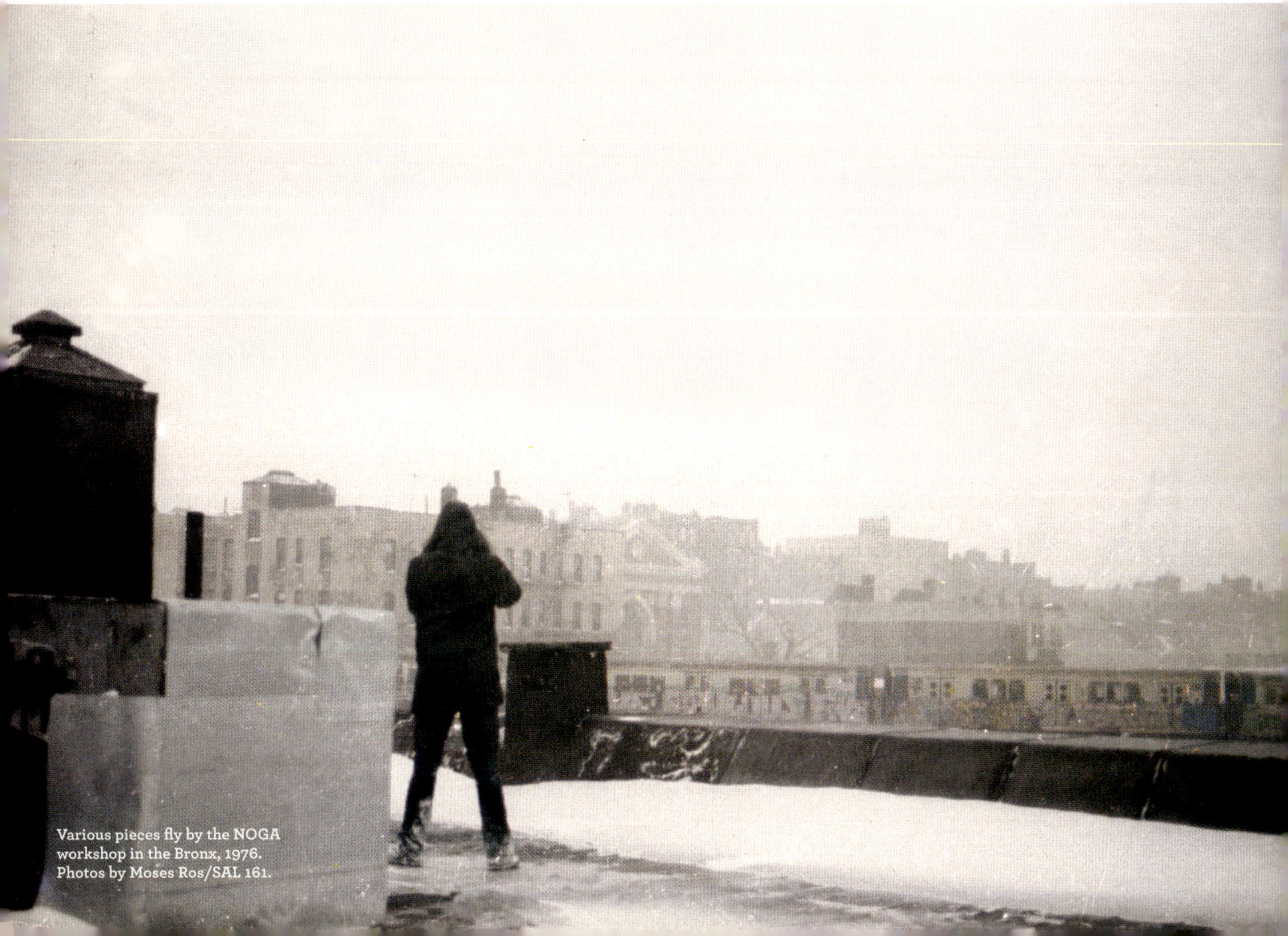

Various pieces fly by the NOGA
workshop in the Bronx, 1976.
Photos by Moses Ros/SAL 161.

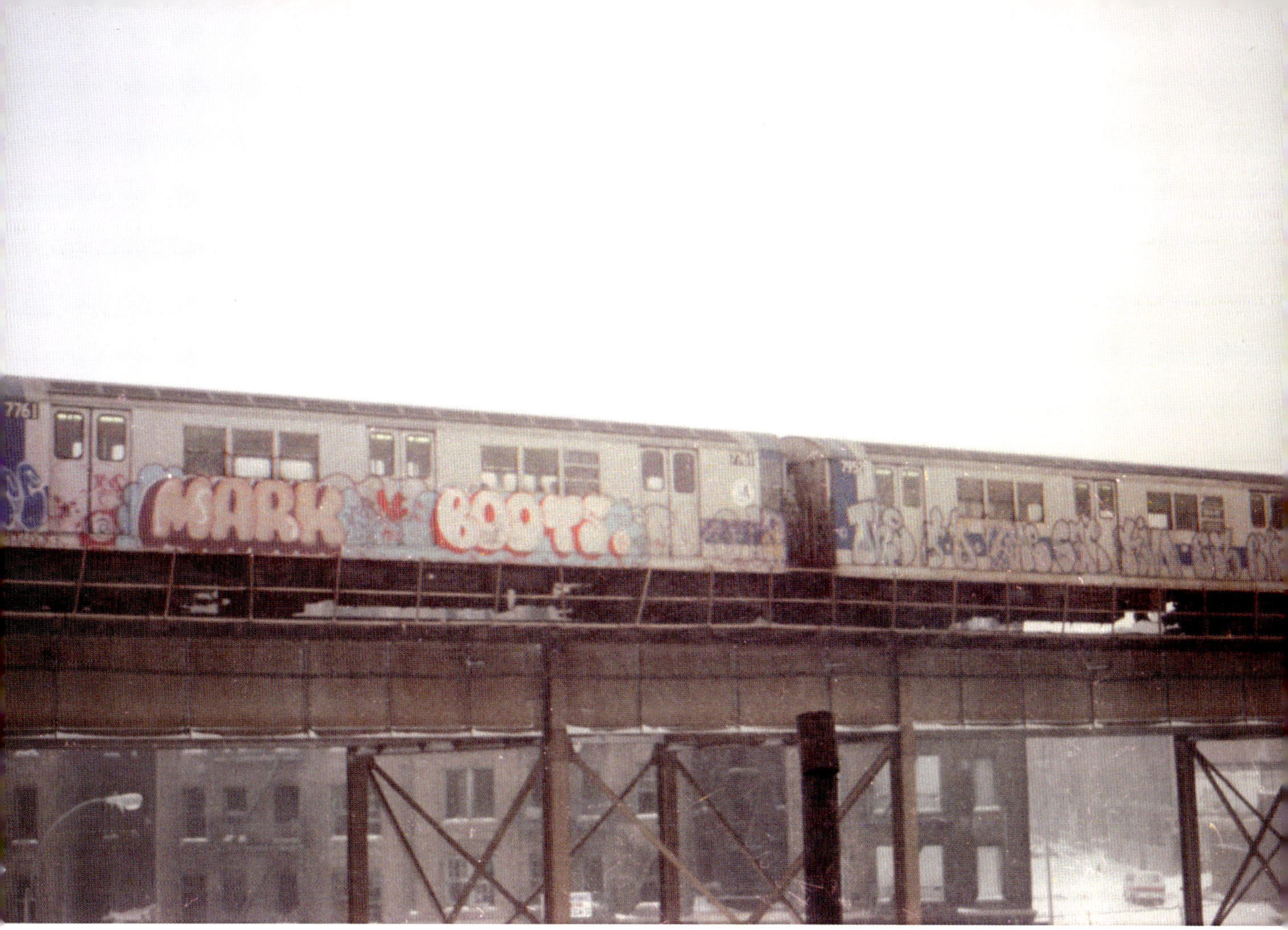

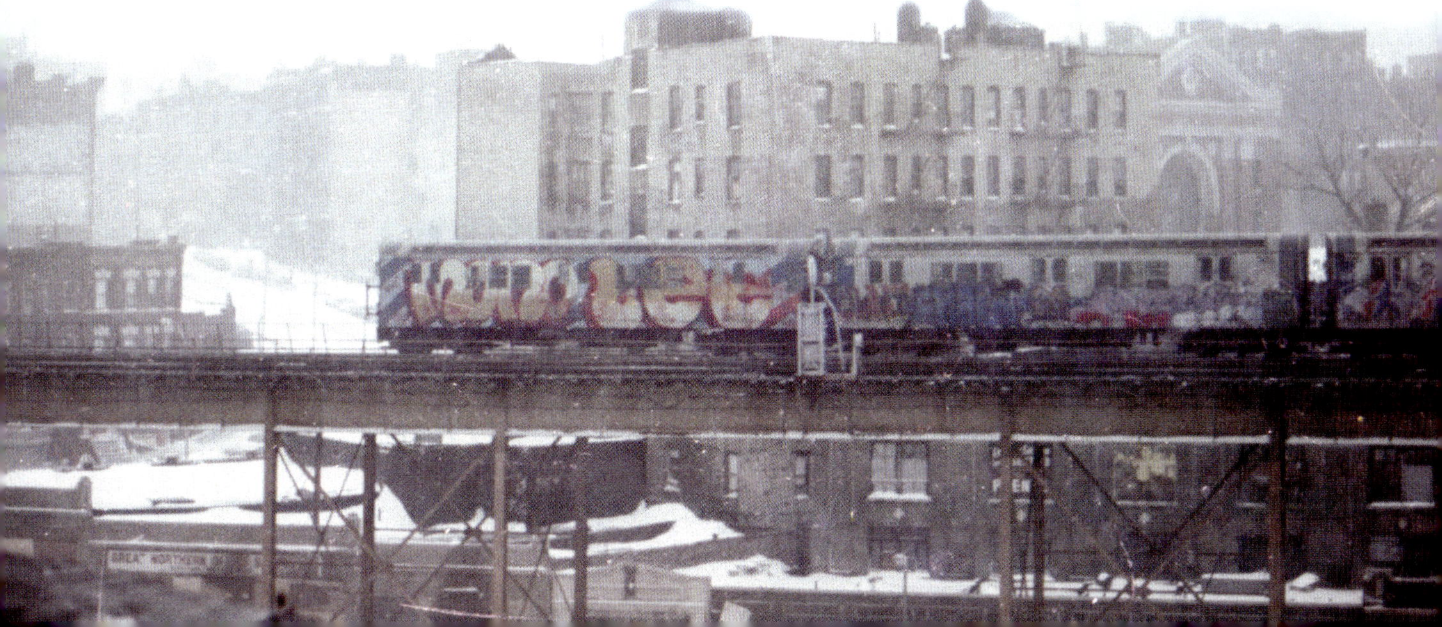

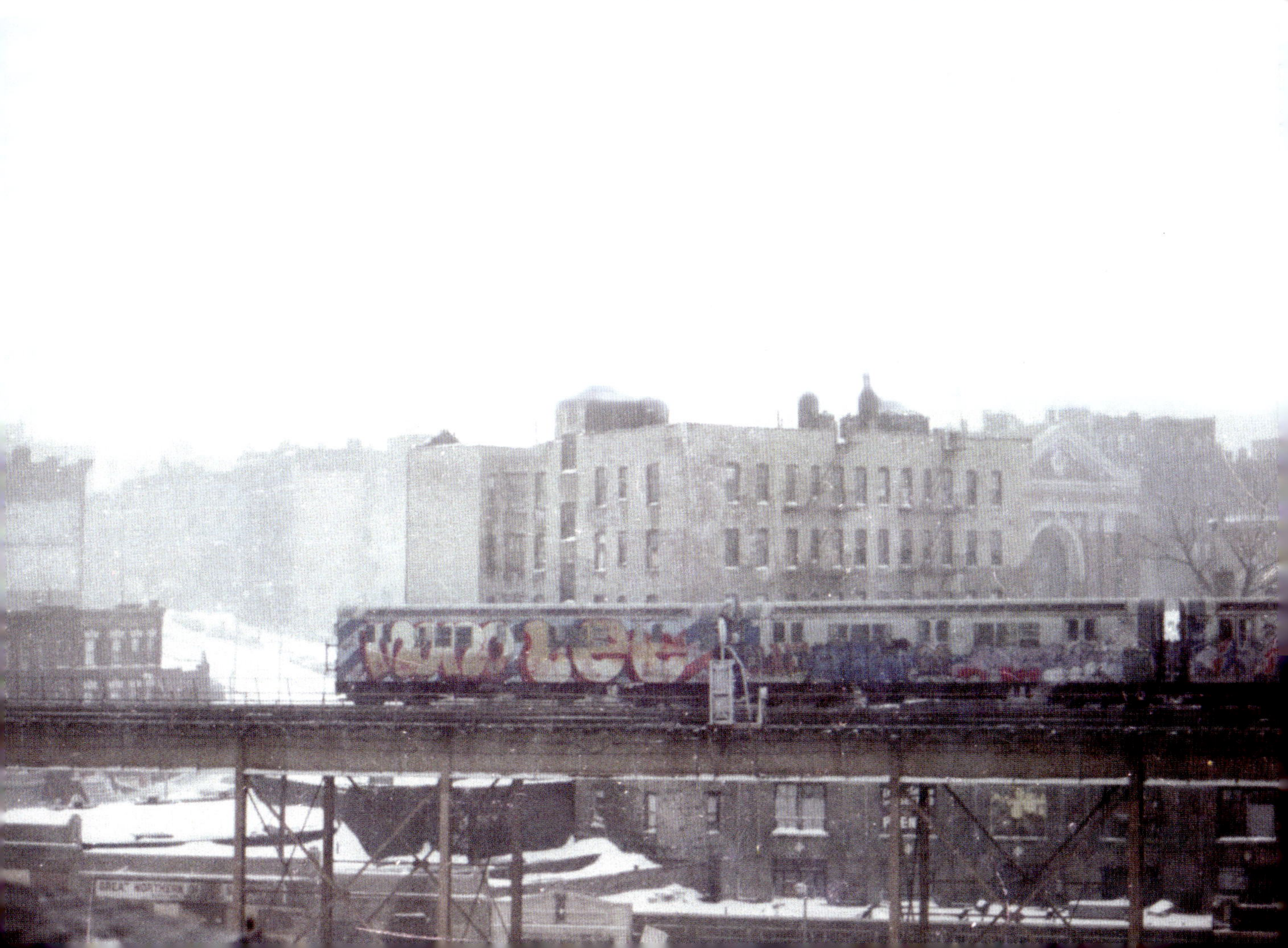

"I HAD A PRACTICE WALL NEARBY IN THE ELEMENTARY SCHOOL I HAD GONE TO."
–REE 2

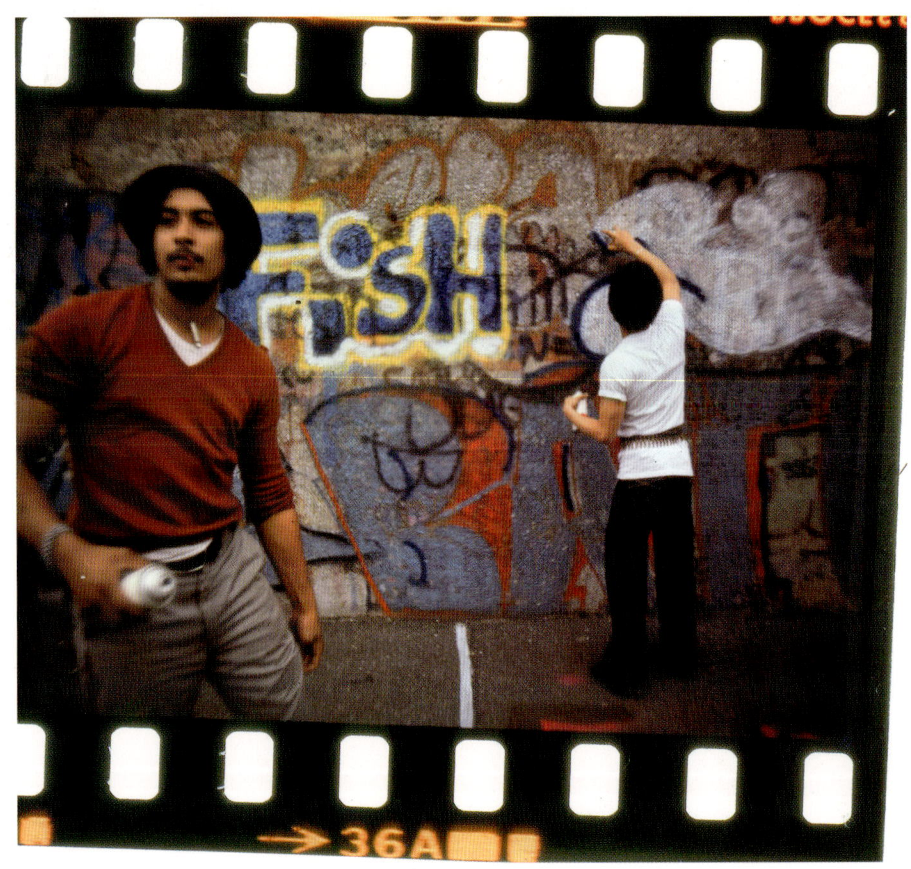

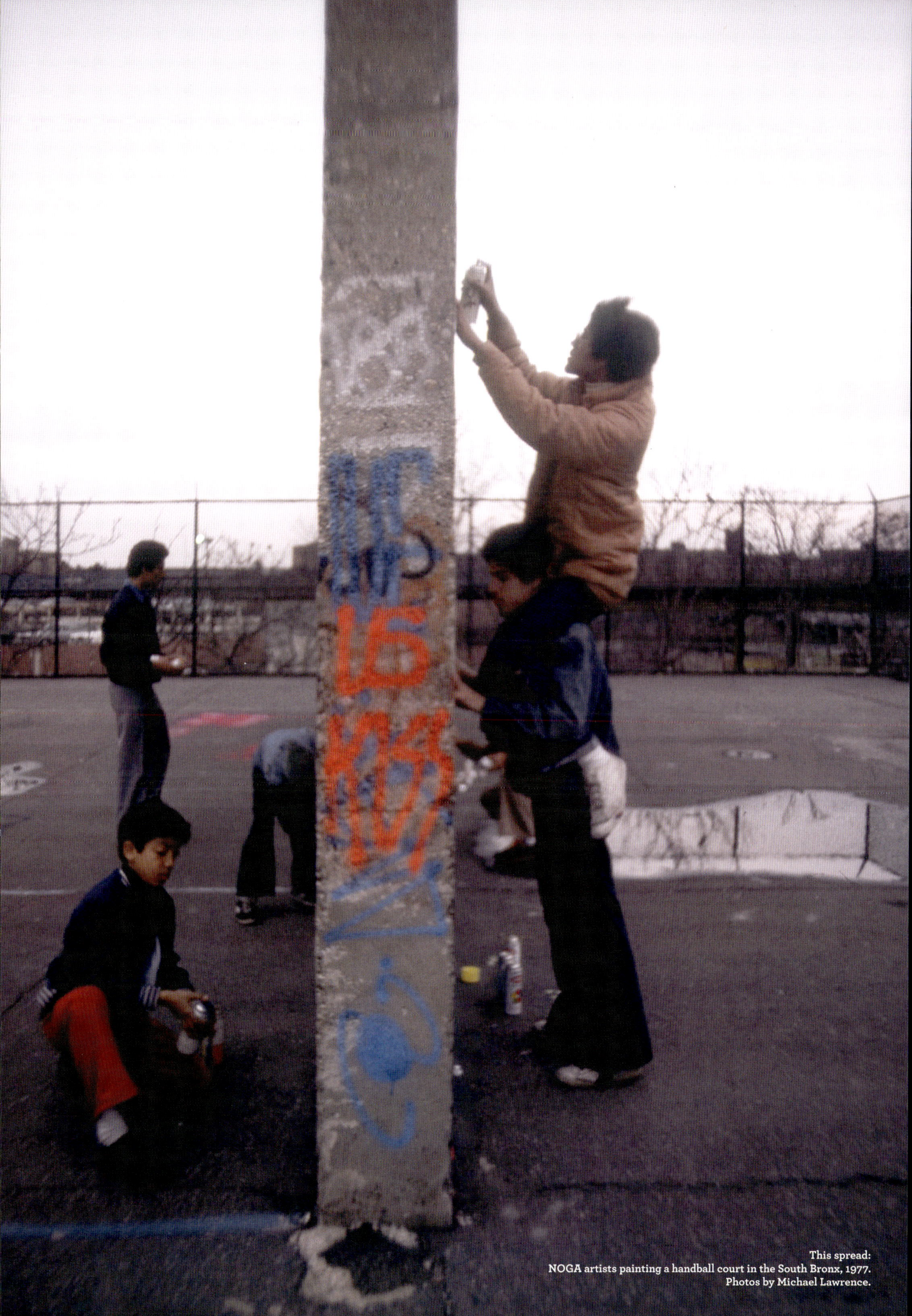

This spread:
NOGA artists painting a handball court in the South Bronx, 1977.
Photos by Michael Lawrence.

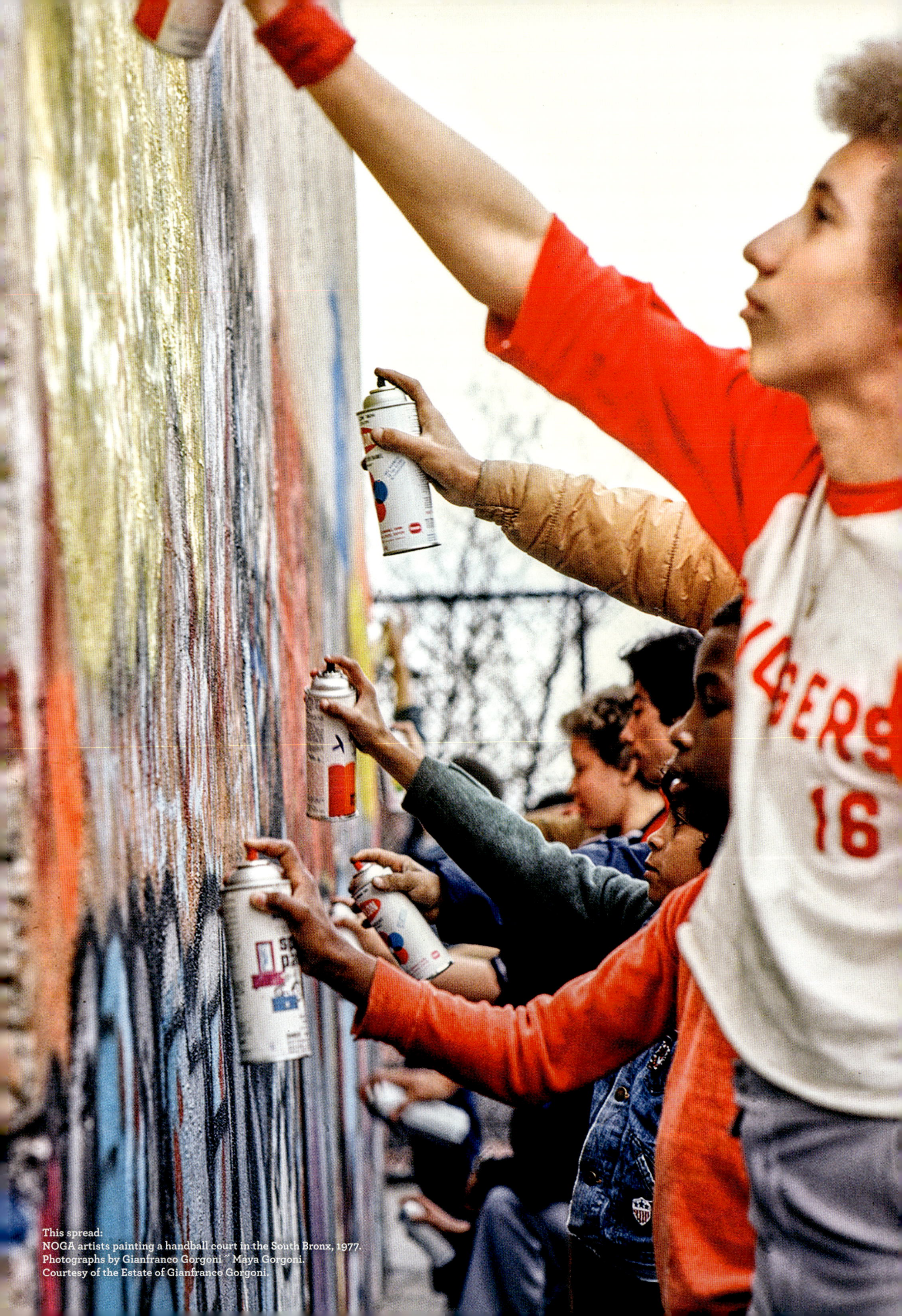

This spread:
NOGA artists painting a handball court in the South Bronx, 1977.
Photographs by Gianfranco Gorgoni \ Maya Gorgoni.
Courtesy of the Estate of Gianfranco Gorgoni.

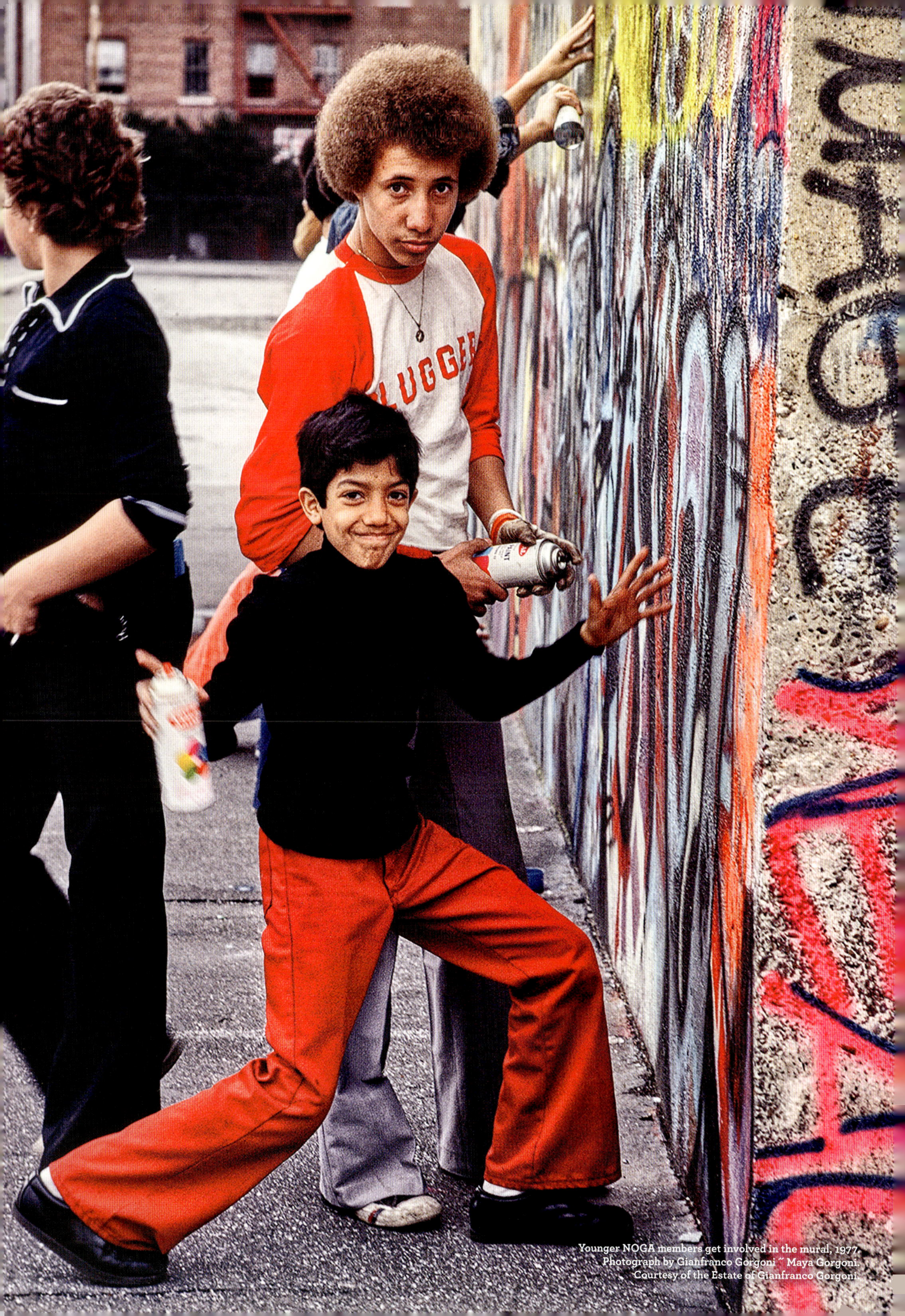

Younger NOGA members get involved in the mural, 1977
Photograph by Gianfranco Gorgoni ~ Maya Gorgoni.
Courtesy of the Estate of Gianfranco Gorgoni.

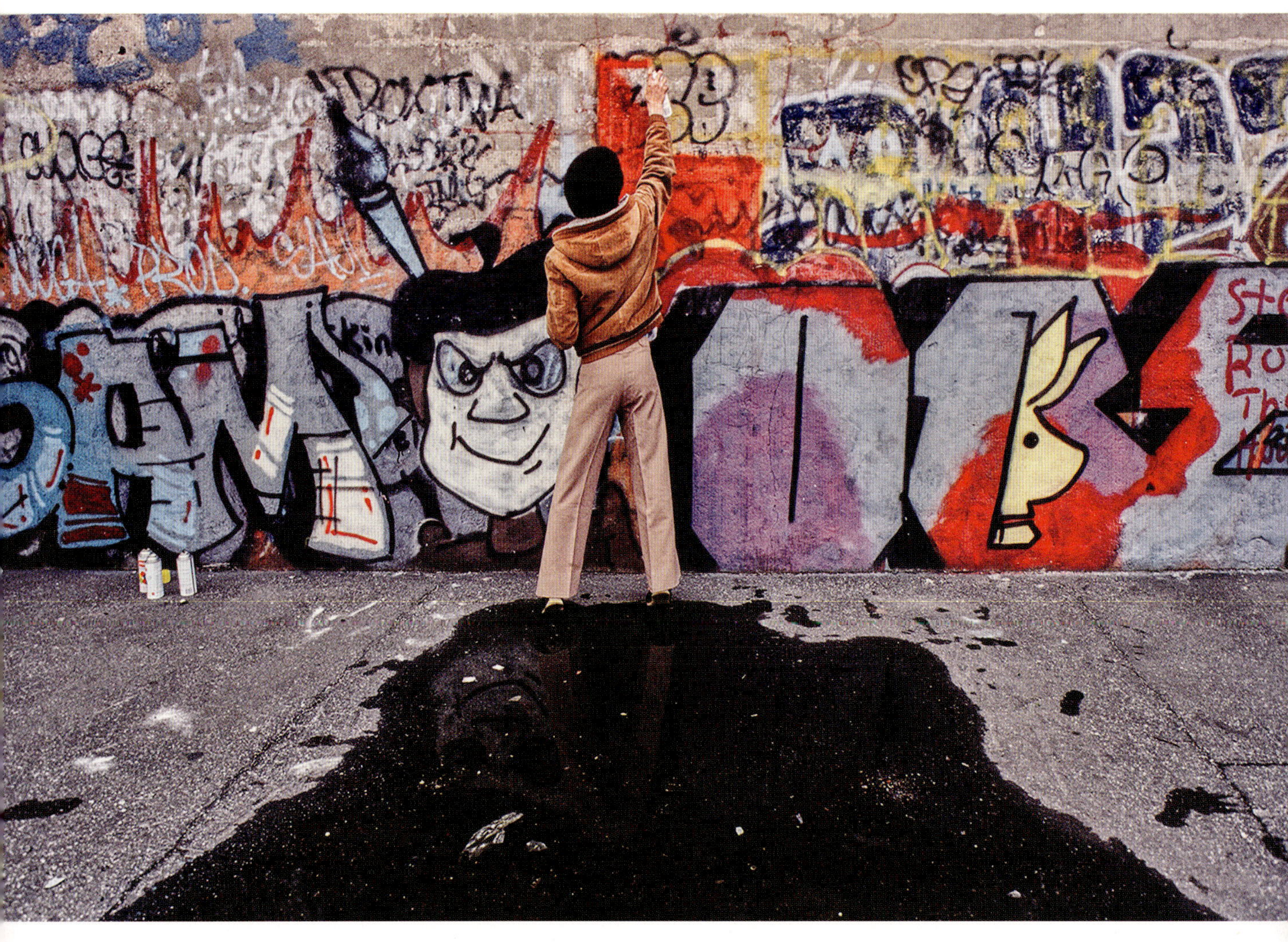

This spread:
NOGA artists painting a handball court in the South Bronx, 1977.
Photographs by Gianfranco Gorgoni ″ Maya Gorgoni.
Courtesy of the Estate of Gianfranco Gorgoni.

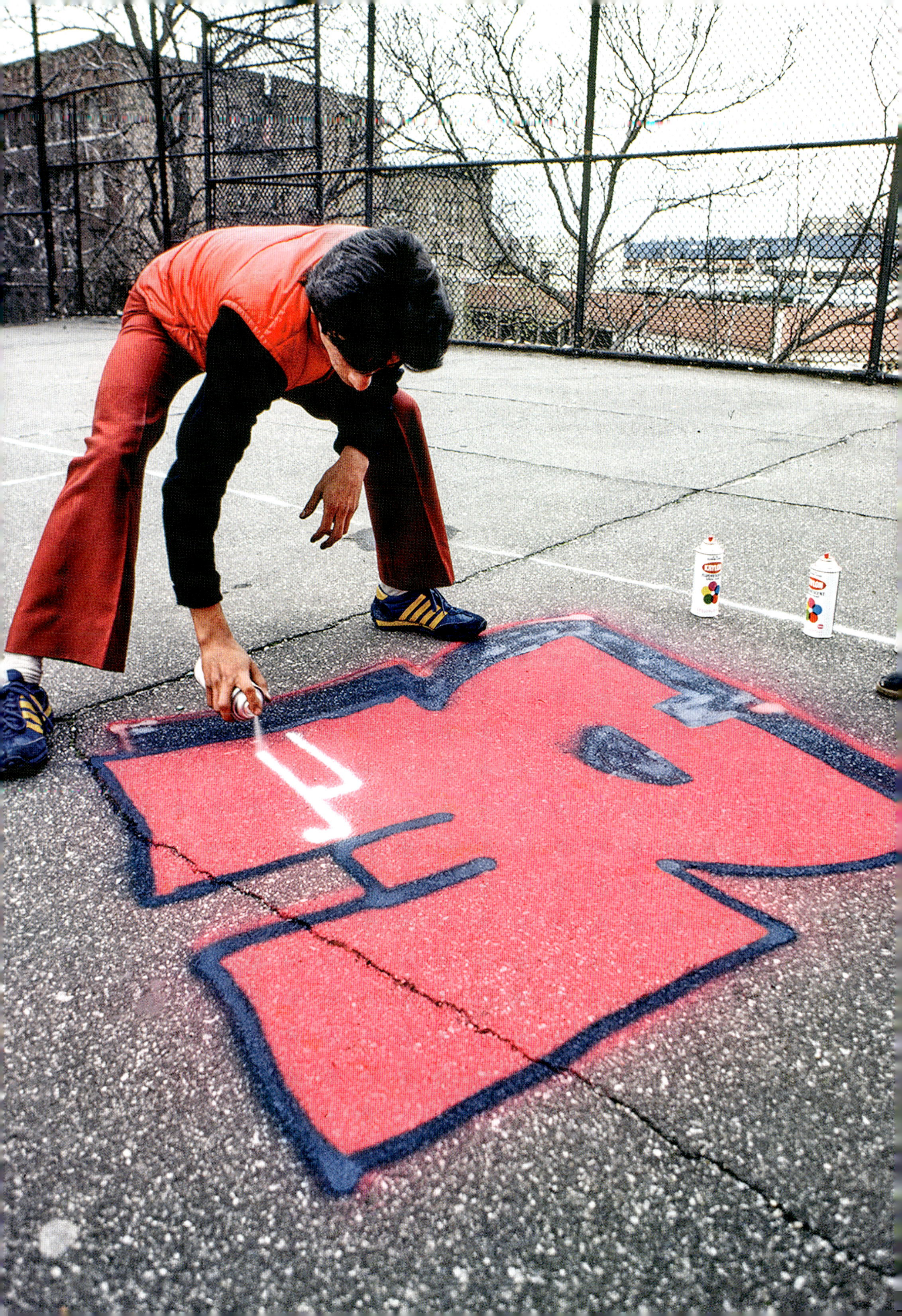

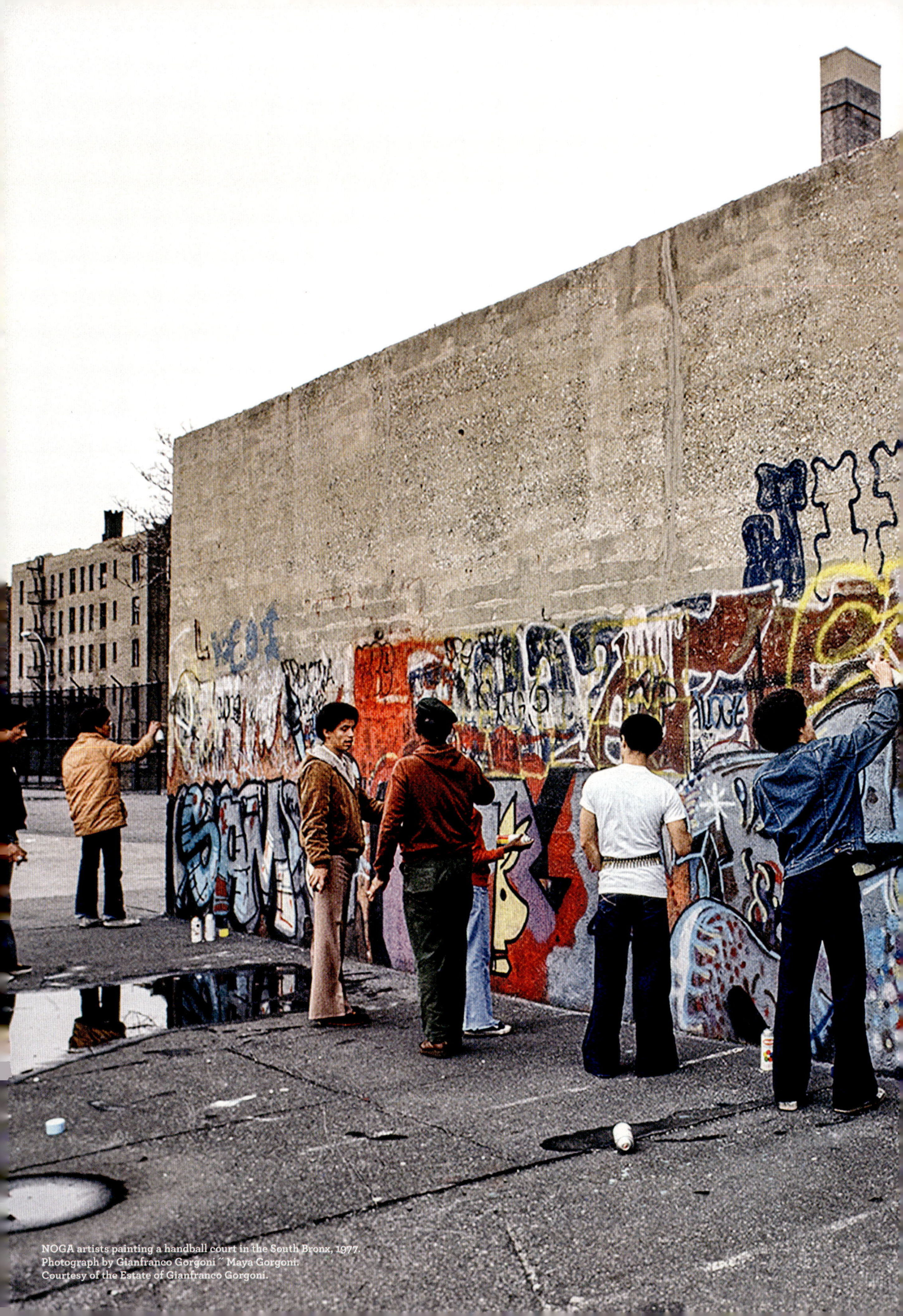

NOGA artists painting a handball court in the South Bronx, 1977.
Photograph by Gianfranco Gorgoni © Maya Gorgoni.
Courtesy of the Estate of Gianfranco Gorgoni.

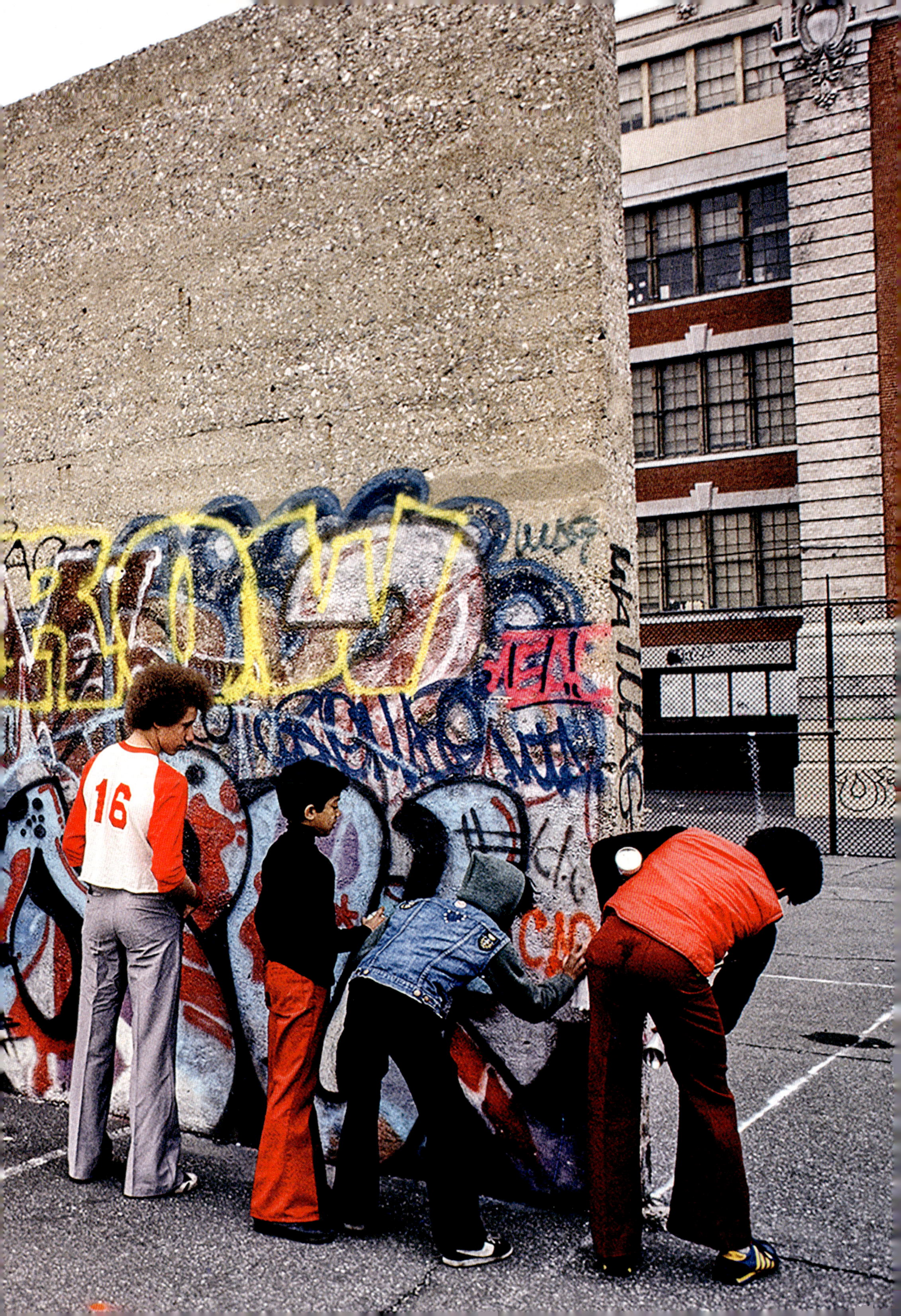

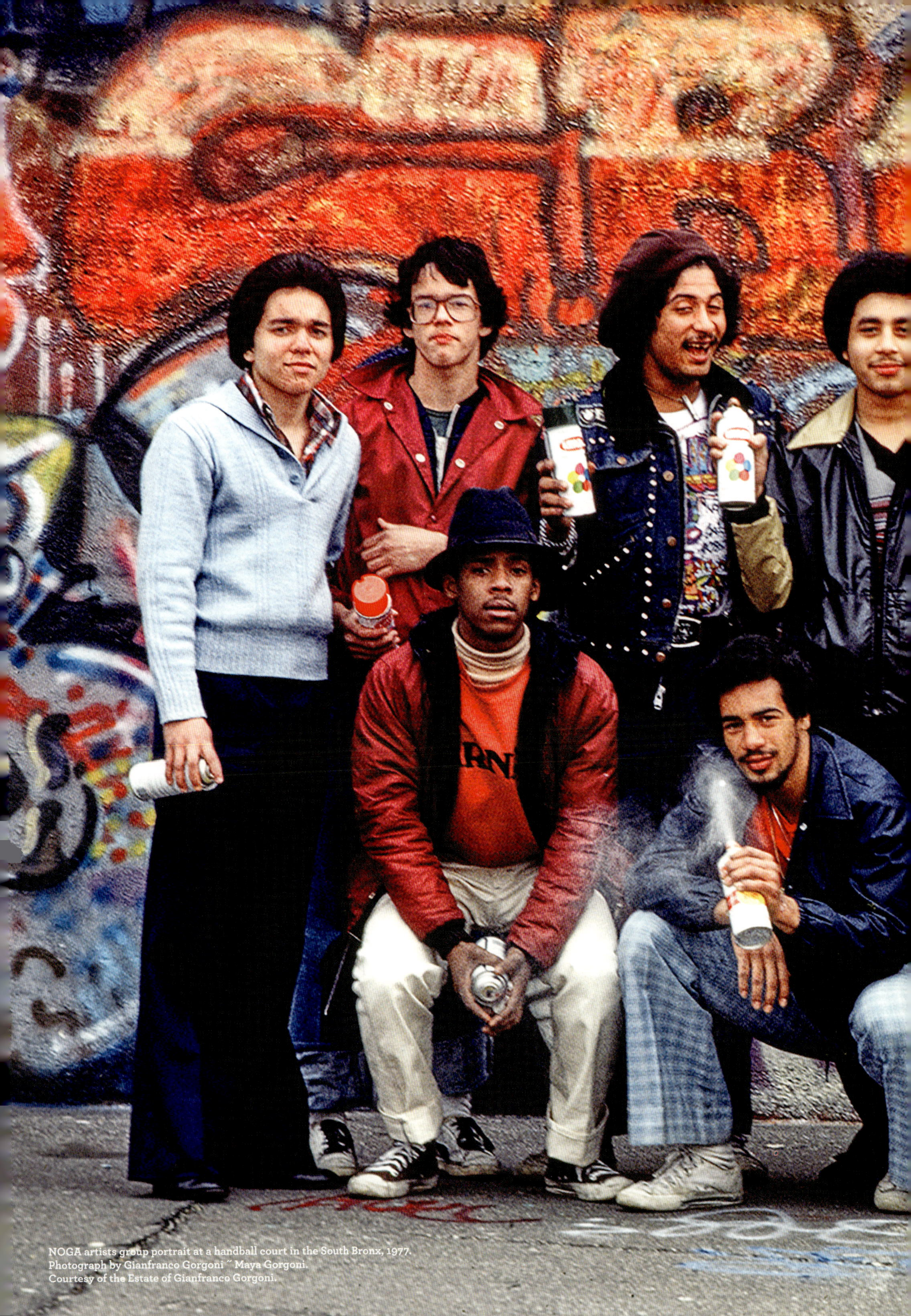

NOGA artists group portrait at a handball court in the South Bronx, 1977.
Photograph by Gianfranco Gorgoni ´´ Maya Gorgoni.
Courtesy of the Estate of Gianfranco Gorgoni.

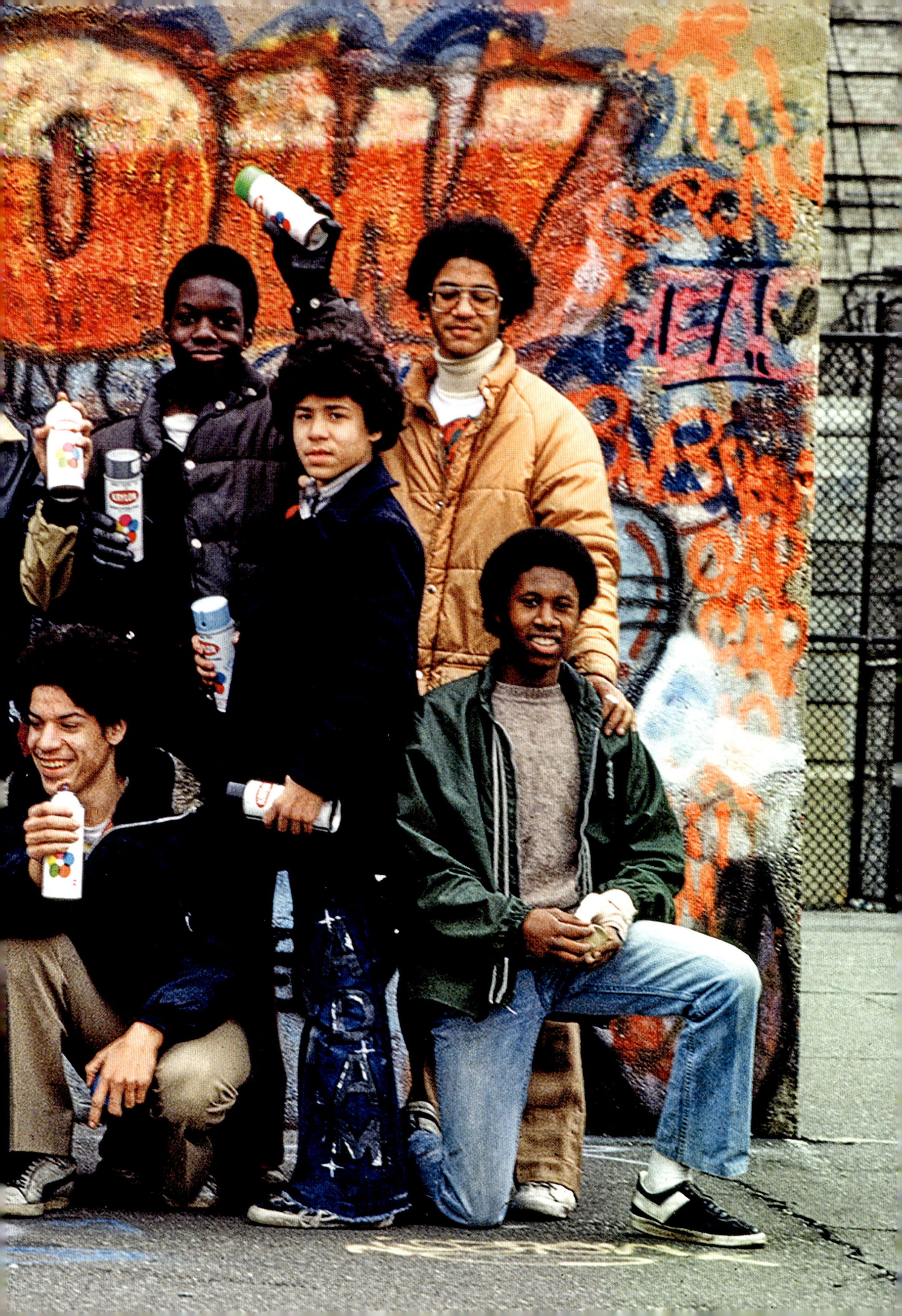

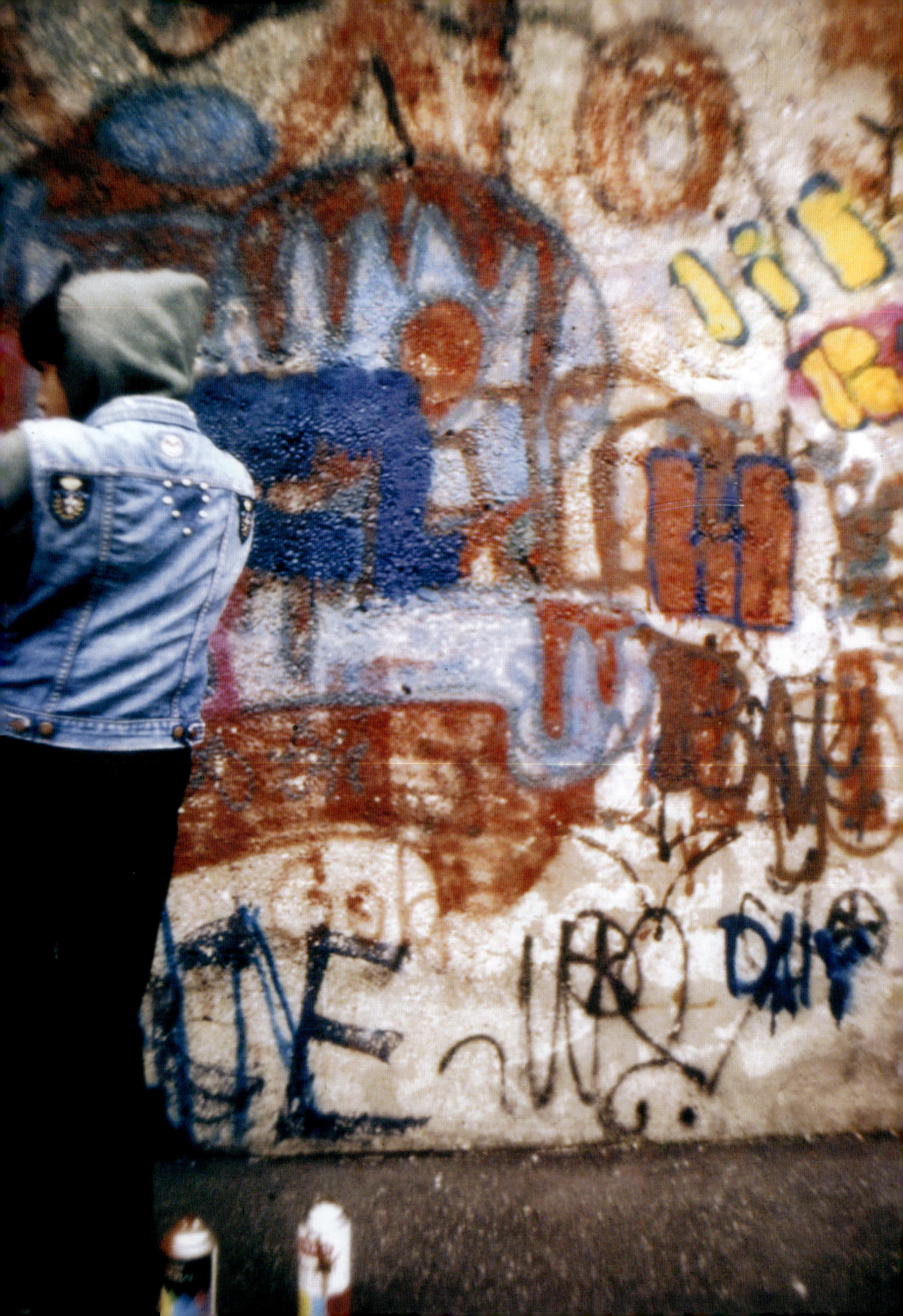

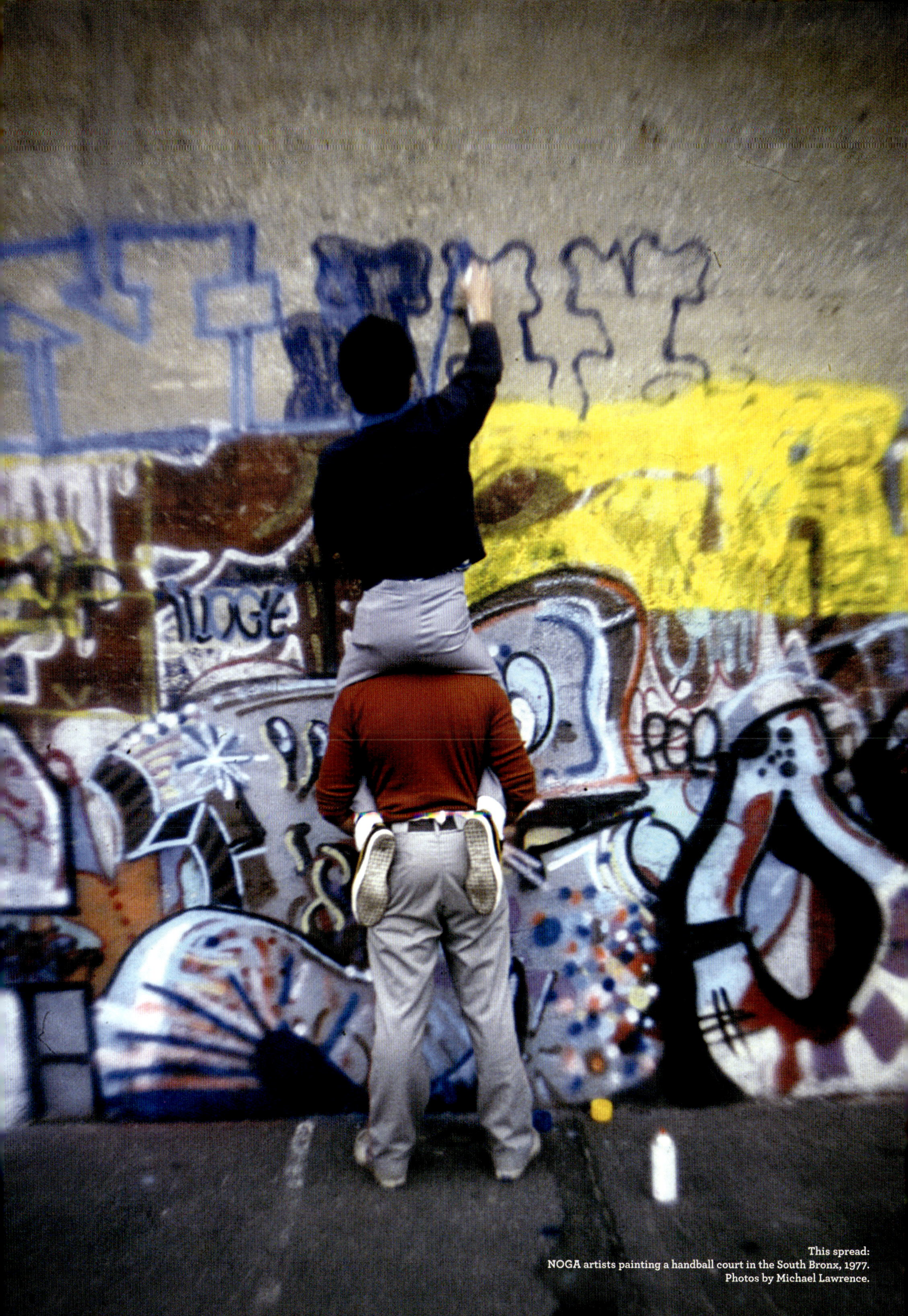

This spread:
NOGA artists painting a handball court in the South Bronx, 1977.
Photos by Michael Lawrence.

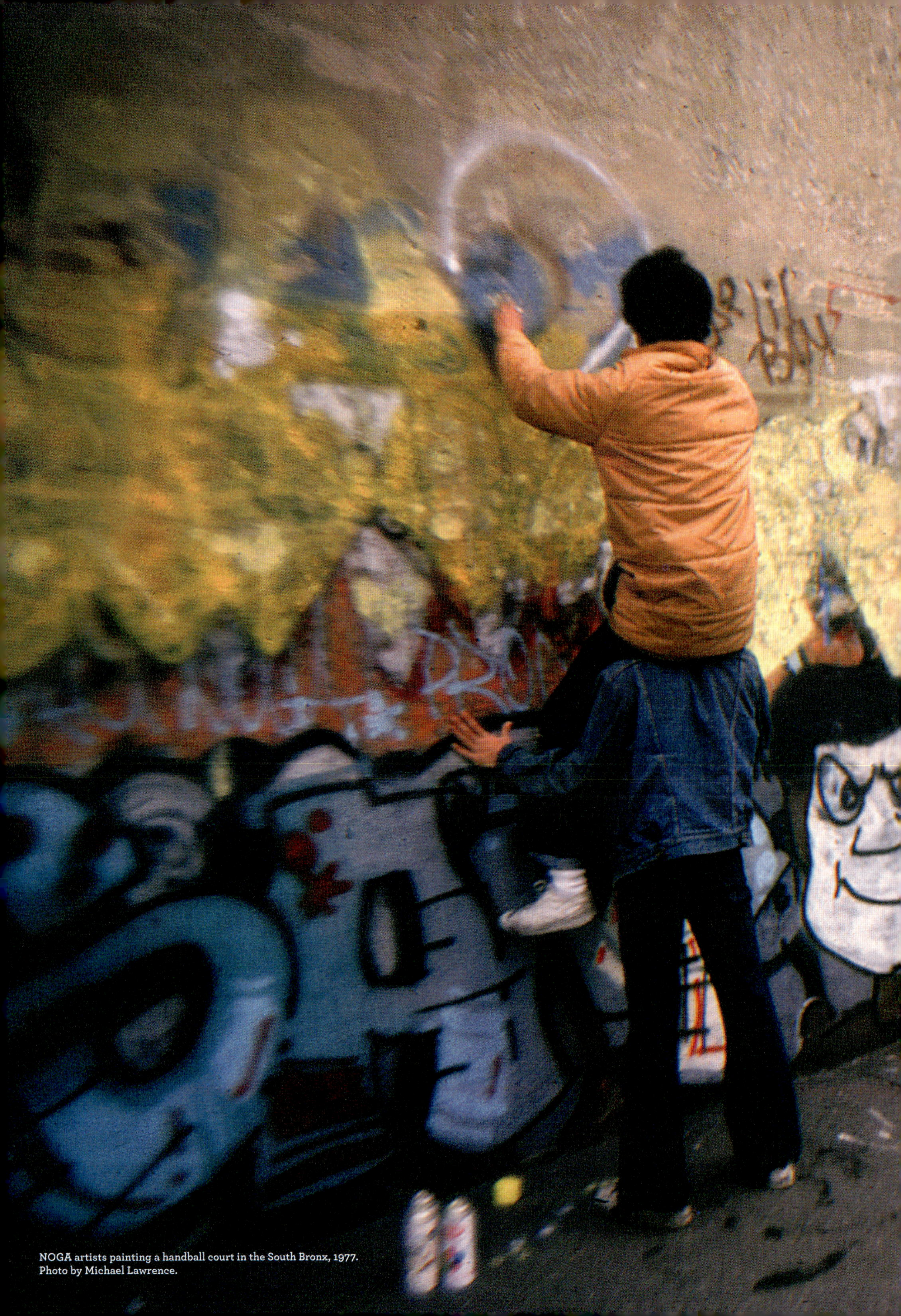

NOGA artists painting a handball court in the South Bronx, 1977.
Photo by Michael Lawrence.

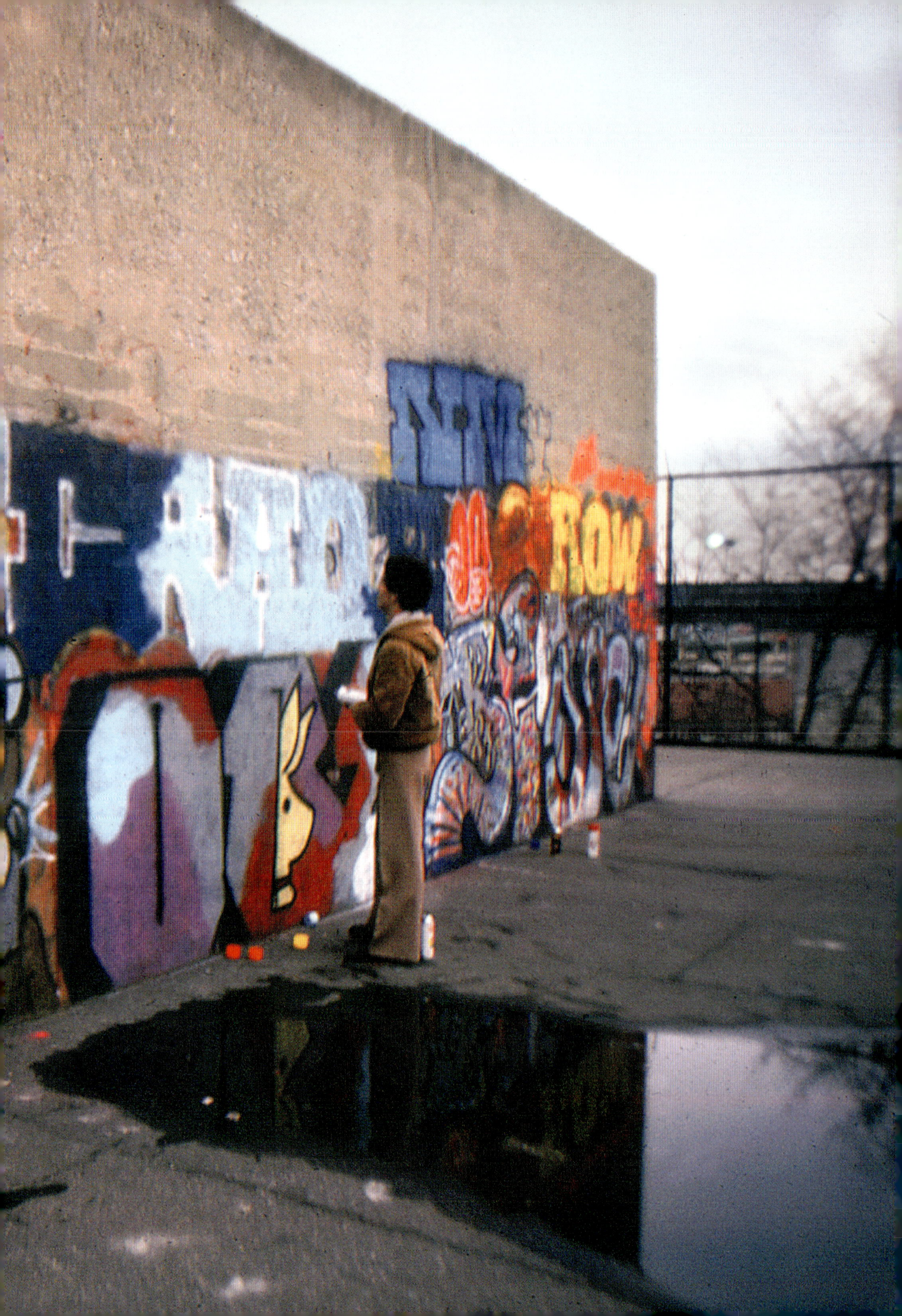

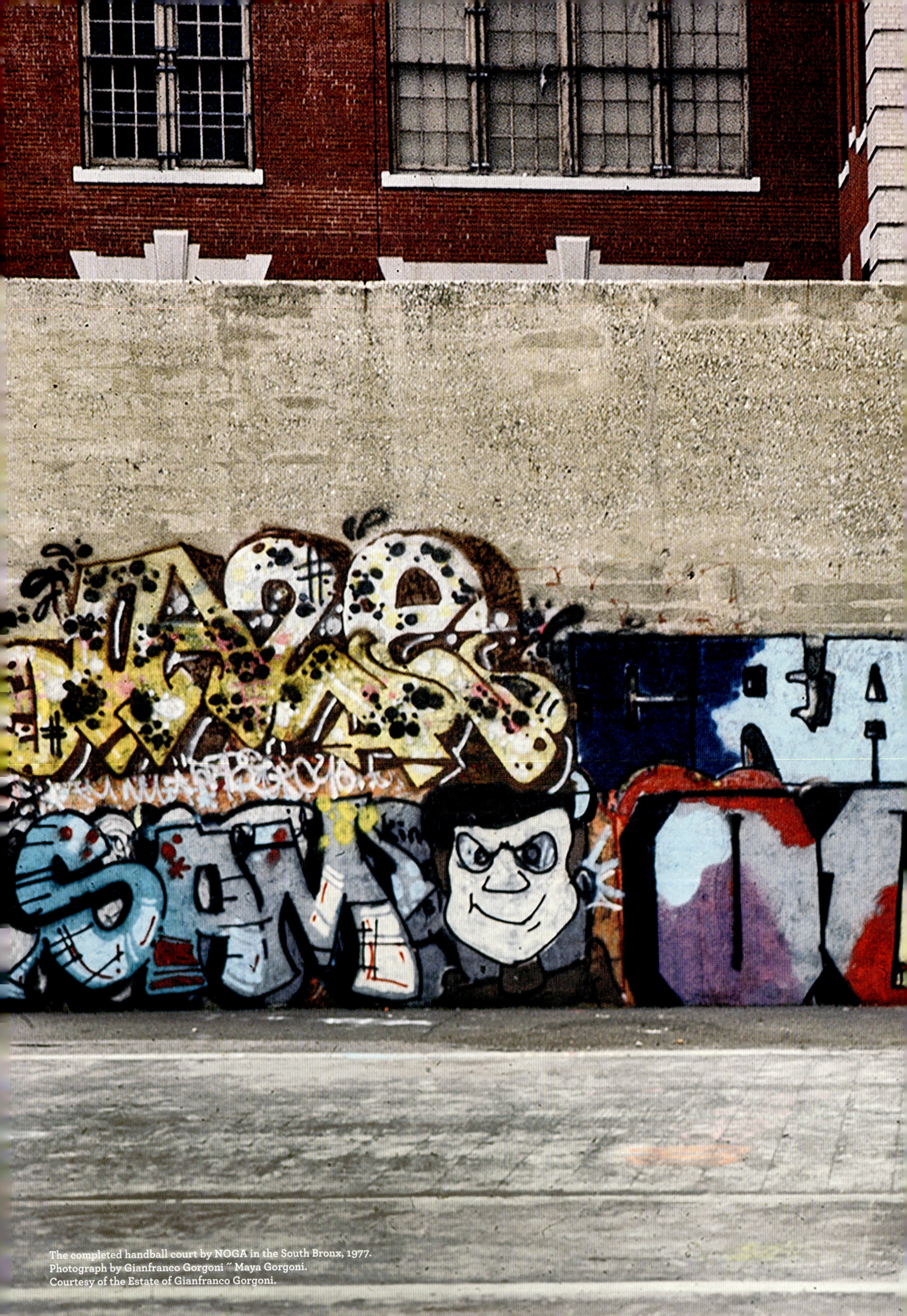

The completed handball court by NOGA in the South Bronx, 1977.
Photograph by Gianfranco Gorgoni ~ Maya Gorgoni.
Courtesy of the Estate of Gianfranco Gorgoni.

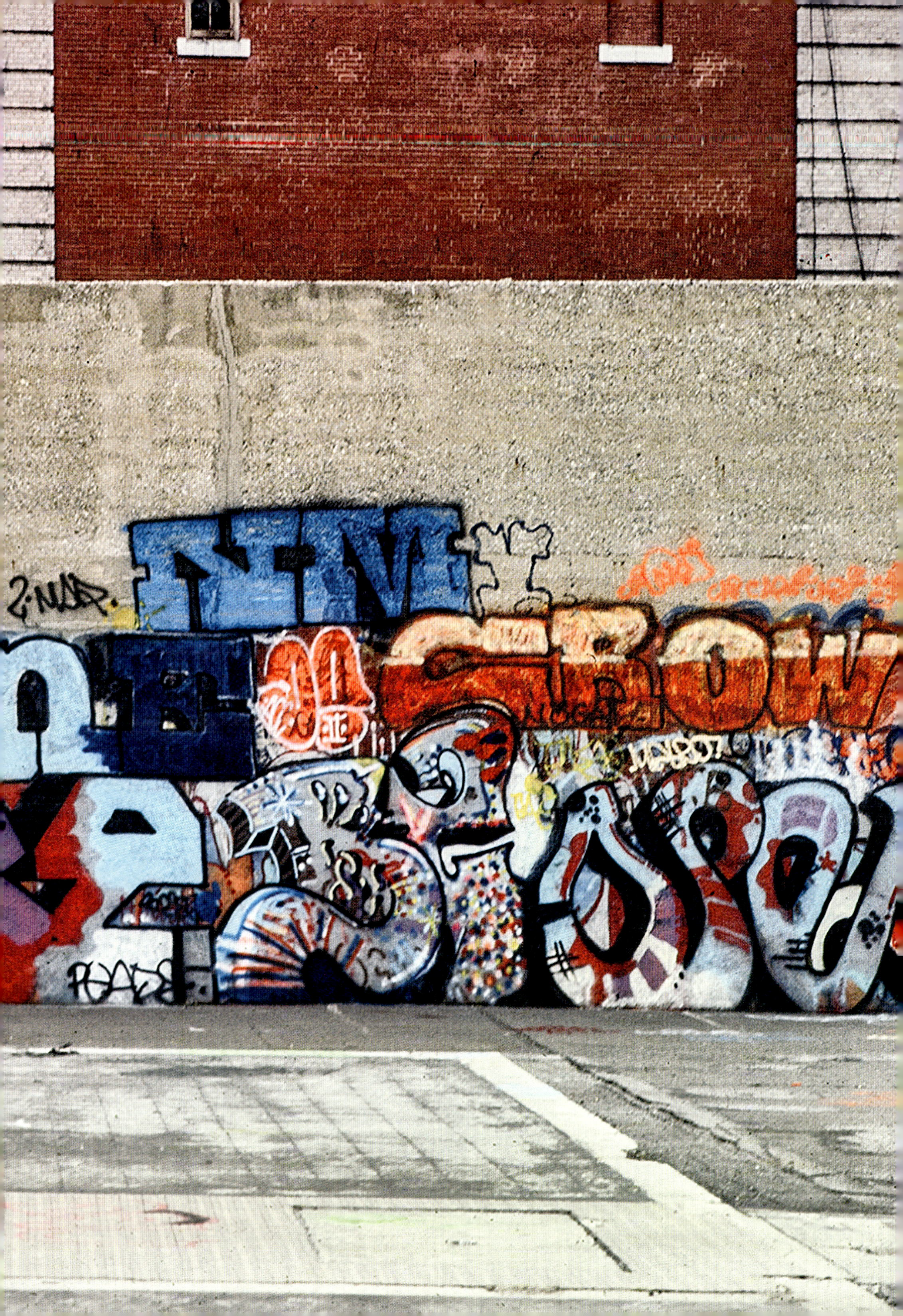

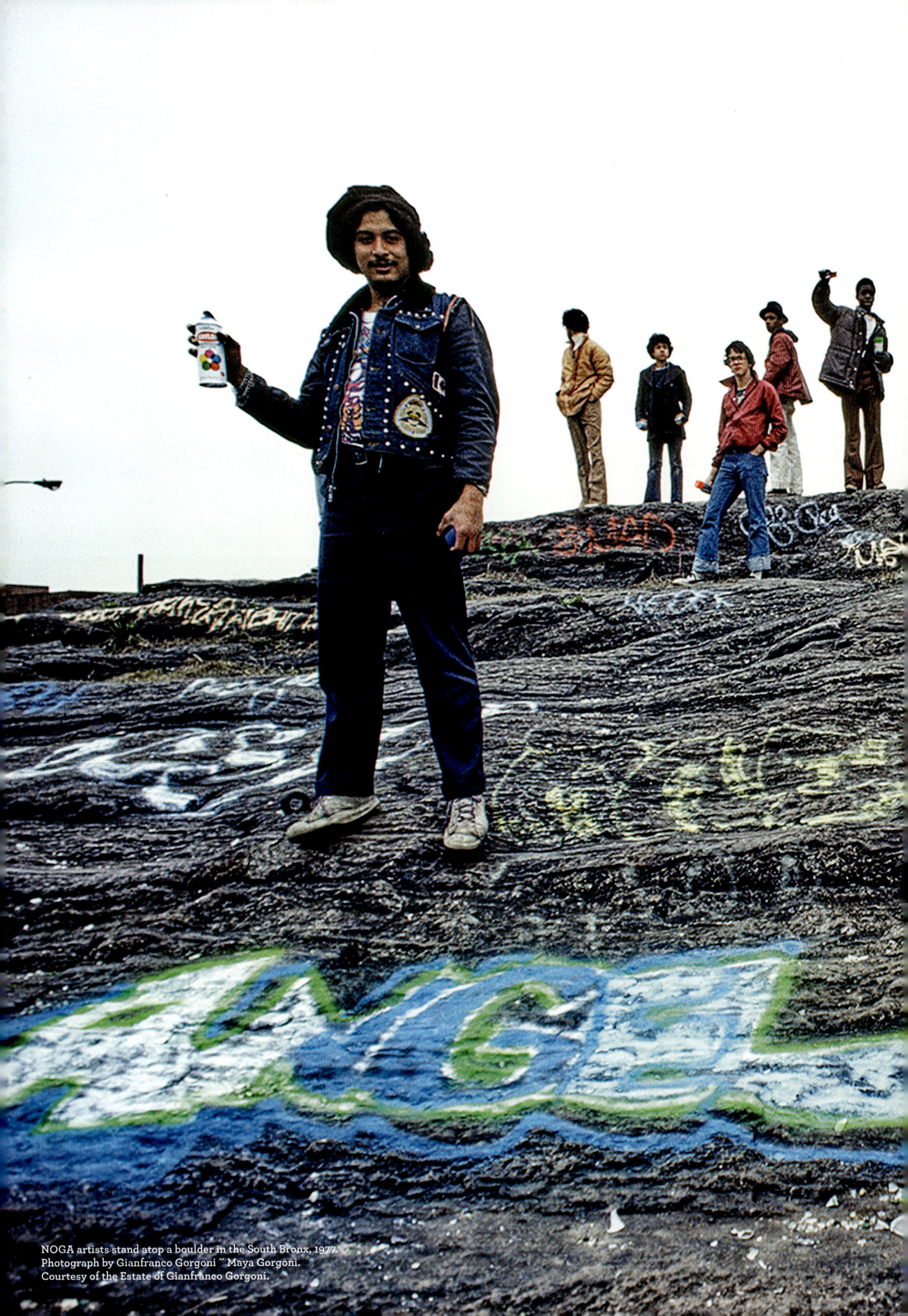

NOGA artists stand atop a boulder in the South Bronx, 1977.
Photograph by Gianfranco Gorgoni ˝ Maya Gorgoni.
Courtesy of the Estate of Gianfranco Gorgoni.

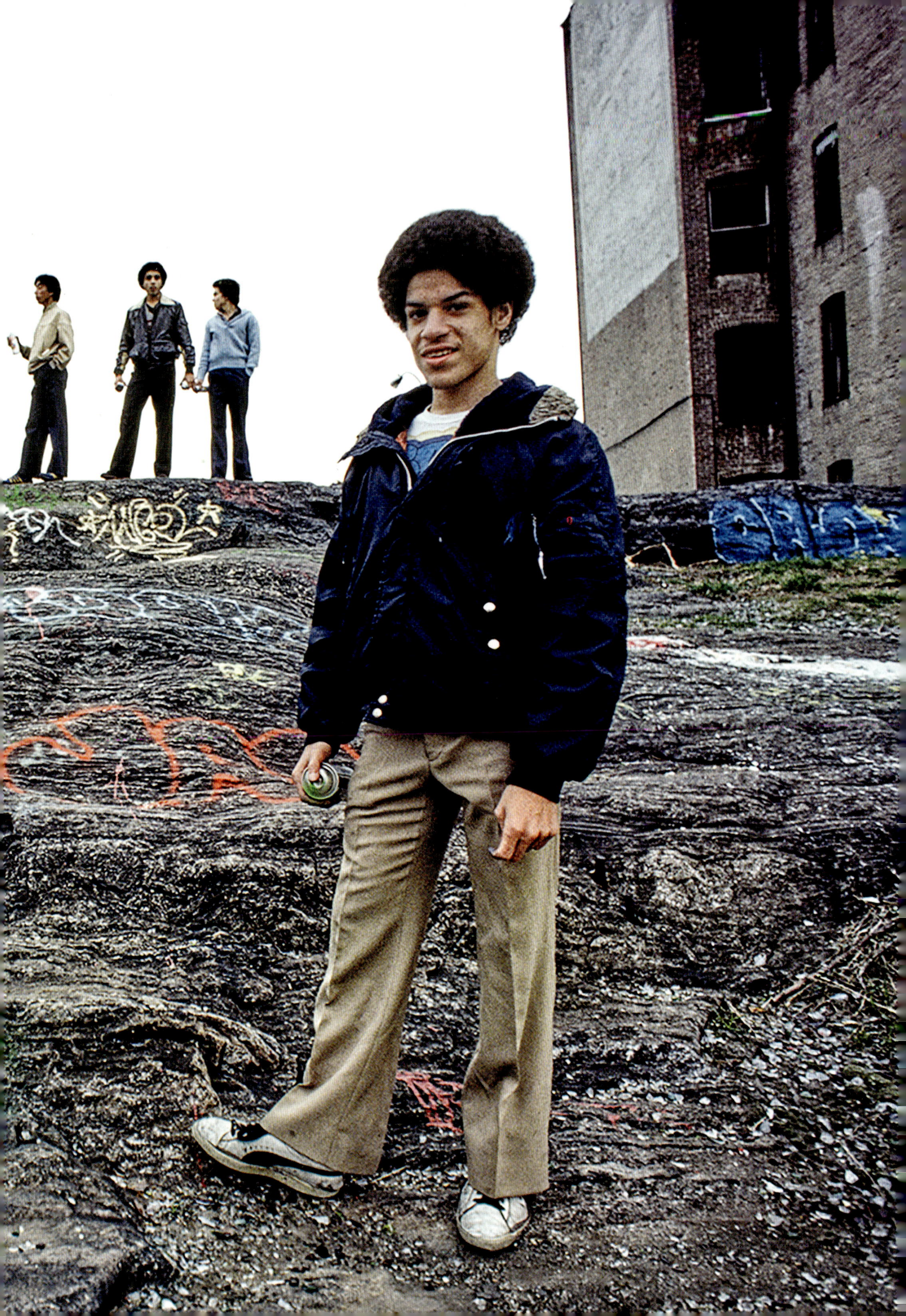

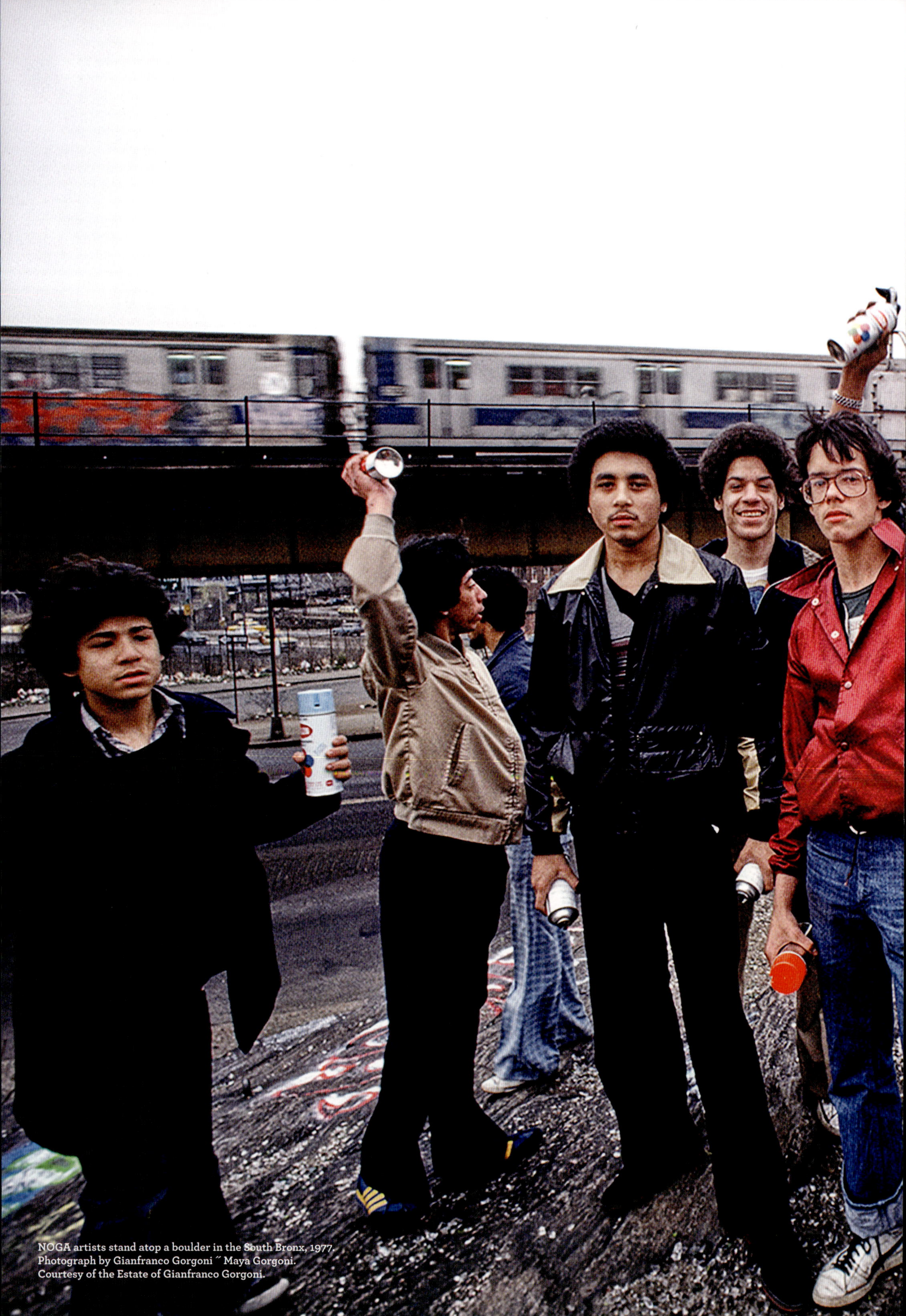

NOGA artists stand atop a boulder in the South Bronx, 1977.
Photograph by Gianfranco Gorgoni ~ Maya Gorgoni.
Courtesy of the Estate of Gianfranco Gorgoni.

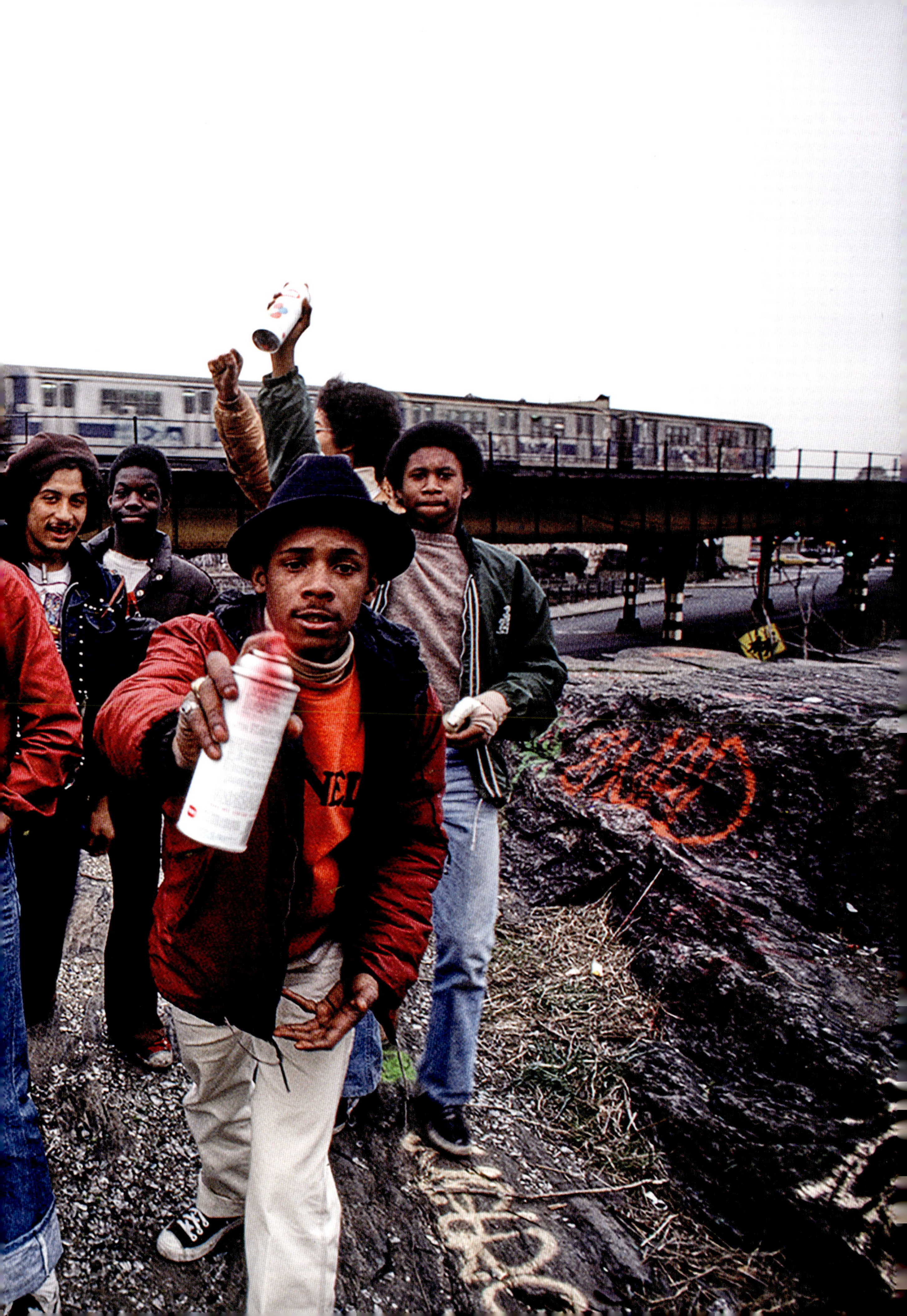

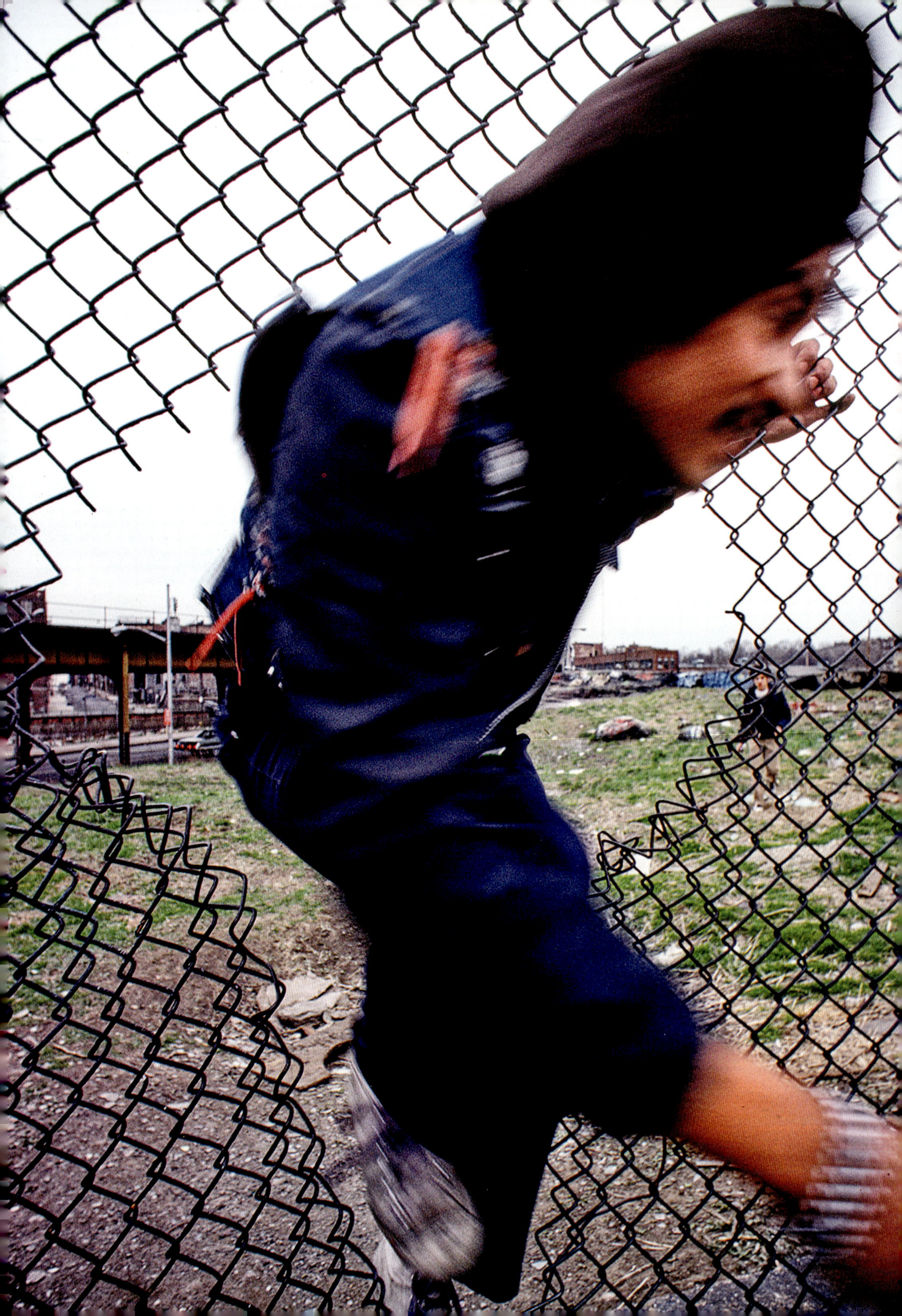

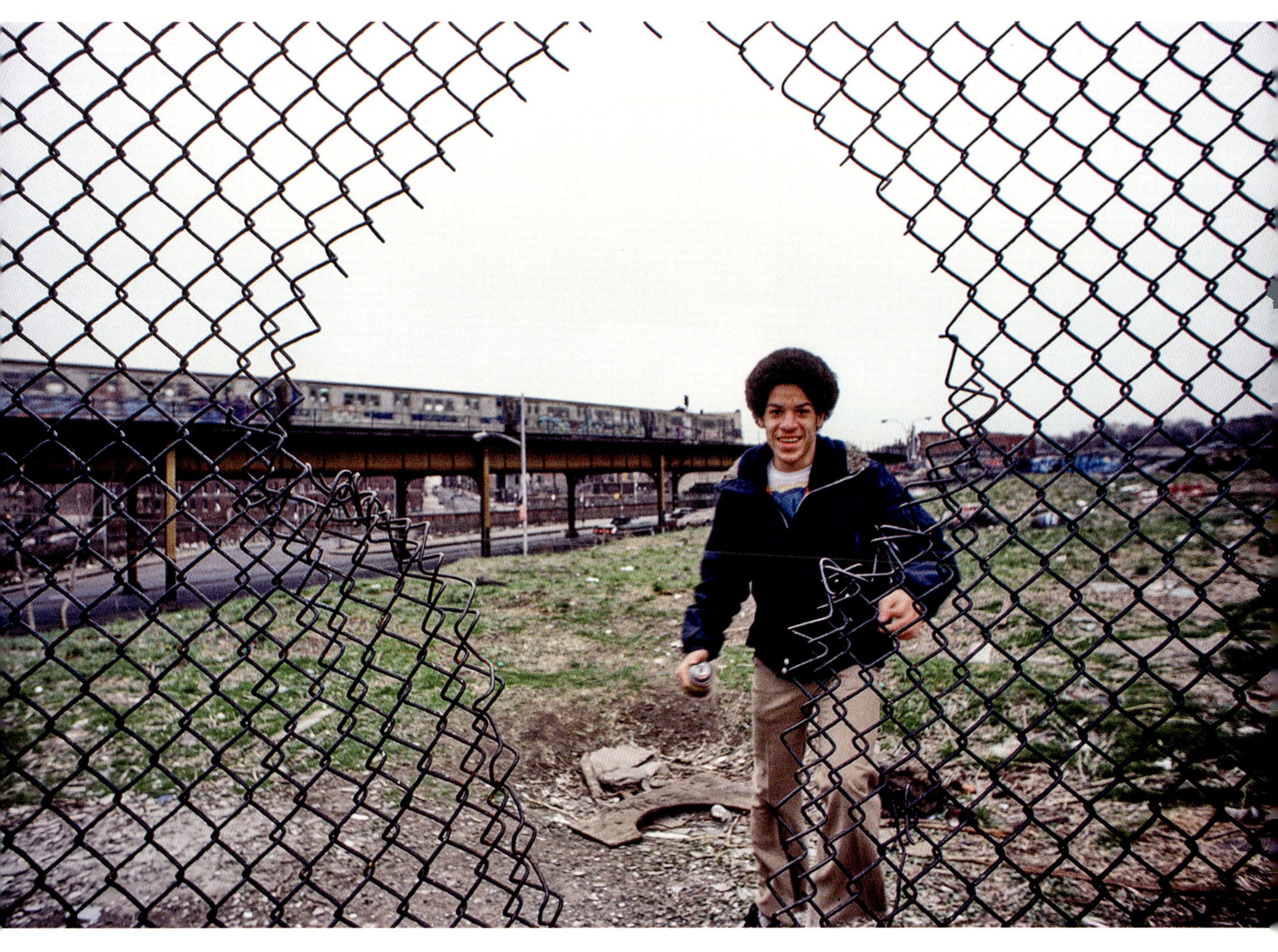

This spread:
KADE 198 and a NOGA member climb through a hole in the fence to
view the trains in the South Bronx, 1977.
Photographs by Gianfranco Gorgoni ~ Maya Gorgoni.
Courtesy of the Estate of Gianfranco Gorgoni.

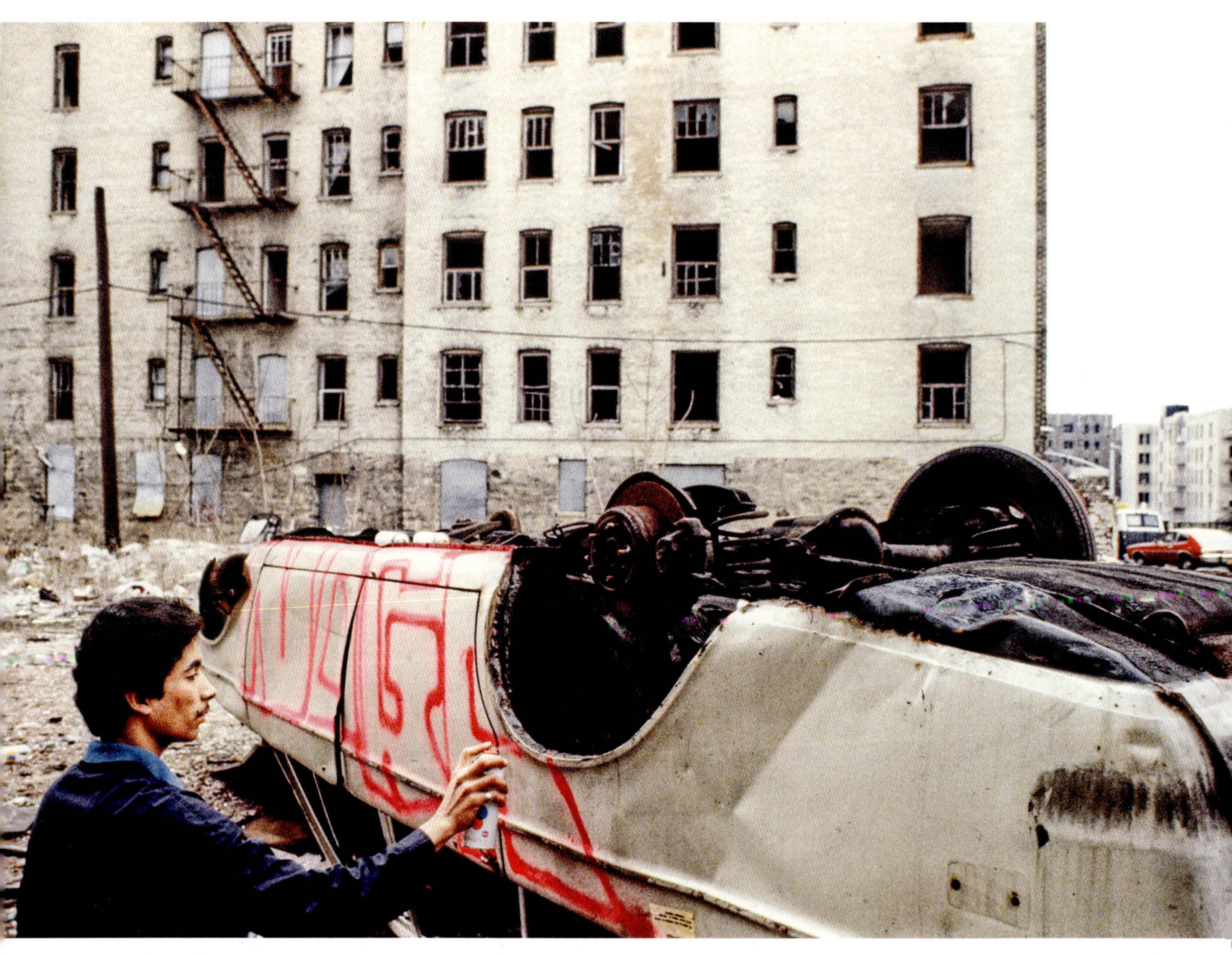

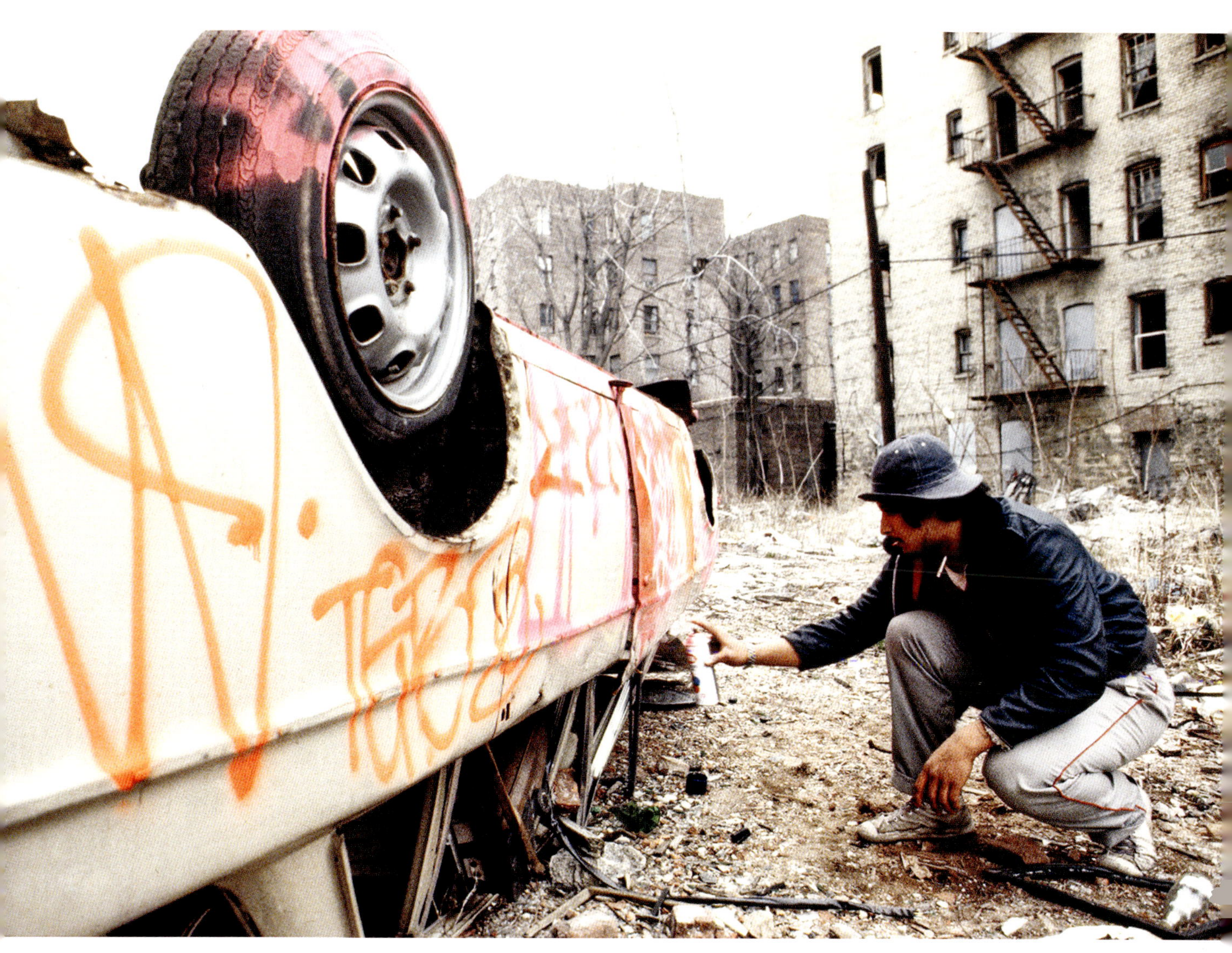

This spread:
A NOGA artist and **KADE** 198 paint an abandoned car in the South Bronx, 1977.
Photographs by Gianfranco Gorgoni ˜ Maya Gorgoni.
Courtesy of the Estate of Gianfranco Gorgoni.

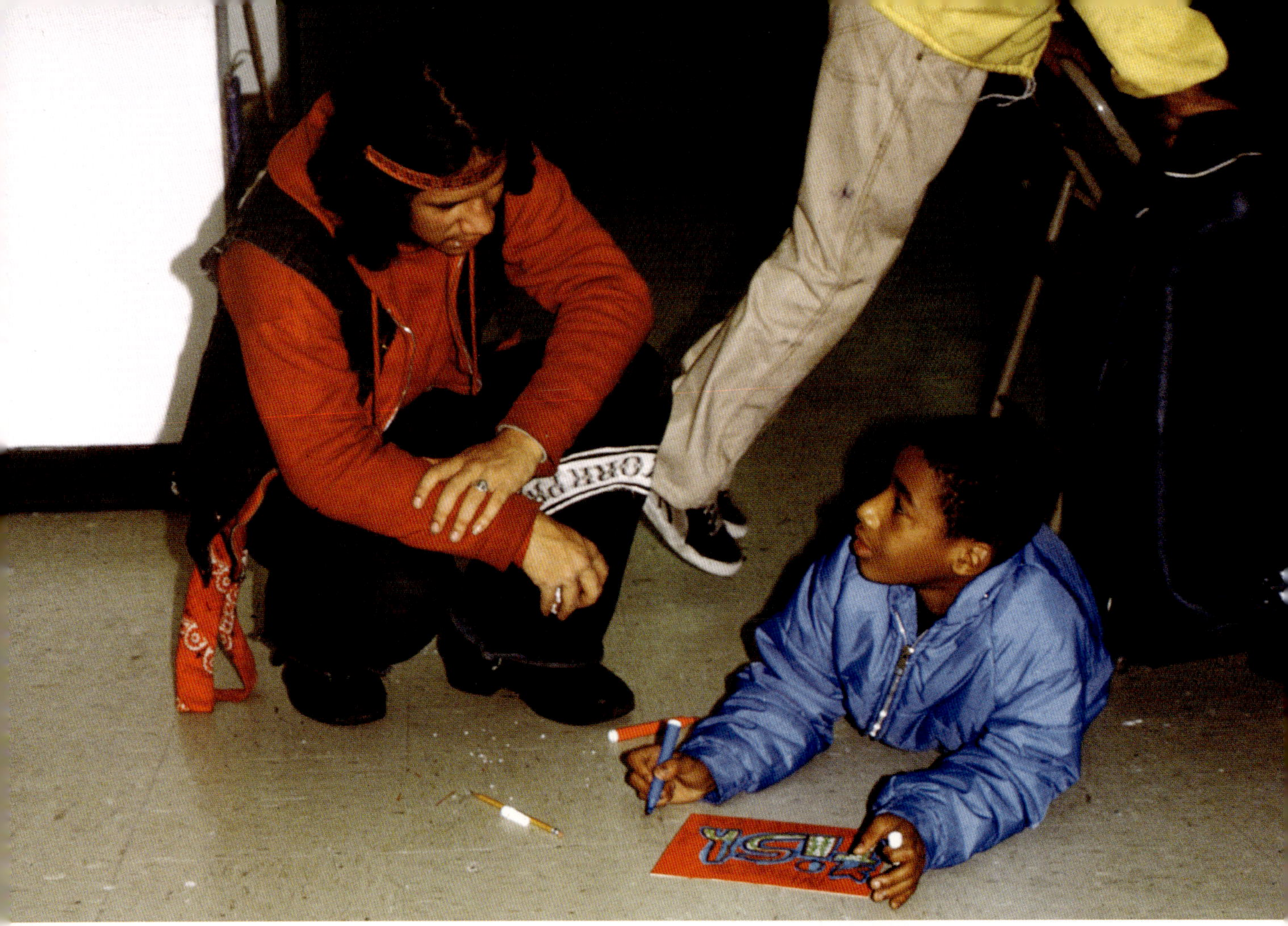

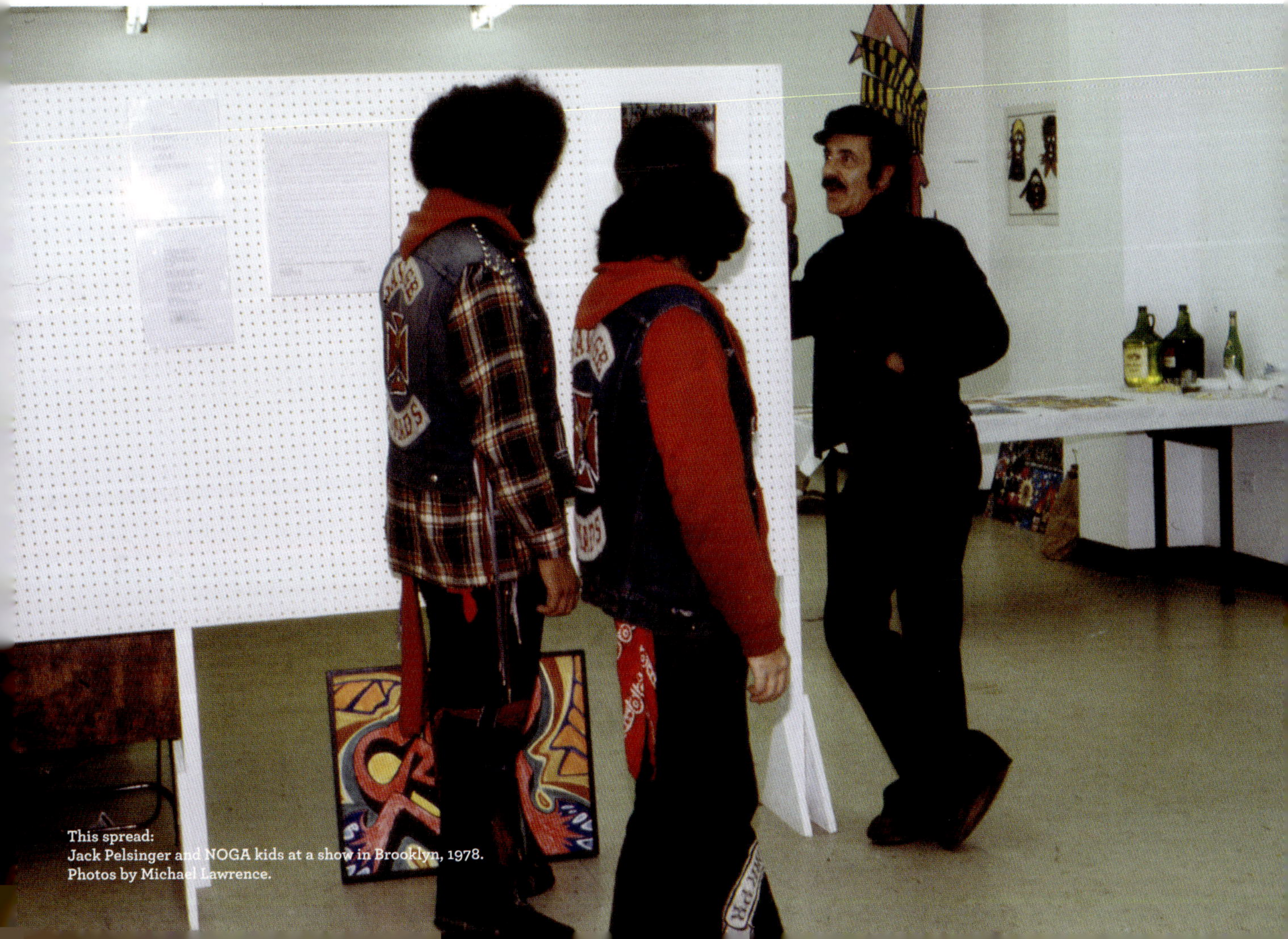

This spread:
Jack Pelsinger and NOGA kids at a show in Brooklyn, 1978.
Photos by Michael Lawrence.

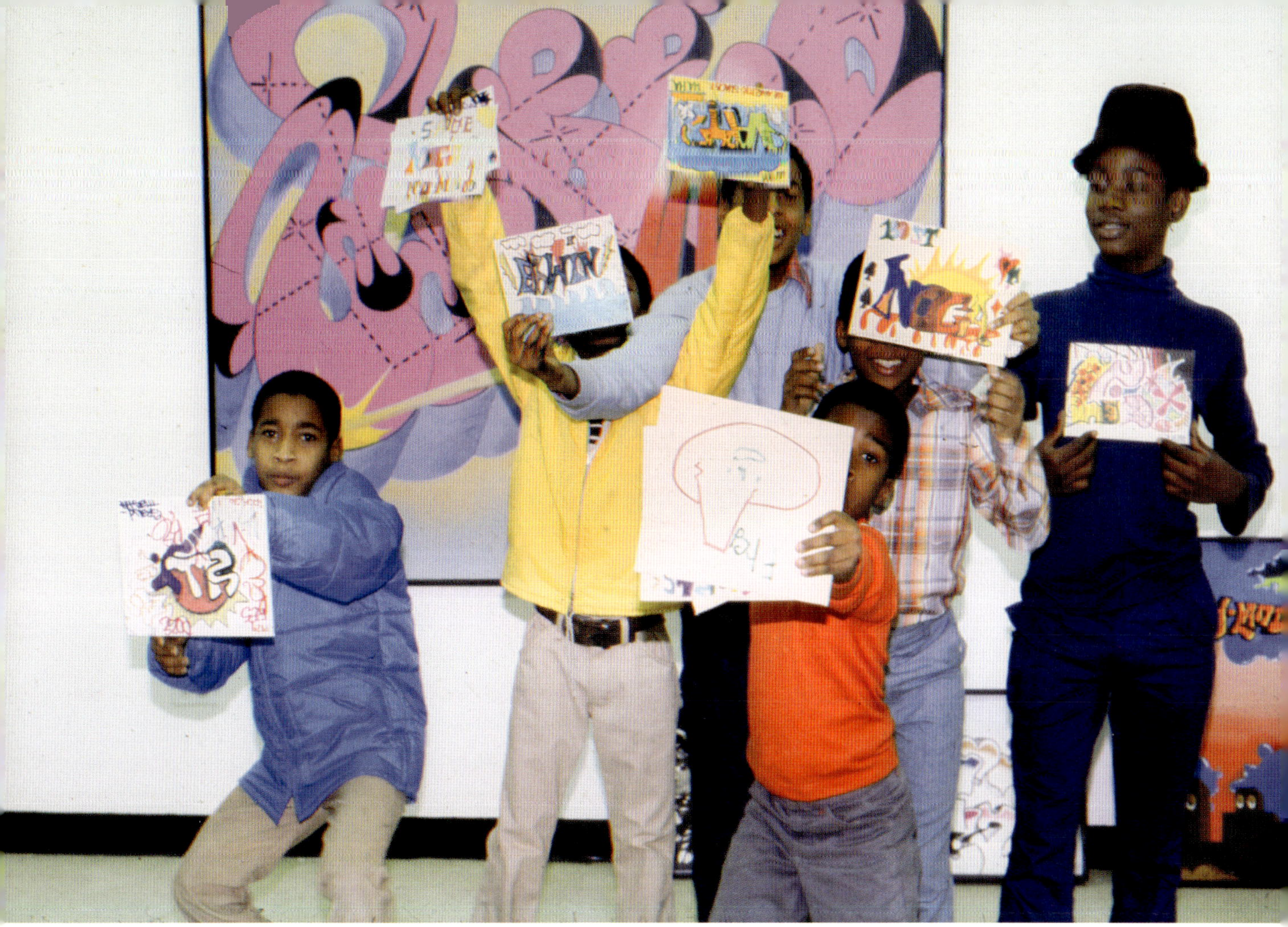

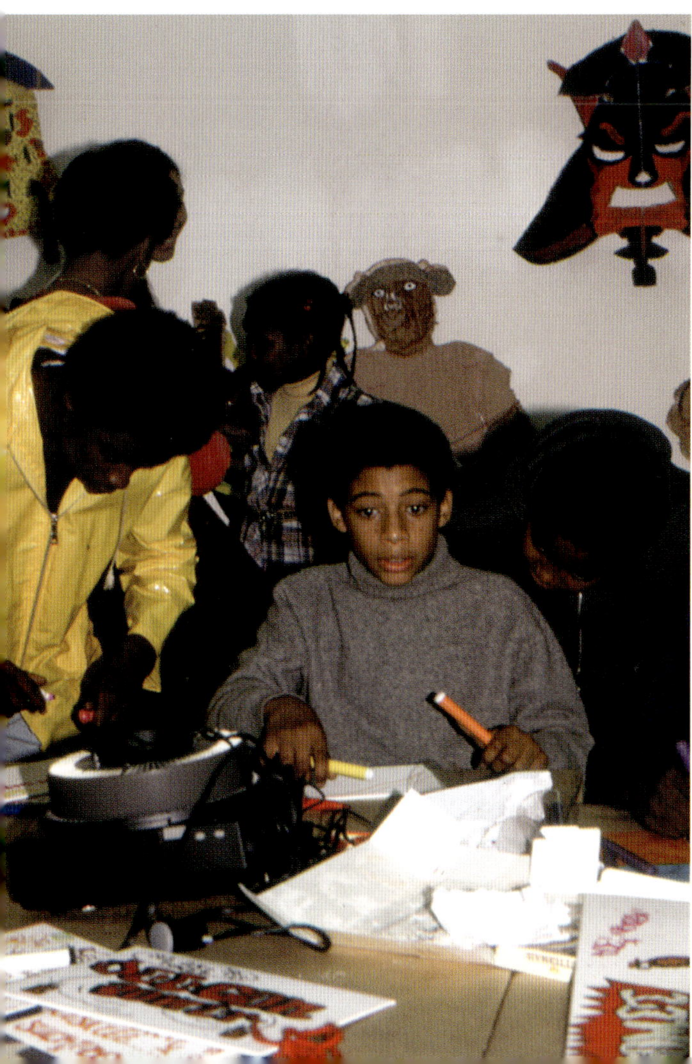
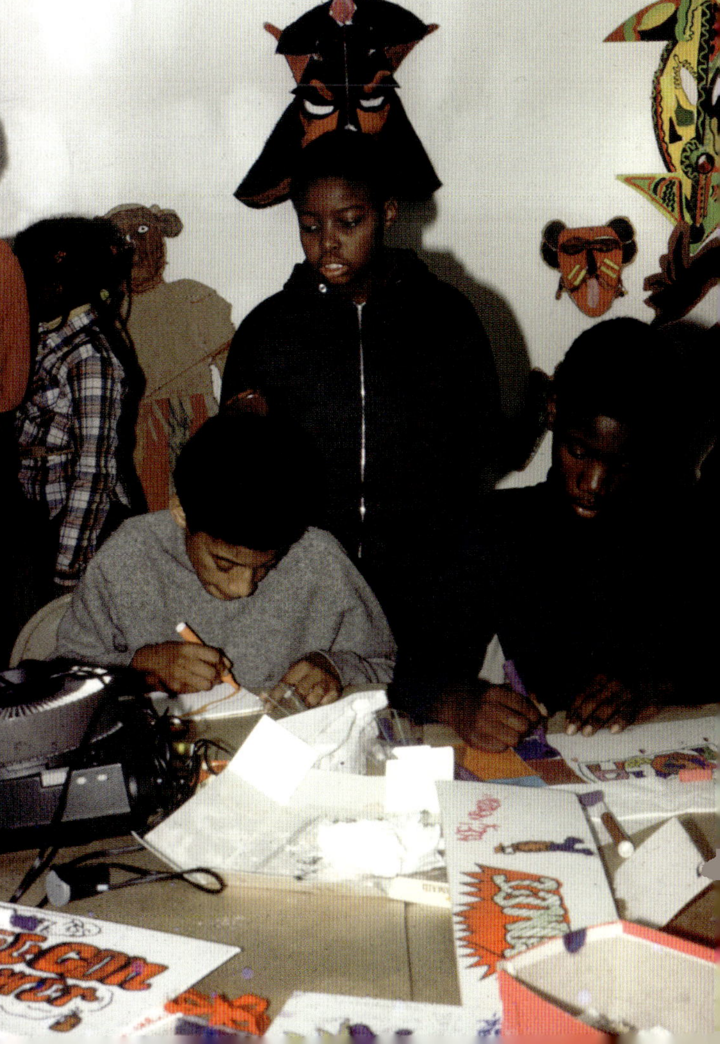

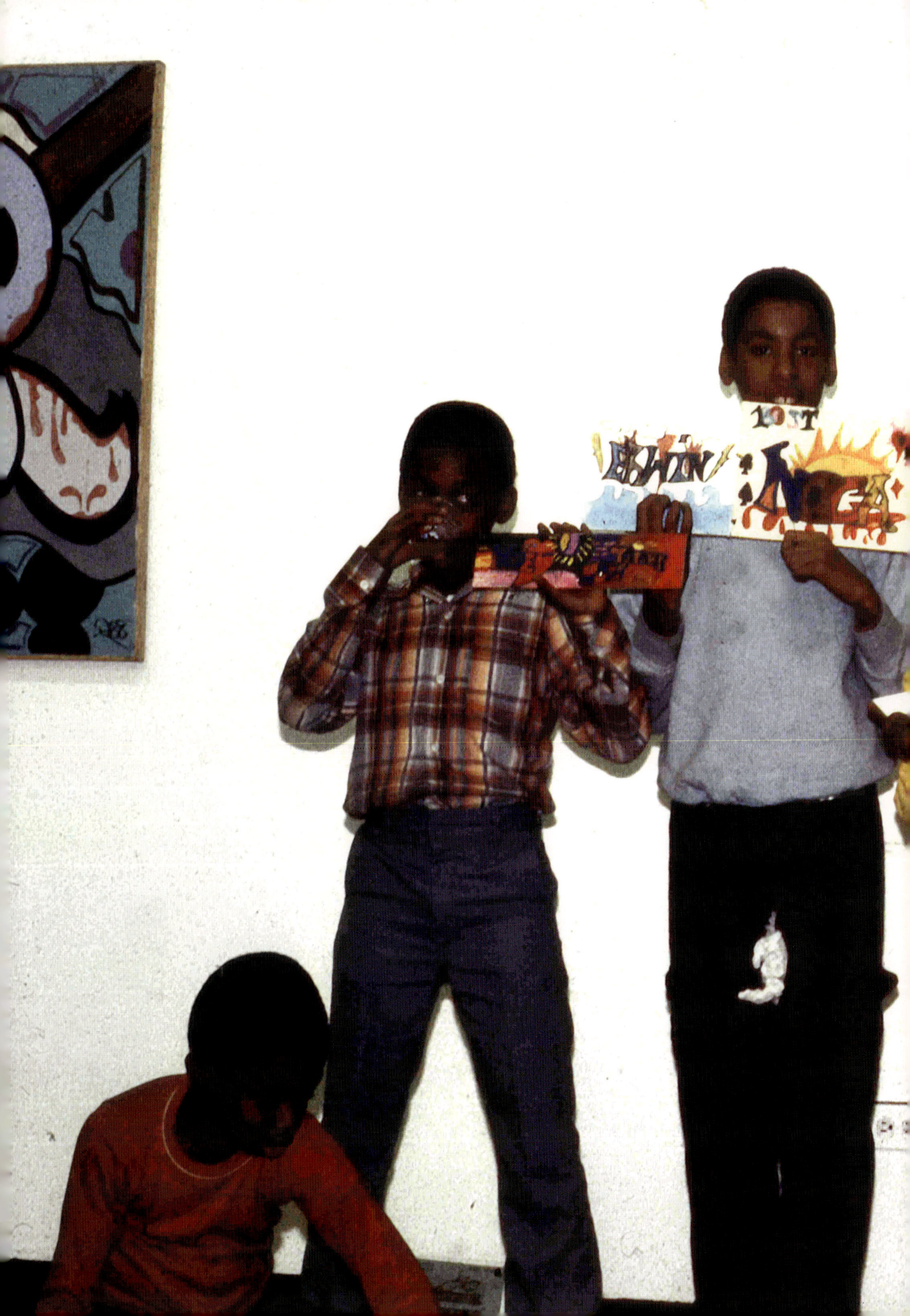
1ST
BHIN
NGA

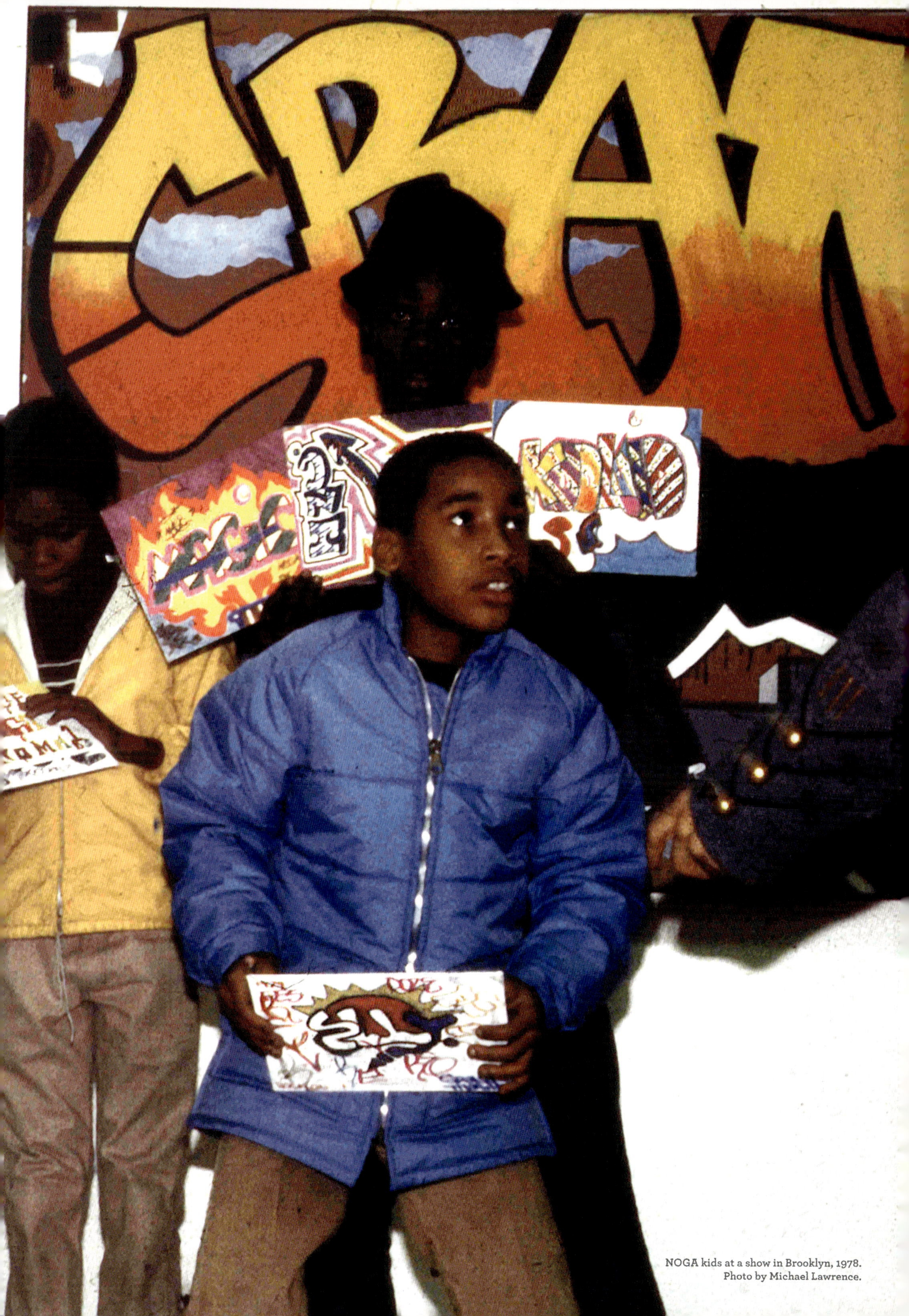

NOGA kids at a show in Brooklyn, 1978.
Photo by Michael Lawrence.

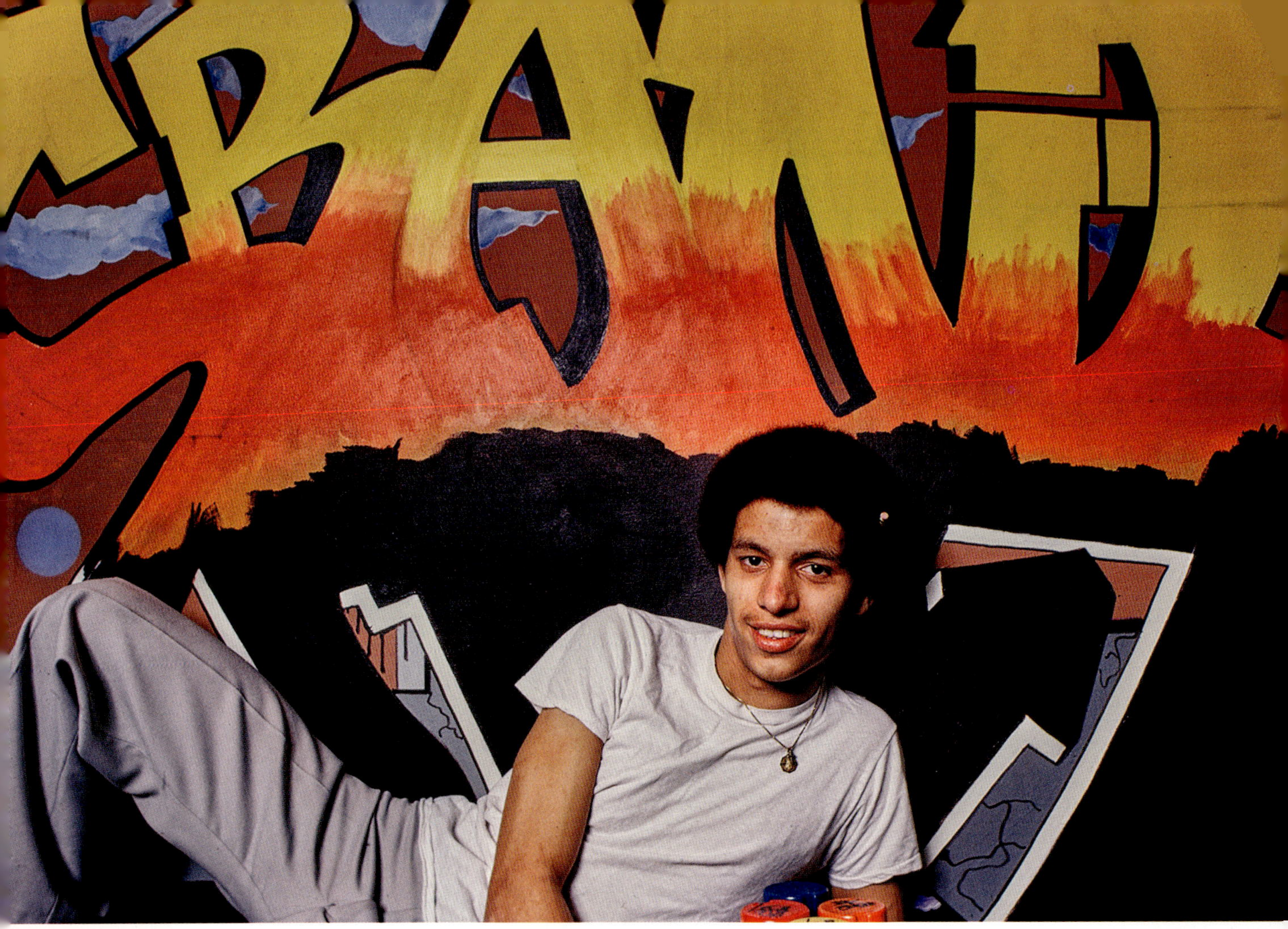

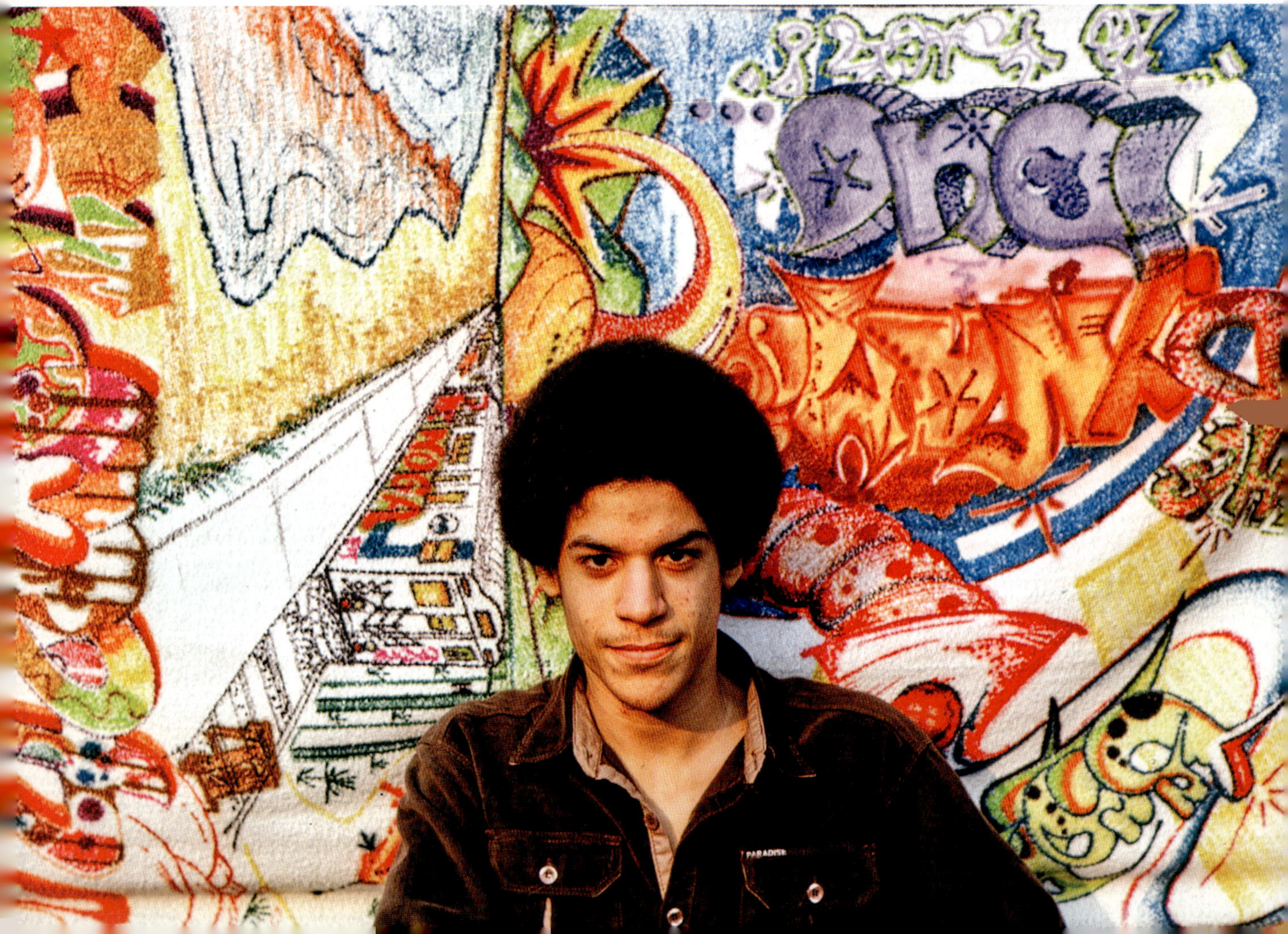

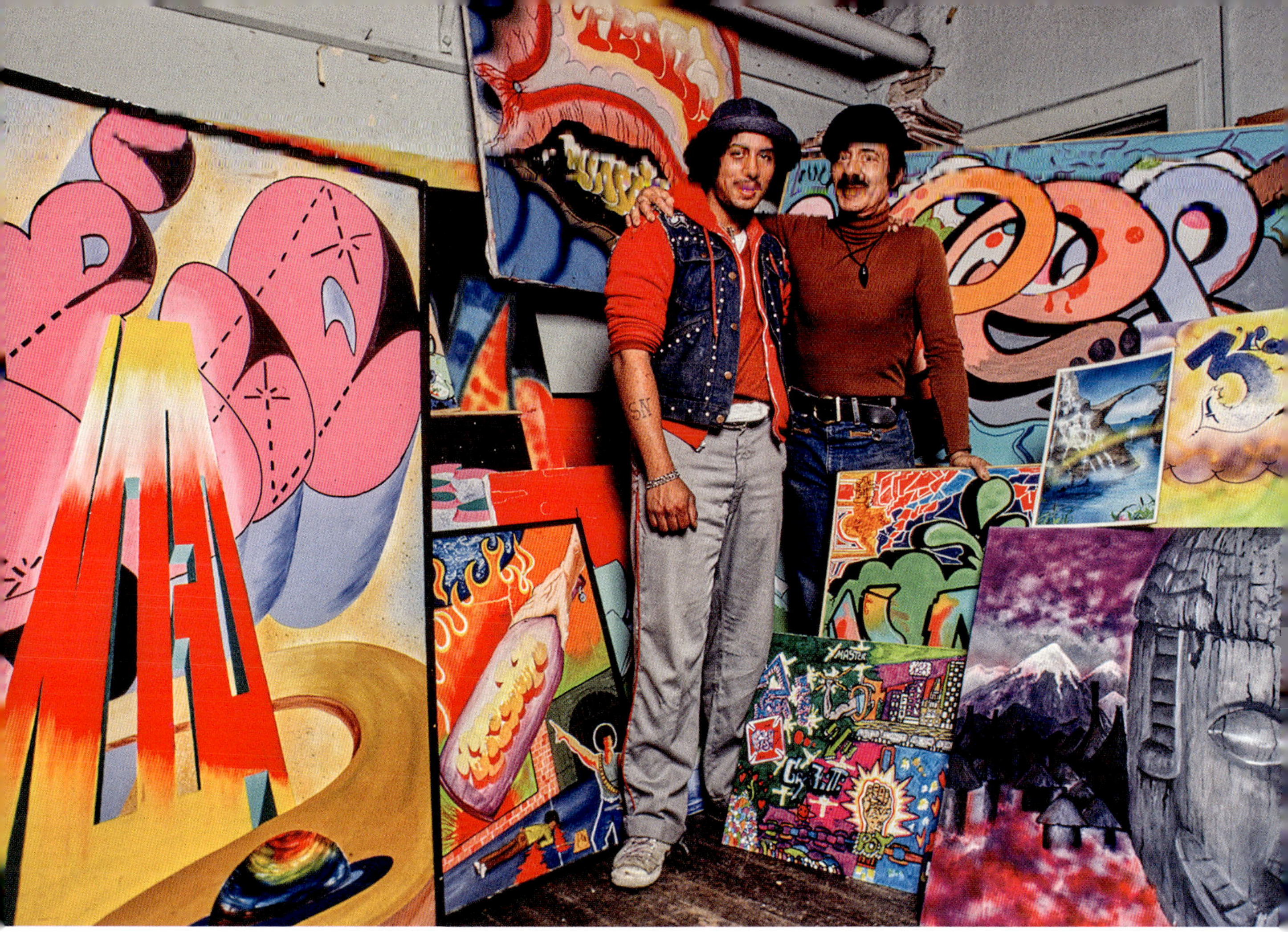

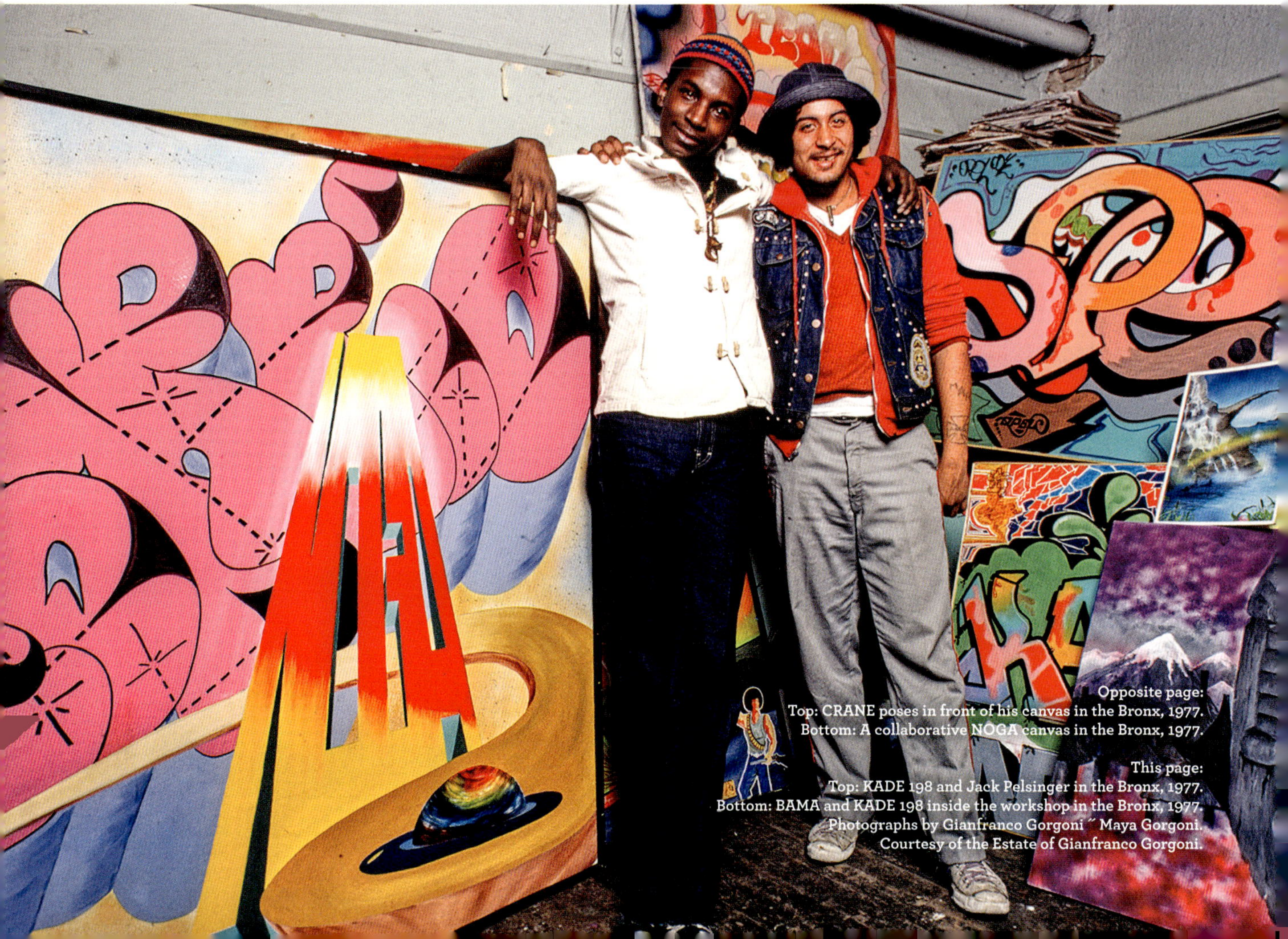

Opposite page:
Top: CRANE poses in front of his canvas in the Bronx, 1977.
Bottom: A collaborative NOGA canvas in the Bronx, 1977.

This page:
Top: KADE 198 and Jack Pelsinger in the Bronx, 1977.
Bottom: BAMA and KADE 198 inside the workshop in the Bronx, 1977.
Photographs by Gianfranco Gorgoni ˝ Maya Gorgoni.
Courtesy of the Estate of Gianfranco Gorgoni.

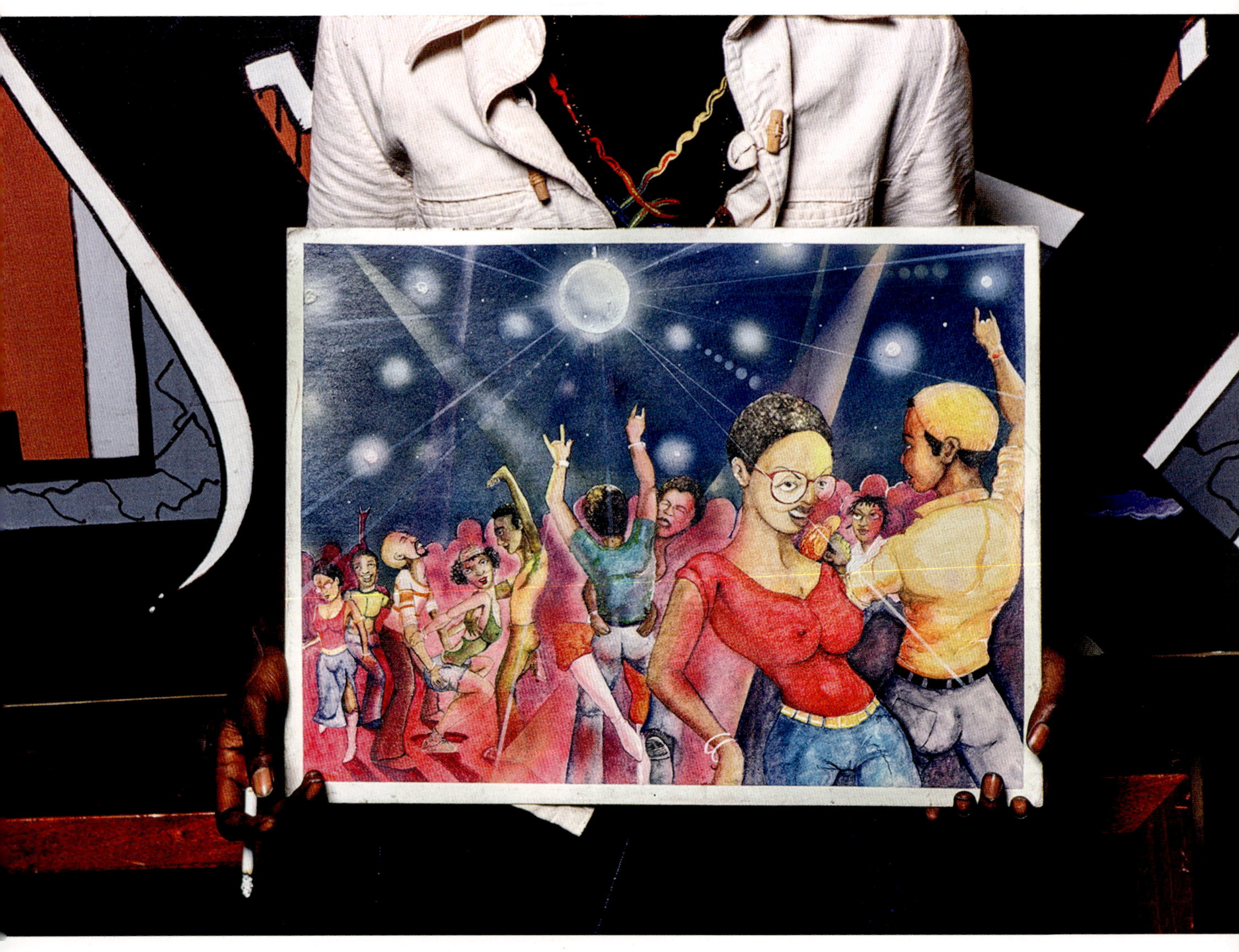

This page:
BAMA holding up one of his paintings in the Bronx, 1977.

Opposite page:
KADE 198 and BAMA reflect two different generations of writers on the Bronx, 1977.
Photographs by Gianfranco Gorgoni ˜ Maya Gorgoni.
Courtesy of the Estate of Gianfranco Gorgoni.

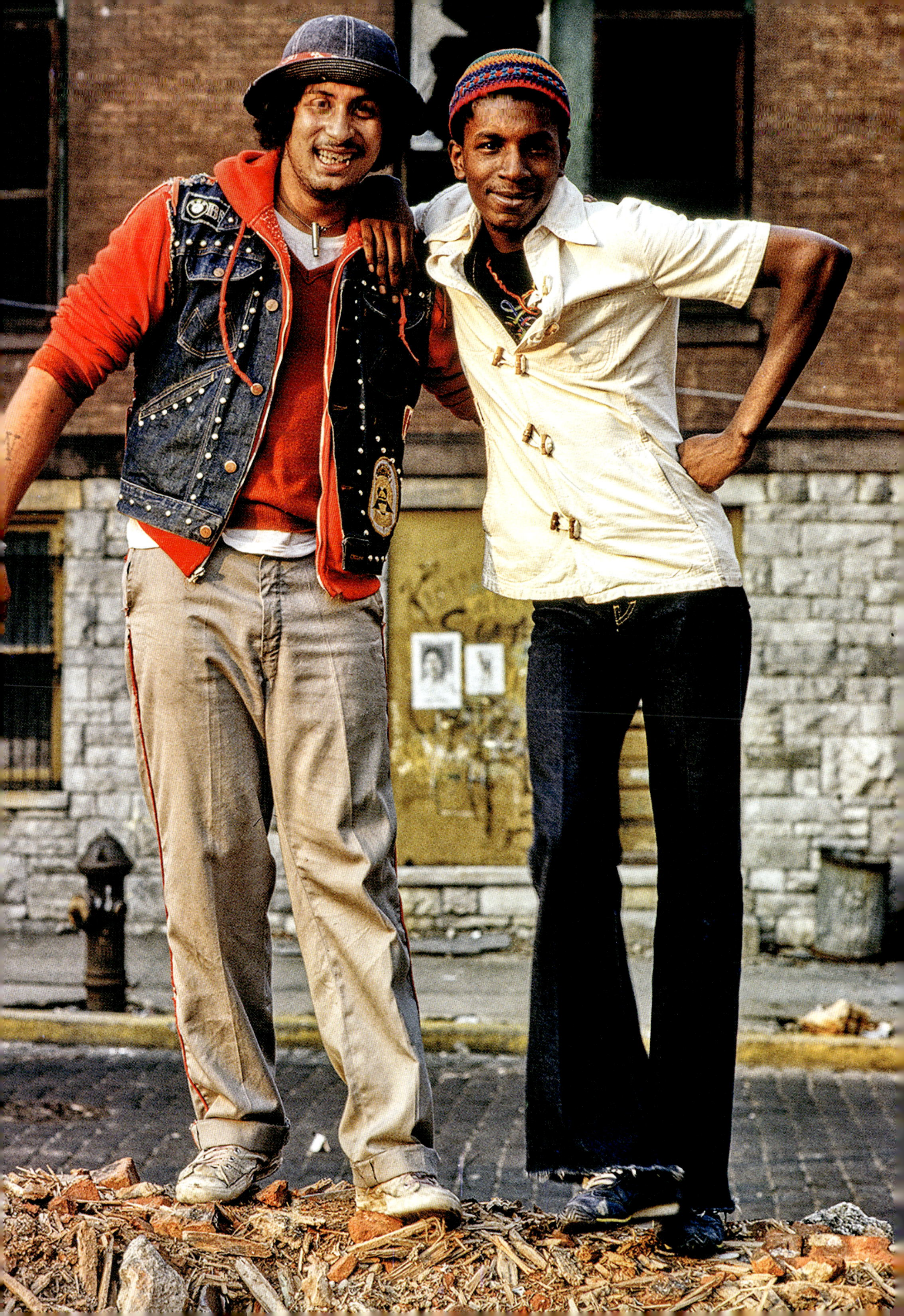

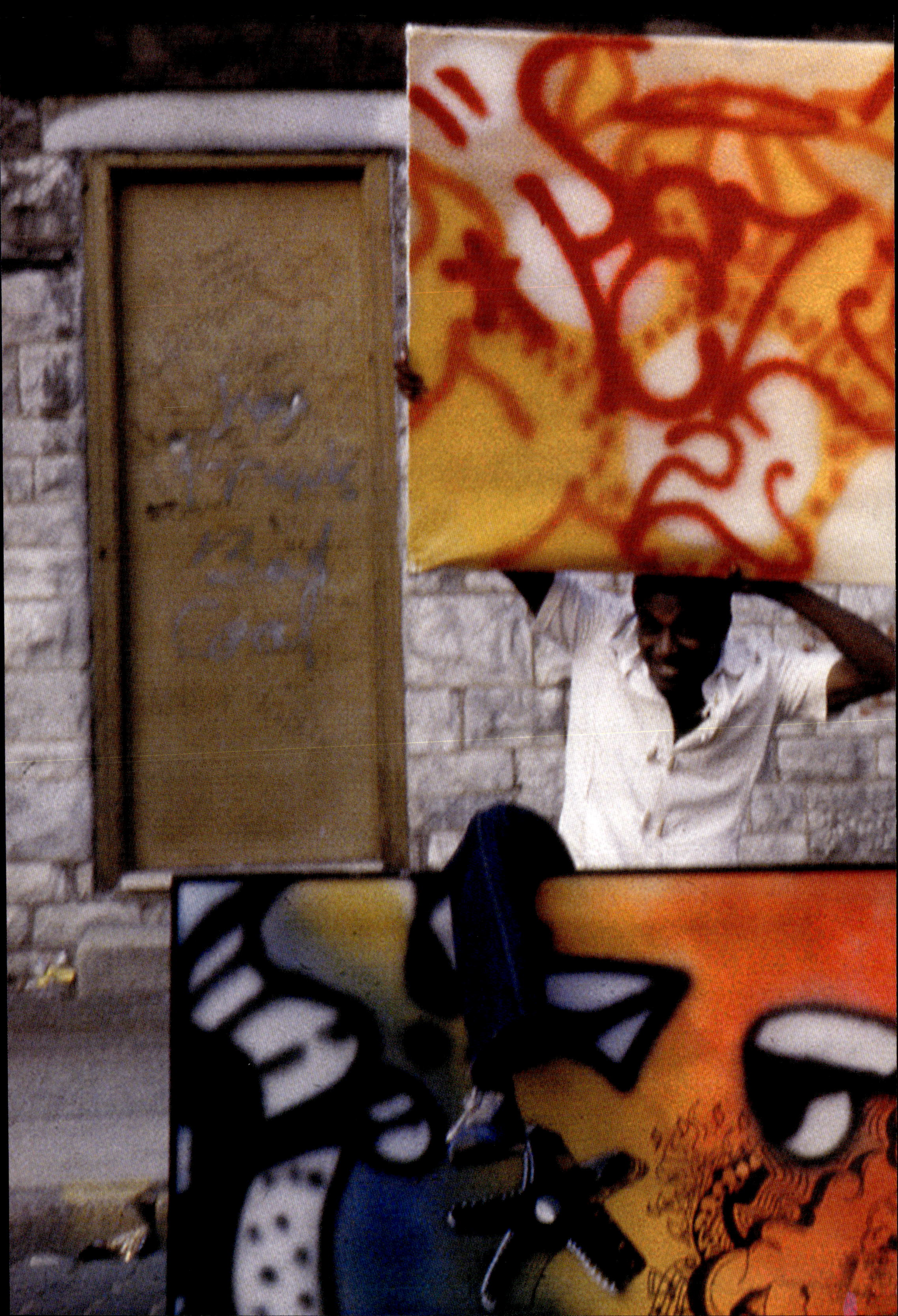

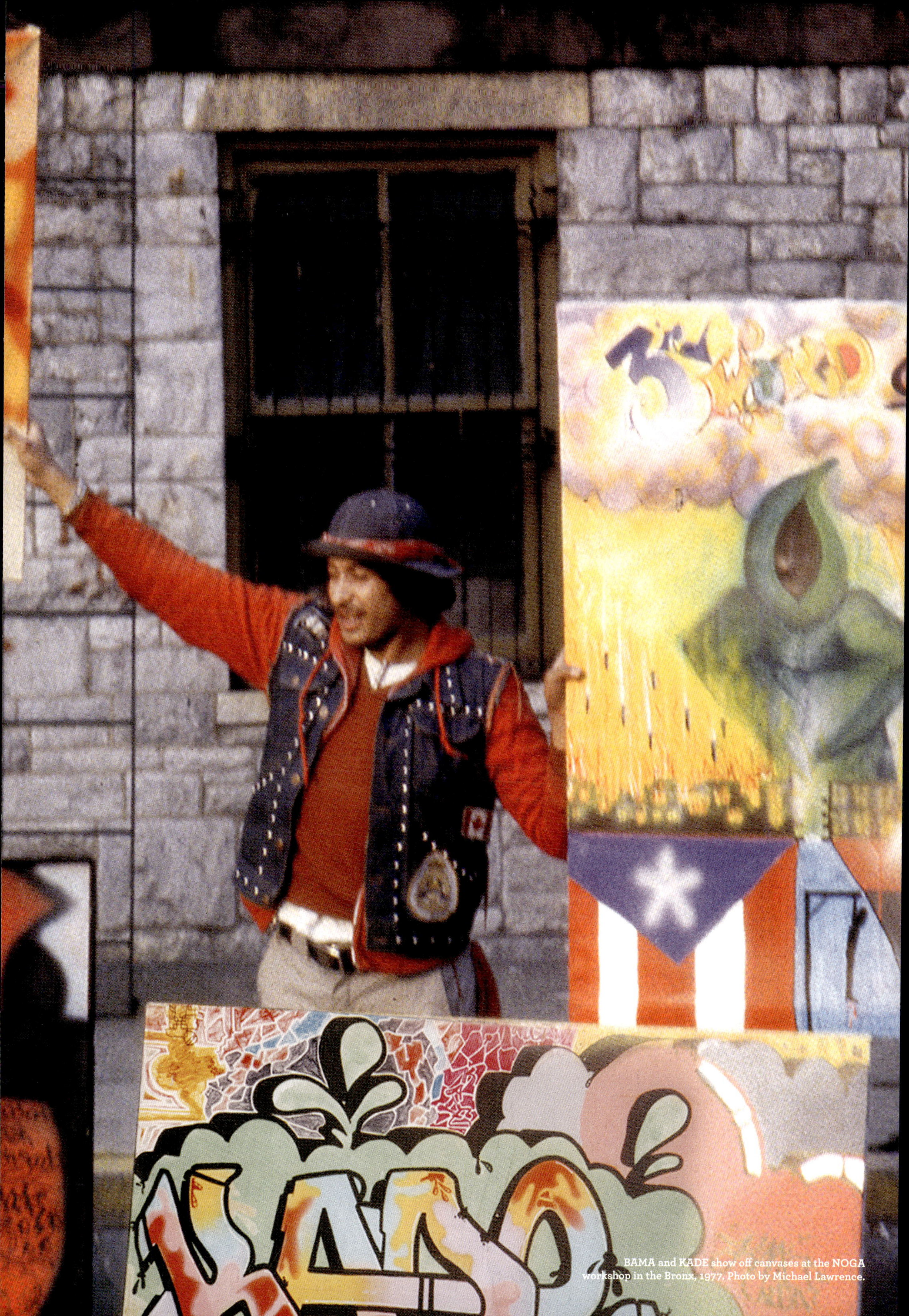

BAMA and KADE show off canvases at the NOGA workshop in the Bronx, 1977. Photo by Michael Lawrence.

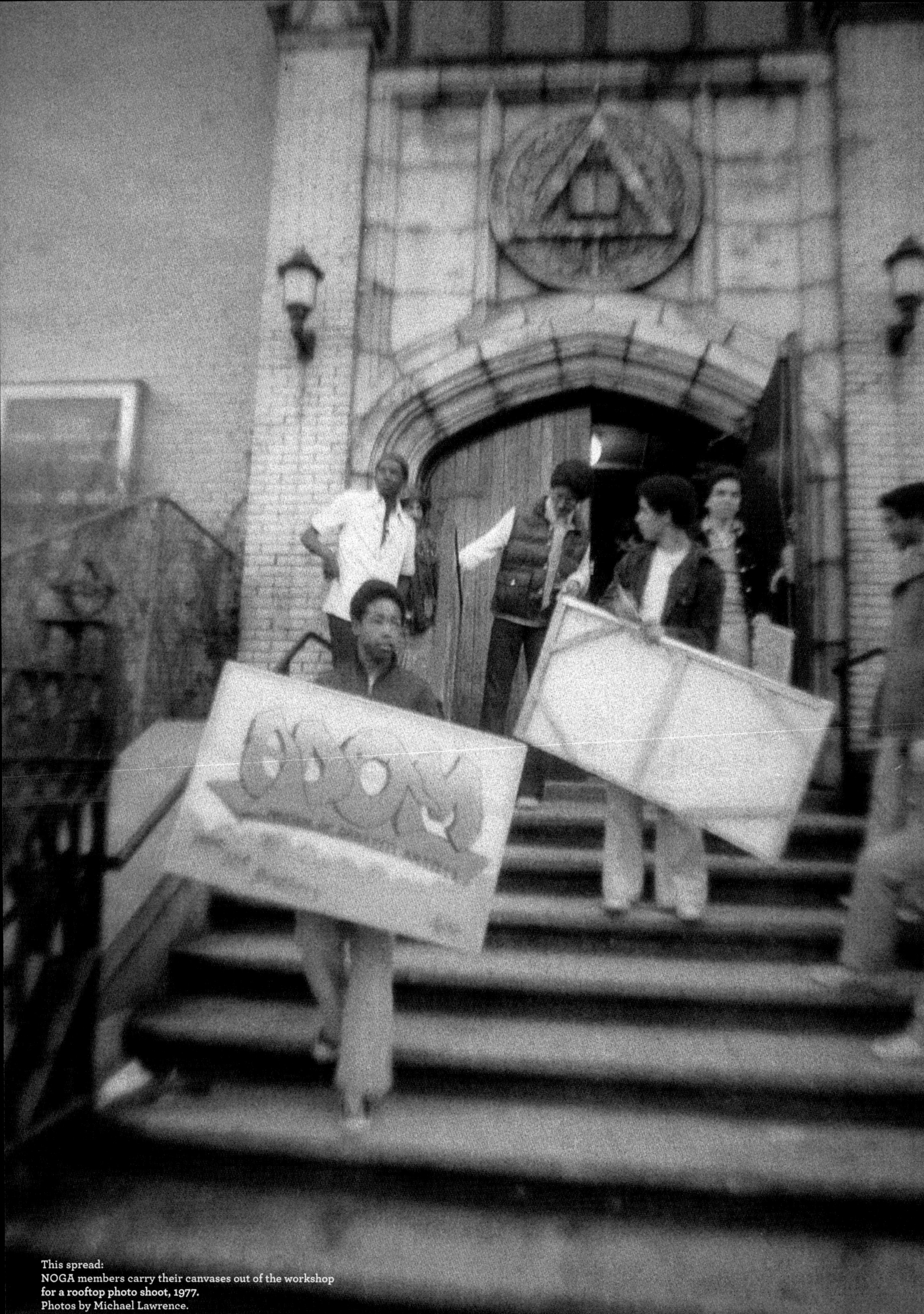

This spread:
NOGA members carry their canvases out of the workshop
for a rooftop photo shoot, 1977.
Photos by Michael Lawrence.

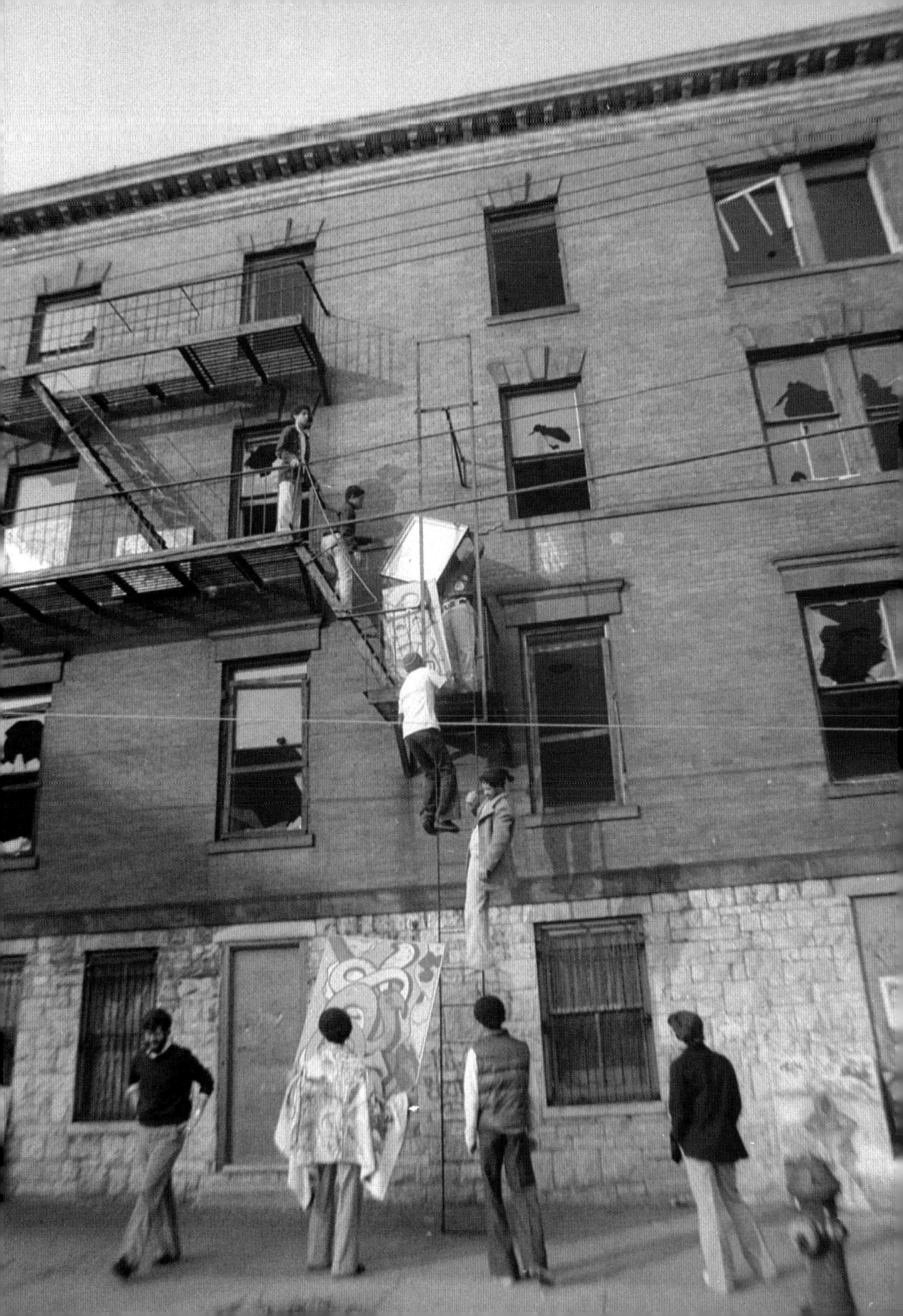

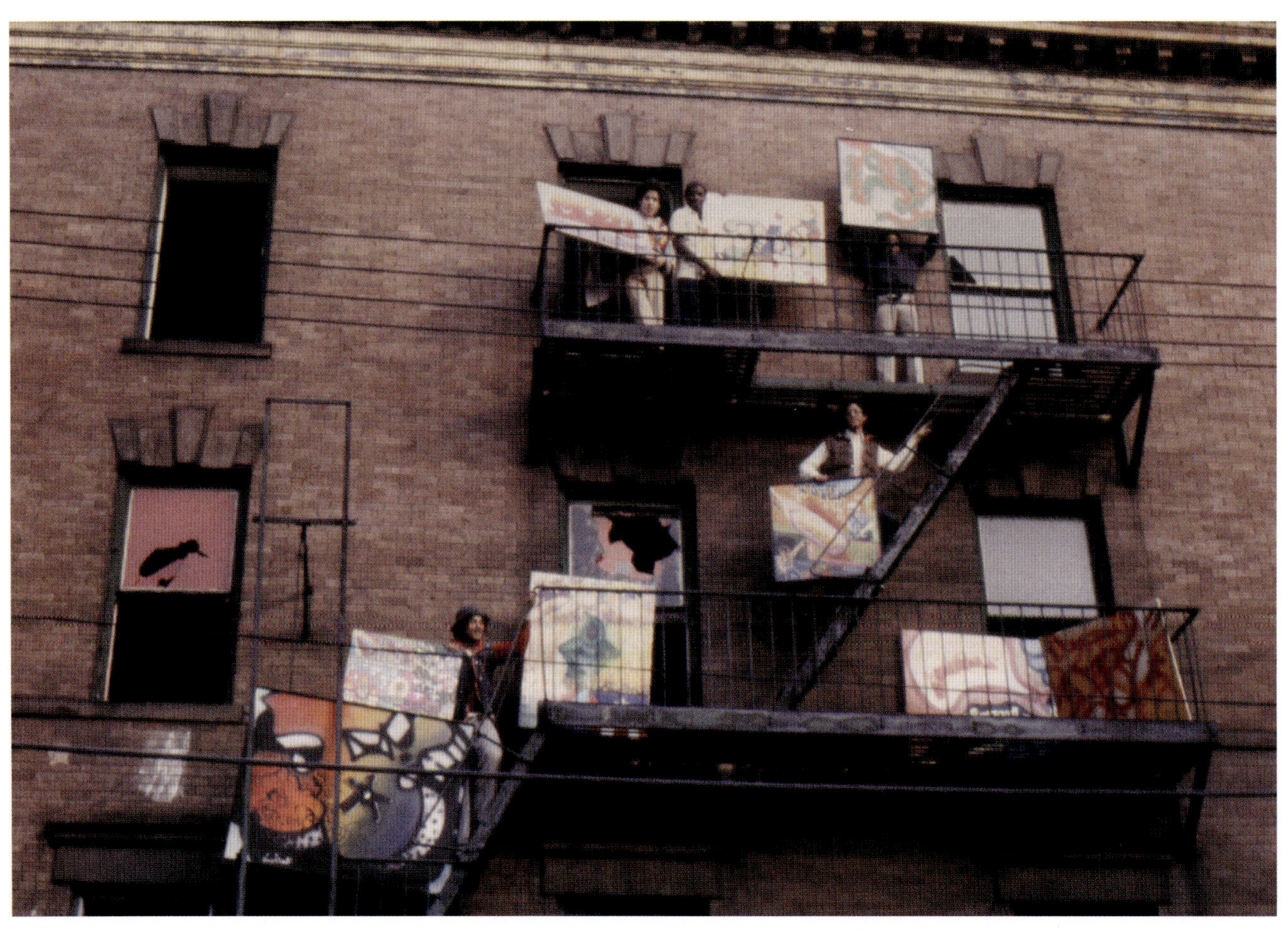

BAMA, KADE and DAZE show off
canvases on a fire escape near NOGA, 1977.
Photo by Michael Lawrence.

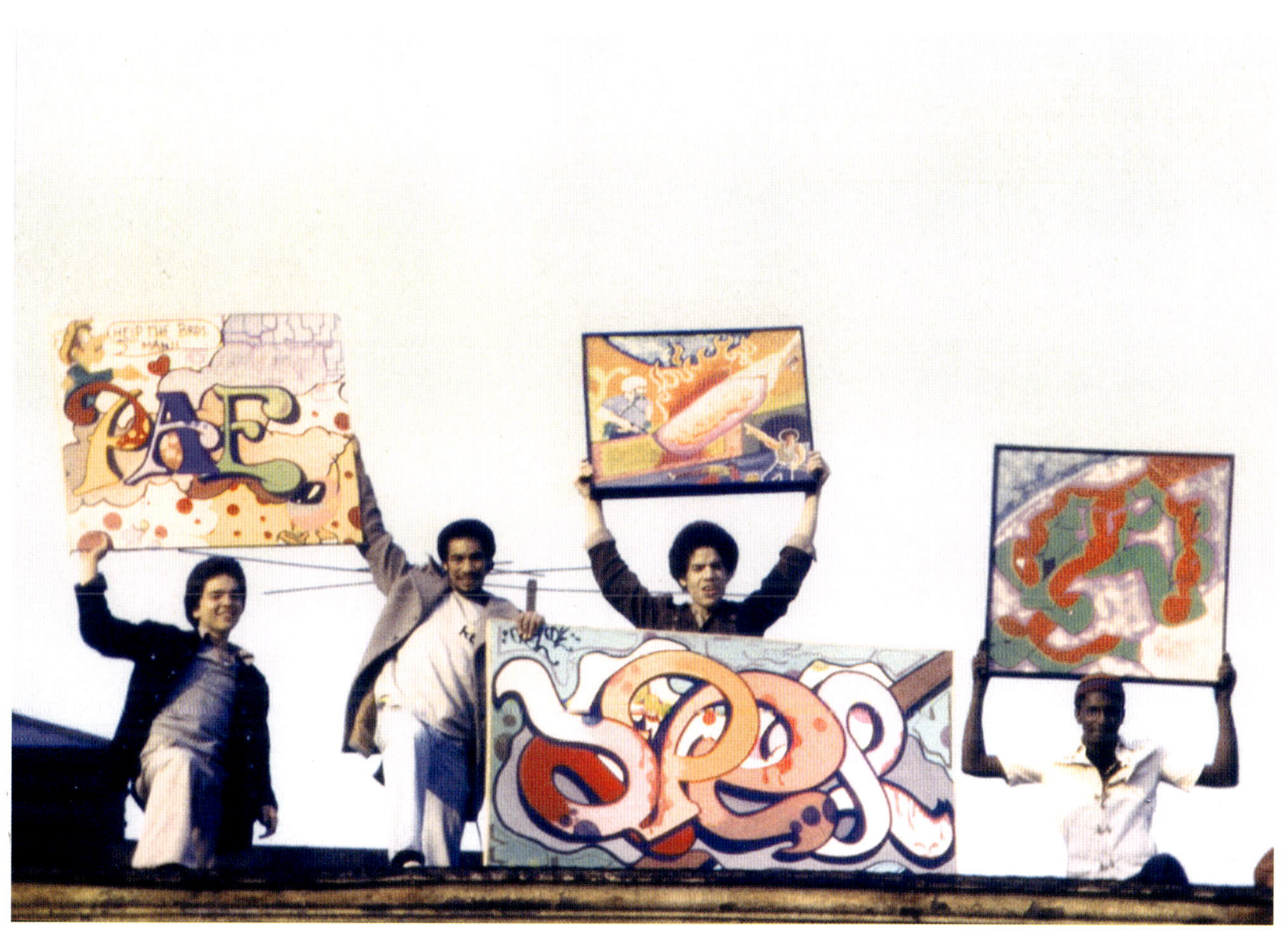

PAE, REE 2 and BAMA show new paintings on a rooftop in the Bronx, 1977.
Photo by Michael Lawrence.

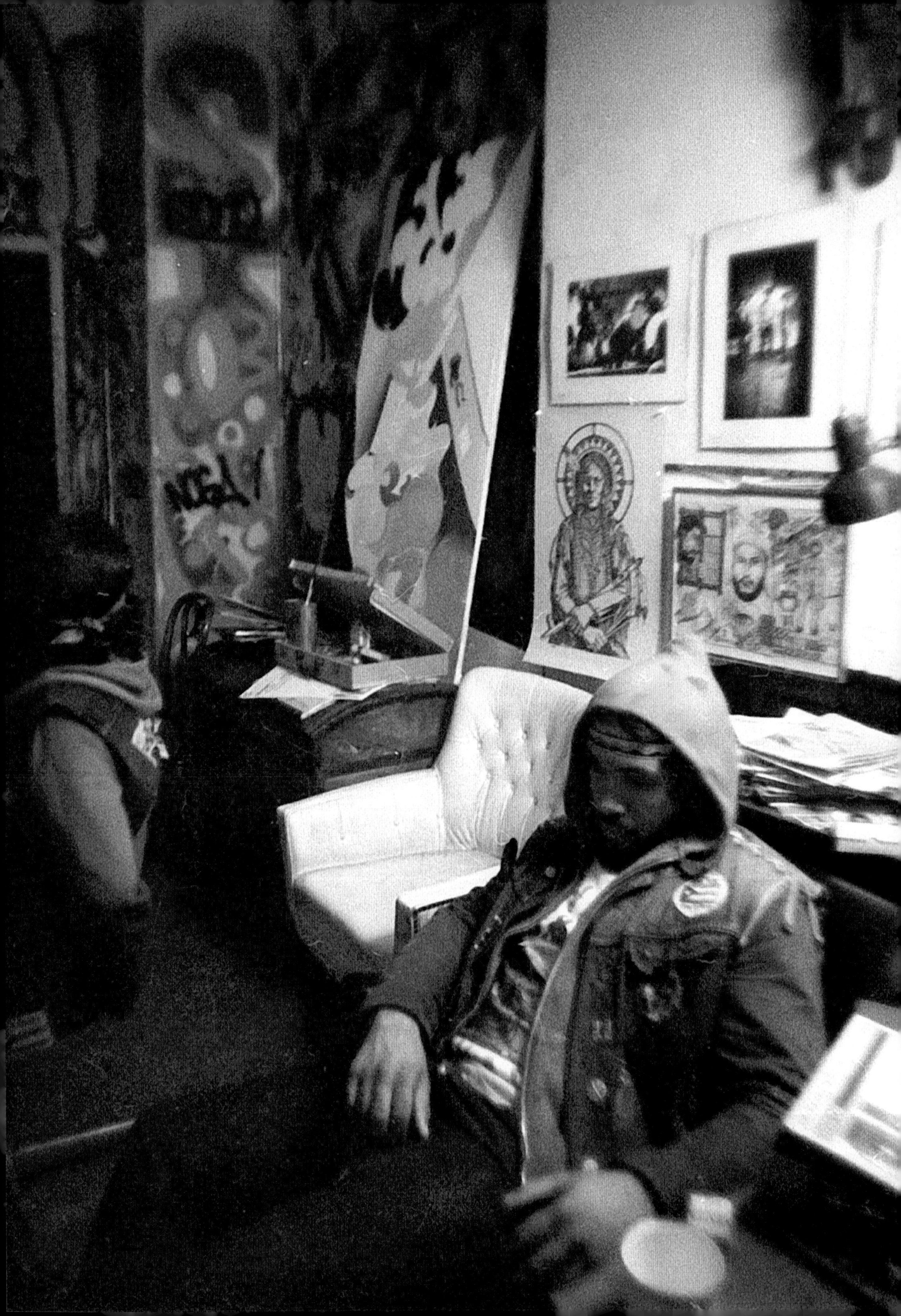

OUTLAWS

Things didn't always go so well when it came to selling the canvases, though. REE tells of one such incident: "We didn't really care about the money. At least I wasn't painting for money — we just wanted a chance to paint. One time we went out to East New York to a gallery that was showing our work, something Jack had set up. When we got there, all of the canvases were out on the sidewalk just sitting there. Jack said that there had been a mistake and that we could sell the paintings on the street. Some of us hung around for a while, then we took the train home. Sometimes the paintings would disappear; we thought they were going to City Corp and we were getting funding in return. Jack would take us all down to Pearl Paints and we'd buy a roll of canvas and build our own stretchers and paint some more."

Ironically, NOGA was getting funding from a more dubious source. Pelsinger and Lawrence had had enough of struggling to get their respective projects off the ground — life would be so much simpler with a little money floating around. Michael Lawrence tells of their newfound wealth:

"I remember that we were struggling. NOGA kept closing, my photography projects would get started and then remain unfinished — they were tough times. But it was the '70s, and everybody smoked weed. There was no stigma to it, and I had a way into that world. I knew some guys in Massachusetts that would sell me large quantities of high-quality weed that they grew in their backyards, so Jack and I went in on this together. We'd pool our money and I'd drive up there and get the weed and bring it back. Each morning I'd roll about 100 joints and pack 30 nickel bags and by ten o'clock there was a line outside our door.

"Things turned around quickly for us; we had a huge profit margin and I put most of mine back into my work. Once, when I was away, Jack was held up at gunpoint, and that was a problem we had to solve. Jack had connections with both the SAVAGE NO-MADS and the SAVAGE SKULLS. He had always wanted to work with the gangs in a positive way, so he started to invite them over more frequently. They got free weed, and we were never robbed again. We became friendly with most of the gang members and that allowed me to get good shots of them while they were relaxed and at ease. Dealing weed lasted about two years for us and while the money was good, it took up a lot of time from our own projects. It was also becoming a problem because Jack took great pains to make sure no one at NOGA knew. He understood he was dealing with young people and took that seriously."

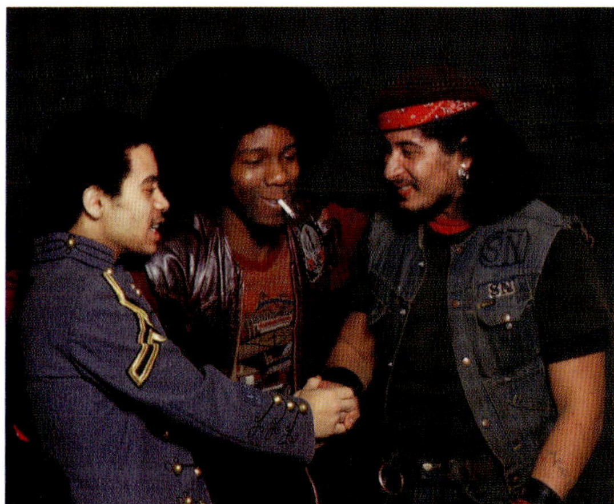

BLOOD TEA with SAVAGE NOMADS, 1980. Photo by Michael Lawrence.

By 1978, REE had become a father and hanging out at NOGA was no longer a priority. The organization moved one final time, into a Boys Club nearby. The newer generation of writers had moved from NOGA to the Writers Bench at 149th Street, where they could view the subways where their masterpieces ran. With few supplies and sparse attendance, Jack Pelsinger could no longer afford to keep NOGA open. Its doors were shut for good in 1979. Pelsinger continued to work from his home, looking for more grant money, but gave up the next year. In the early '80s he took a full-time job as a fundraiser with the National Organization for Women.

In 1980, graffiti would emerge above ground in various ways, most notably with the *GAS (Graffiti Art Success for America)* show at Fashion Moda, curated by CRASH. There was a buzz in the city as graffiti became a commodity. Writers left the subways and started painting on canvas. It is possible that if Pelsinger had just hung on a few more years, NOGA would've reaped those dividends, but it's also unlikely. Pelsinger and NOGA seemed defined by the social mores of the '60s and '70s, where money took a back seat to social activism. For those who were there, it seemed that NOGA was at its best when everyone had a chance to paint, and BLOOD TEA pounded out his ubiquitous rhythm on the conga drums.

Opposite page:
SHOTGUN, a SAVAGE NOMAD, at Jack Pelsinger's apartment in Manhattan, 1979.
Photo by Michael Lawrence.

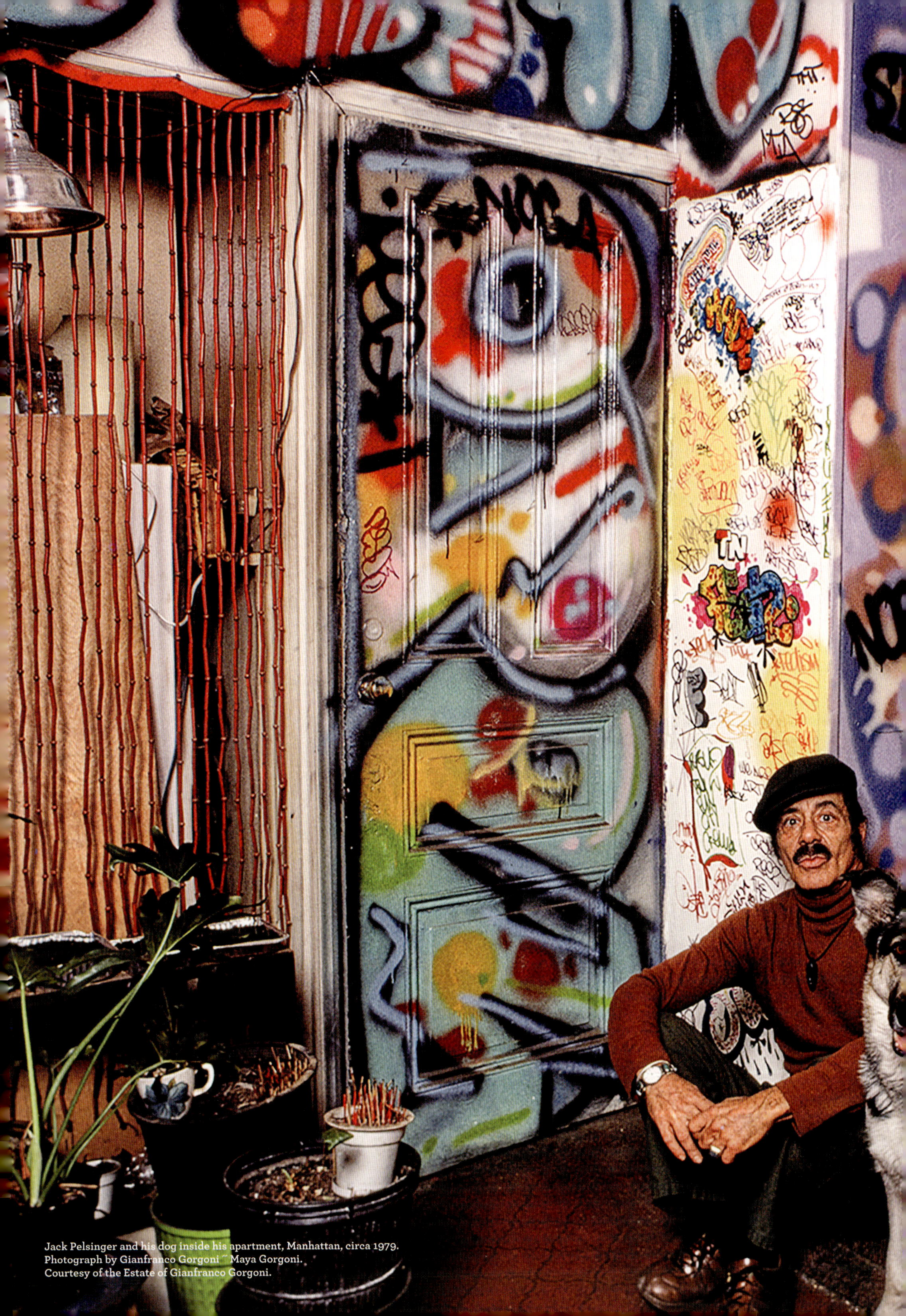

Jack Pelsinger and his dog inside his apartment, Manhattan, circa 1979.
Photograph by Gianfranco Gorgoni ˜ Maya Gorgoni.
Courtesy of the Estate of Gianfranco Gorgoni.

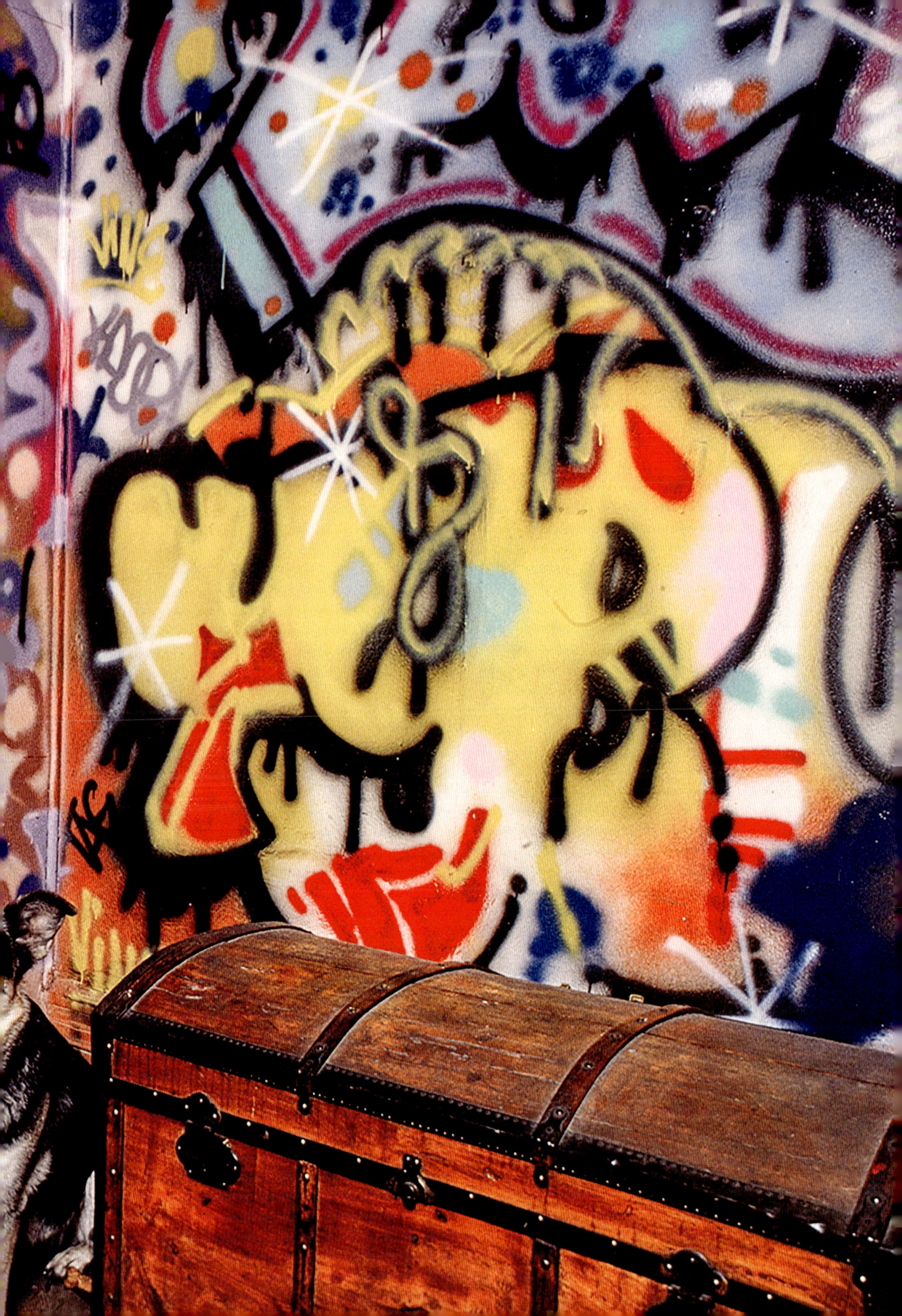

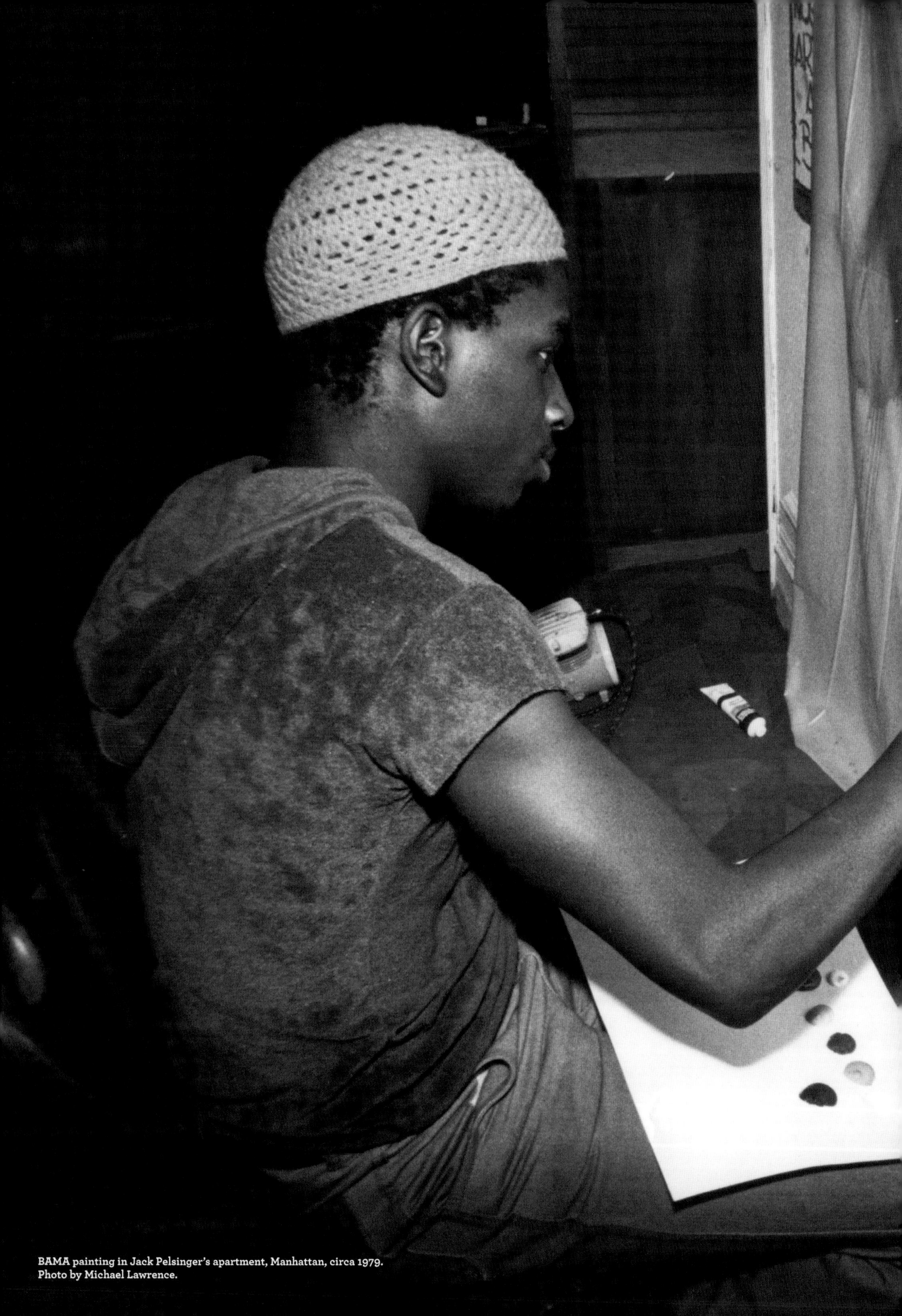

BAMA painting in Jack Pelsinger's apartment, Manhattan, circa 1979.
Photo by Michael Lawrence.

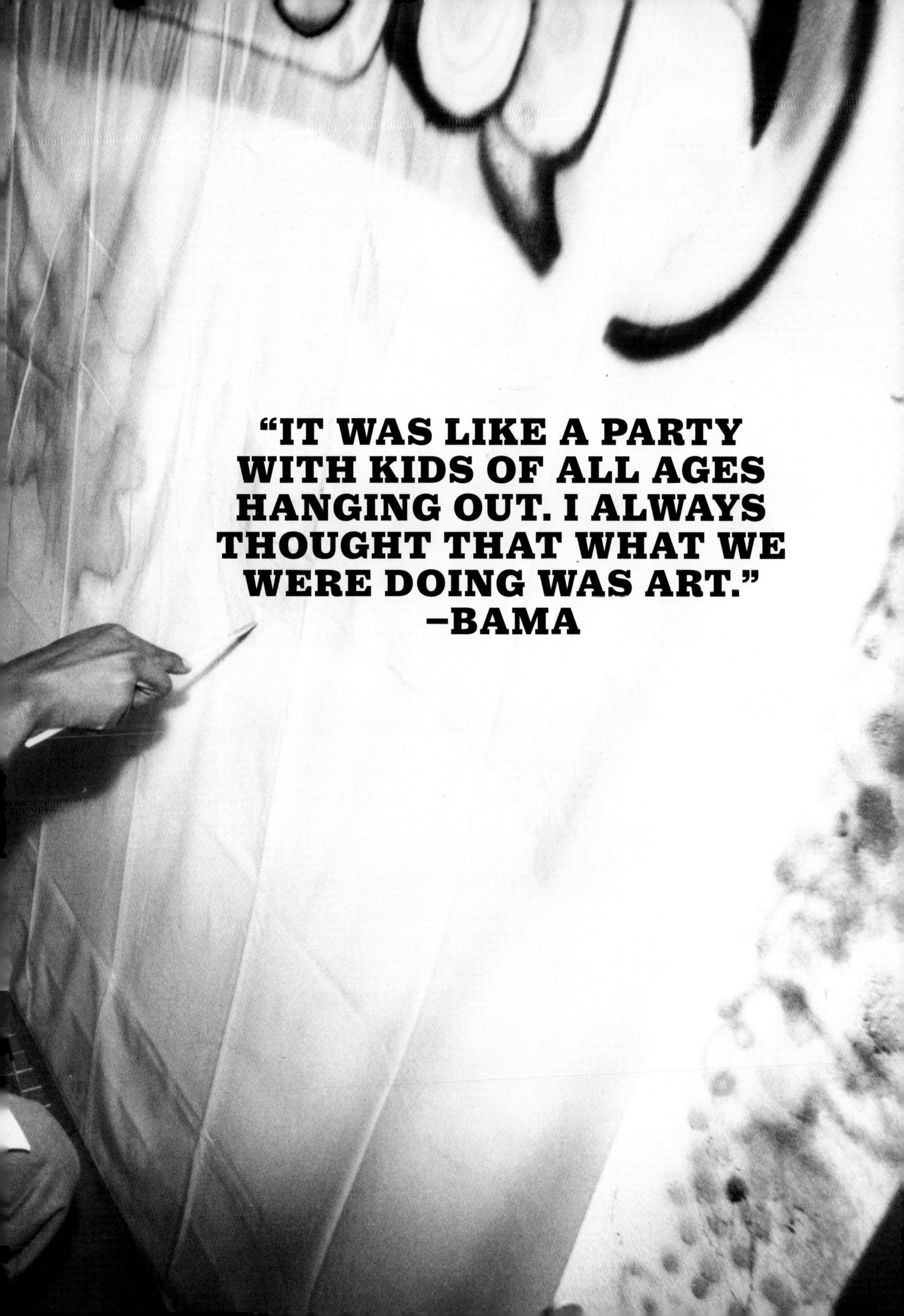

"IT WAS LIKE A PARTY WITH KIDS OF ALL AGES HANGING OUT. I ALWAYS THOUGHT THAT WHAT WE WERE DOING WAS ART."
–BAMA

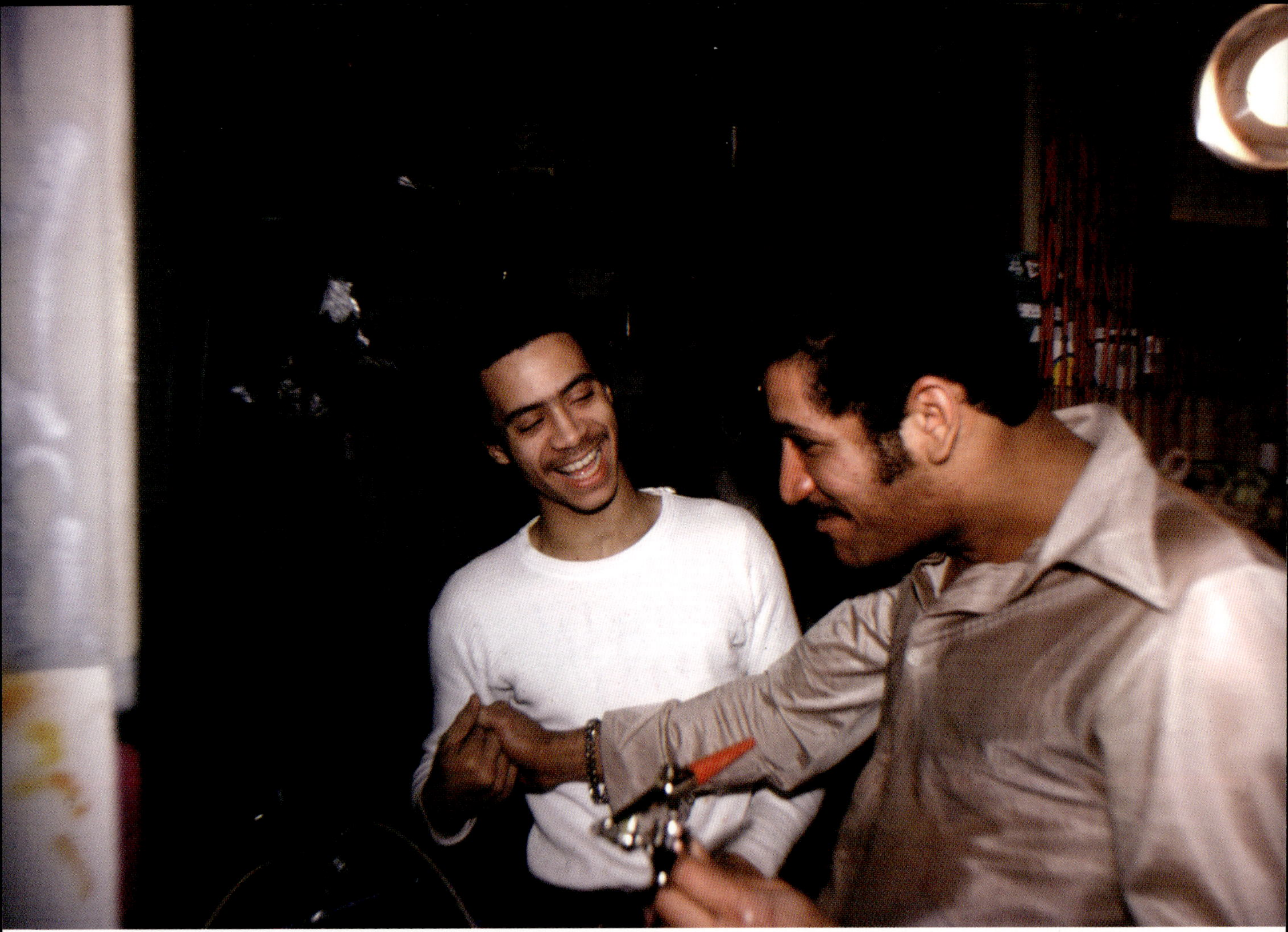

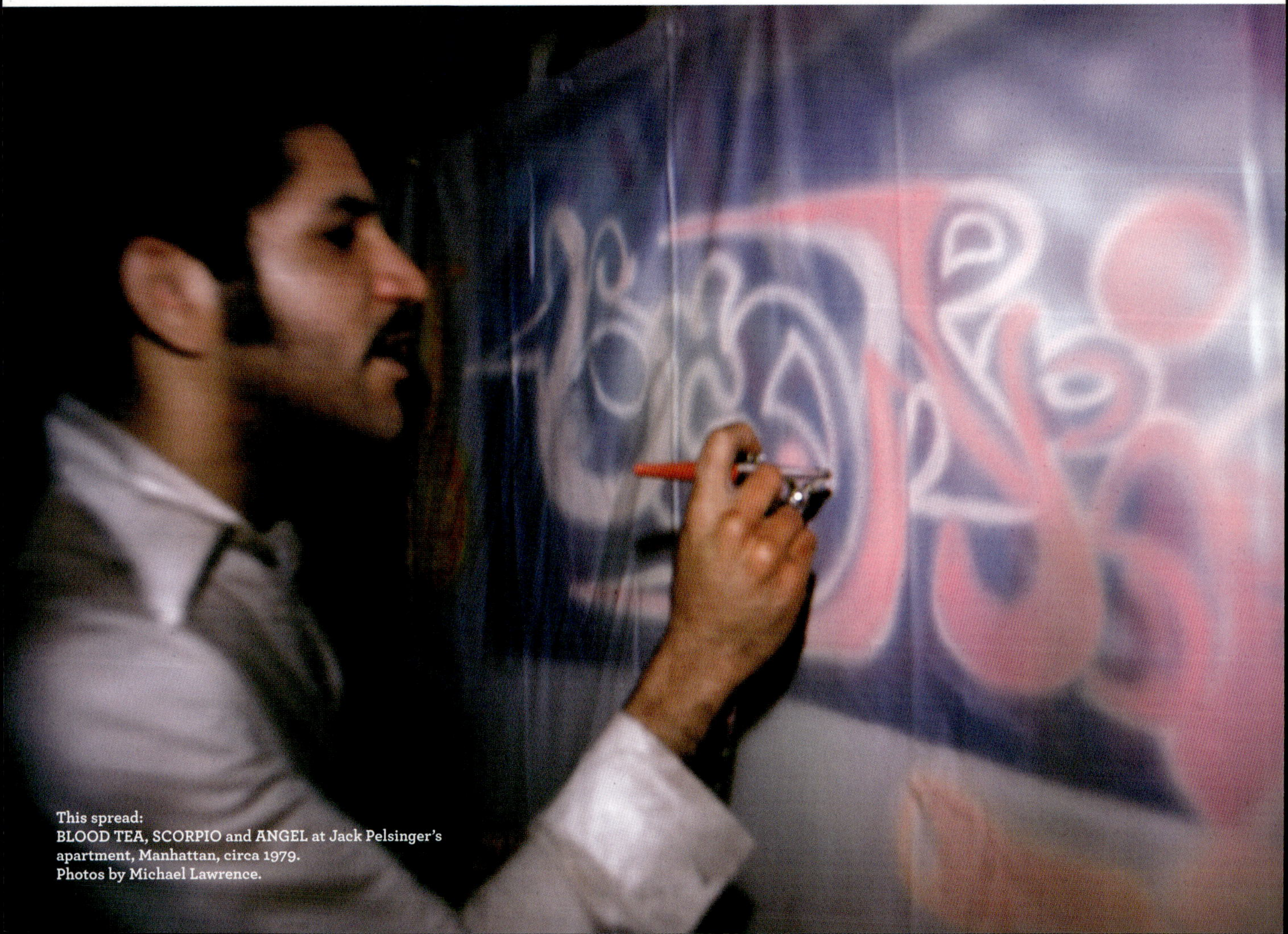

This spread:
BLOOD TEA, SCORPIO and ANGEL at Jack Pelsinger's
apartment, Manhattan, circa 1979.
Photos by Michael Lawrence.

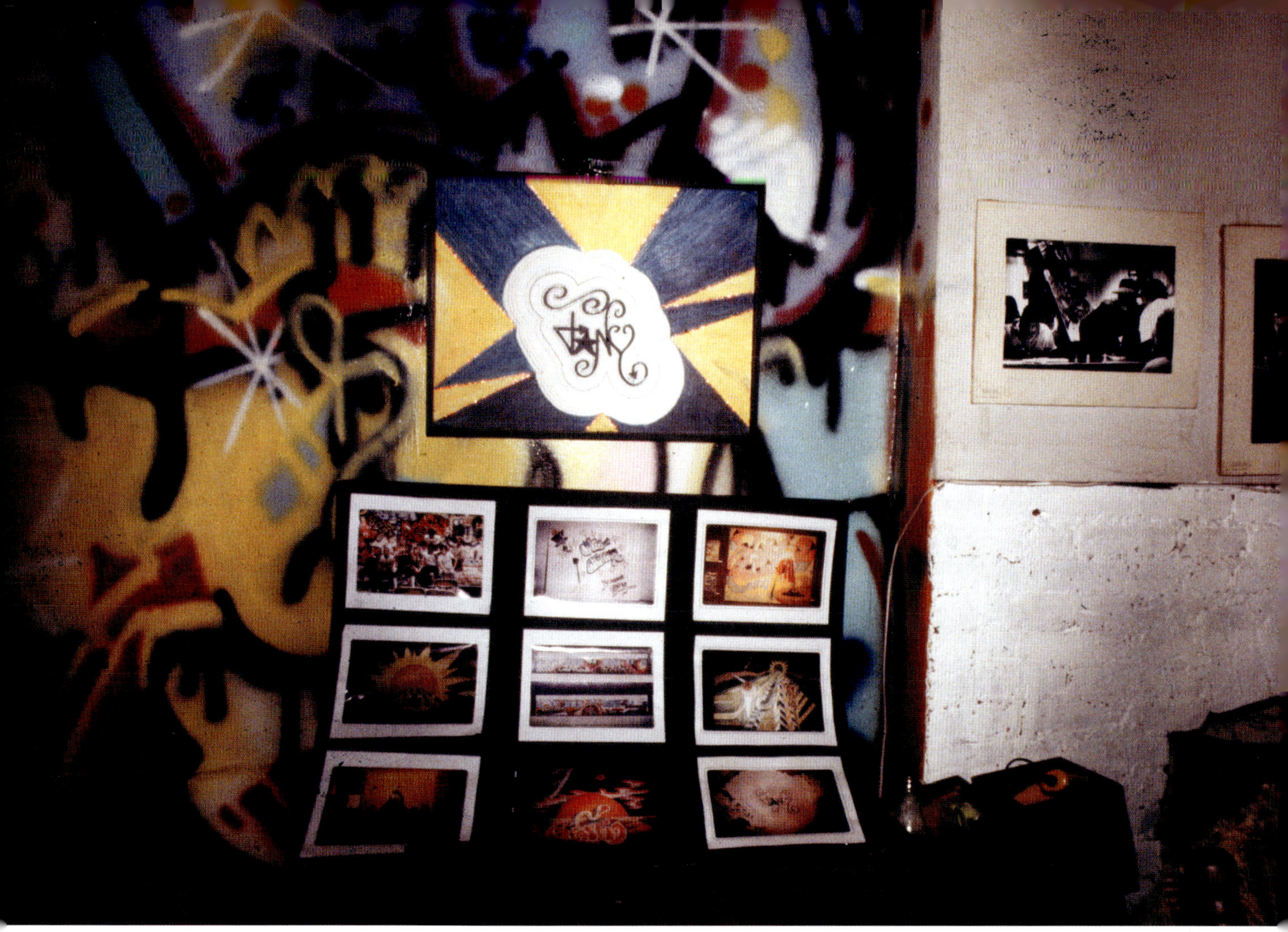

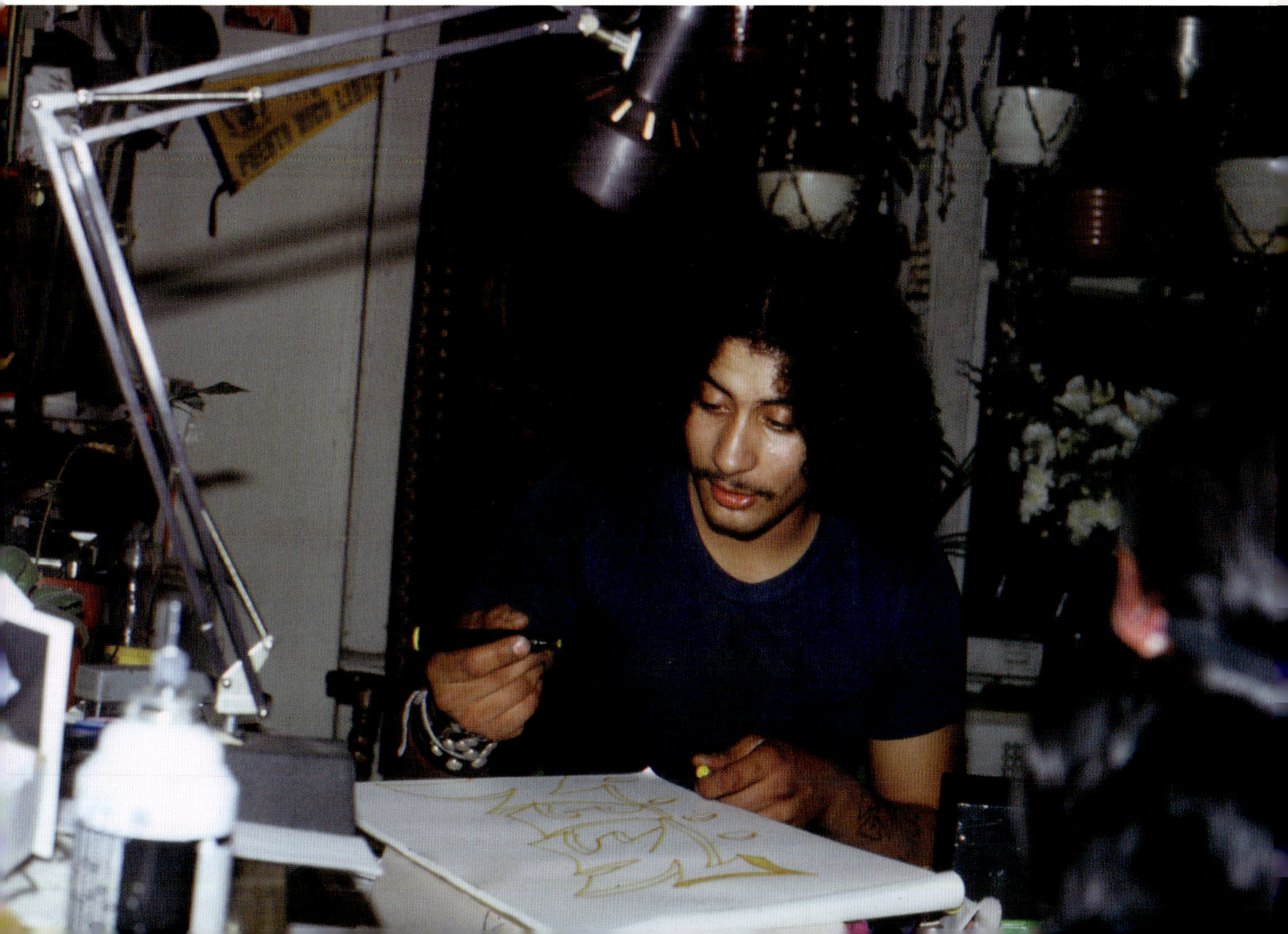

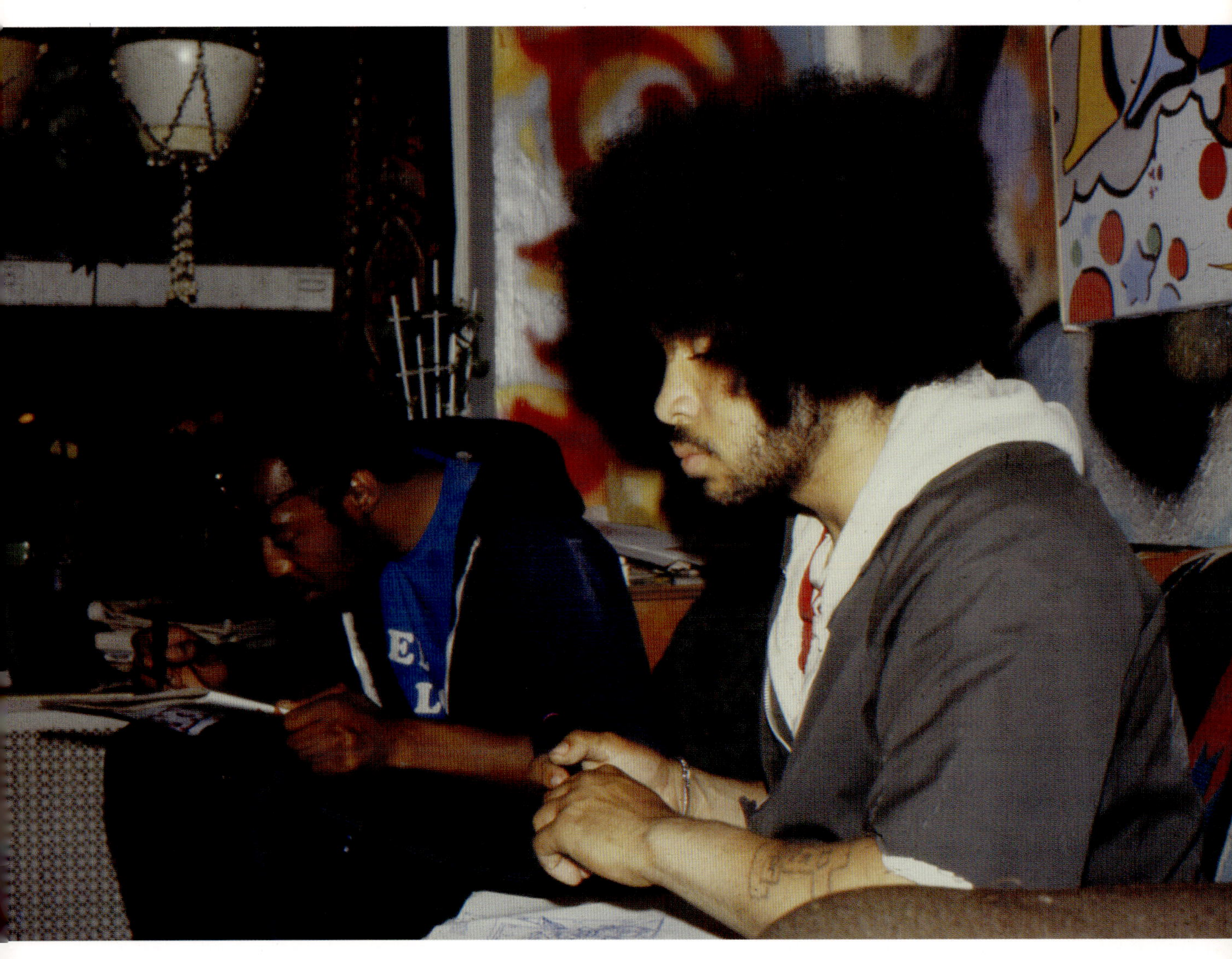

This spread:
NOGA artists at Jack Pelsinger's apartment, Manhattan, circa 1979.
Photos by Michael Lawrence.

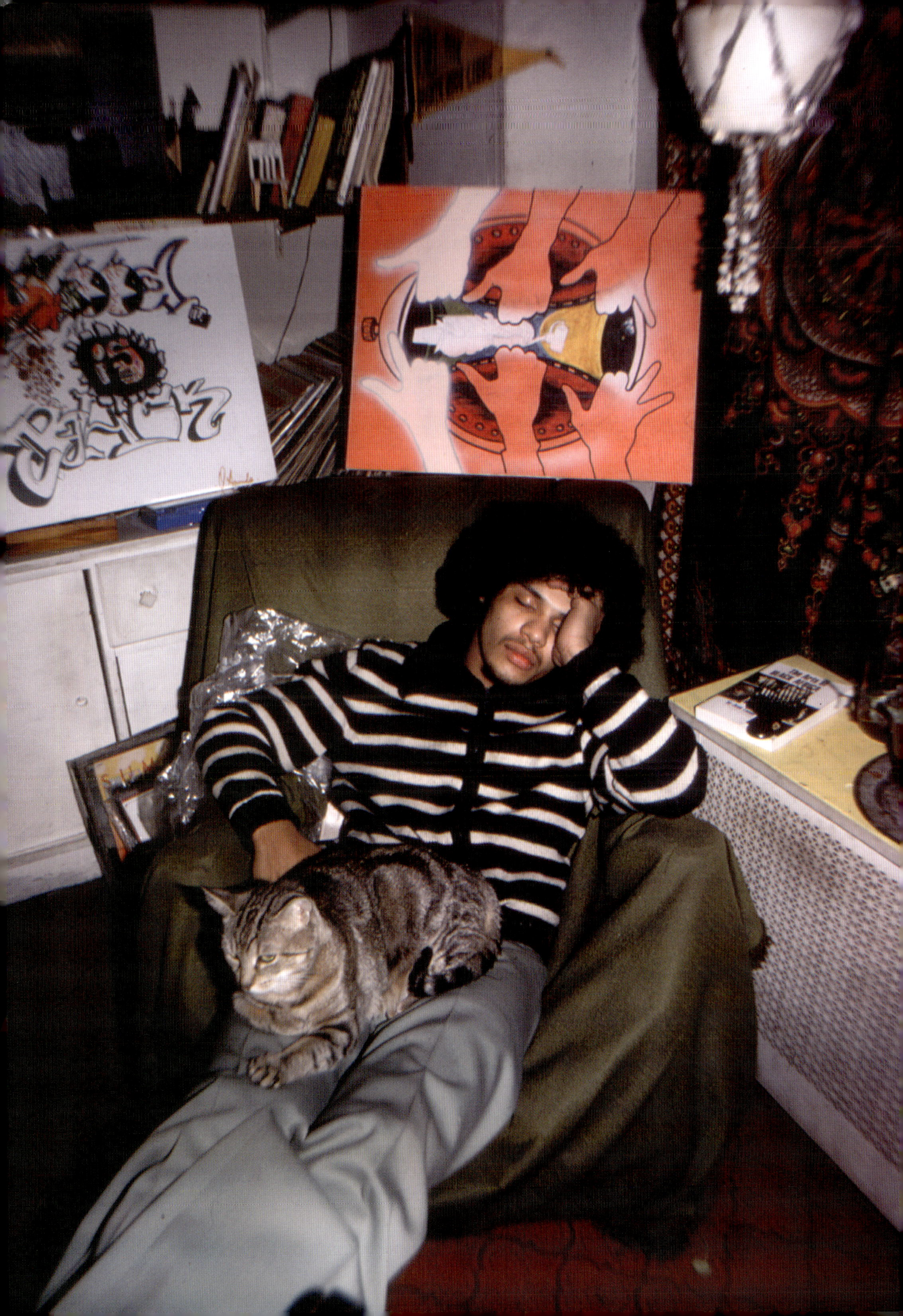

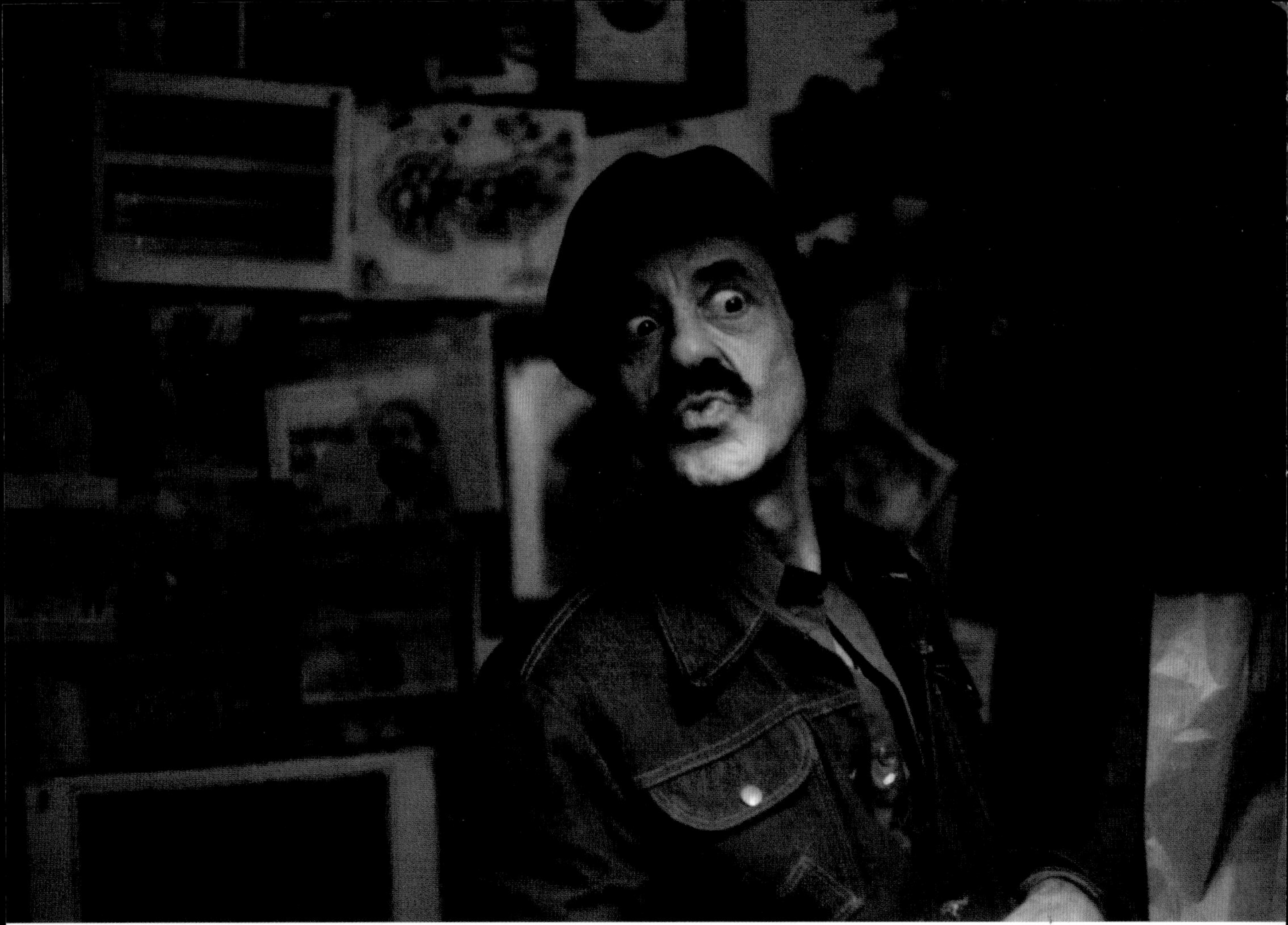

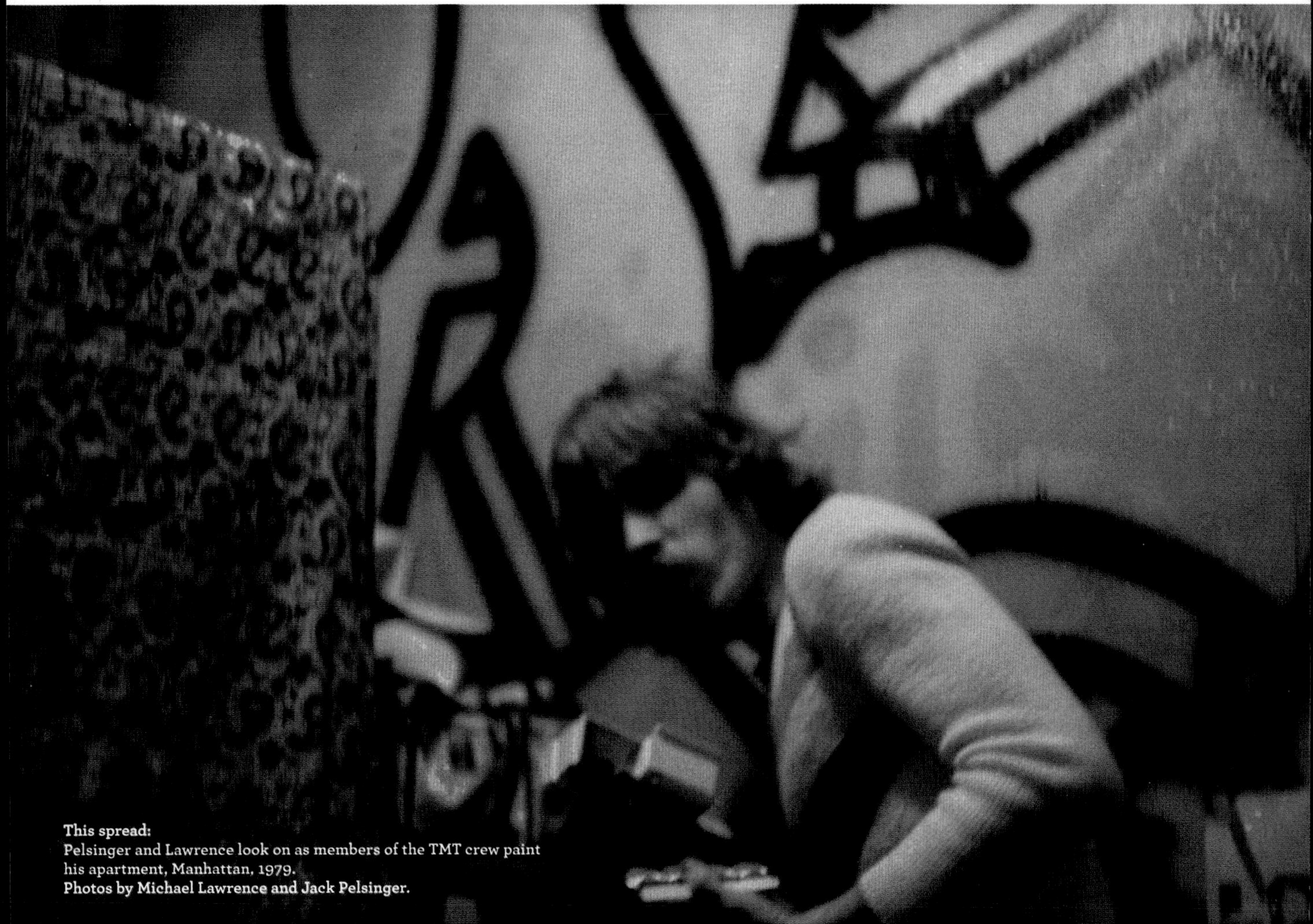

This spread:
Pelsinger and Lawrence look on as members of the TMT crew paint
his apartment, Manhattan, 1979.
Photos by Michael Lawrence and Jack Pelsinger.

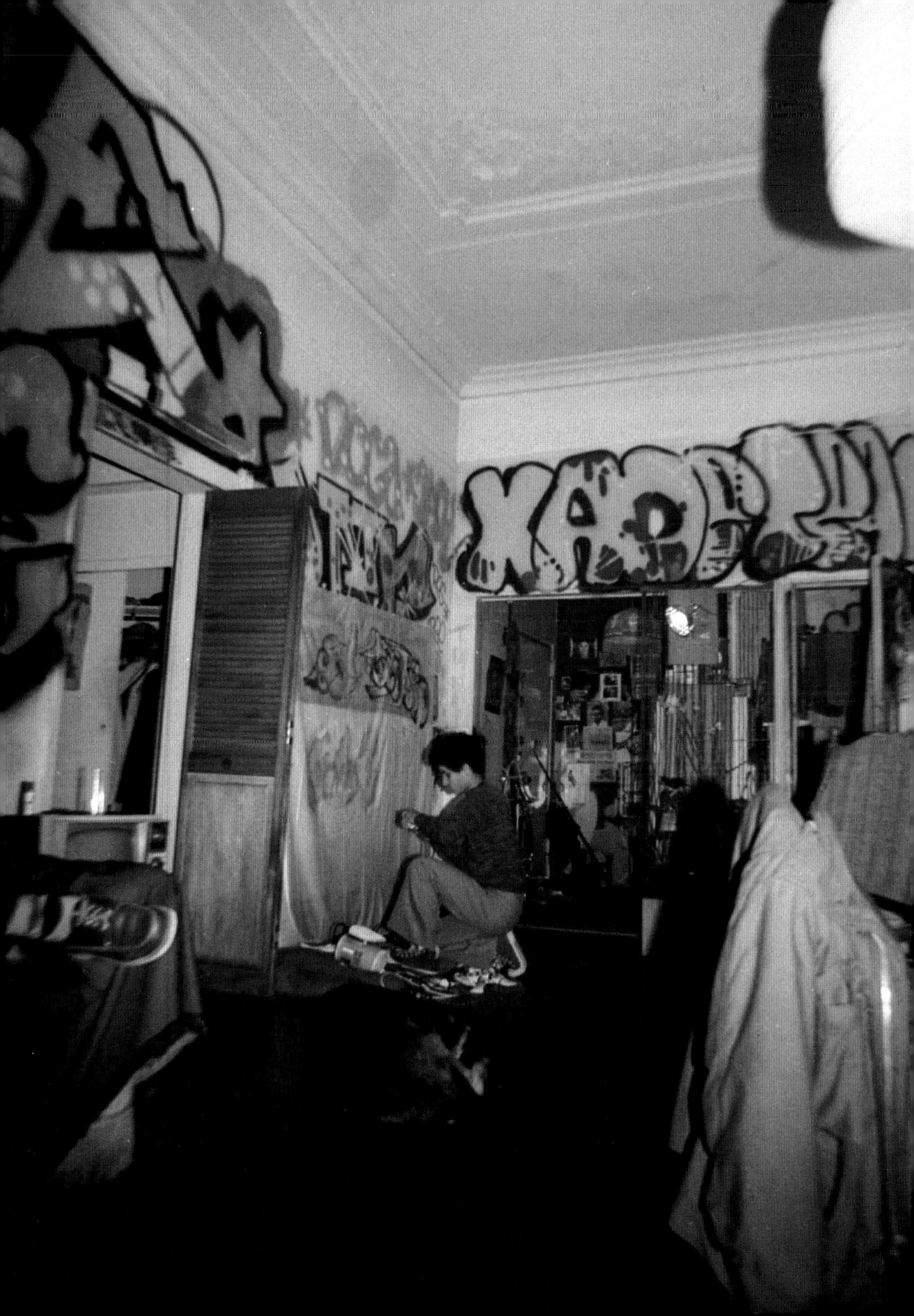

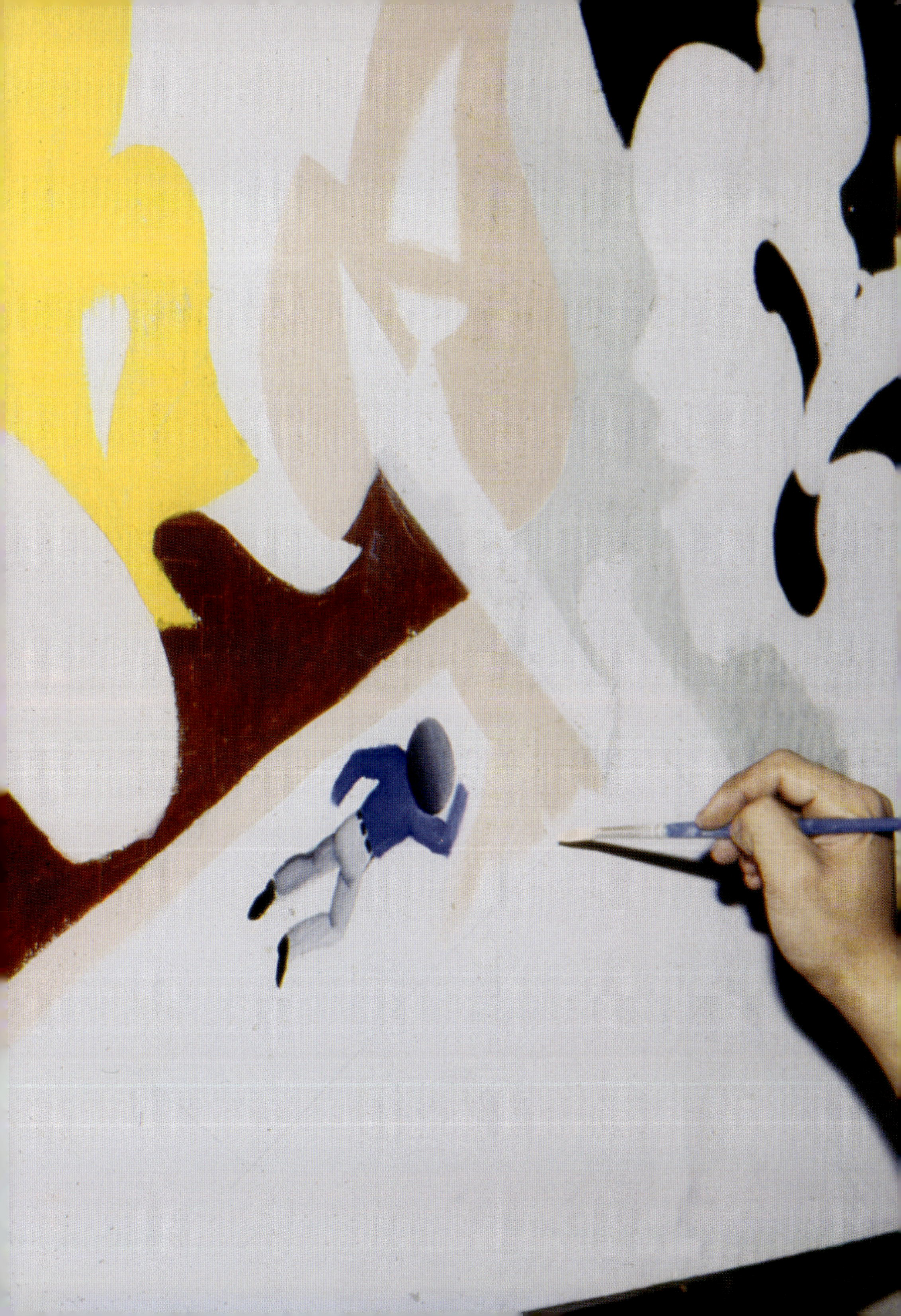

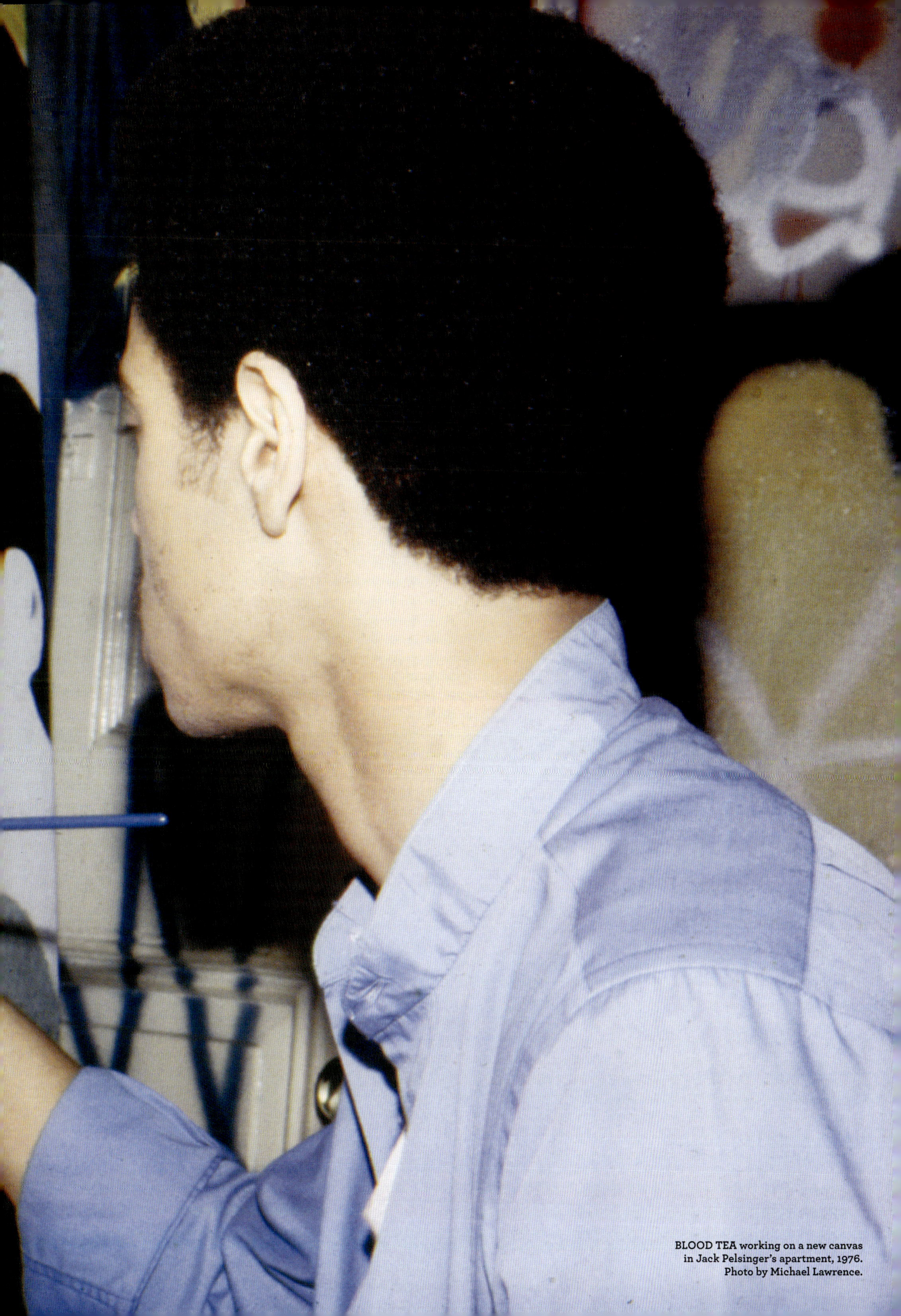

BLOOD TEA working on a new canvas
in Jack Pelsinger's apartment, 1976.
Photo by Michael Lawrence.

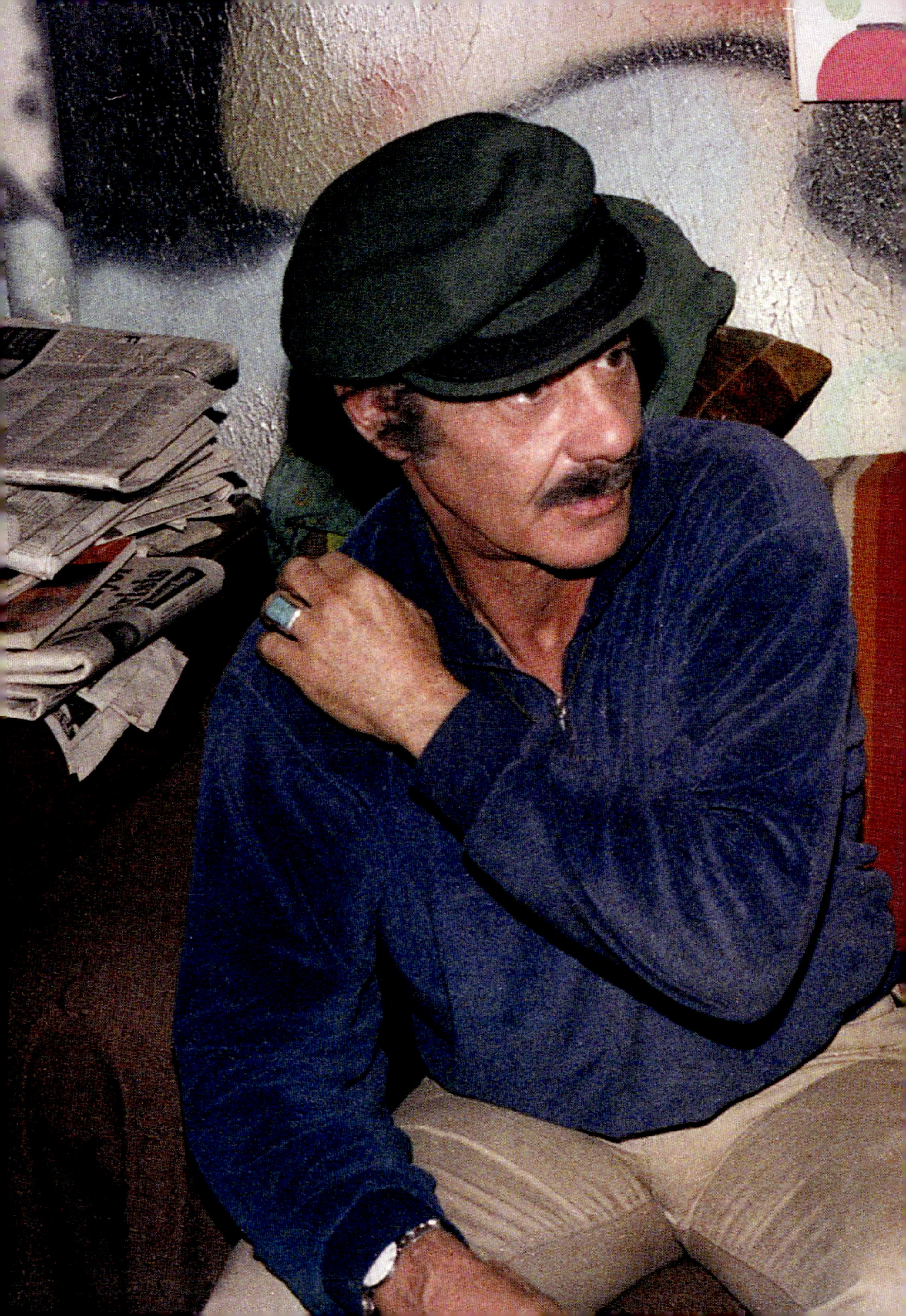

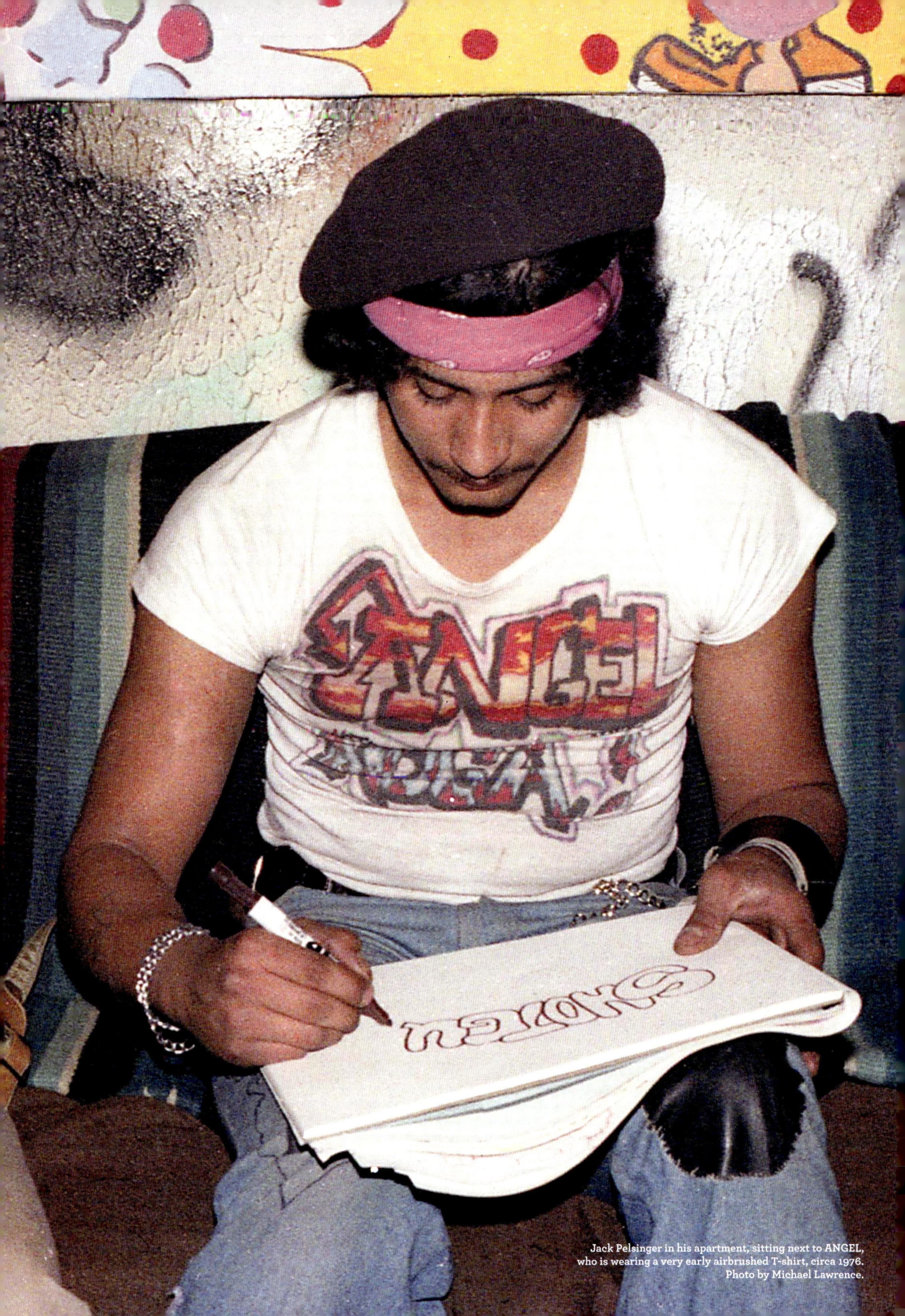

Jack Pelsinger in his apartment, sitting next to ANGEL,
who is wearing a very early airbrushed T-shirt, circa 1976.
Photo by Michael Lawrence.

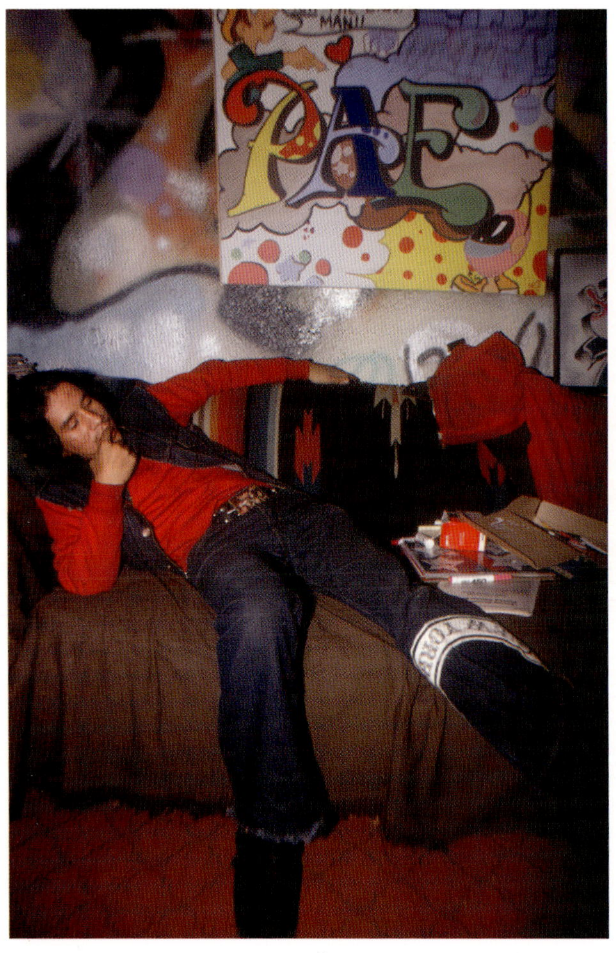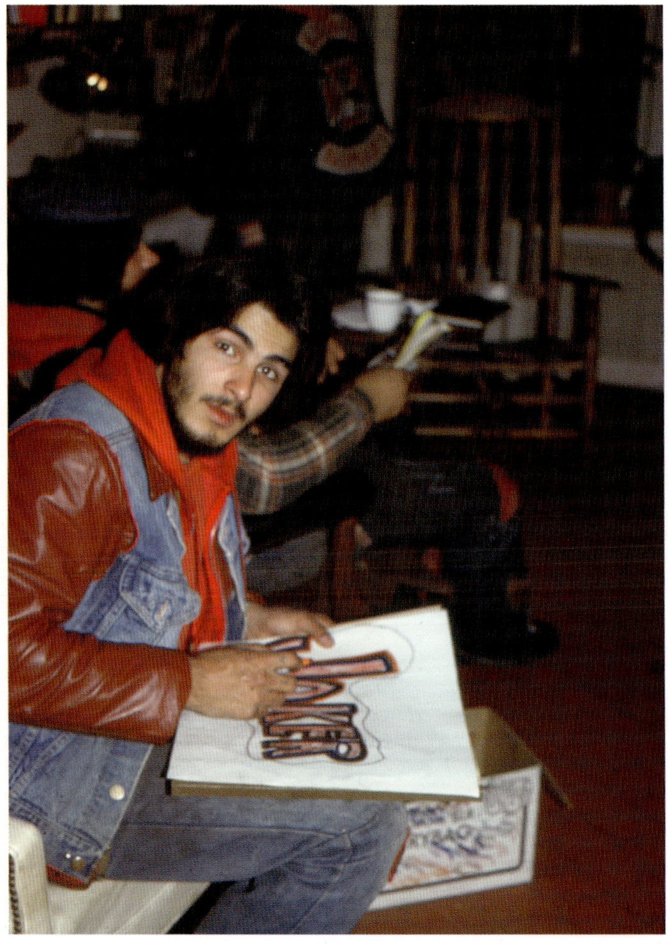

This spread:
SAVAGE NOMADS drawing at Jack Pelsinger's apartment, 1979.
Photos by Michael Lawrence.

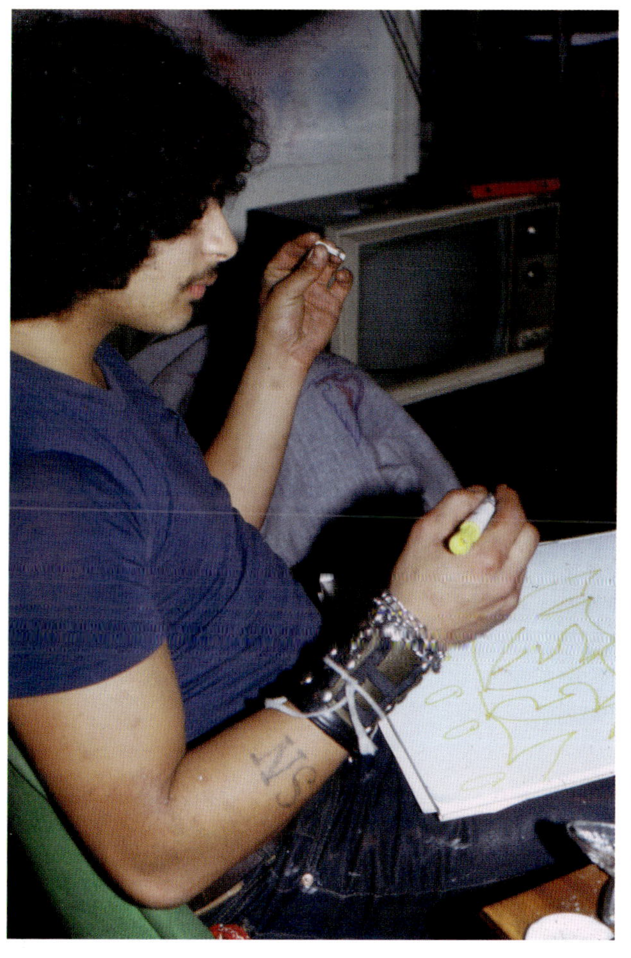 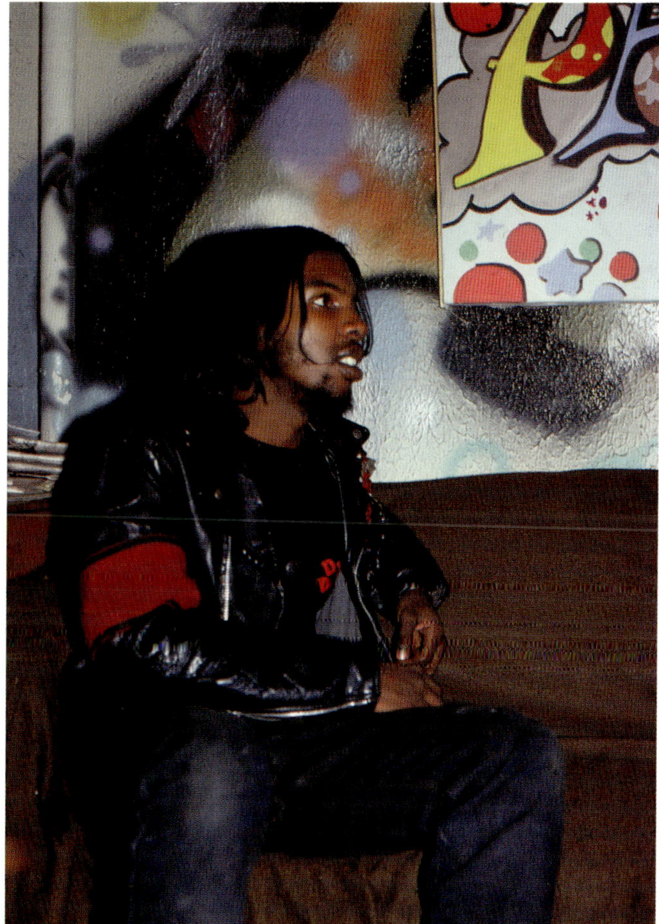

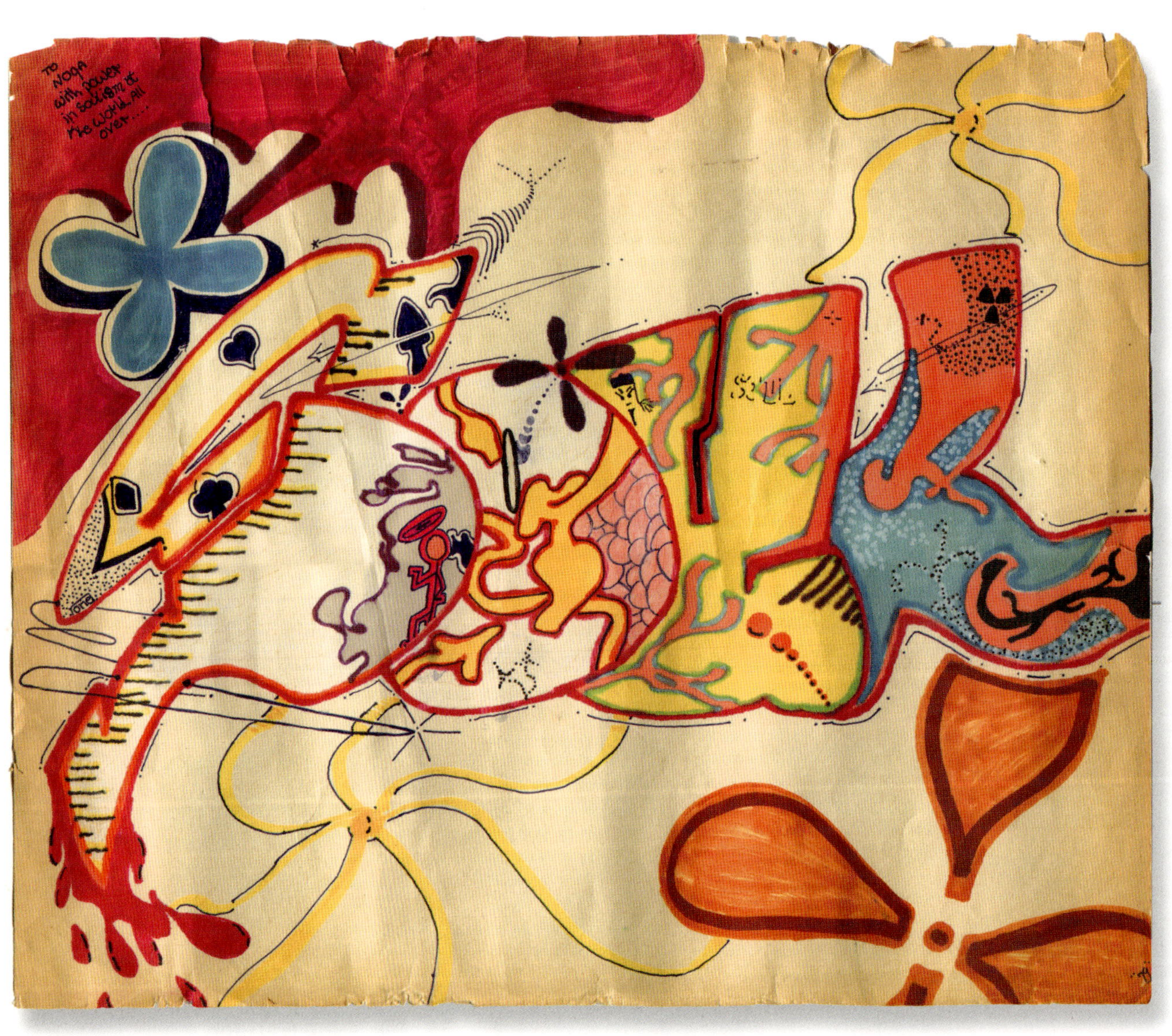

SOUL sketch, 1979.

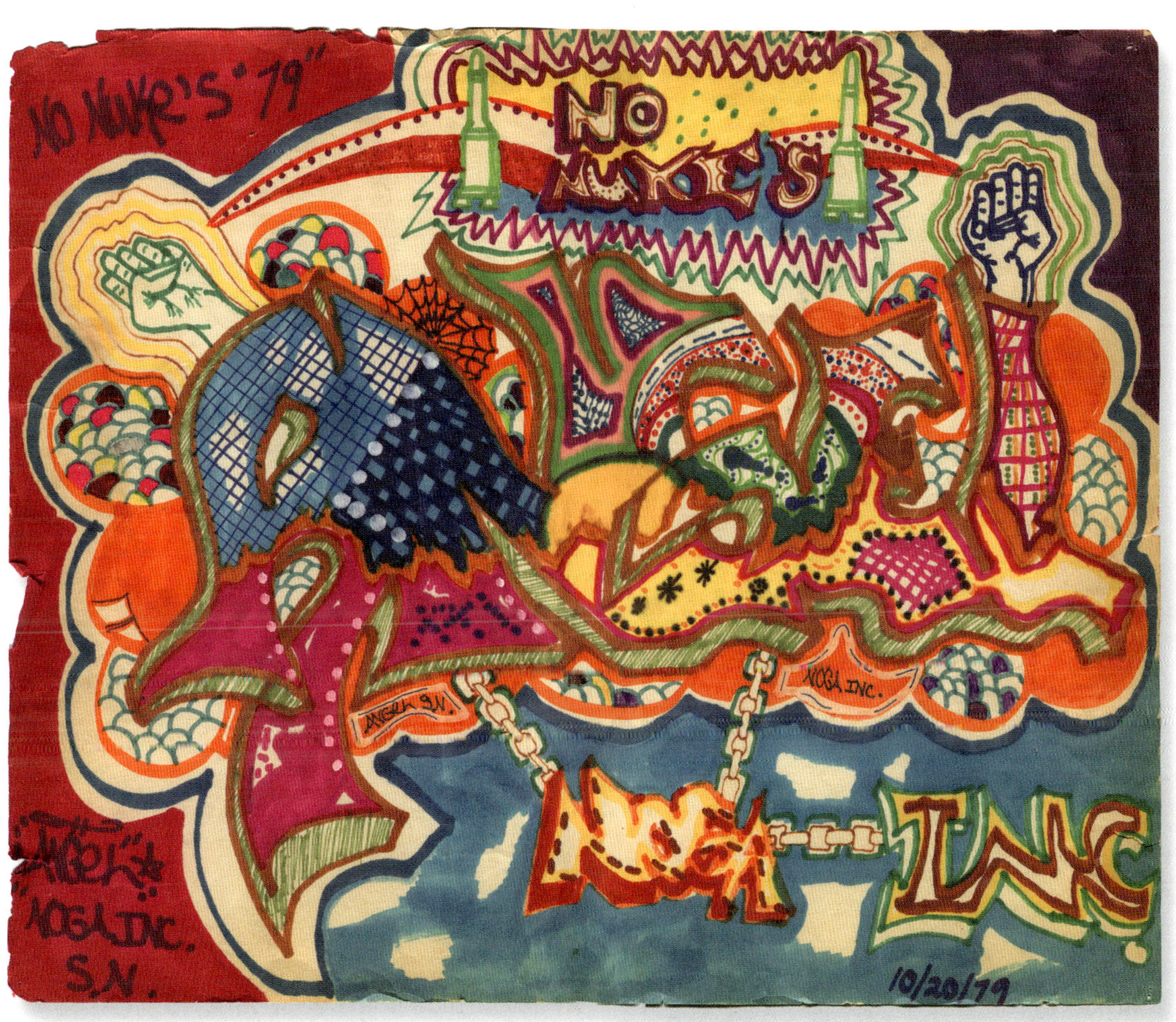

ANGEL sketch, 1979.

August 8, 1979

Mr. Jack Pelsinger
Executive Director
Nation of Graffiti Artists
149 West 80th Street
New York, New York 10024

Dear Jack:

Pursuant to our conversation on August 7, 1979, this letter is to inform you and prospective suppliers that the Nation of Graffiti Artists has surveyed five Open Space sites for the construction of murals. The Task Force expects N.O.G.A. to assess the amount of work and also assist the Task Force in selecting the best and fairest company to contract business with. The Task Force hopes this letter will expediate the process of construction and selection of a supplier.

Thank you for your cooperation.

Sincerely,

Andre Green
Assistant Field Supervisior

AG/nc

SENATOR TARKY LOMBARDI, JR.
CHAIRMAN

SENATOR ROY M. GOODMAN
VICE-CHAIRMAN

SENATE SPECIAL COMMITTEE
ON THE CULTURE INDUSTRY
STATE OF NEW YORK
ALBANY
12247

LEGISLATIVE OFFICE BUILDING
(518) 455-2911

October 25, 1979

Mr. Jack Pelsinger
Executive Director
Nation of Graffiti Artists, Inc.
P.O. Box 119
New York, New York 10028

Dear Mr. Pelsinger:

On behalf of the Senate Special Committee on the Culture Industry I would like to thank you for your participation in the recent hearing on the New York State Arts Council's decentralization program.

Your testimony reflected your special experience in dealing with the arts at the local level, and provided the Committee with a perspective valuable to its efforts in assessing the future of decentralization in New York State. You can be assured that your statement will be part of the permanent record and will be a basis of our report to the Legislature and the Governor.

Kindest regards.

Sincerely,

Tarky Lombardi, Jr.
Chairman

TL/sh

IN THE END

Telling the story of NOGA is best left to the wonderful photographs of Michael Lawrence. Sadly, many of the major participants are deceased, including Jack Pelsinger — who died in the late 1980s — CLIFF 159, SCORPIO and ALI. Many more have simply fallen off the grid. I'm thankful to those writers who were generous enough to share their memories with me.

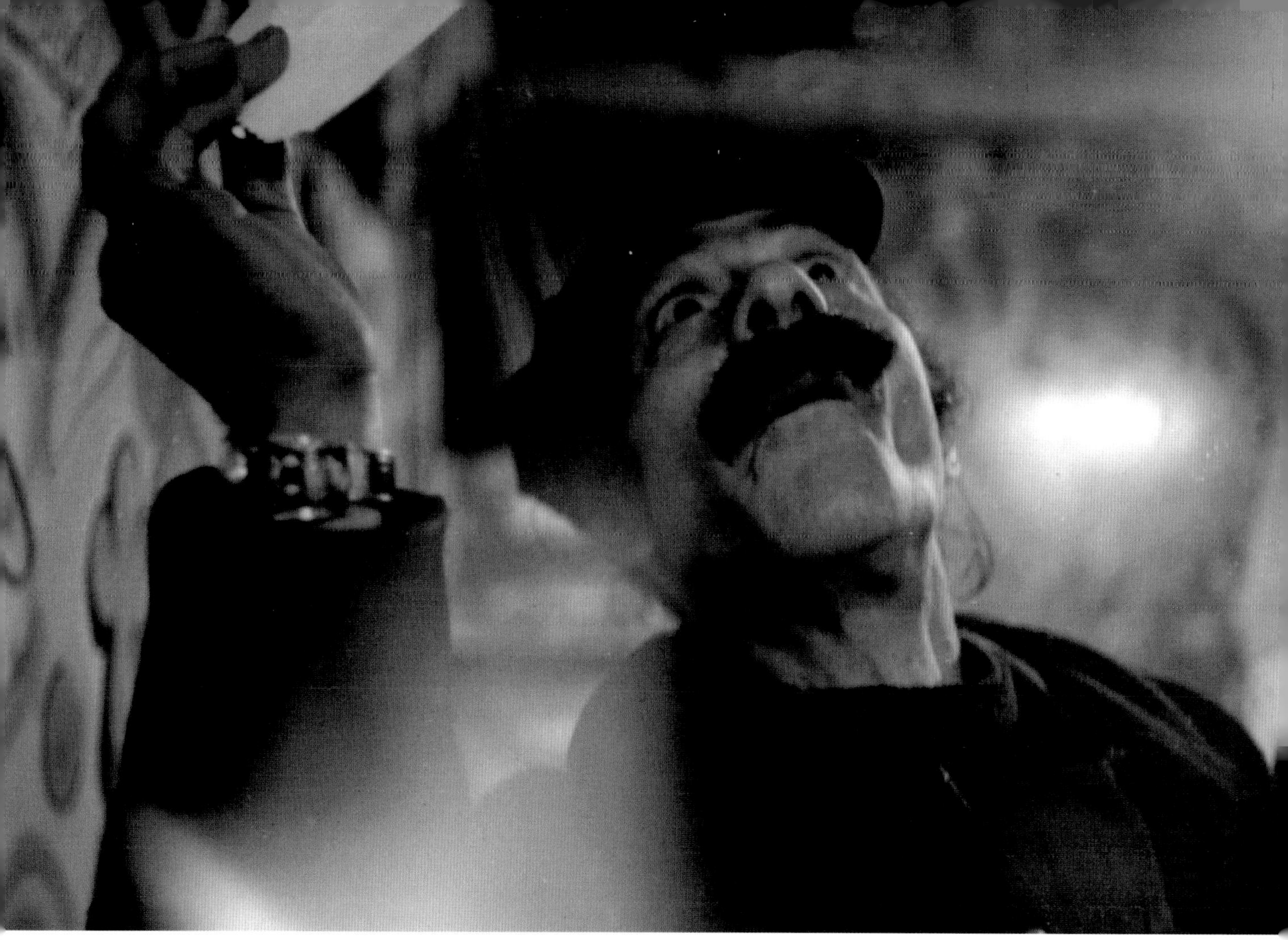

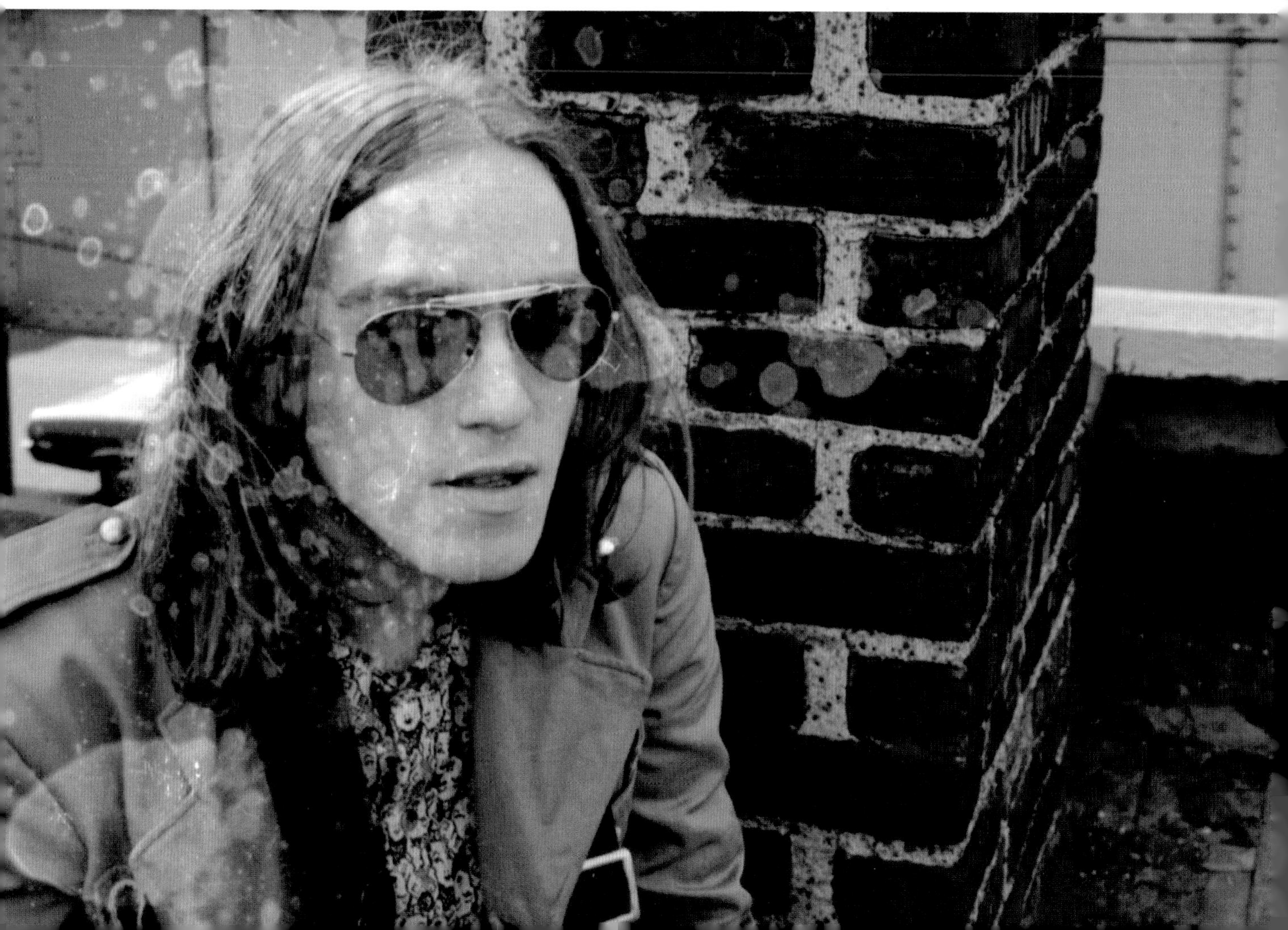

TIMELINE

AUGUST 1974:

NOGA opens on Columbus Avenue.

DECEMBER 1974:

First show at Central Savings Bank.

DECEMBER 1974:

Warm Up Music Studio mural job.

JANUARY 1975:

STIM 1 dies.

SPRING 1975:

NOGA exterior painted for STIM 1.

JUNE 1975:

Outdoor exhibition at the 88th Street Fair.

MARCH 1976:

Bank Street College show.

SUMMER 1976:

Prospect Hospital mural performance.

FALL 1976:

NOGA loses its space at Columbus Avenue.

WINTER 1976:

NOGA relocates briefly to the West Village.

FEBRUARY 1977:

NOGA moves into second floor of the Alianza Civica Tropical Day Care and Senior Citizen Center in the Bronx.

SUMMER 1977:

NOGA moves to the church in the Bronx.

SUMMER 1977:

REE, KADE and TEAN paint Jack's apartment.

FALL 1978:

NOGA moves to the nearby Boys Club in the Bronx.

FALL 1979:

NOGA closes.

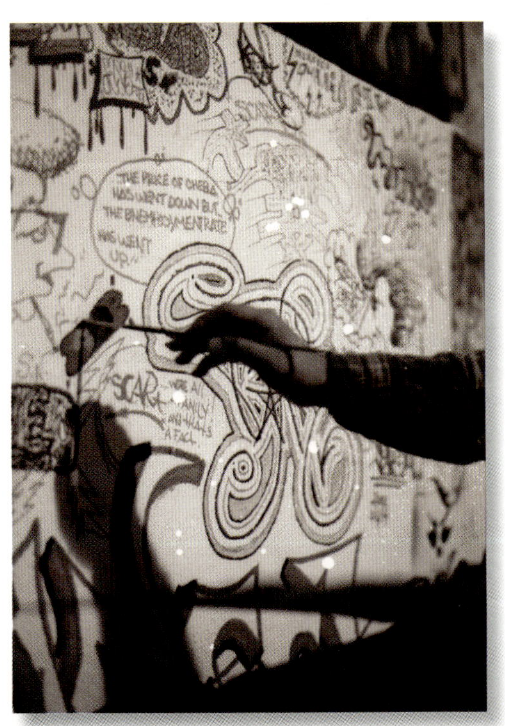

LOVE adds his name to a collaborative canvas, 1977.
Photo by Michael Lawrence.

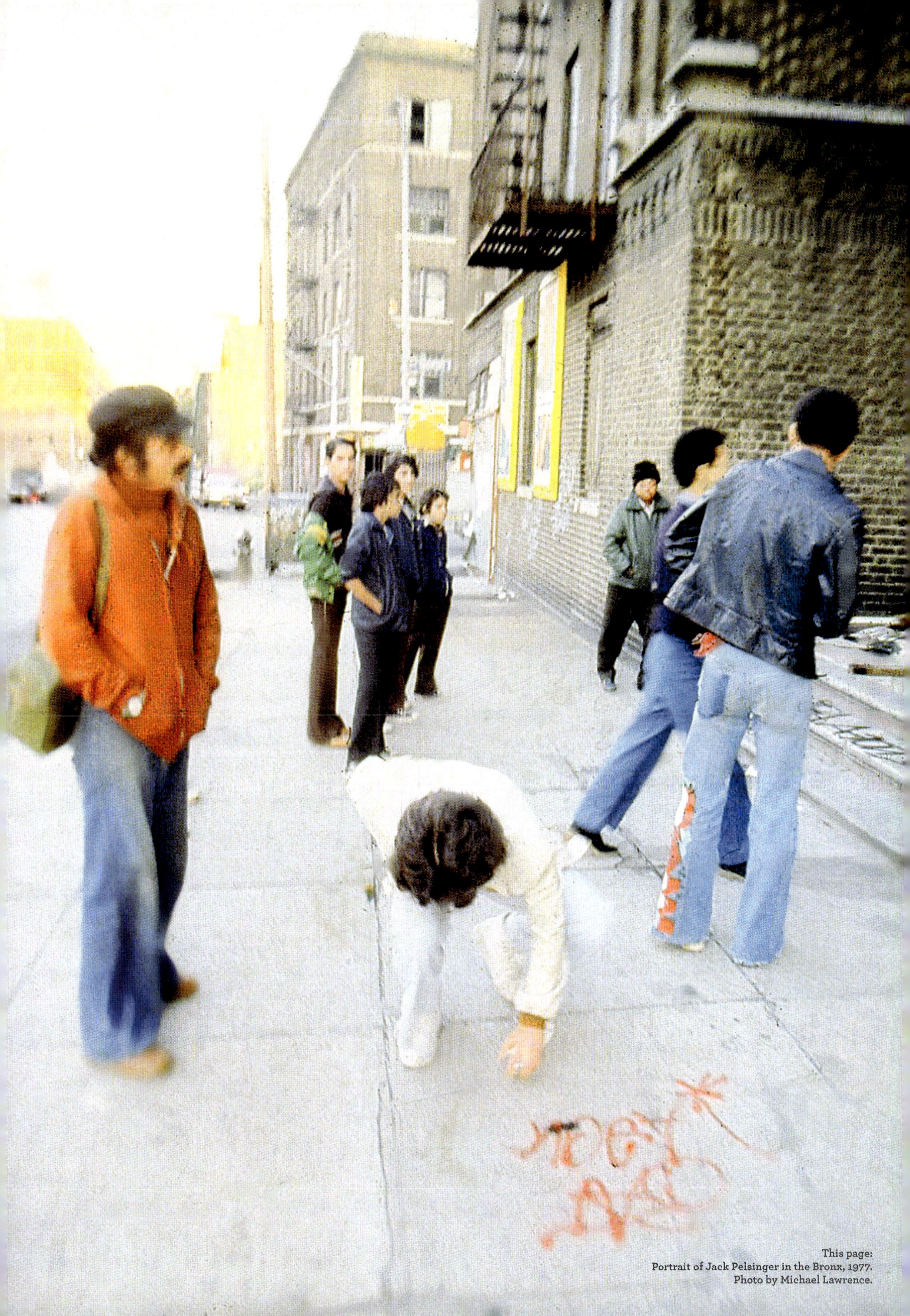

This page:
Portrait of Jack Pelsinger in the Bronx, 1977.
Photo by Michael Lawrence.

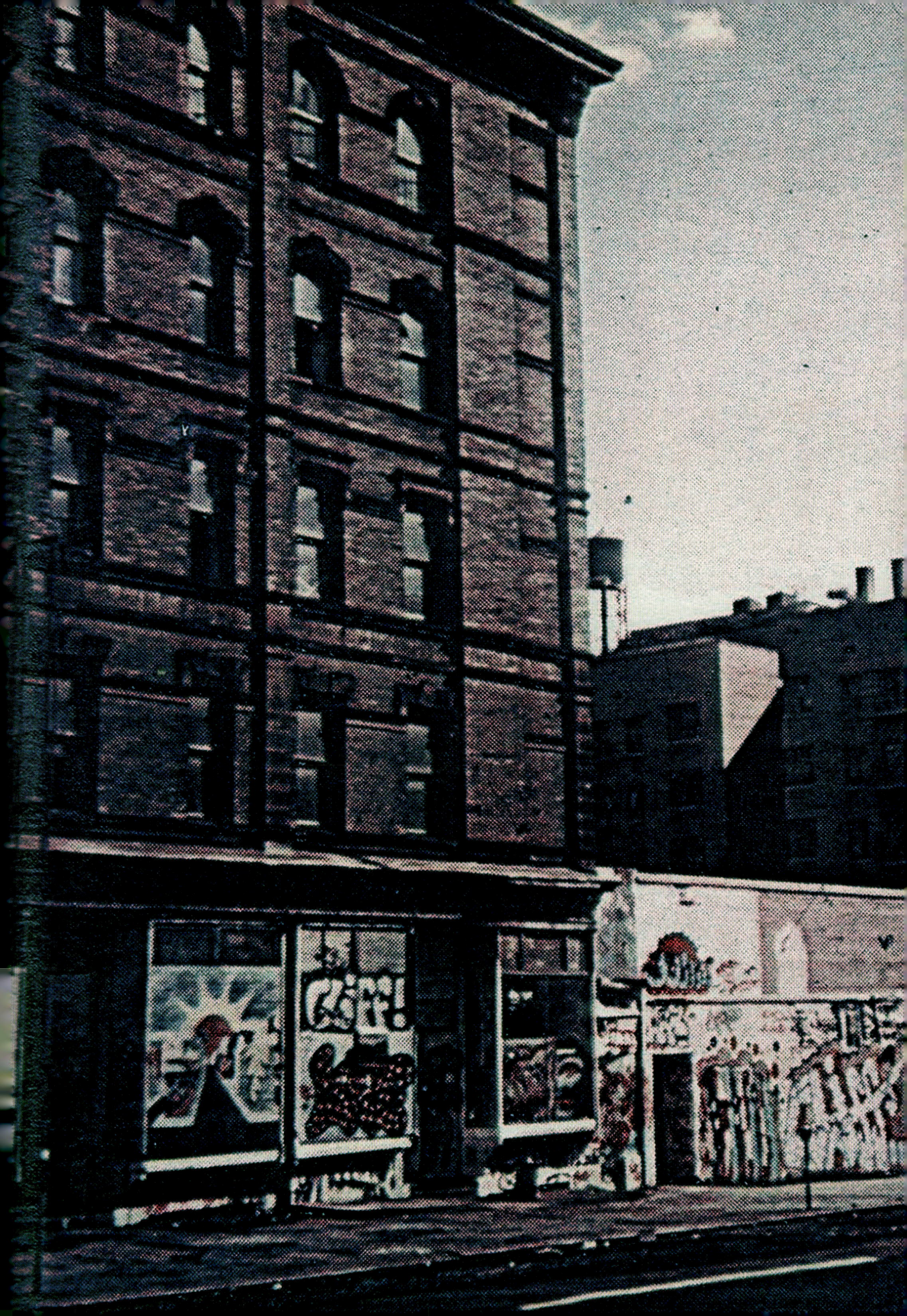

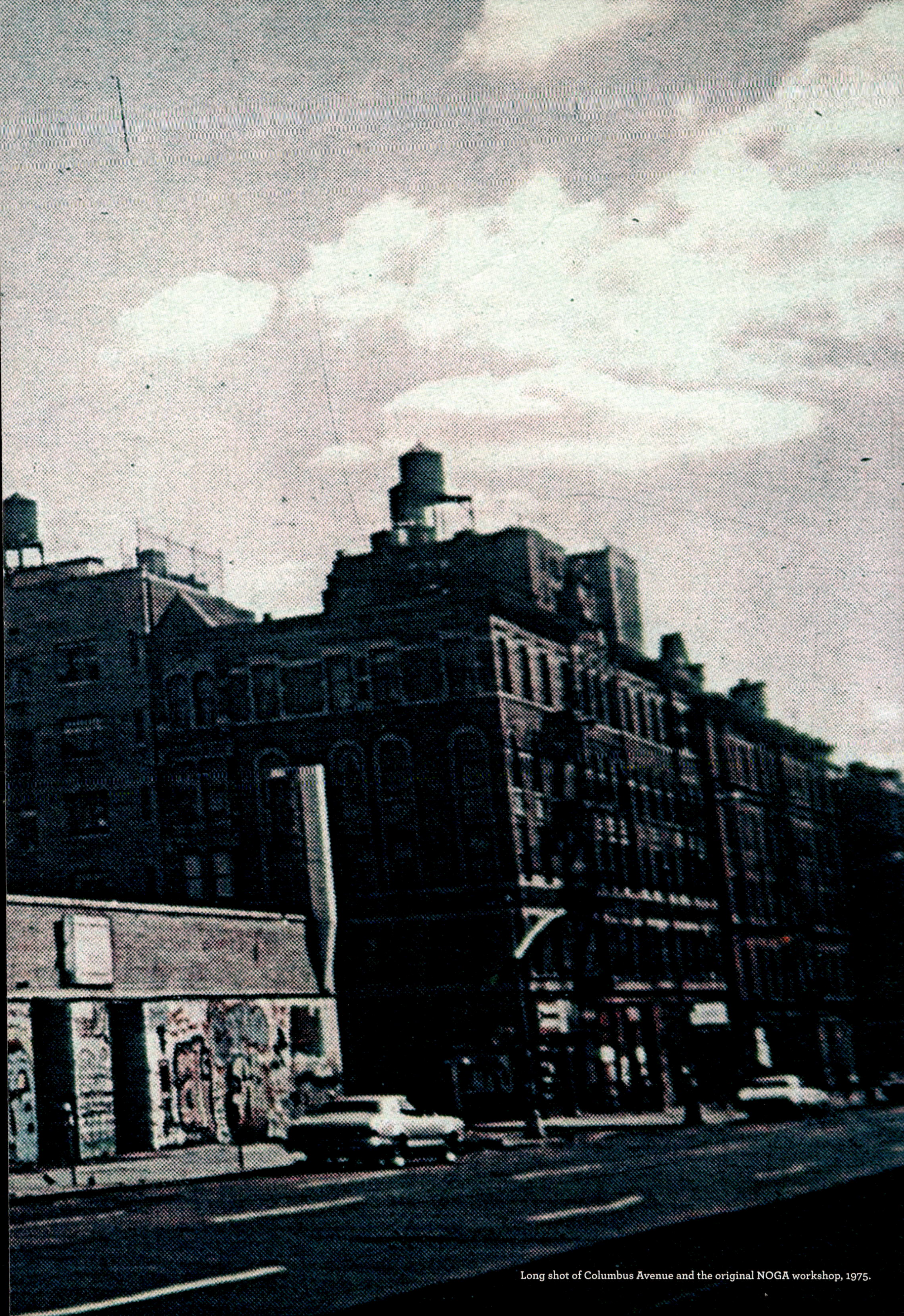

Long shot of Columbus Avenue and the original NOGA workshop, 1975.

Published by: BEYOND THE STREETS

Creative Direction: Roger Gastman

Design & Production: Leon Gonzalez

Title Design: Dustin Ames

Photography ©Michael Lawrence

Written by: Chris Pape

Additional Photos by: Martha Cooper,
Moses Ros/SAL 161, The Harald Hamrin Estate,
Gianfranco Gorgoni, Herbert Migdoll, and
Yolanda Rodriguez.

Special Thanks: REE 2, Michael Lawrence, NOC 167,
DAZE, PART, JEAN 13, SAL 161, Martha Cooper,
STAN 153 (RIP), BAMA, Amanda Bessette & ZOOEY,
Tobias Barenthin Lindblad, Bethesda, Houston's,
Christopher Lewis & Maya Gorgoni of The Estate
of Gianfranco Gorgoni, Real Friends – Same Enemies
and Jack for the vision!

Michael Lawrence would like to thank: David Archer of
Gallery West for all of the free prints and processing done
for NOGA over the years, as well as Robert Joffrey and
Twyla Tharp for letting me be a part of Deuce Coupe and
the history of New York graffiti.

Front Cover: An older SCORPIO shows off one of
his early airbrushed shirts in Jack's apartment, South
Bronx, 1979.

Back Cover: SCORPIO at NOGA, 1975.

Opposite Page: FED 2 collab canvas, 1979.

*Best efforts were made to identify and credit all
artists. Corrections and updates will be made in future
editions.*

Second Edition
098765432

Published in association with
Gingko Press
ISBN: 978-1-58423-779-2

Copyright ©2023 BEYOND THE STREETS

BEYONDTHESTREETS.COM

Printed in China

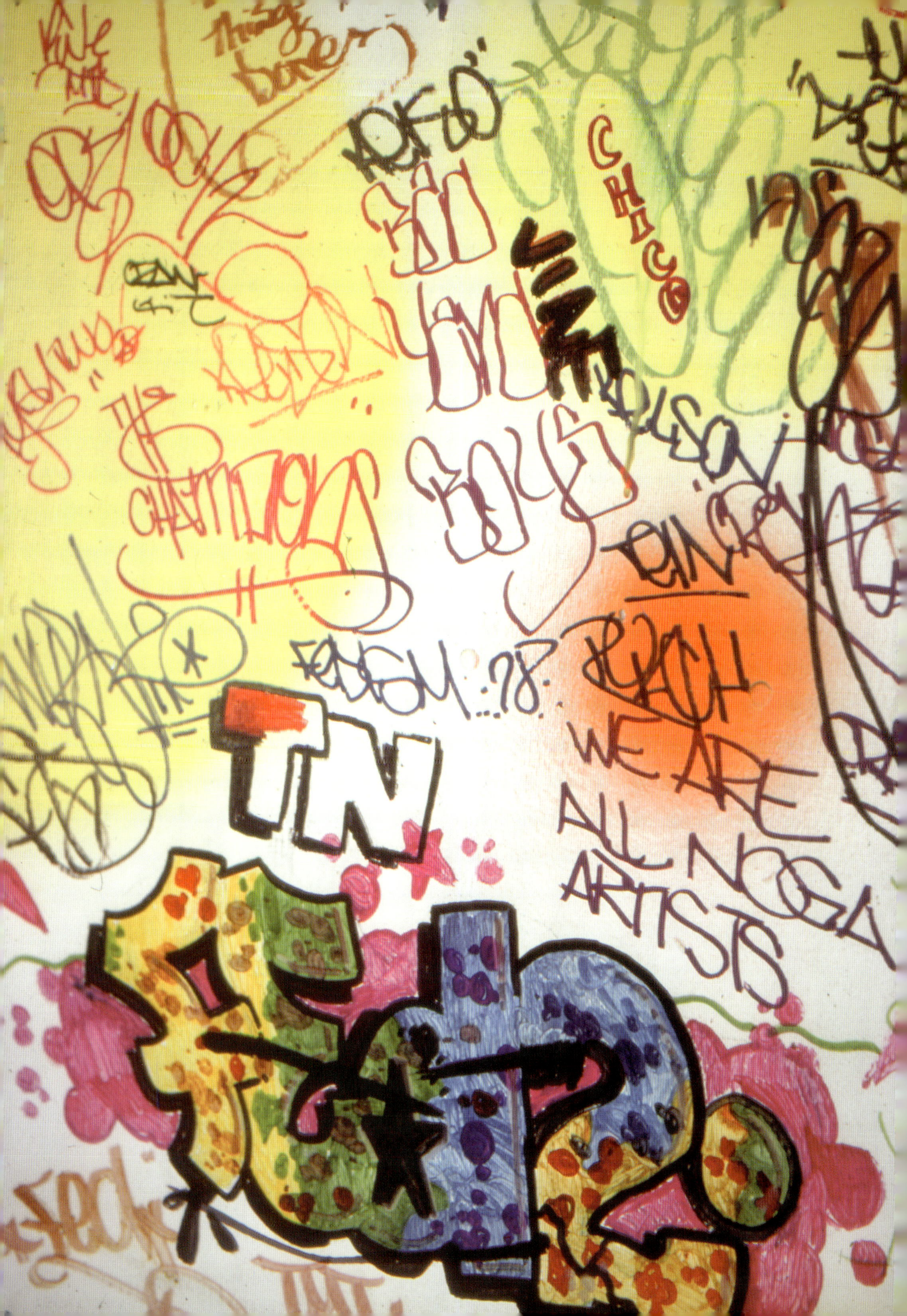

CHICO
CHAMPIONS
TN
WE ARE ALL NOGA ARTISTS

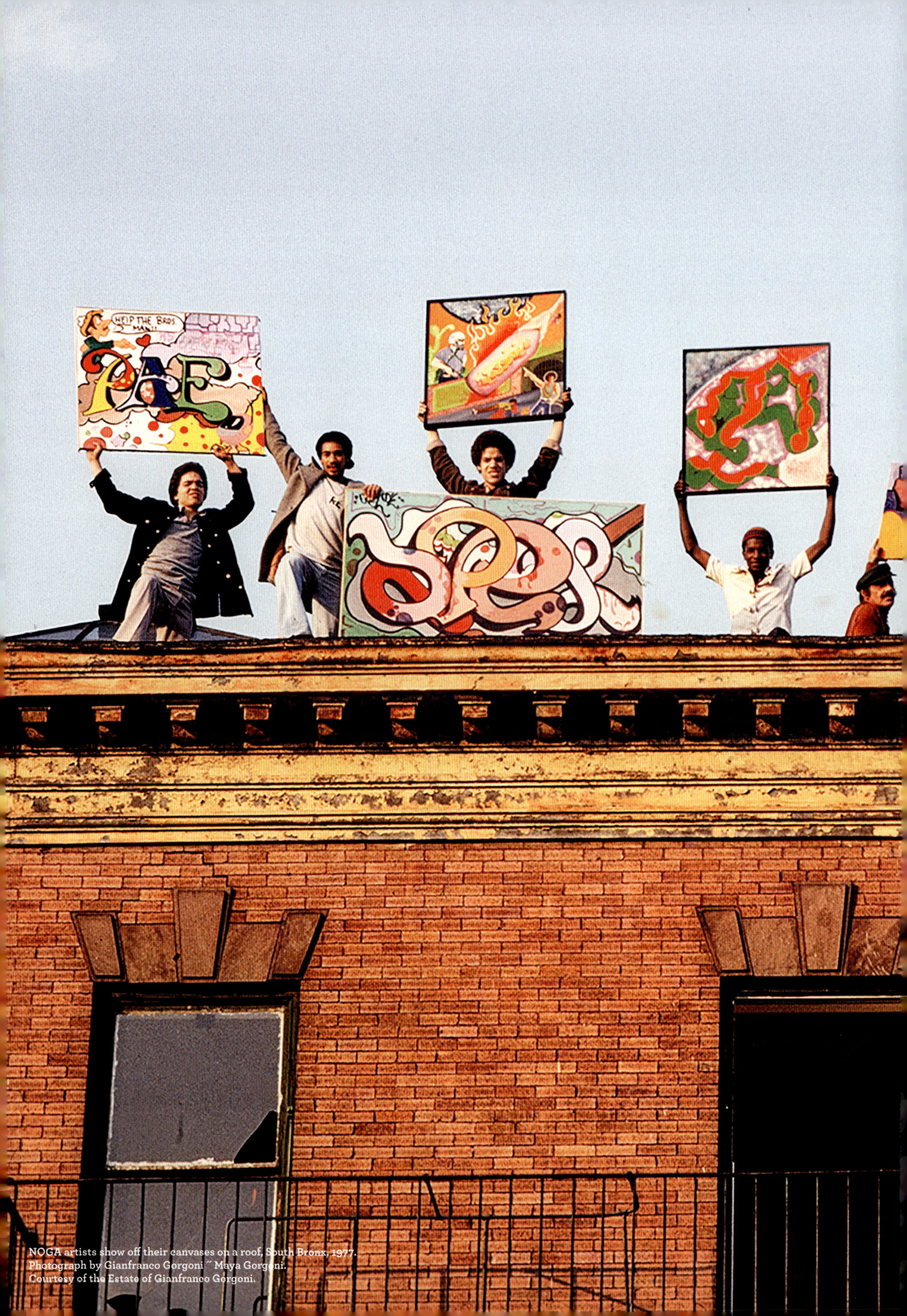

NOGA artists show off their canvases on a roof, South Bronx, 1977.
Photograph by Gianfranco Gorgoni ˜ Maya Gorgoni.
Courtesy of the Estate of Gianfranco Gorgoni.

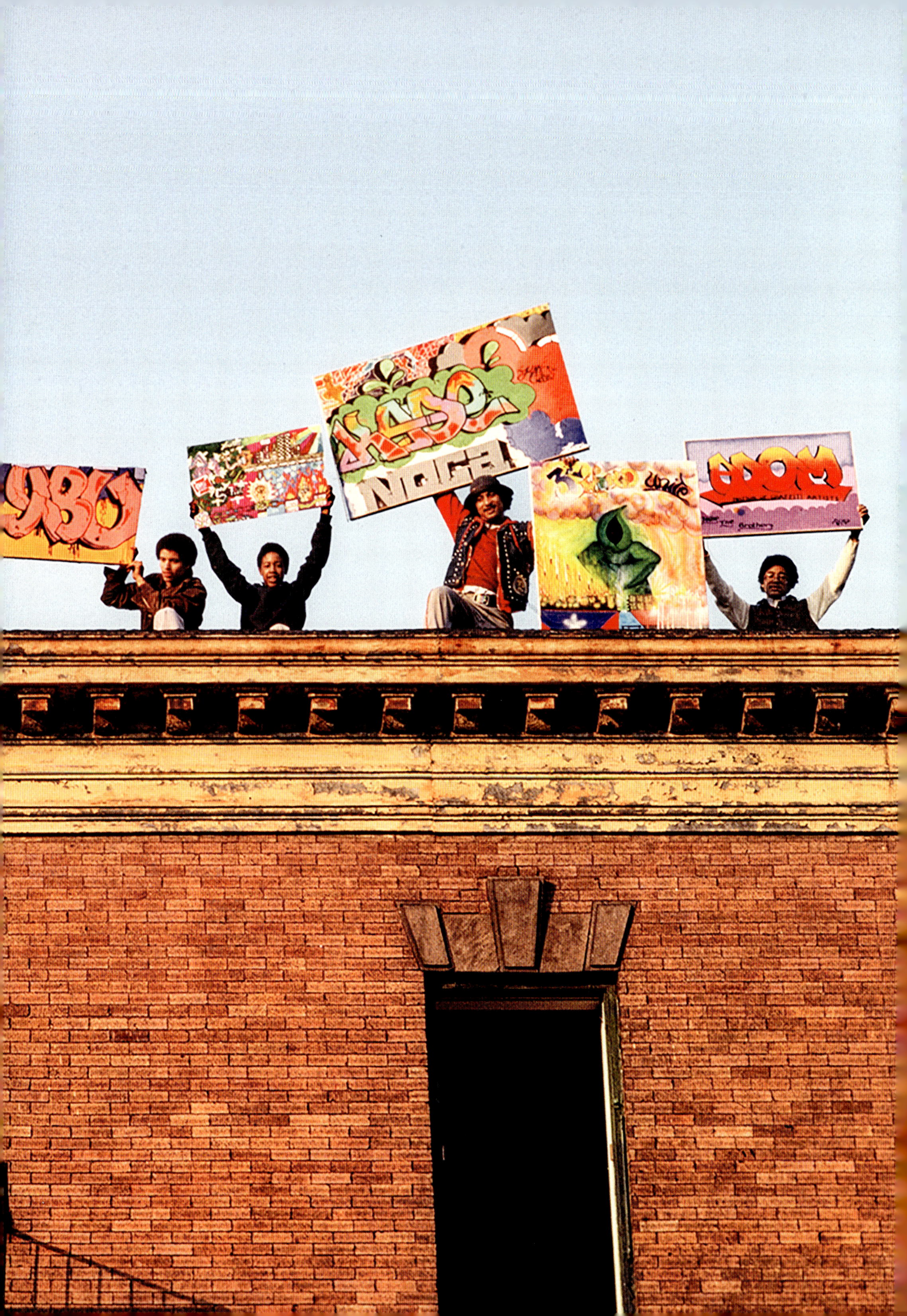

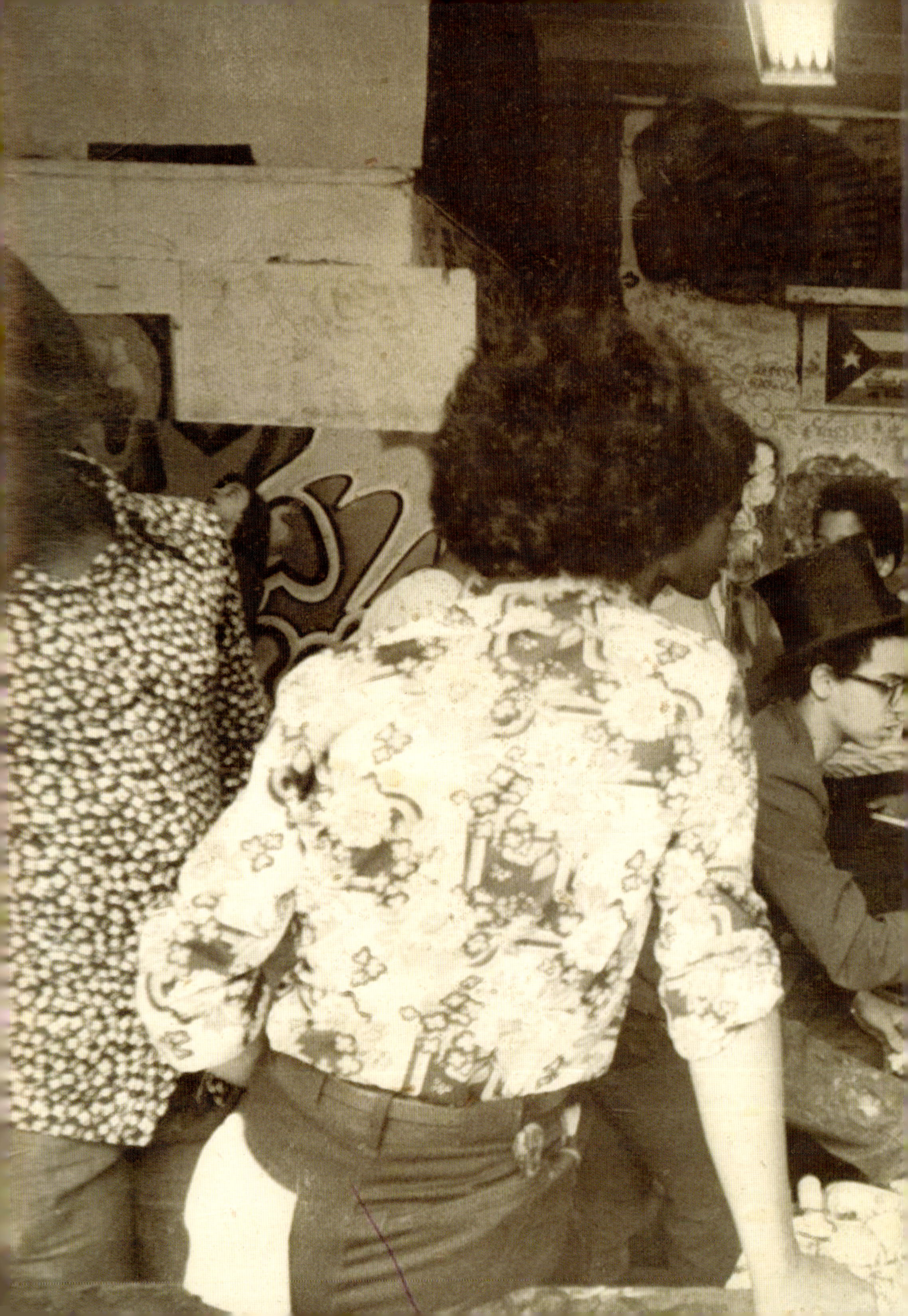

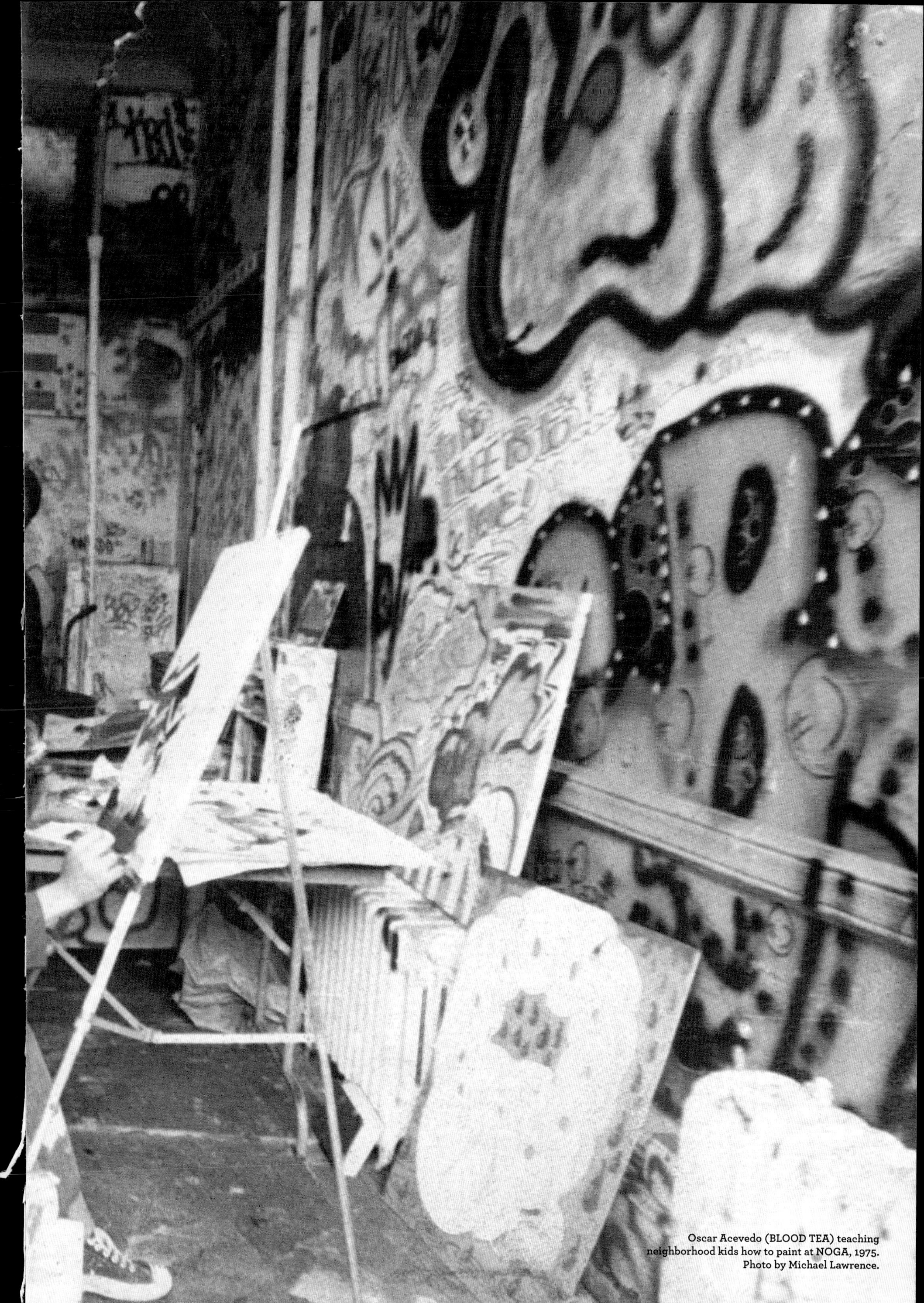

Oscar Acevedo (BLOOD TEA) teaching
neighborhood kids how to paint at NOGA, 1975.
Photo by Michael Lawrence.

NATION
OF
GRAFFITI
ARTISTS